INFORMATION TECHNOLOGY PROJECT MANAGEMENT

WITHDRAWN

INFORMATION TECHNOLOGY PROJECT MANAGEMENT

BENNET P. LIENTZ
Professor, Anderson School of Management, University of California, Los Angeles (UCLA)

palgrave
macmillan

© Bennet P. Lientz 2011

All rights reserved. No reproduction, copy or transmission of this publication may be made without written permission.

No portion of this publication may be reproduced, copied or transmitted save with written permission or in accordance with the provisions of the Copyright, Designs and Patents Act 1988, or under the terms of any licence permitting limited copying issued by the Copyright Licensing Agency, Saffron House, 6-10 Kirby Street, London EC1N 8TS.

Any person who does any unauthorized act in relation to this publication may be liable to criminal prosecution and civil claims for damages.

The author has asserted his right to be identified as the author of this work in accordance with the Copyright, Designs and Patents Act 1988.

First published 2011 by
PALGRAVE MACMILLAN

Palgrave Macmillan in the UK is an imprint of Macmillan Publishers Limited, registered in England, company number 785998, of Houndmills, Basingstoke, Hampshire RG21 6XS.

Palgrave Macmillan in the US is a division of St Martin's Press LLC, 175 Fifth Avenue, New York, NY 10010.

Palgrave Macmillan is the global academic imprint of the above companies and has companies and representatives throughout the world.

Palgrave® and Macmillan® are registered trademarks in the United States, the United Kingdom, Europe and other countries.

ISBN 978–0–230–30036–1

This book is printed on paper suitable for recycling and made from fully managed and sustained forest sources. Logging, pulping and manufacturing processes are expected to conform to the environmental regulations of the country of origin.

A catalogue record for this book is available from the British Library.

A catalog record for this book is available from the Library of Congress.

10   9   8   7   6   5   4   3   2   1
20   19   18   17   16   15   14   13   12   11

Printed and bound in China

Contents

Part six: What to do next

List of figures

Preface

Information Technology (IT) Projects fail too often

Studies repeatedly point out that 30–45 percent of systems projects fail prior to completion. Over half of all systems projects overrun their budgets and schedules by up to 200 percent or more. Combined costs of failure and overruns total in the hundreds of billions of dollars. Failures and problems continue despite improved tools and technology. Data also indicate that the failed projects were viewed as critically important by management. Over the past years, these statistics have hardly improved. A major Japanese bank recently experienced a total failure in implementing new systems that cost over US$120 million.

Failure statistics are staggering

The results of several surveys were published in *Computerworld,* a leading systems magazine. Here are some of their results:

- Failed systems projects cost more than $100 billion per year.
- One in every two projects overrun its budget by 180 percent or more.
- A survey of what was missing in the project management process indicated the following:

    Project office—42 percent
    Integrated methods—41 percent
    Training and mentoring—38 percent
    Policies and procedures—35 percent
    Implementation plans—23 percent
    Executive support—22 percent

Why are IT projects different from projects of the past?

Many of the methods and techniques of the past are still being used today, even though the technology, methods, management, and entire environment have changed. What are some of the differences?

There is a need to employ a modern project management approach to reflect the modern environment.

Systems and technology implementation and support are complex and involve many elements, necessitating planning and project management. Project management for these projects is different from that for some standard projects in industries such as construction or engineering. The projects often involve new technology with which the

Factors	Traditional	Modern
Focus	Single project	Multiple projects
Management attention	Critical path	Mgmt. Critical path focusing on risk and issues
Staffing/resources	Full time/dedicated	Part-time/full-time mix; shared
Project	Side by side to business	Processes and systems are linked
Staffing	Best people	Average people with energy
Milestones	Assume that they can be reviewed	Reviews must be selective due to time and resources
Project status	Budget versus actual; % complete	Unresolved issues; future tasks with risk and issues
Large projects	Divide by organization	Divide by risk
Small projects	Often not treated as project	Include as projects
Risk	Often treated in a fuzzy way	Treated tangibly through issues
Lessons learned	Each project treated as unique so that lessons learned are not stressed	Major emphasis on lessons learned
Management expectations	Moderate	High
IT projects	Critical to departments	Critical to the enterprise

project team is unfamiliar. The projects include interfaces with existing systems and other, incompatible technologies. Integration is often required. Given that many people treat software development and programming as an art, it is easy to see why systems projects become even more complex. Nor are the requirements for the systems stable. Business-, technology-, and externally generated changes can arise right in the middle of the project. Systems projects require extensive cooperation between business units, IT, and management.

Therefore, it is not surprising that many major IT projects fail or that almost as many reengineering and Six Sigma projects suffer the same fate. Managers at more than 60 percent of the firms in one survey thought that they had implemented purchased software packages incorrectly and had achieved little or no benefit. Firms indicate that when a failure occurs, the direct losses can be in the million of dollars and the total indirect losses in business are often much more (because the firm was depending on the results of the completed projects for revenue or for cost reductions).

E-Business failure is significant

There is no doubt that E-Business is a major force and trend for the early twenty-first century. Benefits of E-Business are well-known in all of the media. There is a dark side that many don't want to discuss—E-Business failures. Most of these are not publicized. After all, what would happen to a company's stock price if the failure were widely known? Some of the causes of E-Business failure are as follows:

- E-Business implementation is treated like a traditional project—a bad idea.
- The scope of the E-Business effort is defined as IT only. Business process and organization change are not included.

- There is an inadequate provision for change in direction. The project is inflexible to change.

This book addresses these and more.

Why do many technology projects fail?

Why do so many technology and systems fail? Why don't people learn from their mistakes and those of others? Complexity is part of the answer. Also, people get caught up in their work. They move from one project or piece of work to the next. Although they continue to use many of the same tools, they do not gather or apply lessons learned. Were this not enough, management and the business depend on technology today as never before. Technologies not only must be implemented correctly but also must be integrated. The bars of standards and expectations have been raised.

Failure also occurs because people manage technology projects the same way as they manage other projects. However, technology projects are different. The duration of the project can be long. During that time, the technology advances and can affect the project. The requirements of the business can change. Typically, technology projects are not carried out from scratch. There is always the integration of the new project into the fabric of the current systems and technology—called the *infrastructure* or *architecture* in this book. As part of the project, the project team members may have to learn the technology as they go. These characteristics are different from what one encounters when building bridges, launching new products, or undertaking other, more common projects. On the other hand, many of the lessons learned from the project management can be applied to systems and technology projects.

Another reason for failure is that projects are managed singly—like disjoint construction projects. This does not work for technology because (1) the projects are often interdependent, (2) many projects depend on the same technology and resources, and (3) issues that cross many projects are resolved in contradictory or conflicting ways between projects. A fundamental theme of this book is that technology projects must be managed as a whole, not as individual or isolated projects.

What are the benefits of project success?

With all of this talk about failure, why do projects at all fail? There are many reasons, including complexity, duration of the work, and the need for organization of the work. If you are successful in better managing single and multiple projects, experience and lessons learned point to the following benefits:

- There are greater benefits to the business, because the purpose and scope are set and supported to provide tangible business benefits.
- Risk can be minimized and managed better because all projects are being managed collectively as well as individually.

- Resources are better managed, utilization increases, and critical resources can be spread across multiple projects.
- There are fewer surprises in project work and schedules, allowing more predictability.
- You get more productivity and results from investment in technology and systems.

Purpose and scope of the book

The purpose of this book is to answer the following questions:

- How can the overall project management process be improved?
- Which systems projects should be given resources and approved for action?
- How can you better manage all systems and technology projects together?
- How can individual projects be better managed and more successful?
- What are the specific guidelines for managing different types of projects?
- What steps can you take to ensure that change occurs after the project is completed?
- How can you achieve a greater likelihood of project success?
- What are the useful guidelines that can supplement using a project management methodology such as the PM body of knowledge(PMBOK) or PRINCE2?

We answer these along with other specific questions, such as follows:

- What projects should be approved?
- How do you formulate and start projects effectively?
- How do you manage single and multiple projects?
- How do you identify, analyze, and address specific project issues and risks?
- How do you communicate effectively with management, team members, staff, and vendors to obtain results?
- How do you address quality concerns in IT projects?

Two leading project management methodologies have emerged: the PMBOK and PRINCE2. Others include Agile, Critical Chain Project Management, and Extreme Project Management. We will examine all of these and more. These are very helpful in indicating "what" is to be done. They do not, however, address the "how". This book helps to address the "how" for systems and technology-related projects. As such, the methods, lessons learned, guidelines, and issues in this book are consistent and supportive of all of the methodologies.

Trends in IT projects

Because this book focuses on a project management approach different from the single project monolithic methods of the past that addressed single projects, we assumed that there were dedicated resources to the project, and supposed that the purpose, scope, and requirements were fixed. We don't think that this world ever existed in IT, but if it at all did, then those days are long gone. Modern project management methods have to succeed in the following world.

- Technology is changing rapidly.
- Management changes business direction in response to pressures.
- Competition and industry change create more stress.
- There is limited staff to work on projects.
- People who work on projects also must do their normal non-project work.

The approach in the book is common sense. It is a breakthrough in that it is different from the normal project management books by dealing extensively with the "how." This approach has the following themes.

- You have to manage multiple projects not single projects.
- You derive benefit by having the project team use modern software tools for project management.
- Team members on the project work in a collaborative way where they participate in defining and updating their work and working on issues.
- Risk management is a major focus through identifying, addressing, and tracking issues and risks.
- A high-level structure through project templates and standardization supports cumulative improvement in project performance. Standardization supports analysis and management reporting. However, at the detailed level of all projects there is flexibility to accommodate the individual characteristics of the project.
- Lessons learned are gathered throughout the projects and applied to project templates and work so that project performance is improved.

All of these themes must be self-reinforcing across the life of the projects. This is shown in the following table. Here the rows are some of the major activities involved in a project. The columns are four elements of the focus of this book. Note how the themes are mutually reinforcing across all of the areas.

Area	Templates	Issues/lessons learned	Collaborative work
Getting started	Project template needed to start	Project concept	Concept analysis
Meetings	Updating areas of the template	Subject of the meetings	Each person defines and updates
Presentations	Structure	Format defined	Joint presentations
Getting the people	Standardization for what is needed	Use issues as a way to get people; use lessons learned for retention	Joint tasks where they can make friends
Vendor management	Templates fit with our schedule	Common database; vendor participate in lessons learned in the meetings	Joint tasks between vendor staff and internal staff
Changes to the plan	Fit within template	Manage through issues	Joint definition of the change

The audience and what you will get out of the book

Who can use this book? Anyone who is involved in any type of systems and technology project in either private or public sectors—organizations large and small. We do mean organizations of all sizes. The methods developed in this book have been applied to companies with 10 to more than 45,000 employees. Although this seems very general, the lessons learned have been applied in a variety of companies and industries. In addition, the materials have been tested and employed in project management, software, and technology classes in business and management, engineering, computer science, library and information science, architecture, public policy, and medical schools. We have taught over 4500 people in over 20 countries using these techniques.

You will obtain guidelines that can help you achieve greater success and reduce the risk of problems and failure in projects. These guidelines are lessons learned from more than 100 projects over the past 25 years. Lessons learned are a part of knowledge management, in which a firm attempts to leverage from its experience, expertise, and knowledge for competitive advantage.

This book has specific advantages and features over others:

- The book addresses the "how" in systems and technology project management. Most other books address the "what."
- The material in the chapters is related to project management methodologies including both the PMBOK and PRINCE2.
- Many specific examples from different industries are featured, ranging across the industries of banking, insurance, manufacturing, distribution, transportation, government, retailing, medical services, and energy and natural resources.
- The book is written in user-friendly style. Many books are very dry. The style here is intended to make the material more interesting and useful.
- More than 300 individual guidelines and lessons learned are provided along with ways you can employ them to be more effective.
- Projects involving software acquisition, development, operations, maintenance, enhancement, and technology are addressed in depth.

How is the book organized?

The book is divided into six logical parts:

- Part one: What should your project management strategy be and how should you address multiple projects?
- Part two: How do you establish projects and project plans?
- Part three: How do you manage projects after getting started to avoid failure and ensure success? How do you implement change so that project benefits are realized?
- Part four: How do you successfully manage software development (client-server, intranet, data warehousing), operations, maintenance, and enhancement, software package implementation, and technology (including networking) projects?

- Part five: How do you cope with specific issues related to personnel, management, technology, quality, global projects, and vendors/contractors?
- Part six: How do you implement the materials in the book and deal with resistance to change?

Chapters are generally organized in the same manner and include:

- *Introduction.* This lays the groundwork for the chapter and discusses what has been attempted in the past.
- The core of the chapter, which gives detailed methods, follows.
- *Cases and examples.* One or more examples are included along with discussion questions.
- *Mapping to the PM body of knowledge and PRINCE2.* Indicates how the chapter material fits in with these methodologies (in Parts one–three).
- *Lessons learned.* Tips gained from experience that have proven very useful.
- *Guidelines.* These are specific suggestions and lessons learned from experience.
- *Questions.* Questions for students are provided for follow-up.
- *What to do next.* These are steps that you can take after reading the chapter.
- *Summary.*

Throughout the book, examples appear that employ specific technologies involved in various industries, including retailing, distribution, manufacturing, education, banking, and transportation. These examples are not your typical successful case type examples. Often, those are not of the real world. Here we deal with the dysfunctional, struggling, and failing companies as well as successful organizations. And can you guess why? You often learn more from failure than success.

What are some key features?

Here are some of the major features cited by reviewers:

- There is a chapter on the various project management methodologies.
- There is a discussion in each chapter as to how the material fits with the leading project management methodologies: the PMBOK and PRINCE2.
- Too often a project ends, but there are no benefits because the business did not change to fit the results of the project. There is a chapter dealing with change management after a project is over.
- A chapter has been created for managing risk and issues.
- Many projects fail for political and cultural reasons. To address this, there is a chapter on specific issues in these areas that apply to global projects.
- Many IT and technology-related projects suffer because of poor communications and misunderstandings. So there is a chapter that provides guidelines for both formal and informal communications.

- Quality assessment and assurance have been a significant problem in many technological efforts. There is a chapter that has been added on quality management. There is also a chapter that has been added on commonly faced quality issues.
- Seventeen checklists and score cards to measure all aspects of projects and the project management process have been included in a chapter on performance measurement.
- Useful Web sites and references have been included along with guidelines on how to get the most of these.

There are over 300 specific proven guidelines and tips to help you achieve greater success in your projects and work. As important, these ideas will help you accomplish a key goal in your life—cumulative improvement and greater success in your project work.

Acknowledgments

I would like to point out that the roots of this book are in the two editions of the book *Breakthrough Technology Project Management* published by Elsevier-Butterworth-Heinemann. My co-author of this book, Kathryn P. Rea, passed away due to cancer some years ago. She provided insights and contributed much to that book.

I also owe many thanks to students, seminar attendees, colleagues, and consulting clients who provided ideas, criticism, and examples that contributed much to this book.

Part one
Project strategy

1
Introduction

Project management concepts

Let's start by defining some basic concepts related to projects and project management for single projects. A *project* consists of work that is focused on specific purposes within the boundaries of a defined *scope*. The scope defines the boundaries of a project and determines what is included in and excluded from the project. Projects can be of any size or type. A *purpose* for a project can be a narrow goal related to a specific system or technology, or it can be more extensive to include improvements in a business process. A *business process* is a set of regularly performed, integrated business tasks that produce specific outputs. Payroll, sales, and planning analysis are examples of business processes. The *project plan* consists of related tasks or activities and milestones together with resources, costs or budget, benefits, roles and responsibilities, and schedules.

Moving up to multiple projects, the *project portfolio* is the set of approved projects that will be funded and provided with resources. It is often the case that the portfolio is approved by a *management steering committee* or group. *Resource management* is the coordination, management, and control of resources across the projects. How to resolve competing demands among projects for the same resources will be called *resource deconflicting*. If you place all of the schedules together, the result will be called the *master schedule*.

Turning to systems concepts, the systems organization will be referred to as *information technology* or IT. Many other terms have been used over the years: information systems (IS), management information systems (MIS), and data processing (DP). The business organization staff members have often been referred to as *users*. This term can be viewed as derogatory so the business organizations will be considered as *business units*. The employees in the business units will mostly be referred to as *business staff* or employees.

Both the systems and business organizations have objectives and strategies. An *objective* here is a directional goal that is timeless. Examples relate to profitability, costs, effectiveness, and efficiency. These are general and have to be supported by strategies. A *strategy* provides the focus for supporting objectives. Projects then support strategies that in turn support objectives. A strategy might be to expand market share. In information systems an objective is to be responsive to the business. A strategy might be to implement a Web-based solution.

The collection and structure of the hardware, software and systems, and network will be referred to as the *infrastructure*. How the pieces of technology go together is critical to the infrastructure and its flexibility and capabilities. A poor infrastructure, for example, might have either missing pieces or parts that do not integrate or interface with each other.

Before and during a project, problems, situations, and opportunities can arise. These will be referred to as *issues*. Effective issue management is a key attribute of good project managers. Issues have symptoms that are signs of problems as well as the problem or opportunity itself. Examples of issues are how to allocate a scarce personnel resource among projects, how to address a gap in technology, and how to deal with a specific requirement change. To address issues, management makes *decisions*. Decisions are implemented or followed up by taking *actions*. Some tasks in projects have *risk* in that there is a significant likelihood that there may be problems or slippage. Here we will treat the reason behind the risk as an issue. Thus, if you resolve the issues behind a risky task, you have reduced or removed the risk. This is a key association in the book and has been found to be an effective means of dealing with the more fuzzy concept of risk.

A goal in project management is to gather lessons from experience and then apply these to current and future projects so as to be more effective. These will be referred to as *lessons learned*. Lessons learned can take many forms: policies, guidelines, procedures, and techniques. In systems, lessons learned include how to work with a specific business process or how to effectively use a software tool. In traditional project management, lessons learned are collected at the end of a project—a bad idea. In this book you will gather these as the work is performed.

Figure 1.1 puts the components together. As can be seen, the IT and business components mirror each other. The business processes correspond to the systems and infrastructure.

In the diagram, business issues are reflected in systems issues (on the left). The organization interface is shown on the right. In the center, the systems and the architecture

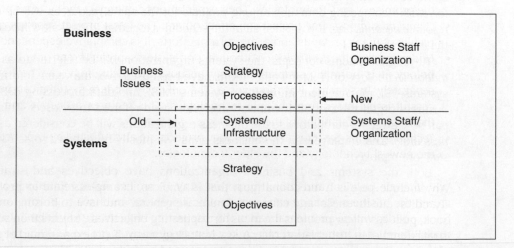

Figure 1.1   Systems and business components

(structure of the technology) support the business processes. This diagram will be employed to relate business-oriented topics to those in systems. This figure has two dashed boxes. One represents the traditional project approach of focusing only on systems and the architecture (labeled "Old"). The second, larger one is the more modern view of including the business processes along with systems and architecture (labeled "New"). In the past, systems often worked alongside the processes. Today, they are integrated with and embedded in the processes.

Differences between standard and IT projects

In the preface some general differences between standard projects and systems and technology were identified. These can now be made more precise.

- *Purpose.* The goals of a system and technology project are often not as clearly defined as those in engineering or other projects. The goals may not be well-defined at the start of the systems project if only technical purposes are defined. So in this book, three other purposes are specified—business, political, and social.
- *Scope.* Systems projects sometimes lack clear boundaries. Is the business process within the project? With what systems must the project interface? Moreover, the scope can creep and expand.
- *Parallel work.* While a new system is being created or installed, work can continue on the current system, creating changing requirements. This is not as true in standard projects.
- *Interfacing projects.* Systems projects are more likely to have complex interfaces.
- *Technology dependence.* It seems that only in systems and technology projects do people attempt to use new technology or technology with which they have no or only limited experience, raising the level of risk.
- *Management expectations.* Upper-level managers attend seminars and read about the promise of new technologies. Their expectations can impact the systems project.
- *Cumulative impact.* One project can affect others. The latest project depends on the results of many previous and some current efforts. It is cumulative dependence.
- *Understanding the technology.* Although non-systems projects can involve technology, it is normally simpler to apply because the technology can be handled separately. In systems, it is the reverse. The only way modern systems can be successful is by integrating multiple technologies. This requires a deeper and more thorough understanding of the technology.
- *Technology gaps.* Systems and technology projects are also affected by gaps between the newest technology and the older technologies.

Why include political and social purposes? Any IT project results in change within IT and the business. Change can create political problems and issues. Throughout the book, politics will be an integral part of the discussion. Projects are often the only times that different departments interact. A key benefit of many IT projects is that they provide for collaborative effort among departments and business units. Thus, you want to have a social purpose.

Trends in business

Certain business trends have emerged and persisted, affecting systems projects.

- *Accountability.* Business has become more sensitive to accountability and has a greater drive for results impacting which projects are funded and their schedules.
- *Downsizing/rightsizing.* IT has been hit by this trend as have the business units. The impact is that many organizations have to make up for the decline in staff with automation by putting more pressure on IT projects.
- *Importance of business processes.* Whereas in the past the focus was on the business organization, now the attention has shifted to the basic business processes. This new focus has been spurred by the successes of Wal-Mart, Federal Express, and other firms, and it impacts the scope and focus of systems projects.
- *Reengineering, Six Sigma, and process change.* Changes in business processes are almost always linked to changes in systems and technology.
- *Global competition.* Companies are faced with competing in multiple, diverse markets. This requires flexibility on the part of the technology and systems.
- *Outsourcing/supplier–customer links.* With electronic commerce and electronic data interchange (EDI), firms seek to tighten their links with suppliers and customers. In addition, more functions are being outsourced (in some cases to suppliers and customers).
- *Thirst for information.* Firms desire to get at the information for management, strategic, and tactical/operational purposes. Data warehousing and the spread of database management systems have created new projects that pull information from multiple sources for analysis in support of knowledge management.
- *E-Business implementation.* Implementing E-Business combines system implementation, process improvement, and organizational change.

These factors lead to the creation of more projects that are of increased complexity compared to traditional systems work. Success with the first project in a given area typically leads to more projects in the same areas. For example, a firm that has been successful in reengineering its accounts payable processes is then a firm that has been tempted to move to other accounting areas. Thus, it is not surprising that the number of projects and their interdependencies are growing.

Trends in systems and technology

Examine some of the key technology trends that have affected project management.

- *Cloud computing.* In cloud computing, an organization uses the hardware, network, staffing, and software resources of one or more vendors to do their data processing.
- *Integration of application systems.* More and more firms employ integrated software to meet their business needs. Benefits include more consistent and complete information as well as structured business processes. Examples are Enterprise Resource

Planning (ERP), Supply Chain Management (SCM), and Customer Relationship Management (CRM) systems.

- *Widespread use of networks*. Today, integration is supported through the wide area networks. Stand-alone computing for business processes is largely a thing of the past.
- *Web-based solutions*. Since most people know how to use the Web and browsers, this is just a natural evolution. These replaced traditional client-server systems.
- *Increased management expectations*. Managers are acutely aware of the importance of IT and systems. They expect much more from IT and systems to support the business.
- *Cumulative impacts*. With a growing dependence on technology, companies need to manage the cumulative efforts and cross-impacts of the technology.

To many business managers these trends combine to support their beliefs that technology and systems can respond to business trends and needs rapidly and easily. This raises expectations and requirements for systems and technology projects.

Trends in project management

These trends further influence the nature of systems and technology projects. Overall, the trends have the following impacts:

- Projects involve more business aspects due to reengineering, process improvement, and E-Business.
- Projects are more complex in general in terms of technology.
- Projects are more integrated with each other and with current work.
- Staff members have to be assigned to multiple projects due to limited budgets and resources. In addition, there is competition for staff time between projects and normal work such as network support, maintenance, enhancements, and operations support.

More tools are used for project management nowadays than were available 15 years ago. Some highlights are the following:

- Project management software is now network based to support sharing of project information among project teams and with others outside of the project.
- Groupware allows for project teams to share information on issues, project status, action items, and other project information.
- Electronic mail, voice mail, and videoconferencing support the dissemination and sharing of information more rapidly.
- Databases support the storage and organization of information related to projects.

Note that these all enable sharing of project information and collaborative effort.

In the distant past, each company had to come up with its own methods for managing projects. Today, the use of structured project management methodologies is more widespread. The two most popular methodologies are the PMBOK and PRINCE2. More unconventional methodologies are Agile, Critical Chain Project Management, and Extreme Project Management. These will be examined in the next chapter.

Common IT project management myths

The preceding trends help to explode some of the myths that have arisen around project management over the years.

- **Myth 1: To be successful, projects require dedicated resources.**
  This was true 20 years ago. It is no longer the case. Systems projects require a variety of different skills from different people over the life of the project. For most companies, having any substantial number of full-time staff dedicated to the length of the project is not possible.
- **Myth 2: Project leaders must be allowed a great deal of autonomy to get work done.**
  This myth is based on the idea that projects have a stand-alone nature and that project leaders are fully responsible for the project. Today, this is not realistic. Projects are interdependent; resources are shared. Project leaders may even be shared and split among multiple projects.
- **Myth 3: Success in a project is to achieve the implementation of the system or technology.**
  This is the traditional narrow definition of *success*. It is why many systems people think that a project was a success, while the business managers view it as a failure. It is a matter of perspective. Many systems people think that the job ends when the software runs; however, business managers think that the project ends when the business processes are improved with the implementation of the systems. A fundamental point in this book is although much of the costs of a project occur in the systems aspects, the benefits largely are realized in the changes and improvements to the business. Thus, if a project stops with the completion of the system, there may be no project benefits. If the business processes and organization do not change when the new system is implemented, then there are likely to be few benefits, making the project a waste of time.
- **Myth 4: Projects depend on stable, defined requirements and technology.**
  The traditional system life cycle emphasized getting the requirements right. If this were done, then the design and development are more likely to be successful because they met the requirements. This is nice in theory and terribly wrong in practice. The business managers and staff may not know what is needed until they see something. As they see and experience the systems and technology, their requirements naturally evolve and change. It is part of life. It is also true that you must plan for technological improvement and change in any long-running project.
- **Myth 5: You can measure a project in terms of percentage complete and budgeted versus actual results.**

This is the traditional and accepted approach that students are taught in project management classes. Unfortunately, in systems projects it is difficult, if not impossible to clearly identify the percentage complete. In addition, much of the expense in a systems project is in fixed costs associated with networks, hardware, and software. The variable that mostly indicates problems is staff time. Thus, budget is a trailing indicator. You will see better measures for a project in terms of assessing outstanding and remaining issues and problems.

- **Myth 6: Each IT project is unique.**
  This is a seemingly innocent statement. However, if you accept it, then you tend to manage projects independently and fail to gain from lessons learned. Projects have unique attributes, but underneath the veneer of the new technology they have much in common.
- **Myth 7: You can throw resources and money at systems projects to good effect.**
  In some business projects this is true. It is seldom the case in systems management. People's skills and knowledge are not interchangeable. Throwing people into a systems project often just slows the project down due to time consumed for coordination and bringing people up to speed.
- **Myth 8: Things will work out all right if you use the magic tool or software.**
  Any tool requires a substantial learning curve. A tool expert should be identified and on board. People not only must gain familiarity with the tool, but also expertise. Were this not enough, many tools would not have been complete. Staff members are forced to deal with multiple tools from different suppliers, making the job worse.

Traditional project process

From lessons learned, a major cause of failure occurs when an organization maintains the old project management process and methods to manage modern-day projects. Let's consider the problems with the traditional project management process. In general, the project management process can be divided into the following parts:

- **Ideas and proposals for projects.**
  In most organizations ideas for projects are often expected to come from the business. The assumption here is that business units know their needs and so will formulate their requirements. These will then go to the systems organization for review and estimate of effort and schedule.
- **Project approval.**
  Several approaches are employed for approval. One is to use a steering committee that meets to approve or change priorities recommended by information systems. Although it may appear to be a slate of related projects, this is often a list of individual projects. Another approach is to negotiate and approve, defer, or reject requests individually. This is the "let's make a deal" approach.
- **Project kick-off and start.**
  Because the elapsed time between initial request and start of the project can be long, the project may get off to a very slow start. Generally an extensive planning effort

is launched to develop a detailed project plan. Then this plan must be approved. Individuals must be signed up to be on the team. After considering the initial idea for the project, the idea is often found to be incomplete and more work must be done to define the scope of the project and end products. The project leader and team are often dedicated to the project. They have not been told to interface with other projects. That will, it is hoped, occur later. The project leaders are left to define their own tasks and milestones for each project, resulting in little or no uniformity across projects.

- **Project execution, monitoring, reporting, and management.**
  Many people make a big deal out of the size of the project in terms of project monitoring and reporting. Larger projects get more attention while smaller projects get it less. Project managers are often trained to focus on administrative matters such as tracking, reporting, and estimating for the project. Historically, several factors contributed to this. Project teams were larger. The software and other project management tools were primitive so that much of the project manager's time was consumed gathering status and using the software. Even today, there is often no organized approach to deal with problems. As problems appear, the project leader uses his or her own experience and knowledge to address the problems one at a time.
  When it comes to review, managers consider the projects one at a time. They do the same with the problems and issues. More attention is given to projects that are over budget or behind schedule.
- **Project end or termination.**
  The project progresses toward its milestones. At the end of the project, the business unit that wanted the project is asked to sign off. This can be a rushed affair. Both the business unit and the systems unit do not want the project to appear as a failure, which would reflect badly on them both. After sign-off, it is too seldom the case that management insists on determining the benefits of the system. If asked, the response is often in terms of soft, fuzzy benefits. Normally no effort is made to extract lessons learned from the project. The business unit goes back to its normal work. The system staff moves on to another project.

Twenty-six reasons why projects fail

Many flaws are in the traditional approach that contribute to failure. Let's now build a list of 26 reasons why systems projects fail. These will be discussed in more detail in later chapters.

1. *IT is reactive.* The IT organization responds in a reactive mode to project requests. There is little or no proactive effort to search out good projects with major benefits.
2. *There is a lack of a project strategy.* Without an overall plan, many of the projects submitted and approved may provide only marginal benefits. Major projects involving the underlying technology and architecture infrastructure are ignored or viewed as impossible because no one business unit supports them.

3. *Project ideas are not well-organized.* When you open up project idea development to any department, you are likely to attract those who are most interested in automation. These people tend to be younger and manage smaller departments (due to less seniority). As a result, the project ideas sometimes do not stem from a clear business need, but rather from a desire to acquire a benefit that would be nice but may not be necessary.

4. *Projects goals are not understood or agreed on.* There is sometimes a lack of understanding and agreement about the goals of the project. Business, technical, and organizational objectives might overlap and conflict.

5. *Small projects are not allowed to be projects.* Because of the fear of administrative overhead and the desire for results, management allows small projects to exist without the controls and direction associated with project management. As the scope of the project grows, the stage is set for collapse because no organized structure is in place. This occurs in business units that attempt to carry out projects informally.

6. *The business unit role is ill-defined.* The role of the business unit is ignored or is assumed to be known. As a result, the business unit staff members struggle to find out what they are supposed to do. With few responsibilities, they are less committed to making the project successful. The potential tasks that they can address in terms of business process are not included in the project.

7. *Work is being done on the wrong projects.* The information systems unit is reacting to business units individually. Thus, many projects that involve critical business processes that span multiple organizations are left out because there is not one owner. Resources are consumed by intradepartment work.

8. *Projects arc not closely linked to the business processes.* Projects are carried out with the attention on the technical side of the puzzle. The business process side is too often ignored. No tasks are related to reengineering. This can also be a problem with too narrow a scope.

9. *Benefits are not as they seem.* The benefits cited in the project are often estimated based on only the systems side without any business process change. Thus, often very few actual benefits are achieved.

10. *The scope of project is not defined.* The scope of the project is not well-defined until substantial work has been done. Additional requirements that surface then enlarge the scope.

11. *The purpose of the project does not match the scope.* The goals of a project can be ambitious as reflected in the estimated benefits. Yet the scope of the project is too narrow, making it impossible to reach the goal.

12. *Projects are approved individually based on individual benefits.* This results from direct negotiation between the manager of systems and the business unit manager. This practice tends to encourage stand-alone projects, reducing the possibilities of economies of scale. This also makes the process of review political and biased toward specific business units that are on good terms with information systems.

13. *Projects that are approved by a committee are often approved based on fairness.* It is logical that the approved projects represent the desires of the committee members. Fairness says that each area receives some project support. This dilutes resources across many projects and turns them away from more important projects.

14. *Projects adopt tools without methods.* A tool supports a method. Without the method there is less likelihood of getting all of the value out of the tools.
15. *Projects are too rigid in either rejecting or accepting new technology during the project.* In some projects, there is an overwillingness to adopt a new tool—particularly if the project is in trouble. Adopting a tool then can just mask the underlying problems. In other projects, there is a rigidity to anything new or improved. In either case, the project is affected adversely.
16. *There is a lack of review of project ideas and plans.* No thorough and formal approach to reviewing a project idea or plan may exist. Often, the project is only reviewed by itself in a vacuum.
17. *The project team is weak.* The project team is weak or lacks technical knowledge and experience. No provision is in place for assigning senior people to the project.
18. *The project team was identified and gathered too early.* The project team members are identified and committed too early in the project. This leads to their under-utilization. Morale can be depressed.
19. *Resources cannot be managed or shared across projects.* This is due to several factors. First, the resources are often dedicated to single projects. Second, when a high-priority task appears, the project team is stripped to handle the emergency—delaying the project. Third, no mechanism has been established to manage resources across multiple projects.
20. *Project resources are robbed to handle emergencies.* This occurs in non-systems projects as well. The problem with systems projects is that the only apparent downside of taking resources from a project is a delay in the project. Because the benefits are not clearly identified and the business unit is getting along without the systems or technology, there does not seem to be much harm. Don't kid yourself. There is. The people left on the project may work slower and may feel that they are working on a low-priority effort.
21. *The project manager spends too much time in administration.* The project manager is assumed to be carrying out the administrative tasks identified earlier. In many organizations this is assumed to be sufficient. The project manager may lose touch with the actual work on the project and fail to build rapport with the team.
22. *Issues are inconsistently handled.* Because issues are handled in an *ad hoc* manner based on the style of the project manager and his or her experience, analysis, results, and actions related to problems vary widely.
23. *Tracking multiple projects is difficult.* If each of five projects uses a different task plan with different task descriptions for the same work and different resource names, it is almost impossible to put the five schedules together for analysis.
24. *The mathematical critical path receives too much attention.* As you know, the critical path is the longest path in the project such that if any task on this path is delayed, the project is delayed. Who says that this path contains the tasks with greatest risk? It usually does not.
25. *Few or no lessons are learned.* With no formal or organized process to learn from the projects and a lack of incentives and management support, it is not surprising that few devote any time to gathering, organizing, or disseminating lessons learned.
26. *Lack of resource management between projects and regular work.* The problem here is that there is a lack of active management of staffing resources between normal work and project work.

Guidelines for success

Let's turn from failure to success. Take the same phases of a project management process and consider a more modern method. This is the core of the approach in this book. All of the concepts that are discussed here will be expanded upon later. Here you will see the overall road map.

Modern project management process

Ideas and proposals for projects

Although departments can still submit project ideas, information systems works with departments to assess the current state of key business processes and their supporting systems and technology. The result is a *process plan* that leads to projects that involve process improvement as well as systems work. A complete *project concept* is developed that identifies business roles, purpose, scope, general costs, benefits, general schedule, and issues to be addressed in the project. The current processes are measured to assess the problems and to support the determination of benefits.

The IT function plans how to manage resources across multiple projects. The objective is to form project teams that are as small and flexible as possible. Analysis is also performed to identify and analyze the interdependencies between projects. Improvements to the architecture and technology base are identified and related to the business processes.

Project approval

A group of projects or the project portfolio is reviewed and approved by management with an emphasis on interrelationships among projects. Project approval is tentative and subject to review at three-to-four-month intervals. When project concepts and plans are reviewed, their potential impact on resources and other projects is considered.

Project kick-off and start

Projects are initiated by developing detailed project plans based on standard templates. A *template* includes standardized high-level tasks, resources, resources assigned to tasks, and dependencies. This is more than a *work breakdown structure* (WBS), which is a general list of tasks. It paves the way for increased standardization and the ability to analyze data from multiple projects. Team members are placed on teams in a just-in-time mode. The core team for any project is no more than three to four people. Other team members are on the projects part time for performing specific tasks. Lessons learned can be linked to tasks in the template. Issues can be linked to tasks in the project plan that is created from the template.

Project monitoring, reporting, and management

Standardized electronic reporting is employed for all projects. A *project coordinator* analyzes the data from all projects. This person also reviews the active issues across the projects and presents the results of the analysis to the project leaders as well as to management. The project coordinator facilitates the release of resources from projects and their redeployment to other projects. A project leader or IT manager can act as a coordinator.

Project leaders share their schedules with each other in a network environment. They work together in joint meetings chaired by the project coordinator to resolve conflicts for resources.

Project leaders do work on the projects. They also work on all active issues and support the gathering and dissemination of lessons learned. Project updating is done by team members through the network, releasing some of the project leader's time from administration.

Measurement of the project is based on open issues and their impacts on the projects. Percentage complete and budget status are still important but are considered secondarily.

Project end or termination

Although a project can end, it is usually just the end of a phase to support the business processes. As you know, making large-scale improvements in major systems involves creating and managing multiple projects.

Why projects succeed

Based on experience from many projects, there are other ingredients to project success.

- *Requirements.* Requirements in the modern setting come from the changes to the business processes. Business processes tend to be more stable than requirements created in the old manner. Requirements are often tied to business transactions. The requirements have less change and more stability. Moreover, any changes to requirements can be evaluated and justified based on an assessment of their effect and impact on business processes. In doing requirements, you identify the problems and their impacts on the current processes and work. This helps to generate support for change.
- *Team building.* By having team members more active in project management they have a greater sense of commitment. The same is true for business units. Project leaders are encouraged to work together in a cooperative mode.
- *Issue and risk-oriented.* This process makes management more issue-oriented rather than status-oriented. Issues that cannot be resolved by individual or multiple project managers are considered by management.
- *Overall focus of projects.* Because the projects are based on major business processes that cross multiple departments, the projects will consume most of the available

resources. This means that many of the smaller, enhancement type projects will fall by the wayside due to a lower priority.

- *Impact on IT.* With this new project focus, information systems becomes a key supporter, if not owner, of processes that involve multiple departments.
- *Overall resource assignment.* Resources are actively and regularly allocated among projects and normal non-project work.

Organization of the book

The organization of this book reflects the modern approach defined in this chapter. Part one (Project Strategy) focuses on the project management process. Here you will view the details of the process and get help and guidance in transitioning to the new process. How you can better manage multiple projects is considered here as well. Most books might not consider this factor because their attention is drawn to single projects. The specific chapters after this one are:

- Project management methodologies (Chapter 2);
- Developing your project management process and strategy (Chapter 3);
- Managing multiple projects and the project portfolio (Chapter 4).

Part two (Project Planning) of the book deals with developing project plans, assembling the project team, and defining the new roles of the business units as well as the project leader. These support the project concept defined in Part one. The specific chapters are:

- The project concept (Chapter 5);
- The right project leader (Chapter 6);
- Project human resource management (Chapter 7);
- Developing the project plan (Chapter 8).

Tracking, monitoring, and managing the projects are the thrust of Part three (Project Execution), along with coverage of the following:

- Effective project tracking and coordination (Chapter 9);
- Implementation of project results – project change management (Chapter 10);
- Project communications management (Chapter 11);
- Project risk management (Chapter 12);
- Project quality management (Chapter 13);
- Project procurement management (Chapter 14);
- Measuring projects and project management (Chapter 15).

Part four (IT Activities) contains an analysis of specific types of IT projects, including:

- Software development (Chapter 16);
- Operations, maintenance, and enhancement (Chapter 17);
- Software packages (Chapter 18);
- Technology projects (Chapter 19).

Part five (How to Successfully Address Project Issues) deals with issues in the following areas:

- Business issues (Chapter 20);
- Human resource issues (Chapter 21);
- Management issues (Chapter 22);
- Technical issues (Chapter 23);
- Vendor and consultant issues (Chapter 24);
- Global, cultural, and political issues (Chapter 25);
- Quality issues (Chapter 26).

Part six of the book contains one chapter (Chapter 27) on what to do next. Here we discuss your vision and mission. The implementation of Quick Wins as well as change both intermediate and longer-term are addressed. Another section deals with resistance to change.

There are several appendices and materials at the end of the book that include the following:

- Bibliography;
- Useful Web sites;
- Project management software (Appendix 1);
- War strategies applied to project management (Appendix 2).

You might find the last one curious and wonder why it appears here. War campaigns are large projects that have been studied for thousands of years. Unfortunately, war and conflict are some of the most frequently recurring projects in human history. So we should gather lessons learned from experts who developed strategies for planning and conducting wars. Eight of the expert sources are considered spanning a period of 2500 years.

The chapters have been written in a down-to-earth style so that you can put the materials to work for you and your organization immediately. The scope of the book not only includes business and technical dimensions, but also political and social ones.

Cases and examples

For reasons of space limitations, the discussion of cases and examples has been restricted to the critical points. Each of the chapters in Parts one–four contains these. Several questions for discussion are included as well. These are drawn from real life. Names have been changed. These are useful sources for information on issues as well as lessons learned.

Lessons learned

Each chapter in Parts one–four contains specific lessons learned from our past experience over the past 40 years. These are in addition to the tips and lessons contained in the body of the chapter.

Guidelines

Guidelines are generally more detailed than lessons learned. A number of these are provided in each chapter of Parts one–four. As such, they help you in implementing the methods contained in the chapter.

Questions

In each of the chapters of the first four parts of the book, five questions are posed for further research addressing key areas of the chapter. Here are some questions for this chapter.

1. Using the Web, define several alternative definitions of projects, project management, and the project portfolio. Evaluate these in terms of technical, business, political, and social perspectives.
2. Many people treat small projects as regular work and not as projects. What problems can arise if this is done?
3. Using the Web, find alternative definitions of *project success*. Compare and contrast these with the definition in this chapter. Project success is discussed also in the Summary.
4. Using the Web, find alternative definitions of *project failure*. Compare and contrast these with the definition provided in this chapter. Project failure is also covered in the Summary.
5. Apply the definitions of project success and failure to activities in your own personal life. Answer the following questions:

   • Have you learned from your successes and failures?
   • Do you see the same problems and issues recurring again and again?
   • Do you gather lessons learned from experience and apply them to future work?
   • Do you plan out major activities in your life?
   • Do you encounter the same surprises again and again?

What to do next

Each chapter in Parts one–four contains specific actions a business or IT reader can do as follow-up after reading the chapter. Here are actions for this chapter.

1. A logical first step is to assess the current project management process in your organization. Here is a list of questions to consider:

   • Is there a formal process for managing groups of projects?
   • Is each project managed differently based on the individual project manager?
   • Is there any effort to employ standardized project templates?
   • Is it possible to integrate several schedules and perform analysis?
   • Is there any effort to gather lessons learned from past and current projects?

- How are project ideas generated? Are the same people always generating new project ideas?
- How are projects approved?
- How are benefits of projects determined?
- Is there any effort to measure a project to ensure that the benefits are achieved?
- Is there a standardized project reporting process across projects of all sizes?
- How many of the current, active projects relate to key business processes?
- How many business processes lack any projects?
- Can people be moved between project teams?
- What is the size of project teams?
- What is the role of the business unit staff in projects? Is it consistent across multiple projects?
- How are issues defined and addressed? Is there an effort to see which issues apply across multiple projects?

2. Consider some recent projects that were failures. Ask the following questions:

- Was there an effort to learn from the failure?
- Did the project management process change as a result of the failure?
- At what point did people know that the project was a failure? How long was it before the failure was acknowledged?
- How was the failure announced?
- What was the reaction among team members of other projects?
- What were the dependencies between the failed projects and others?
- What major issues contributed to failure? How long had they remained unresolved?

3. Consider some recent projects that were successes. Ask the following questions:

- Was the project only a technical success?
- Was success announced at the conclusion of the project or after the new system had been in place and measured?
- Were there any lessons learned from the success?
- What do you think were the major factors that contributed to success?

Summary

The road map of this book and approach has been laid out. It is a modern approach that relies on the network technology of today and the future. The thrust is on empowerment and effectiveness in the new world of IT and business. The approach is much more related to the business environment than to technical factors. In Figure 1.1 you can see that business issues relating to business processes can be translated into systems issues and the systems and architecture. Overall, you seek to mesh the objectives and strategies of systems with those of the business through the link between systems and business processes. Here is a basic point to remember:

The goal of a project is to implement lasting change as well as to achieve high quality results on-time and within budget.

More specifically,

- The technical purpose is to get the project work done with high quality and that experience from the project is employed to improve later project and non-project work through management of issues and lessons learned.
- The business purpose is to achieve change that is persistent and long-lasting within budget, resource, and time constraints.
- The political purpose is to gain support for change that is lasting.
- The social purpose is to achieve a better working relationship between IT, business units, and management.

Similar purposes apply to the project portfolio.

- Technical purpose. It is to achieve synergy across projects as well as economies of scale for work improvement.
- Business purpose. The benefit and impact on the business of the projects achieve more than the sum of the parts. Moreover, there is cumulative improvement in business process performance.
- Political purpose. The management of the organization and business units acts more responsibly in overseeing and being involved in IT work and projects.
- Social purpose. There is a healthier and more collaborative approach to work related to IT among managers of IT, business units, and management.

It is no longer sufficient to just get the work done with good quality. If you did not achieve change, then why was the project done in the first place? If the change is not lasting, then why was the project done in the first place?

With success being lasting change, what is project failure. Of course, it is the flip side of the coin to the purposes. Also,

- A project fails if it does not generate enthusiasm for change. Without enthusiasm based on self-interest, the change may be implemented, but will not be long-lasting.
- A project fails if later projects and non-project work make or encounter the same problems. Then there are no lessons learned.
- There is failure if experience in the form of lessons learned, templates, and issues and risk management is not improved on a cumulative basis.

2
Project management methodologies

Introduction

Let's start by looking back at the history of project management. Project management was first applied to large engineering and military systems projects. Here you would have found a great deal of structure. Requirements were well-defined. The project teams were large with a diverse set of knowledge and skills. Managing projects such as these on an *ad hoc*, individual basis resulted in many problems, including:

- There was a great deal of variation in project management techniques, methods, and tools.
- Management of multiple similar projects was made difficult due to the first bullet.
- It was discovered that the same mistakes recurred again and again.
- Lessons learned may be gathered, but there was no structure in their use or updating them.

There were several early methodology attempts at individual firms. An example was at the old firm, NCR-National Cash Register. Here were some of their ingredients for project management.

- A project life cycle was defined in four stages: concept, planning, implementation, and closeout.
- Project management was treated as a professional discipline.
- Projects and project management were required to have management reviews and to give approvals and buy-in for projects.
- Project management was made mandatory across all business units.
- The project management function was viewed as neutral and not responsible for profit and loss.
- The position of project manager was formalized. It was supported by training and certification. A promotion path was established for project managers.
- Tools and guidelines were identified and specified for:

  o Project team communications;
  o Cost and schedule controls;

- Risk management;
- Knowledge management;
- Change management;
- Configuration management.

One of the first methodologies originated with the Project Management Institute (PMI). The members along with other professionals involved in project management produced the first version of the *Project Management Body of Knowledge* (known universally as the acronym PMBOK). Several iterations of PMBOK were carried out. The latest was issued in 2008 and is the fourth edition.

In Great Britain, the government was having many problems with projects of all kinds. There were many cost and schedule overruns that were played up in the media. A government agency, the Office of Government Commerce (OGC), developed a methodology called PRINCE. PRINCE is an acronym for PRojects IN Controlled Environments. It was first issued in 1989 for government projects. Based on both success and support, it evolved into PRINCE2. Like the PMBOK it has evolved over time. The latest version was issued in 2009.

For both of these, expansion moved from the government to large firms and more countries. Today, both methodologies are employed in projects in almost every country in the world.

Both of these methodologies are very formal. In real life it was found that in many software and IT projects, there was not a good fit due to the nature of the projects. To the developers and managers the methodologies seemed overbearing and bureaucratic. In 1991 a group of them gathered and issued the Agile manifesto. This was an attempt to begin to specify a more flexible approach to project management for projects that exhibited characteristics that required flexibility in project structure. Extreme Project Management represents one of the most popular implementation of the Agile concepts. In parallel, another methodology was devised that, like Agile, focused on resources in the project—the Critical Chain Project Methodology.

In this chapter we briefly review each of these. We say briefly because space does not permit a detailed description or discussion of any of these. For more detail, consult the references in the Bibliography of this book.

On the structure of the chapter, we first examine the costs, benefits, and issues and risks of using any project management methodology. This is followed by a discussion of some of the leading methodologies: PMBOK, PRINCE2, Agile, Extreme Project Management, and Critical Chain Project Management. Logically, the next step is to compare them. That is the next section.

The following sections address the following questions:

- How do you evaluate and select a methodology for project management?
- How do you market and sell a methodology?
- How do you implement the selected project management methodology?
- How do you enforce effective use of a methodology?
- How do you measure the use of a methodology?

Keep in mind that using a project management methodology helps to make projects managed in a more structured way. This is good and valuable. But,

Using a project management methodology does not ensure or guarantee project success.

This statement is critical. Success of a project or the project portfolio depends on:

- The effective use of the methodology;
- The guidelines, methods, and tools that are used in project work;
- The roles and responsibilities of upper management, IT, business units, and vendors;
- The skills and knowledge of the individuals involved in the project(s);
- The extent and quality of the people as reflected in their work;
- The ability of management, project leaders, and teams to deal with issues and risks;
- The ability to gather, use, and improve on lessons learned.

These are the critical success factors for project success and for long-term, cumulative project success. Here the project management methodology is an important ingredient for success—but also one of the many ingredients needed for success. Failure of a project can result if one of these parts fails. To prove any one element on the list was more important than another, you would like to create exact clones of projects and conduct parallel project trials. This is both technically infeasible and economically unaffordable.

Costs and benefits of using a methodology

We can first turn to the costs of implementing and using a project management methodology. Figure 2.1 gives a list of cost elements for implementation. Figure 2.2 provides a list of the recurring cost elements in using a methodology on an ongoing basis.

- Research effort to investigate different methodologies. This includes good and bad experiences.
- Evaluation and selection effort required. This should involve not just IT and management, but also managers from key business units.
- Marketing and sales work need to gain support for using a methodology. People often don't consider this.
- Outside help in planning the implementation of the methodology. It is useful and shorter to involve a consultant who knows the methodology and has implementation experience to be in the planning.
- Training and certification for project leaders.
- Training in the methodology for business unit managers and upper management.
- Training of IT staff.

Figure 2.1   Cost elements related to project management methodology implementation

Now look for the benefits. Figure 2.3 gives a list of benefits you should consider.

Having stated these benefits, it is often the case that the most compelling benefits are the problems you avoid by having a methodology. These can be gathered from past experience.

- Personnel costs associated with enforcement and monitoring in the use of the methodology.
- Retraining in updates and new releases of the methodology.
- Training and certification of new project leaders.
- Research into best practices of firms using the same methodology.

Figure 2.2   Cost elements for ongoing use of a project management methodology

- Extra effort required to do multiple project analysis without a methodology.
- Impact of surprises and issues on projects. You can use past project experience here.
- Increased ability of management—general, IT, and business unit—to track projects and work.
- Improved understanding of IT projects and project management. This can lead to faster decision-making and more clear actions.

Figure 2.3   List of benefits from the adoption and use of a project management methodology

Issues and risks in using a methodology

There are many potential issues and risks that organizations have encountered in using a specific project management methodology. Figure 2.4 presents a list of these along with comments.

- The wrong methodology is selected. It does not suit or fit with your projects.
- The methodology is implemented in exactly the same way for projects of all sizes and types. This can kill smaller projects.
- There is a lack of enforcement and monitoring of the use of the methodology. So the use of the methodology declines. People pay lip service to it, but don't follow it in their work.
- The appearance of bureaucracy associated with the methodology discourages new project ideas.
- Following from the previous bullet, managers don't refer to projects as projects to avoid the methodology.
- The people who implement the methodology lack experience. When problems arise and questions posed, there is no qualified response.
- The methodology is only imposed on a few, larger projects. This can lead to inconsistent use.
- The methodology is only applied to large projects. The problems here are several. What is large? What is small? What is the dividing line? Why is size used as the measure? Why not risk and issues? In one organization, the mandate was to use the methodology for projects over US$500,000. The IT group left one project that large. For other even larger projects they circumvented the rule by breaking up projects into US$350,000 increments.

Figure 2.4   List of potential issues and risks in using a project management methodology

PMBOK

In *PMBOK* there are five process groups: initiating, planning, executing monitoring, controlling, and closing. The *PMBOK* is divided into two parts. The first part provides information on the project life cycle, project organization, and the project management processes. Twenty areas are defined and discussed in a section on the process planning group. These define the sequence in which the plan is to be developed. These include the following:

- Develop project management plan
- Collect requirements
- Define scope
- Create WBS (work breakdown structure)
- Define activities
- Sequence activities
- Estimate activity resources
- Estimate activity durations
- Develop schedule
- Estimate costs
- Determine budget
- Plan quality
- Develop human resource plan
- Plan communications
- Plan risk management
- Identify risks
- Perform qualitative risk analysis
- Perform quantitative risk analysis
- Plan risk responses
- Plan procurements

Subsequent sections deal with execution, monitoring, and controlling the process group.

The second part of PMBOK addresses specific knowledge areas of project management. These are:

- Project Integration Management (Chapter 4). This contains information on developing the charter of a project and the plan, managing the execution of the project and work, managing project change, and closing a project. Think of this as an umbrella chapter.
- Project Scope Management (Chapter 5). Here the definition of scope, its control, and the setup of the Work Breakdown Structure (WBS) are addressed.
- Project Time Management (Chapter 6). This includes task estimation, schedule development, and schedule control.
- Project Cost Management (Chapter 7). Here costs and budgets are set and managed.
- Project Quality Management (Chapter 8). Quality is planned. Quality assurance steps are addressed along with quality control.

- Project Human Resources Management (Chapter 9). The human resource plan is defined along with acquiring, developing, and managing the team.
- Project Communications Management (Chapter 10).
- Project Risk Management (Chapter 11). Risks are identified along with quantitative and qualitative risk assessment. Responses are planned along with the monitoring and controlling of risks.
- Project Procurement Management (Chapter 12). This covers the following areas for outsourcing: planning, conducting procurements, administration, and closing.

PRINCE2

Space only permits an overview of this methodology. PRINCE2 has seven principles:

- Continued business justification;
- Lessons learned;
- Defined roles and responsibilities;
- Project management by project stages;
- Management by exception;
- Focus on the products of work;
- Customization to fit a project's characteristics.

There are seven PRINCE2 themes:

- Business case;
- Organization;
- Quality;
- Plans;
- Risk;
- Change;
- Progress (formerly called "controls").

Under the methodology these principles need to be referred to during the project to ensure effectiveness. If they are not adhered to throughout the project, then there is a high likelihood of failure. In this book we would associate risk with issues that give rise to risks.

There are seven management processes, listed below. The processes refer to the steps to be followed in the project. As such, PRINCE2 is known as a process-based methodology.

- Starting up a project (covers work through the project concept);
- Directing a project (applies to the entire project life cycle);
- Initiating a project (covers the steps through development of the project plan);
- Controlling a stage of a project (covers the daily management of the work);
- Managing product delivery (includes the detailed planning, tracking, and controlling of parts of the work—called "work packages");

- Managing a stage boundary (covers activities to prepare for the next stage of work as well as addressing exceptions);
- Closing a project (covers the end of the project, measurement of benefits, and lessons learned).

Each process is in turn divided into three to eight activities or subprocesses. Each activity is described in terms of purpose, objectives, context, overview of relationships with other activities, and recommended actions for the activity.

There are three types of management products that are updated through change control. The first category is called "baseline" and includes such items as the risk management strategy, plan, quality management strategy, and configuration management strategy. The second category is that of records for lessons learned, quality, risk, and so on. The third category consists of various reports. An example is the end of stage report.

In the latest version of PRINCE2 there is now a central chapter that discusses how to embed the methodology in the organization and how to fit the methodology to a specific project.

Agile project management

Agile concepts and principles were developed as a response to using the traditional project management methodologies. People felt that more effective project work could be accomplished by following different principles. Here are four principles of Agile methods.

- Individual people and their interactions should be given attention. Traditional project management methods, by contrast, focus on processes and tools. Agile supports team members expressing their views and getting rapid feedback. The goal is to reduce the communications time. In traditional projects, there are only weekly meetings to exchange views except for casual contact.
- Working products or software is the focus. Traditional project management favors documentation. The argument is that a working system is more important than a lot of documentation.
- Customer or business unit collaboration is the key throughout the project. In traditional projects, there is a strong user role at the start and end, but not as much in the middle.
- Success is achieved through iterations. The duration of time between iterations is short. This applies to requirements and development. There are no large time gaps.
- Change during a project is encouraged. In traditional project management, you want to stick with the plan. Change can disrupt the plan.

Agile emphasizes that the project team should be an integrated unit or entity. This is difficult if many of the team members are toiling on other projects and non-project work.

The Agile project leader does not overrule the decisions taken by experienced team members. Decisions are made with the team—not on behalf of the team. The project leader is not involved in technical decision-making. Motivation and coordination are the key roles for the Agile project leader.

Extreme Project Management

Extreme Project Management is one of several ways to implement the Agile principles. Extreme Project Management (often abbreviated XPM) is employed on complex projects that do not have a clearly defined end point. Examples can be in research and development environments for automobiles, weapons systems, and software. In such projects requirements start out as being partially defined. They will be refined and changed during the project. Project success can be defined and then changed during the project due to market changes, new information, and other factors. XPM, like Agile, is based on a close, daily working relationship between the project team members and the consumers, users, or business unit staff. As the work is done, features and capabilities can change. As the consumers of the project learn more about what is possible, they make changes. In traditional project management, the requirements are set and changes discouraged. Here they are encouraged.

Another type of project in which this method can be employed is that of very complex projects. In such projects, gathering all requirements would take months. Documenting and getting them approved—more months. The project is likely to be dropped before it really got started. However, under XPM you get started with some of the key requirements and start building based on these. Each new iteration of the product incorporates more capabilities and features.

There are some principles embraced by many involved in XPM. These include the following:

- What happens after a project is completed is more important than activities during the project. This is a focus on change management. You get no benefits until the processes are affected by the project change. With no change, no benefit.
- The more time a project leader spends with business units involved in the project, the better. This is an emphasis on collaboration with the business.
- A project plan must be developed with the participation of all stakeholders—business units, team members, and so on.
- You must define project success at the start of the project to ensure that you will eventually achieve it.
- As a project leader, your best allies are with the stakeholders. If you don't adhere to this, they can be enemies.

All of these are parts of the approach in this book. However, that being said, there are some more controversial ideas with XPM.

- You should have fear if the project has not changed. This is not necessarily true. It depends on the project. If you have worked on many different projects of the same type, then there should be little change.
- If you cannot predict the future, do not plan it. This is true at the detailed level of a plan. However, at the summary level tasks and milestones should remain the same.

XPM puts an emphasis on teamwork, collaboration, participation, change, and being results oriented.

As you read this, it sounds good, right? XPM and Agile offer flexibility. There are some downside risks to consider:

- One problem is to determine when this iteration approach will end.
- Another is that it ignores the political world. Customer staff involved in the project may not want at all and so may propose so many changes that the project dies a slow, painful death.
- Experience shows that to make this method work, you have to have a high-level business manager involved—not just at the start as in traditional projects. Instead, they have to be fully engaged and committed at all times. They have to be able to quickly and, we mean, quickly, assign priorities for the work. They have to perform rapid trade-offs of function versus cost and schedule.
- The project leader is much more engaged. In traditional projects, a project leader may manage several projects at one time. Here, the project leader must really be on top of the work and actively negotiate with the business customer.
- In some projects if you demonstrate too much flexibility, there will be excessive change. Political factors could rip both the project and you to shreds.

In XPM, iterations of work are demonstrated to the customer/business unit. The feedback provides input for the next iterations. Requirements such as business rules for transactions are refined. The project plan is updated and refined.

The project plan for XPM and Agile is different than a traditional project plan. Traditionally, for example, in system development or other projects, you develop requirements and then proceed to design and programming. Here, in both Agile and XPM, the beginning and end of the project plan remain the same or similar. In the middle of the plan, there are project subplans—one per iteration.

Critical Chain Project Management (CCPM)

The *critical chain* of a project consists of the tasks that define the lowest possible lead time. The critical chain is composed of sequentially dependent tasks. There are two types of dependencies between tasks. The first is when the output of a task is required as input by another (called "hands-off dependency"). The second is a resource dependency. The person cannot start the next task until he or she finishes the first task. In project management terms, you can think of this as the resource-constrained critical path. Focus is on resource-dependent tasks that affect the completion date of the project. The critical chain is the set of resource-leveled tasks. If resources are unlimited, then it is identical to the traditional critical path of project management.

In CCPM, you seek to optimize the schedule by working with the safety margin that people build into task estimation. You look at individual tasks to see if the time durations can be reduced. If you don't do this, then you cannot easily change the schedule. You are locked in. Thus, the first step in optimization is to remove the safety margins from the tasks. The method then places buffers or time periods at specific points in the project schedule. Individual tasks are forced to be completed in the least possible time. There are four buffer types:

- Project buffer. Some of the time acquired by reducing task duration at the task level is placed in a buffer task. This task is put in at the end of the project schedule. It is adjusted based on the experience in the project.
- Feeding buffer. This is a buffer inserted at points where inputs from non-critical tasks merge with critical chain tasks.
- Resource buffer. This is a warning issued to critical resources to ensure that they complete their current work and start to prepare for a critical chain task. This allows work to start on the critical chain task as soon as their current work is finished.
- Capacity buffer. This places on-call resources into the schedule if they are needed to prevent delays in the schedule. This buffer adds costs to the project. This one is most commonly used in a multi-project setting.

These buffers are tracked and adjusted by the project leader during the work.
To implement the buffers, the following steps are employed.

- You must reduce task estimates dramatically so as to have time for the buffers.
- You must resource level the project to eliminate conflicts over resources.
- Part of the time saved in reduced estimates is placed in a project buffer.
- You insert feeding buffers at points in the schedule where non-critical chain tasks intersect the critical chain.
- You put in resource buffers to reduce the likelihood that a critical resource will be unavailable when needed.
- Multitasking is reduced or eliminated.
- Tasks with no predecessor tasks are to be scheduled as late as possible.
- As project leader, you want to push for task completion as soon as possible — before the scheduled time, if possible.

Comparison of methodologies

You can first divide up the methodologies into two groups. One, consisting of PMBOK and PRINCE2 are the formal methodologies. The others in the second group are less formal and stand in high contrast to the first group. Note that it is possible to have several methodologies used by one organization. For example, there could be a formal methodology for most projects. For projects that have certain characteristics, you could employ Agile or XPM. The risk of doing this, however, is not only confusion, but potential interface problems between projects adhering to different methodologies.

PMBOK covers a wider range of project activities and provides more guidance in some areas than PRINCE2. For example, PMBOK contains a Precedence Diagramming Method for identifying dependencies, while PRINCE2 identifies a list of activities together with dependencies. PMBOK has a more extensive treatment of project estimation. If the overall schedule is not acceptable, PMBOK gives more complete treatment of methods to deal with than PRINCE2. Similar remarks can be made for performance measurement methods. Here PRINCE2 does not address Earned Value Analysis while PMBOK does. PMBOK provides more detail with respect to project quality, human resources, and communications.

Overall, both PRINCE2 and PMBOK are complimentary. PRINCE2 is process focused while PMBOK can be considered as an encyclopedia for project management. The differences in the methodologies lie in the details. In PRINCE2 the project leader manages day-to-day work, while in PMBOK the range of responsibility of the project leader is greater. PRINCE2 has a greater emphasis on project oversight.

You can map the processes in both methodologies to each other. The result is as follows:

- Initiating a process group (PMBOK)—starting up a project and directing a project (PRINCE2);
- Planning process group—initiating a project;
- Executing process group—managing product delivery and managing a stage boundary;
- Monitoring and controlling process group—directing a project, controlling a stage; managing product delivery, managing a stage boundary;
- Closing process group—managing a stage boundary and closing a project.

The following list helps to understand how the knowledge areas of PMBOK map to PRINCE2:

- Project integration management (PMBOK)—themes of organization, plans, change, and progress;
- Project scope management—themes of the business case, plans, and change;
- Project time management—plans, change, and progress;
- Project cost management—plans, change, and progress;
- Project quality management—plans, quality, and change;
- Project human resource management—organization and plans;
- Project communications management—plans, change, and progress;
- Project risk management—risk, change, and progress;
- Project procurement management—business case, plans, change, and progress.

Evaluation and selection of a methodology

There are a number of factors to consider when evaluating project management methodologies. These are divided into two groups. The first addresses whether to adopt any formal methodology. A list of questions for this is contained in Figure 2.5. Why is a formal approach needed? One reason is obvious—to select the methodology that is best suited to the organization. Another reason is to head off upper management expectations that all projects will now be done quicker, with higher quality, and not fail. Emphasize the negative. What will happen if we adopt no methodology and continue as we are? This is the fear factor. It can be very compelling in organizations that have failed projects.

- What is the nature of our projects in terms of duration, size, scope, and risk?
- What is our project track record in terms of successes, partial successes, and failures?
- Is a variety of different methods used for project management so that it is difficult or almost impossible to manage multiple projects and the project portfolio consistently?
- Do you have the resources available to implement and enforce the methodology?

Through answers to these questions, you answer the two questions.

- What will happen over time if you continue as you are without a methodology?
- What will be the short- and long-term impacts of no change?

Figure 2.5   Questions to consider in adopting any project management methodology

The second group of questions deals with the evaluation and selection of a specific methodology. To get to this point, it is assumed that you have gotten through the items in Figure 2.5 and have decided that you want a methodology. The items to consider for methodology evaluation and selection are given in Figure 2.6.

- How will you become familiar with the jargon and acronyms of the methodology?
- How will you determine if a specific methodology fits your projects?
- What level of support is available for implementing a methodology?
- Are their companies or agencies that are in our industry segment using the methodology? What has been their experience?

Figure 2.6   Questions related to methodology evaluation and selection

You can almost view this process as similar to application software package evaluation and selection (see Chapter 18 on Software Packages). Why not just pick one methodology without all of this work? There are several reasons. First, you have to have a good fit between what is in the methodology and your projects. Otherwise, the methodology will not be used. Second, you head off and prevent people from later saying, "We picked the wrong method."

Marketing and selling a methodology

You may be thinking about the necessity of a sales and marketing campaign. One approach is to preach the benefits of using a methodology. There is more order to the work. All projects will follow a standardized approach. The project leaders acquire more skills and knowledge by becoming certified in the methodology and so on. Often, this won't work—especially with senior project leaders. You need another approach—negative selling. Taking this method might entail the following:

- Have project leaders discuss problems and issues that were encountered in the past. Show how things would have been different if the methodology had been in place.

- Take a recent failed project and, again, demonstrate how the outcome for the project could have been different if the methodology had been used.
- Use the fear factor. What will happen to them if the methodology is not followed? Will they be removed from their project management role?

Emphasize that the methodology is just the "what." The "how" in terms of project management methods and tools will be largely unchanged or improved.

If you think marketing and sales must be done one time, forget it? Drop this idea. Marketing and sales continue on an ongoing basis as new projects arise that are urgent.

Implementation of a methodology

OK, the methodology has been selected. Through marketing and sales efforts, it has been approved. Now you are ready for implementation. You could just buy books related to the methodology and distribute them to project leaders, IT managers and supervisors, business unit managers, and upper-level managers. However, you would get into the communications problems discussed in Chapter 11 on Project Communications Management. It is clear that preparations are needed and a planned, organized approach is required if you are going to have the methodology employed effectively.

Suppose that you have several people who have worked in firms that have used the methodology you chose. Why not just use them? A bad idea. They are professionals with in-depth implementation experience. They also may lack training skills. They can be intimidated by more senior staff and project leaders. Experience demonstrates the value of outside help in implementation. They not only know the methodology, but also how to implement it in great details. They also know how to deal with indifference, resistance, and any other questions that arise. They have seen and heard it before.

With the consultant, you want to sit down and map out a project plan. Have them identify and list at least 20 problems and issues that they have seen in the past. Use these to create an initial list of issues.

Apply the methodology to one current project to support the understanding of the methodology. The example can be useful in the training. Moreover, assuming that the project leader supports the methodology, he or she can be a reference sell and give the benefits and make remarks on the ease of transition to the methodology.

Conduct training in the methodology. This should not be some dry lecture. You should start with the problems in the current and past projects. Then you can expand this to discuss the impacts on their work. Through their own eyes, they see the need for change. Now you can proceed through the steps or phases in the methodology. Prior to this, the IT manager and some of the project leaders should have attended training in the methodology. They can then reinforce the internal training and answer questions. It is best sometimes if the audience hears answers from their own management rather than the trainer.

Develop guidelines for how the methodology will be applied to current projects. Some are so small or are almost completed that applying the methodology makes no sense. Cover separately for how it will be handled for new projects. Discuss the enforcement and monitoring that will be done.

Establish a database of guidelines for how best to use the methodology. Start with ideas supplied by the consultant. The more and faster that the guidelines can be deployed, the more the use of the methodology is reinforced.

Enforcement of a methodology

At first thought, if something is adopted by IT, upper management, and business unit management, it would not be necessary to consider enforcement. However, the following factors point to the need to consider enforcement of a methodology.

- Senior project leaders will be among the most resistant. They have managed many different projects before without the methodology or using a different one. They see no need to change something that works.
- Junior project managers will adopt the methodology—even embrace it word for word. Just as they were trained to do when they worked toward certification.
- The urgency of project work and the press of project deadlines may encourage people to bypass steps in the methodology—to get the work done faster.
- Management may view a project as critical and needed fast. They also may perceive the methodology is bureaucratic. These two, when combined, put pressure on getting the work done—don't use the methodology.

From experience, each of these will likely arise. Thus, in anticipation of problems, you have to think about how the project management methodology will be enforced. There are several parts to enforcement. You have to first decide what to enforce and how to do it. Then you have to think of what to do if there are violations in use. Are there any effective penalties and actions that will reduce the likelihood of the problems in the future.

Someone in IT has to have responsibility for enforcement or, more politically correct, for monitoring the use of the methodology. Until everyone gets into the habit of using any methodology, you will not be able to rely on self-policing or self-enforcement.

Having identified someone, what should they do? Where do they begin? To get them up to speed with some experience, have them first review several recently completed projects for which information is fresh. You should select a successful project and one that was partially so or failure. Both large and small projects should be considered. Another variable is the experience level of the project leaders involved.

Once you have selected these past projects, the person can review the milestones first. Do the milestone content and quality mesh with what is said in the methodology? You cannot review the work since it is over. So turn to surrogates—the issues in the project. How were they addressed? Was it consistent with the methodology? Were any problems recurrent and persistent? Were there any project surprises? Could these have been prevented if the methodology had been followed? Answering these questions prepares you to deal with current and new projects.

For new projects, you want to have the project leader state how their project concept and project plan follow the methodology in terms of project definition, planning, methods and tools, quality, communications, cost control, and risk management. Here you seek detailed answers—not just vague statements. To get more precise responses, a tip is to pose potential problems that the project might encounter. The project leader should answer in the context of the methodology. If he or she does not, then you can probably anticipate that when issues arise, they will resort to methods outside of the methodology.

Let's turn to ongoing projects. Start with a small project. It is easier to review. Consider the past milestones as was discussed above. For current work you can start with how problems, issues, and surprises were handled. You will likely not have time to examine all of the current project work. So concentrate on tasks for which the project management methodology provides guidance.

"Enforcement" is often viewed as a nasty, negative word. However, if there is no enforcement or monitoring, then project leaders may get the wrong impression. Regardless of what is said about the importance and application of the methodology, in reality through actions they see that little value is placed on using the methodology. It is like the old adage, "Actions speak louder than words."

Measurement of the use of a methodology

Suppose you are in an organization that employs a project management methodology. How do you determine if it is useful? Are you getting the benefits? By answering the questions in Figure 2.7, you can improve and refine the use of the methodology to achieve greater effectiveness. Note that this scorecard could have been placed in Chapter 15 on performance measures. Instead, it is here because of its value to the discussion of methodologies and it is very specific to the contents of this chapter.

- Is the methodology used on all projects? If not, what are the reasons and justify for the variance in use?
- Is there a formal approach to grant exception status to a project?
- Before a project starts, is there planning on how to use the methodology? If not, then this could be a sign that people pay lip service to the methodology, but do not really follow it.
- Is there recurring training for project leaders and others on the methodology? New staff and project managers would seem to require this. Refresher training would be useful for the existing project leaders.
- Is certification in the methodology required for all project leaders? If not, is it at least encouraged? Does certification lead to higher pay? Or, how is a certificate holder rewarded?
- Is there formal training in the new version or release of the methodology? If not, there is a danger of uneven and inconsistent usage.
- Is there measurement taken of the use of the methodology in projects?
- Are measurements related to methodology use collected and put in a database?
- Are management reports prepared and issued on the use of the methodology?

Figure 2.7 Scorecard for evaluating methodology use

> - Are guidelines defined, organized, and issued that relate to more effective use of the methodology?
> - Related to the preceding, are lessons learned gathered and employed relative to the methodology?
> - What is the method in project review to assess adherence to the methodology?
> - What are the "on the street" views about the methodology? What are the subjective remarks that you can pick up casually from IT managers and staff as well as those in business units?
> - Does someone have as their roles and responsibilities the task of keeping up with project methodologies in general and the one you are using in particular?
> - Related to the previous question, are best practices gathered and used from other organizations using the same methodology?

Figure 2.7   (Continued)

So you answer these questions. Now what?

Cases and examples

A European manufacturing firm, Omega Industries, acquires Bodega Manufacturing based in the US. Omega uses PRINCE2 and has had mixed success with its use. Bodega uses the PMBOK and has had greater success. After the merger, Omega management must make decisions regarding the following questions:

- Should a single methodology be made standard across the merged firm?
- If so, how do you select which methodology should be used?
- Assuming that only one methodology is to be used, how can they transition to one methodology without disrupting current work?

While there are some joint projects between the firms, most of the projects will be performed by employees in the separate organization as separate projects.

Questions:

1. Discuss the feasibility of using elements of both PMBOK and PRINCE2 to get a hybrid methodology.
2. What are characteristics of the projects that would favor one methodology over the other?
3. What steps would be required to transition Bodega to PRINCE2?

Lessons learned

There are political ramifications to the use of a methodology. First, it shows management that IT is following a structured approach to projects. Second, this is likely to prevent management from imposing a methodology themselves or through consultants.

A third use that we have seen is in intimidation of business units. If a structured methodology is employed, then they will be less likely to resist. You may think that this discussion is unnecessary since you are doing technical projects. Such is not the case. In one firm we observed, the IT manager adopted a methodology and started to use it on projects in a partial way. Even so, he received the following benefits:

- There was less resistance and complaint from business unit managers and staff members.
- Management posed questions about his and IT's performance.

Did project performance improve with the methodology? The answer is no if you consider technical work and progress. The answer is yes if you consider politics. The project leaders and teams were subject to fewer questions and less interference. This example is a good reason to adopt a methodology.

In our experience, the best and most successful implementations of methodologies occurred in firms that produced guidelines and lessons learned on how best to apply and use the various detailed parts of the methodology. There was much less success in firms that just stressed enforcement. In those firms, the methodology was viewed as negative and often given as a reason for project delays.

Guidelines

- Experience shows that the selection and implementation of a project management methodology is just the start of the work or tip of the iceberg. To gain value, you not only have to have management endorsement and technical support, but you also have to have ground rules for deciding whether a project can avoid using the methodology. If you have none of these, then the decision will be made on a project-by-project basis. This *ad hoc* approach leads to inconsistency and sometimes to collapse in the use of the methods.
- Many times a firm implements a methodology for projects without measuring their current projects, policies, procedures, and work before the methodology was implemented. This is a very bad practice. Everyone—IT, business units, and management—must see that change is needed. Use the scorecards in Chapter 15 on performance measurement to do this.
- Assume that you have conducted the measurements, then you should repeat the measurements at six-month intervals. One benefit is that you demonstrate the before and after difference due to the use of the methodology. Another benefit is that you can collect lessons learned to refine how you are using the methodology. A third benefit is that you uncover areas of issues and weakness that can then be addressed.

Questions

1. Using the Web, find examples of completed projects where success was attributed to using a project management methodology.

2. Using the Web, find examples of failed projects that employed a project management methodology.
3. Select one of the project management methodologies and apply it to your personal life. For example, you could use one in a project to buy a car or truck.
4. Using the Web, find an example of project success using the Agile methods. Were there aspects of the project that took advantage of Agile? What would have happened if one of the two formal methodologies had been used?
5. It has been argued that a project management methodology is necessary if you are to have successful projects. However, it is widely agreed that using a methodology is not sufficient to guarantee success. Give some reasons for why this is true.

What to do next

1. If your organization uses a project management methodology, address the following questions:

   - Is the methodology employed on small projects? If not, what is the cut-off point, under which the methodology is not used?
   - At the time that the methodology was selected, were alternatives considered? Why or why not?
   - How is the use of the methodology enforced? Can a new project that is urgent and important get around using the methodology?
   - Have there been more lessons learned gathered with the methodology in place? Has the rate of project success increased?
   - Do formal guidelines exist alongside of the methodology?

2. If your firm does not employ a formal project management methodology, address the following questions:

   - Why hasn't a methodology been adopted? What is the success rate of projects?
   - Without a standard methodology, each project is managed and overseen individually. What problems have you observed from this?
   - If management was to select and mandate the use of a project management methodology, what would be some of the issues to be addressed in the transition?

3. Let's suppose that you are using either PMBOK or PRINCE2. A new update or version becomes available. Now when a newer release of a software package comes out, you quickly implement it because it will have some of the following benefits: (1) fix bugs and errors detected in the previous version; (2) provide for new features and capabilities; (3) have increased performance. With a methodology this is not the case. Answer the following questions:

   - What would be the criteria for making the decision on upgrading to the new version of the methodology?
   - What would be cost elements involved in the upgrading?
   - What you do with current projects? Would you make project management changes in the middle of the projects? If so, why?

Summary

In this chapter you have seen a variety of project management methodologies. Each has benefit in certain circumstances. The content of this book deals with the "how" of project management and supports all of them. The theme of collaboration follows closely to that of Agile-type methods by encouraging business unit involvement throughout the project life cycle. The use of templates supports the more structured methodologies. The use of issues and lessons learned is mentioned as part of the "What to do" in all of the methods.

In Chapter 10 we address change management. Here as requirements are gathered, Quick Wins are identified and can be implemented while the project is ongoing. Quick Wins fix problems related to the business processes. Quick Wins can also result in changes that mitigate or handle some of the requirements. These have proven often to then reduce the requirements and future project work since they have already been addressed through the Quick Wins.

3
Developing your project management process and strategy

Introduction

The purpose of this chapter is to provide you with guidelines to the following:

- Evaluate your current project management process;
- Develop a project strategy;
- Determine improvements to project management;
- Transition the current project management process to an improved one.

What is a *project strategy*? It is your overall approach for setting up and managing projects. What you decide to do here will be carried out in your new project management process. All of your projects will then be managed within the process and follow the strategy.

To better understand what a strategy is, let's consider some alternatives.

- **Alternative strategy 1: No strategy at all.**
  Here project ideas are generated and projects are started on an individual negotiated basis. Each project is managed and measured on its own. Interfaces are very difficult because no collaborative culture exists. It is everyone for oneself. You are unable to combine the data in different projects or gather lessons learned across projects.

  Without a strategy, the entire process of managing the projects can become disorganized. Results will be at best uneven. Because there is no overall vision or view, there is more likelihood that major projects will be missed or left out. Also, critical infrastructure projects to establish or improve networks will be more difficult to approve because they lack a specific business department client or owner.

- **Alternative strategy 2: Carefully select which projects are funded, but then manage each separately after they start.**
  Many organizations have drifted into this approach. Management has become aware of the importance of projects, so the project receives a great deal of management attention at the front end. Unfortunately, this attention is not carried through during the project. There is often an underlying assumption that if you start the projects out correctly, then the project managers and teams will see them through. This is not the case with systems and technology projects that are highly interdependent. Issues that are unresolved in one project can quickly impact other projects. How will upper management become aware of the impacts of such an issue? If no mechanism is in place to deal with issues, they can mature into crises.
- **Alternative strategy 3: Proactively determine which projects are funded based on tangible business benefits and then manage the projects collectively.**
  This strategy assumes that the whole of the projects is greater than the sum of the individual projects. This strategy results in a collaborative management approach that involves the management of issues, resources, and schedules across multiple projects. As you can imagine, this consumes more management time and effort in dealing with issues. Results and project success in a number of firms indicate that this is the approach to consider for your organization. Benefits can be seen tangibly in the business process improvement. This applies in E-Business where the implementation is very large in scope so that E-Business implementation consists of a number of projects.

You probably have most often observed the first two alternatives. However, from the previous chapter you learned that substantial benefits can be derived from the third alternative. Thus, restating part of the purpose of the chapter, you seek to find ways to migrate from alternatives 1 and 2 to alternative 3. Why haven't more firms adopted more aspects of the collaborative strategy? Experience reveals many reasons. First, the organizational culture may reinforce the old systems mentality of separate projects (dating back to stand-alone batch and limited online systems). Culture is hard to change. Second, if you work on maintenance and fail to take on major projects, then you can avoid developing a strategy. Third, there may be a lack of tools and support for shared work.

A project strategy leads to defining the *project management process*. The *project management process* is how you manage all of the systems projects from their conception through completion or termination, as was informally discussed in Chapter 1. If you assume that the third strategy applies, then the project management process includes the following goals:

- Ensure a proactive approach in identifying potential projects that link to key business processes.
- Encourage wide participation and commitment by business units in projects.
- Obtain upper-management commitment by setting the slate of projects and dealing with major issues that cross projects.
- Enforce uniformity in project plan structure through templates, common databases for issues, action items, lessons learned, and standardized reporting.

- Support information sharing among projects and resolving issues among project leaders.
- Provide analysis of multiple projects and dynamic resource management across projects so as to spread resources effectively across projects.

Now let's make this discussion more formal by putting it into a series of steps. You will be considering each step in the context of the more proactive project strategy. For each step the end products and key questions you must address will be defined. The specific chapters where the steps are covered in detail are also listed.

Step 1: review and select the project management methodology

Given the discussion in Chapter 2 on methodologies, not too much needs to be added. Often, the methodology has already been determined. Even so, there are decisions to be made related to the following: (1) how the methodology will be employed for projects of different sizes; (2) how any exceptions can be reviewed and allowed. These decisions are based upon the following factors:

- What are the issues and risks in the project? If the project is routine and there are few issues, you may want to scale back the methodology to speed the work up. Later, if the project encounters more issues, you can bring back elements of the methodology.
- If the project is small, then you might opt for Agile or one of the other less formal methods that focuses on the team members.
- If the project is substantial with many issues, the tendency would be to use one of the formal methodologies—PMBOK or PRINCE2.

Usually an organization will have adopted only one methodology. However, experience shows that this can leave the organization at a disadvantage since there is little or no flexibility. We recommend the following guidelines:

- Have one formal and one less formal methodology. The default is the formal methodology to reduce risk.
- Use the guidelines in Chapter 2 to help determine if a specific project should follow an informal methodology such as Agile.
- As part of the project concept, the concept should evaluate and recommend the appropriate methodology.
- If the informal methodology is recommended, then criteria should be given for transitioning to the more formal method if there are substantial issues, or there is significant project change in scope or direction.

Changing methodologies in midstream can often be very disruptive to the team and work. Thus, it should only be employed if you are going to make major changes such as changing the project leader or major changes in the makeup of the team.

Step 2: establish basic components of the project management process

The end products are as follows:

- Approaches for managing multiple projects, project reporting, issue management, and lessons learned are defined.
- The project management process (defining what is to be done in each of the nine steps) is documented, presented, and approved.
- A steering committee is appointed.
- A project coordinator is identified.

Additional end products may apply given the methodology selected.

It is important to define the role of the project coordinator(s). The *project coordinator(s)* is responsible for the following activities:

- Assist business departments in developing process plans.
- Support the development of project concepts.
- Provide support for training in project management methods and tools.
- Analyze project concepts and recommend a project slate to the management steering committee.
- Assess project issues and status and present analysis results to management.
- Coordinate the identification, analysis, and resolution of issues.
- Maintain and support the database of issues.
- Support the lessons learned database.

A project coordinator does not have to be a full-time role. It can be filled by a line manager, or on a rotating basis by project managers.

What if you do not have a coordinator for projects? Well, the list of duties listed above still should be performed. Without the coordinator, some of these will be done *ad hoc*. Some may not be done at all. For example, lessons learned and issues analysis may be done on an individual project basis. However, there will be little or no cumulative improvement since there will be reservoir of lessons learned and issues.

Whether the project manager is one person or several depends on the projects, organization, and range of business and system activities. Note that these responsibilities are similar, but expanded from the role of the traditional concept of a *project office*. In the past, the project office typically concentrated on the tracking activities of systems projects and then provided analysis results and reports to management. A project office performs the following functions:

- Provides a centralized review of all projects
- Reports on projects to management
- Sets standards and procedures for project management
- Supports project management software

For some companies, the project office has provided a useful way to gain control over projects and provide uniform reporting. A survey indicated that 15 percent of firms have established project offices. However, by its very nature the project office is pure overhead. It can take on a life of its own and impose major burdens on projects. The project office can also separate project management from project administration.

What are the attributes of a project coordinator? He or she should know project management and see the opportunity to improve the current process. The project manager should also be able to perform a number of tasks in parallel. The candidate does not need to be an expert with project management software and does not need to be technically oriented, because this role will entail working closely with business processes, business units, and business department staff.

Let's consider some defining questions. What will be the general scope of projects? You can arrange alternatives for project scope into levels. Your goal is to have as many projects at higher levels as possible to support the business.

- *Level 1.* The project is restricted to the system itself. This is very narrow and traditional. There is no guarantee that either architecture or business process improvements will be carried out.
- *Level 2.* The project includes infrastructure or architecture along with the system. This is a more modern view and reflective of network-based systems such as client-server or intranet projects as well as data warehousing projects that often involve database management and hardware upgrades.
- *Level 3.* The project includes the system, architecture, and business process improvements. This is the comprehensive scope that is most desirable. Although this scope is larger, you can divide the project up into subprojects.

What is the role of the business units in projects? This is a crucial question. One part of the answer is the involvement of high-level business managers in the management steering committee. Another part consists of the following activities, which are performed by business units:

- Develop process plans—blueprints for the long-term future of the business process.
- Participate in individual projects.
- Support process change linked to new systems projects.
- Insist on measurement of projects—during and after work.
- Strive to prevent deterioration of projects. This is discussed in detail in Chapter 10.

How should the *management steering committee* be constituted and operated? The steering committee consists of high-level business managers, whose duties include the following:

- Review and approve the slate of projects.
- Assist and resolve project issues that cross multiple projects from a business perspective.
- Periodically meet to review and reset project priorities based on current needs and the state of the projects.

The committee can meet from two to four times per year based on issues and the budget cycle. Note that if it meets more often, managers will tend to send lower level replacements. The agenda will start drifting into considering project status. Then the steering committee ceases to be a steering committee and becomes a project oversight group—another layer of red tape. You can scale the number and frequency of meetings based upon the number and urgency of outstanding issues so that there would be more frequent meetings with many important issues. Using this approach, the steering committee would meet more often at the start of the project and toward the end during implementation.

When thinking about the management steering committee, you must consider the budget cycle. Let's suppose that your organization operates on a calendar year. This means that the first cut of the budget will be completed in October or earlier. The project slate must be in place prior to this date. If you back up from October, you might select August or early September as the time for your first meeting. Assume that there are to be four meetings a year equally spaced through the year. The second meeting might be in December, during which time results and issues are to be presented. A third meeting might be in March. This is an important meeting during which project priorities might be realigned. The fourth meeting might be in June and resemble the December meeting. If you think that this is too much detail, you are wrong. The more you can plan and make known to management, the more likely you are to attract the right people to the meetings.

Who are potential candidates for the committee? Assuming that you have identified several major business processes that merit projects, then the business unit managers most involved in these are logical candidates. When selecting between line managers and staff managers, choose the line managers. They command the attention of top management and their support will be critical.

Why do you have to have a formal method for addressing issues? Why not address each issue as it arises? This is the seat of the pants of the reactive approach. It will yield inconsistent actions and sometimes raise even more issues. Proactive issue management aims to track and analyze all issues that have remained unresolved for some time. Issues management also attempts to determine the impact of issues and their resolution across multiple projects. Because risk in tasks and the plan are reflected in the issues, issues management covers traditional risk management in projects.

Step 3: define critical business processes and activities as well as the system architecture and process plans

To be proactive, you must understand what areas are crucial to both the business and the systems in terms of infrastructure and architecture. This is the first step in detailed analysis. The step can help management and the business units focus on what is critical overall. Isn't this done naturally? Not really. Many general managers are uncomfortable with systems. The business processes cross the boundaries between business units; business unit managers may be reluctant to address issues outside of their control.

The end products of this step are as follows:

- Definition of system architecture
- Identification of critical business processes
- Process plans for each critical process

Critical questions here are as follows:

- What is the current systems architecture? What improvements are needed based on current and known projected systems requirements?
- How will critical business processes be determined? You will not be able to generate projects for all processes. In addition, resources will still be required for maintenance and operations support as well as architecture improvement.
- What constitutes a process plan? How will process plans be developed? These questions will be addressed in Chapter 4.

Step 4: review all current projects and associate them with the process plans and architecture

This can be an eye-opening experience. You may find that many of the projects do not fit with the business processes and architecture. They may instead be directed toward enhancements and maintenance or minor systems development. The importance of this step lies in showing management and the business units that the way things are currently being prioritized needs to be revisited. This can help set the stage for the new project management process.

The end products are as follows:

- Assessment of current projects along with necessary changes and recommendations in relation to the process plans and architecture;
- Recommendations on which projects can be terminated due to limited benefits.

It is in this step that the shortcomings of the current projects are identified. From lessons learned, several problems can occur:

- The scope of the current project is too narrow and does not include business processes.
- The business role in the project is not defined.
- There are few, if any, tangible benefits to the project as it stands.
- The interdependencies between projects have not been completely specified.
- When you add up all of the projects, there are insufficient resources and substantial unplanned work.

As a result, you will likely recommend that some projects be killed, others restructured, and still more combined. Killing a project has several benefits. First, resources are released to work on other projects. Second, management shows that it is serious about insisting on project results. Third, the organization has an opportunity to learn lessons from the experience.

Step 5: develop project concepts for new project ideas and current projects

This positive step counteracts the negative previous step. Do not present the results of Step 3 to management without Step 4, balancing the negative with the positive. The project concept provides sufficient information to build management support. The project concept nails down the purpose, scope, general schedule, benefits, and costs. Why to have a project concept and not a detailed project plan? Because the project plan assumes a specific scope and sets too much of the project in concrete. The concept provides a vehicle to negotiate with management on the scope and relationship among projects, for example.

Why to have a project concept for an existing project? The project concepts for existing projects begin to reformulate the projects themselves and provide greater focus from a business perspective. Many surprises may be revealed here. Some encountered in the past include the following:

- The scope of the project had changed and no one had informed management.
- There were hidden or assumed dependencies that now surfaced, which resulted in schedule delays.
- Business unit support evaporated for several projects when they were faced with identifying specific benefits.

The end products are as follows: (1) project concepts for new project ideas and (2) project concepts for current projects.

Step 6: analyze and relate all project concepts

As was stated earlier, projects do not stand alone. The whole is greater than the sum of its parts. In this step you will determine how the projects relate to each other, what gaps have to be filled, and the additional benefits that will accrue if multiple projects are implemented. In this step you will flesh out the project concepts. This means that you are more likely to have a complete view of the benefits of the projects in total. This can prove useful later when you present management with the project slate.

Some examples of results of the analysis are as follows:

- A business unit was going to use two Web-based applications. Hence, a common, standard user interface was required. This was unanticipated before the analysis.
- The wide area network had to be expanded to accommodate additional users.
- Several supporting projects of lesser priority now became higher priority due to the dependence of high-priority projects on them.

The end products are as follows:

- Analysis and determination of relationships and dependencies between project concepts;
- Adjustment of project concepts to cover gaps identified in analysis;
- Analysis of resources across project concepts;
- Recommended prioritization of project concepts.

Step 7: determine which projects will be approved for implementation

With the analysis of Step 5, you are ready to present management with groups of projects. You must avoid wherever possible reverting back to single projects. When you present and market a group of projects, you can enlist the support of multiple high-level managers of business units. These managers will not feel that they are part of a "zero-sum game", in which one party wins while another must lose. The accumulated benefits of the group of projects can be presented. The end products of the step are as follows:

- Approved slate of projects;
- Project leaders identified for all projects.

Step 8: develop detailed project plans for approved projects and begin work

In traditional systems project management, Step 7 might have been Step 1. It is not the case here. With management approval in Step 6, you are ready to develop the detailed project plans and identify project leaders and key team members. The thrust is to give attention to interfaces and other areas of risk from the beginning. Different rules for building the project plan will be defined. The end products are as follows:

- Detailed project plans for all projects;
- Refined budget and schedules for all projects;
- Key team members initially required for each project;
- Management review and approval of all plans.

Step 9: manage, monitor, and report on the project portfolio

In traditional project management, this step normally involves reporting on status and the percentage complete. That is only part of the puzzle and not very revealing at that. Here you will concentrate on three major activities: managing issues, allocating resources across projects, and evaluating actual work results from the projects. This is much more proactive than status reporting.

A wide range of end products are possible. Issues are resolved. Project plans can be changed. Priorities can be reset. The new project management process gives a much more active role to management and the project coordinator in addressing issues and actively overseeing the projects.

Part five of this book contains seven chapters on issues. Why seven chapters? Because this is a book on how to do technology project management. Issues of all types are addressed in this part of the book. These issues are very specific and tend to recur in various forms in different projects. You must know how to recognize the symptoms of these issues, how to analyze and group the issues, how to market for a decision, and how to implement actions that support the decisions.

Step 10: develop and implement criteria for project completion and termination

This is an unpleasant subject that people avoid. It is essential to have termination in mind for almost all projects. You cannot afford to have a failing project drift along. By taking a more proactive approach, you can redirect projects, change their scope, and salvage failing projects. Because projects are more interdependent, the importance of salvage cannot be underestimated. If you manage the issues actively in the previous step, you can start to see the impact of unresolved issues on the project earlier. This will give you time for action.

Critical to killing or abandoning projects is an organized approach for salvaging lessons learned and even end products. How do you do this if you have never had experience? Take a project with which you are familiar and assume that it were to be killed. What can you salvage that might be useful? What would the business unit do if the project were to be killed? What would its fall-back position be?

Transition to the new project management process

With the steps defined, you might wonder how a systems organization can migrate to the project strategy and process. Experience shows that management must see benefits from the potential of a new approach before it would be considered seriously. Here are some suggestions:

- Evaluate your current projects and associate them with major business processes.
- Examine each project to determine if it could be changed, reduced, or eliminated.
- Determine what resources can be freed up if the previous step were taken.
- Develop a model or scenario of a list of projects that you think might yield the most benefits.
- Identify the general benefits of the projects in terms of example business transactions.
- Define comparison tables as discussed below.

- Develop a project plan for making the transition to the new project management process.
- Present the results informally to management to trigger interest.

The differences between the old and new process are revealed through project slate change and the benefits of the new projects on the slate. Here are some comparison tables that have proved effective in the past.

- *Potential new projects versus existing projects.* The table entry consists of comments on how the new project relates to the existing project and reveals how different the new projects are from the existing ones.
- *Potential new projects versus business processes.* This table shows how the new projects support the business processes. Each entry explains how the business is supported by the project.
- *Existing projects versus business processes.* Similar to the preceding table above, this table shows the limitations of the current project for the specific process. Comparing this and the pervious table can be enlightening.
- *Potential new projects versus business units.* This table explains how each new project will benefit the major business units.
- *Potential new projects versus benefits.* The columns are types of tangible benefits. Each entry explains how the project will yield the benefit.
- *Potential new projects versus potential new projects.* This table can be employed to display and explain the interdependence among projects. Each table entry explains how the column project supports the row project. This information is valuable for gaining support for architecture and infrastructure projects.
- *Existing and potential new projects versus issues.* Here you identify what issues the projects have in common. The table entry is a short description of how an issue applies to a project.

Management may have the tendency to just implement the new process. This can be very disruptive to current work and projects. In addition, unless the current project process is a total failure, there will be some, or even many, who would say, "Why do we need to change? It will just cause problems." You should anticipate at least some resistance to change. While Chapter 10 deals with change management within a project, you can use the guidelines there to deal with this problem. Anticipate resistance and plan ahead for each major project.

One example of resistance may come from business units. They may think that a more formal process will just slow things down. Their current projects will be delayed and their future projects will never happen. To ease these concerns and fears, you should emphasize the problems with the current approach and the negative impacts it has on their projects. This negative marketing is often more effective than positive marketing of the benefits of the new project process. We examine this in more detail in the next section.

Marketing the new project management process

Why market the process? Can't a logical new method sell itself? Hardly. A number of barriers need to be overcome, including the following:

- *Internal resistance from the systems staff.* Programmers who are comfortable with maintenance and operations support may not appreciate or want to participate in larger-scale development or software acquisition projects.
- *Internal resistance from systems managers.* Traditional systems managers may like the current process. They will point out that it has worked for some time. Experience shows that they will resist including the business process in their tasks. They also feel uncomfortable with a wider role for the business units. In addition, they may feel that they have lost power in setting priorities.
- *Lack of interest among business units.* Although some business units may "step up to the plate", others will not want to assume any other duties. They may not see anything in it for them by addressing a cross-department business process.
- *Lack of support from management.* Managers may be supportive—up to a point. When issues have to be addressed, their interest may wane.

The attack on the new approach can take many forms. A common tactic is to argue that changing the current projects will be too disruptive. The new process can be phased in later—like next year or beyond. How do you respond to this argument? Point out what potential changes you have identified with the current projects and what the benefits are. Also, point out what will be wasted if management decides to wait. Resistance is often not on the surface. The suggestion is for you to assume that factors such as these exist and that they are addressed.

To help you with marketing, consider the benefits of the new process to each audience. Here are some benefits that have proved useful in the past:

- Business unit managers
  - Work on their critical processes will be more intense and yield greater benefits.
  - They will have a greater role in setting priorities.
  - They can impact the scope of the projects.

- Upper-level managers
  - Reinforce the importance of projects to the organization and business.
  - Indicate that their involvement will be very limited.
  - They will be able to change priorities on a more controlled basis.

- Systems management and staff
  - They will be working on critical projects.
  - Business unit involvement will be more carefully defined.

How do you go about doing sales and marketing? The sequence in how you approach people is important. If you do it wrong, you can create enemies. Here are some specific suggestions:

- Start with business unit managers in line organizations. They have the most to directly gain from the new process. They can help with their own staff and with management.
- Approach the systems managers and point out the benefits of the new process to them.
- Spend time working with the systems staff to build support.

In making presentations, be sensitive to the audience and present the project slate to appeal to their self-interests. Avoid using technical terms. Clearly indicate the business reasons for dependencies between application-oriented projects and technology/infrastructure-related projects.

What can you do to get people to act now, rather than waiting? What is the price of waiting?

- Project resources will be wasted in the projects that you have tagged for cancellation and change. What can be done with these resources in the interim if action were to be taken now?
- Relationships between business units and information systems will be affected if known gaps, interface problems, and other issues are not addressed.

A key here is that once people see that there is a better way to manage the projects, then there will be pressure to move to the new approach.

Cases and examples

Beaumont Insurance

Beaumont Insurance is a standard homeowner and automobile insurance carrier. This example will be discussed in several chapters. Beaumont's key processes are insurance application processing, policy servicing and tracking, payment processing, accounting, and claims. The previous management of Beaumont had decided to establish a major project for application processing and tracking using CASE (computer-aided software engineering) tools. The systems part of the project team started with five people and then grew to more than 20. The business units involved committed more than ten people full-time to the project. The project had gone on for 15 months, yet the company had only a prototype to show for the more than $3 million in expenses. The impact of the drain of resources for this new project was widespread and severe. First, almost all other non-maintenance work was halted. No enhancements were made to other systems. The architecture, which consisted of terminals and some PCs, was frozen to release funds for the project. Business unit managers constantly complained that they could not be competitive because they could not offer new insurance products. The investment in the system provoked a crisis in management. New management was brought in.

The first step was to assess the current project and other systems work. The hardware and network were out of date and too expensive. The large insurance application processing and tracking project was out of control. Efficiency in the business units was very low due to the use of the legacy systems and old procedures without the new system. It was clear that major change was required. All of the business processes identified earlier required major work along with system replacement. No suitable software packages were available that fit Beaumont's situation.

The decision was made to concentrate on those processes that contributed directly to revenue or that incurred large costs. This meant priority went to application processing, policy servicing and tracking, and payment processing. These were the bread and butter of the firm. Accounting was dropped from consideration due to limited resources and the fact that benefits were much less. The claims area was a possibility, but it was not a major problem. A plan was developed for each of these processes. This plan included procedures, business policies, systems, and the infrastructure. The three plans were then applied to the developed project concepts. The current large systems project failed the test when mapped against the project concept. The project might have resulted in a new system that might have been easier to maintain but would not have had added new features. Moreover, it did not employ client-server technology. The assessment was that there might have been no business benefits from continuing.

Given the decision to kill the project, salvage began immediately. Much analysis had been performed to define business rules or the detailed procedures of how the current business processes worked. This had not been done formally before and was useful for the future. What was to be the future? Much of the design had to be dropped. Extensive experimentation on various project concepts resulted in the following projects:

- *Project 1.* Establish a wide area network to replace the terminal network. The benefits were improved response time in accessing the legacy system as well as providing local functions that were now done manually.
- *Project 2.* Reengineer and improve the business processes with the current system as well as in preparation for the new system.
- *Project 3.* Create a client-server system in which the client side of the system was modern whereas the server side was really a front end into the legacy system. This would give the business staff increased productivity while providing interim benefits until the new client-server system was implemented.
- *Project 4.* Develop a new client-server application that would employ the business rules from the failed effort, the client software from the previous project, and database technology along with some object-oriented rules for development.
- *Project 5.* Modernize the host hardware to support client-server, Web-based, and database management technology.

The management steering committee was established, and its members were very unhappy in their first meeting. They were told the extent of failure and what had to be done. Several business unit managers committed to the new projects immediately. They had no real choice. The managers of the units that were to be sidestepped were unanimous in their opposition. This was overruled and work began on all but the fourth project at the start. The infrastructure and client-server front-end system would have to be in place before serious work could be performed on the new system.

The project coordinator role was dedicated to analyzing the business processes and doing the overall project management. Pairs of managers from systems and the business units developed project concepts and detailed plans for each of the projects. The project coordinator put the projects together and performed analysis. This led to more dynamic resource allocation. Initially, resource allocation was reviewed every 2 weeks. When there was more progress, it was stretched first to monthly and then once every 2 months.

From the start the focus was on issues. The previous management had tolerated the project plan even though it was only in a prototype stage, but was listed as 70 percent complete (incredible, but true). The project coordinator worked with staff from the business and systems units to create a list of more than 350 issues. A number of these had nothing to do with systems but involved business procedures and policies. For example, one policy determined when to send out bills to customers. Another established when to terminate coverage for non-payment of insurance premiums. Schedules were managed around the issues to ensure that the issues were addressed.

Overall, the project management process was successful. However, *ad hoc* requests from marketing and other areas often had to be deferred to focus on key requirements. For each request, the manager was required to provide information on direct benefits related to cost savings or revenue generation. This philosophy reduced the backlog of work requests by over 80 percent. More details of the Beaumont Insurance example will be given in later chapters.

Questions

1. What steps could have been taken at the beginning to head off the problems that occurred?
2. Beaumont was forced to change the technology and implement a new project process at the same time. Why is this disruptive? What should have been the order of change?
3. At the start there seemed to be little understanding of the problems and issues to be faced. How could have the problems been identified earlier?
4. There were obvious communications problems between IT and management. How could these have been detected? What steps could have been taken to improve the communications on the problems?
5. The new technologies were poorly understood by IT management. What could have been done to bring the company and IT up to speed on new technologies?

Lessons learned

Many firms have rushed into new, major projects—often with disappointing results. Why does this happen? Among the reasons are that the organization had no project management approach and process in place that could address successful implementation. Having turned around a number of efforts, we have noticed that the following problems are typical.

- The company treats project implementation as a narrow technology project. As such the emphasis is on installing the software, enhancing their network, and adding other software such as firewalls. They ignore changing marketing, purchasing, accounting, ordering, customer service, and other areas.

- The project starts as a single large project. The project leader is often an IT systems analyst. He or she is well-intentioned but treats the project as a standard IT project.
- Issues begin to arise in both the business and technical areas. There is pressure to implement the project fast. Hence, there is a rush to deal with issues as soon as they come up—a big mistake. Decisions and actions on later issues undo those for earlier ones. The project loses focus.
- There is a lack of awareness of the need to address resistance to change and fear among business unit staff.

Turning from problems to success, some critical success factors in project implementation are as follows:

- Recognizing that project implementation is not a one shot deal. It is a continuous program since once you set it up, you have to measure the business processes to prevent deterioration and keep the systems current.
- Having several project leaders who divide up accountabilities and can address both the business and technical sides of the project.
- Setting the scope of the implementation to include process, procedure, policy, and organizational change as well as software and infrastructure implementation.
- Dividing up the implementation project into a number of parts. The division is based on responsibility with a focus on ensuring that task areas with issues and risk are given high exposure in the plan.
- Actively managing issues during the project.
- Gathering lessons learned and experience during the project.

Guidelines

- In completing the analysis steps outlined in this chapter, be careful to limit your visibility. The more visible the potential change in project priorities, the more danger of an attack and confusion.
- If you think about it, the major differences between large and small projects lie in scale, scope, and purpose. There can be more risk in some small projects than in larger ones. Work to have all projects included in the analysis and prioritization. If small projects are allowed to be treated separately, then the resources available for allocation will be reduced. You become locked in.
- It is easy to set aside resources for maintenance and operations support. Often, the most trained and experienced staff are required for these tasks. These activities can then escape being prioritized. With so little of the time of the key people available for new projects, there may be little point in having the projects go forward.
- Even with limited resources, still make a proactive effort to control resource allocation and limit work on current systems and the architecture. Otherwise, each year will just bring more maintenance requests.

- In considering a transition to the new process, you might want to use a department as a pilot case for a project. This will demonstrate the project concept, issue management, and analysis of projects that are parts of the new process.
- In order to test out the resource allocation across projects, take the projects that were approved in the previous year. Go through the analysis suggested here and identify what different priorities could have been set.
- There is resistance to change that we explore in the last chapter. Here be aware that a major source of resisting change is the desire to maintain autonomy and control. The paradox is that the project management process here gives structure at the highest level and flexibility in the detail and in dealing with issues—areas where it is needed.

Questions

1. Let's assume that a company is employing a formal project management methodology. A project arises that is small and urgent. The project leader has experience with Agile methods and pushes for its use. What questions would you ask of the project leader? What preparations would be needed for using a new methodology? How would you determine if it was working?
2. Research the Web to find an example of a firm that changed methodologies. What problems did they encounter? What benefits did they cite with the new methodology?
3. Steering committees appear to be overhead. They can delay decisions on issues, thereby delaying the project. What if you did not use steering committees for projects? How would decisions be made? How would bad decisions be addressed?
4. Suppose that an organization implements the project concept for all project work. What are the advantages and disadvantages of having the project concept for projects that are ongoing? How would you draw the line in terms of project size? What would be the benefits of doing the project concept for a project that is in the implementation stage?
5. Assume that an organization is going to implement both a new project methodology and project management process. However, your internal staff resources are very limited. You are forced to rely on consultants. What questions would you ask in interviewing potential consultants?

What to do next

In Chapter 1, you answered questions about the current systems project management process. The following actions flow from the answers to these questions.

1. Identify the key decision-makers and supporters you require to implement a new process.
   a. Upper management
   b. Staff to general management

      c. Business unit management
      d. Business unit employees
      e. Systems managers
      f. Systems staff

2. Following up on the discussion in this chapter, estimate what types of resistance you will encounter.
3. Identify several potential candidates for the role of project coordinator. Write down what you consider to be the duties of the project coordinator. This will depend on the number and extent of projects. Assuming that it was not a full-time role, what other duties can this person perform?
4. Identify potential members of the management steering committee based on the earlier discussion. Estimate what their schedule of meetings might be. Write down a list of things that they might be required to do. This includes making decisions on issues that only management can solve as well as redirecting resources.

Summary

If the underlying method for managing systems projects is not effective, then being successful with a few projects may not be enough. The cost of a poor process is high—resources that are locked into projects, a higher likelihood of failure due to issues not being managed, and projects that do not deliver tangible benefits because they may lack linkage to business processes and support of business units.

A proactive systems project management approach will attempt to identify the most beneficial project ideas in advance of planning and setting the project slate. Once identified, there must be a step in planning that would allow management to trade off alternative goals and scope. This is the project concept. Having upper management involved in setting the project slate and reviewing it periodically not only increases involvement and commitment, but also provides for a channel to handle *ad hoc* requests for new projects.

4
Managing multiple projects and the project portfolio

Introduction

The new project management process centers on managing a portfolio of projects as opposed to single projects. How to analyze and manage multiple projects in more detail is a critical part of the process and the focus of this chapter. The remaining chapters will develop methods that fit within the framework.

Project Portfolio Management (PPM) is a management method to help an organization collect and use information about all of their projects. Data is first collected on all projects. Then managers are required to review each project and set a priority for the project. The set of all projects is also referred to as the *project slate*. The goal of managing all projects is to determine the best mix of projects that contribute the most to achieving the goals of the organization. A key ingredient is not only the selection of the projects, but also their sequencing. This is sometimes referred to as *pipeline management*.

Here are some signs that a portfolio approach is needed.

- You find that it is very difficult and time consuming to collect, organize, and analyze data from multiple projects.
- You find the project leaders often fight over resources.
- Some IT or business staff are overcommitted across too many projects.
- Too many resources are put into projects with marginal benefits.
- Resources are moved too frequently between projects.
- You find that there is substantial overlap between projects.

Because projects can be widely different from each other, it is often more useful to consider a group of projects that have some specific attributes in common. Then you could follow the PPM techniques for that group. How can we group projects? Here are ten possibilities:

- Select all projects that share the same business units.
- Select all projects that share the same methods and tools.
- Select all projects that affect the same set of customers.
- Select all projects that impact a group of processes.
- Select all projects that share the same IT resources.

- Select all projects that share the same facilities.
- Select all projects that share the same technology.
- Select all projects that have the same issues.
- Select all projects that have a similar schedule.
- Select all projects that use the same vendor.

You would employ the specific grouping based on the situation. For example, the one on issues should be considered on a regular basis so that you solve issues across projects in a consistent manner. You will gain more leverage with a vendor if you consider not one of their projects, but all of them.

This chapter explores how projects are interdependent. Then guidelines are provided for handling analysis, resource allocation and conflicts, issue resolution, and disseminating lessons learned. The scope will cover all of your projects. Do not omit any projects because they are small, large, or have some special characteristic.

What if you try to manage the projects separately? There will be less sharing of resources. Project managers will tend to work with one another only when an issue becomes major or a crisis. Management will have to be more involved because more issues will bubble up. There will be greater incompatibilities between software because there is less coordination among members of teams doing similar development.

What are some of the benefits to managing projects as a whole rather than as individual units?

- Management has a better idea of the value of the projects.
- Information can be shared among projects. This includes lessons learned and issues.
- Project managers can solve issues among themselves because a vehicle for supporting issue resolution is available through the project coordinator. Remember that the coordinator is just a role that can be filled by one of the IT managers.
- Resource shortages and overages can be adjusted by analyzing resource needs across all projects.
- The focus of attention can be placed on interfaces where the risk often lies in systems projects.
- The same methods and tools can be employed across multiple projects faster.

However, there will be resistance as well. Here are some examples by source:

- *Project managers.* Their independence is impacted in several ways. First, they must adhere to a standardized project template with the same resource list and high-level tasks. Second, they must share information with other project leaders. Third, they must contribute and participate in resolving issues and using lessons learned. Fourth, and perhaps more important, they must be prepared to give up resources.
- *Business units.* In the past, a business unit would be assigned a project after management approval. In many cases, the business unit managers felt that they could make changes to the scope, purpose, and structure of the project at will. After all, they controlled it. In an open setting, this control goes away because the project information is more widely known and being tracked. Changes in purpose and scope are subject to more intensive review.
- *Upper management.* In the past, high-level managers could reset priorities more easily because the project information was not as visible. When the portfolio is

managed as a whole and information is visible, then the high-level manager must approach change with more caution.

- *Information systems staff.* Some people working on projects like to work alone on their specific tasks without having to spend time in coordination and planning. This is a luxury that systems departments can little afford. A programmer's work is more complex because he or she must consider the impact across multiple projects.
- *Vendors and consultants.* Vendors hired to work on a project often find it to be in their best interests to keep the project going and even expand it to increase the work. In the process identified here, the change in scope is reflected in the project tasks and schedule. This tips off management that there was an issue here.

How do you disarm resistance? You ignore it at your peril. Involve project leaders in the definition of common issues and the template. A template consists of standard high-level task, resources, and dependencies. Then you can establish a process for sharing information. Sit back and see what happens. Will the managers cooperate on their own? For the business units and upper management, a suggestion is to indicate the impacts of past project changes in purpose and scope on multiple projects. Also, point out lost opportunities in past projects for cooperation that resulted in extra work. An approach for the information systems staff and vendors is to indicate how the nature of systems projects has changed and how interdependent projects are. Point to the challenge of trying to spread the results of work across multiple projects.

Analysis of business vision and mission

To analyze the project portfolio in terms of the business, you have to perform analysis of the business vision and mission. The *business vision* is what a firm sees as its future. An example might be, "to capture xx% of the market by the year 20XX". The *business mission* is the general direction needed to achieve the vision. In our example this could be "by growing our existing store business by Y% and expansion into Z countries or markets".

Business visions and missions are often posted on walls and always appear in annual reports. Suppose you have them in front of you. They look so general. How can one possibly map these words to projects and project concepts? It is very difficult to do directly. You first have to parse or breakdown the wording. Since this is very general, let's take an example. Consider Figure 4.1.

XXX is a company committed to providing a high-quality, one-to-one customer experience that exceeds expectations and exceeds expectations in long-term relationships. We provide excellent customer service and a vast selection of products and services through unique channels and partnerships. We foster high morale among our team members by providing them with an energizing work environment and clear direction, and by valuing all team member contributions. Long-term profitability, creating value for our shareholders and partners, and enhancing the communities we share are essential to our success.

Figure 4.1   Example of a mission statement

This is a real mouthful. Take each sentence and break it down. Doing this we have the following list:

- High quality, one-to-one customer experience;
- Long-term customer relationships;
- Vast selection of products and services;
- Unique channels and partnerships;
- High morale among staff;
- Energizing work environment;
- Clear direction for employees;
- Value all team member contributions;
- Long-term profitability;
- Enhancing communities.

This is just the first step. These are still too general. The second step is to make a list of the business units and their business processes. This particular firm has a focus on catalog and Internet sales. Figure 4.2 gives the business units and their processes.

Marketing

- Customer profiling
- Catalog planning
- Web planning
- Internet promotions
- Catalog/sales promotions
- Airline/hotel relations

Sales

- Sales prospecting
- Contacts and follow-up
- Preparation of the deal
- Contract negotiations and signing

Order Entry/Customer Service

- Order entry
- Customer service (returns, backorders, refunds, cancellations, etc.)
- Customer credit processing
- Fraud

Human Resources

- How people are interviewed and screened
- Familiarization for new employees
- Training in processes
- How people learn about other departments

Figure 4.2   Example business units and key processes

Accounting-Vendor
- Vendor payments
- Reconciliation
- Disputes

Finance
- General ledger
- Accounting systems
- Payroll
- Accounting
- Operations performance information and analysis
- Management information and analysis

Figure 4.2   (Continued)

The third step is to define mission statements for each business process (Figure 4.3). This should be done in a collaborative way with the business unit employees. There are some immediate benefits in doing this. First, the employees get a common vision for their work. Another reason is analytical. You need the process mission statements to relate them to the general company-wide mission elements. That is the next step. Space limitations apply here so we give one example for human resources.

Hiring	Ensure that the most qualified people are hired
Familiarization	Ensure that new and current employees are familiar with the organization, mission, and business processes
Retention	Provide for retention and career paths for dedicated employees, including lessons learned from terminations
Training	Provide training in processes, methods, and tools to support higher productivity
Information sharing	Support the sharing of information and lessons learned among employees

Figure 4.3   Human resource mission statements for processes

With this last table in hand you can now map the mission statements of the departments' processes to the elements of the general mission. The result for Human Resources is shown in Figure 4.4. In the table an "X" means that the process mission supports the general mission element while a blank indicates that it does not.

Some comments on the above steps are useful here. First, you would do this with the supervisors and employees. Second, it is a one-time activity since the mission and visions for both processes and company overall do not change much over time. Third, you will observe that you have mapped the general company mission to the business processes through their missions.

Mission Element	Ensure that the most qualified people are hired	Ensure that new and current employees are familiar with the organization, mission, and business processes	Provide for retention and career paths for dedicated employees, inc. lessons learned from terminations	Provide training in processes, methods, and tools to support higher productivity	Support the sharing of information and lessons learned among staff
High quality, 1–1 customer experience	X				
Long-term customer relationship		X		X	X
Vast selection of products/ services				X	X
Unique channels/ partnerships					
High morale among staff	X	X		X	X
Energizing work environment	X	X	X	X	X
Clear direction for employees		X	X		X
Value all team member contributions		X	X		X
Long-term profitability				X	X
Create value for shareholders and partners					
Enhancing communities					X

Note that training and familiarity with processes maps to the greatest number of mission elements.

Figure 4.4 Mapping of the Human Resource Department mission to the company mission

The next steps are to map the projects and systems to the business processes. You would develop the following tables:

- Systems versus processes. Here the entry is an "X" if a particular system supports a process and blank otherwise.
- Projects versus processes. The table entry is "X" if the project will aid that process and blank otherwise.

The last step is to now combine the tables. You can develop two of these.

- Systems versus mission elements. The table entry is "X" if the system supports the mission element and blank otherwise. This table is derived by combining mission elements versus processes and processes versus systems. This table shows the *positive alignment of systems to the company mission.*
- Projects versus mission elements. The table is "X" if the project will support the attainment of the specific mission element and blank otherwise. This shows the *positive alignment of projects to the mission of the organization.*

In practice you would first carry this analysis out for current projects. Then, later, instead of current projects you could use the project ideas. This will reveal the *positive alignment of the project ideas to the mission.*

Analysis of business issues

The analysis proceeds in a way analogous to that of mission and vision. You first identify key business issues. Then you map these to the missions of the business processes. In that you can identify which processes affect the issues and their severity. Then you proceed to use the mappings of the systems, projects, and project ideas to the process mission elements. As before, you now combine tables to obtain:

- Systems versus business issues. This table reveals which systems are contributing to the business issue. This is the *negative alignment of systems to business issues.*
- Projects versus business issues. This table shows which current projects could improve specific business issues. This is the *negative alignment of current projects to business issues.*
- Project ideas versus business issues. This table reveals which project ideas apply and could relieve specific business issues. This is the *negative alignment of project ideas to business issues.*

You can use the tables in this section to support the selection of projects for work. You can also employ it to identify systems that require attention. Third, you can apply it to evaluate projects in your project portfolio.

Categories of interdependence

How are projects interdependent? In a standard project management context, this is simple. It is the dependence of specific tasks and milestones between several projects. In systems and technology projects it is more complex. Five categories of dependence are identified next. Two projects can be interdependent and fit in multiple categories. Which category a project falls into will help determine how projects can be grouped.

Category 1: technology base

Systems projects here share the same technology base. Some examples are as follows:

- *Sharing the same network*. As an example, suppose that you were implementing a client-server system, upgrading electronic mail, and deploying groupware. These three projects share the same network. By themselves the workload in implementation and testing along with the load on the network is reasonable. Taken together, it is likely that the network will have to be upgraded. After adding this project to the list, you now must prioritize the network staff time among support of the projects.
- *Sharing databases*. There can be several projects involving an application that includes a database. The basic application may be enhanced. There could be a data warehousing project that accesses the database. A client-server or intranet project may also require the data. If you attempt to do these in parallel without tight coordination, then you risk having to do substantial rework when the database is changed.
- *Using a common GPS and GIS system*. In transportation and other areas where geographic information is used by multiple applications, it is important to design the applications as a whole so as to avoid redundant and inconsistent data.

How will you address these issues in managing multiple projects? You want to make sure that a technology project is created and that all interfaces are covered across the projects. You might want to appoint a superproject leader for the group of projects.

Category 2: resources

The most common shared resource is people. In client-server applications, it is logical to use the same programmers to develop all of the client software across multiple applications. It is the same with the design of databases. In intranet and Internet applications involving electronic commerce, you logically want one or several staff members to centerpost all electronic commerce applications from a technical view—regardless of their nature. Network support staff members are also shared. Programmers who maintain legacy systems are often shared between these systems and new, replacement systems. This is because they are the only ones with knowledge. Quality assurance staff members have to be allocated across applications for testing as well. In an intensive development environment, the development and testing hardware, network, and software must also be allocated.

Resource analysis and allocation can be simplified if standard templates for the projects are in place. Then you can combine the projects and extract all tasks for the next 2 months that involve a specific scarce resource.

Category 3: milestones

This is the traditional mode of dependency. Tasks in one project depend on milestones in another project. Is there much to say here? Note that many people have trouble with these dependencies because they do not control them. Some give them little attention and wait for the project leader of the dependent project to inform them of problems and slippage. This, of course, gives the project leader a chance to slip the schedule of the other project.

Lessons learned point to a better method of dealing with these dependencies. First, pull out all of the interfaces from both projects to form a separate project. When the project plans are updated, the new project plan with the dependent tasks and milestones can be updated. Second, have the project coordinator monitor these "interface projects". This gives special attention to interfaces and potential schedule problems.

Category 4: business units

Projects can impact the same business unit. Therefore, the projects can require the same business unit support staff. That is an allocation problem. To cope, insist that business unit resources be included in the resource list for the project and then be scheduled in the template. This will ensure that business unit resources are not bypassed or ignored. The business unit staff issues can be dealt with in the same manner as that of resources in category 2.

The next problem is that implementation of the systems created by the projects can cause havoc in the business unit. In one government agency, separate groups were upgrading the PCs, the software, and the network and loading an online application at the same time. It drove the staff crazy and caused the work in the department to grind to a halt.

Category 5: general business need

Your company can face a major competitive threat. It may be forced to implement a number of major projects at the same time. These systems then affect major parts of the business concurrently. The most effective approach is to establish a superproject that includes tasks from the business viewpoint. This will give attention to the impact on the business effects of the systems.

A common theme runs through the discussion of these categories. It is that the project information must be combined, filtered, and extracted to suit the specific category of dependency. Fortunately, with modern project management software this is easier to do because of increased capability and greater flexibility.

Category 6: business processes

Here the projects aim at improving the same or highly interrelated business processes. An example of this is in E-Business implementation in which there are technical, marketing, and management subprojects that touch on several of the same processes such as customer service. It is very important to manage these projects as a group since otherwise work in one area can undo what was done in another project.

This is an increasingly evident trend among projects since more companies are realizing that their strengths and competitive position are due to their business processes.

Assessment of current projects

The following step-by-step approach will help you to assess your current projects as part of the transition to the new project management process.

Step 1: gather information across projects

Collect the following information for all projects:

- Project plan in software file form
- Issues that are active, resolved, and potential
- Resources currently employed on the project
- Status of the project in terms of schedule and actual expenses versus the plan

Unfortunately, information will be missing because different project leaders have different styles. Information is also likely to be inconsistent. Some projects may not have resources assigned. Different projects may have different levels of detail. Don't let this deter you. Take what you get and move on to Steps 2 through 4 in parallel. Don't keep asking people for more information. They might be embarrassed and defensive. You want them on your side.

Step 2: establish common templates for analysis

Begin with building a resource list. This will be a list of resources including staff, hardware, software, network, vendor, and business unit resources. Identify people by initials as well as generic resources such as programmer and analyst. You will be using the generic resources in the template. When people turn a template into a project plan, they will not only add detail but will also replace the generic resources with actual resources. Circulate the resource list among the project leaders.

While you are getting feedback, divide the projects into groups. The titles for Chapters 13 through 16 give you four categories. Build the templates from the top down and include at least three levels of outlining. (Templates are provided in the later chapters.) Enter the template into the project management software and circulate it as well.

After getting feedback, refine the template and resource list and submit it for another round of reviews. Next comes the detailed work. You must take one of the project plans and fit it into the template. Work with the project manager to do this. Hold a meeting to review this plan with the other project managers. The other projects can now be placed into the templates. You are likely to encounter resistance. If this occurs, then visit these project leaders and work with them one-on-one to develop their schedules.

What is a sign of success from this effort? The project leaders drop their old schedules and begin to update the schedule that you developed using the templates. Make sure that you store the schedules on a network server so that people can view each other's schedules (but can make changes only to their own schedules).

Step 3: identify interdependencies

From the discussion earlier, examine the plans for dependencies. A guideline here is to start from scratch and define these rather than using the existing plans. You can then validate the ones you have identified with the existing plans. How do you insert a dependency? If the templates are not established, then insert tasks into the existing task list that indicates the link. This will be a temporary manual link. If the templates are set up, then you can link the schedules if the project management software allows for this. Also, all should be simple tail-to-head dependencies. Don't try to get cute or exotic with lagging or leading dependencies now.

Test what you have done by extracting all dependent tasks and milestones into a new plan that includes only these dependent elements. From what you know of the schedules, are these complete? Are these logical? If these tasks were performed successfully, would all risk associated with interfaces disappear? You will employ this schedule to analyze the effects of schedule changes. Make sure that you maintain links to the original plans so that when their tasks are updated, the plan of dependencies will automatically be updated. Another guideline is to label each dependency by type according to the categories listed earlier. This will aid your analysis later.

Step 4: define common issues

An issue can be a known problem or opportunity. Don't spend time sorting and comparing these here. Instead, take the issues as they are given to you. For each issue define the following characteristics:

- Descriptive information about the issues
- Related projects and task areas
- Impact and effects of the issue if it is not addressed
- Urgency and priority in solving the issue
- Status of the issue

More detailed data elements will be given in Chapter 7.

Step 5: group projects into categories

Using the templates from Step 2, the dependencies from Step 3, and the grouping of issues in Step 4, you can now try grouping projects in alternative ways. Try different groupings based on technology, business area impacted, common issues, dependencies, and methods and tools employed. Why to group the projects? Because it will help you later when you seek to analyze the data from the different projects. You will want to look at different groups of projects in making your analysis.

Step 6: analyze the issues

You are now ready to analyze the data. Here are some analysis steps:

- Combine issues that are variations of each other.
- Sort all issues by severity and analyze the highest priority issues.
- Sort all issues by business units and analyze the ones for the business units with the most issues.
- Sort all issues by age and severity and analyze the oldest, outstanding major issue.
- Based on the sorting, group the issues so that you can search for a solution to multiple issues at one time.

Specific issues are discussed in Part four. The general analysis approach is to attempt to answer the following questions:

- Why has the issue remained unresolved?
- Which issues require immediate and direct action?
- What problems do business units face?
- Which projects have the most unresolved, serious issues?

Step 7: analyze schedules and resources

There is a useful way to organize the analysis. Divide it into four steps: identification and extraction of the information, visualization of the information on the PC or paper, analysis, and actions that follow from the analysis. Let's consider several commonly encountered examples.

- **Assessing a resource across multiple projects.**
  Let's suppose that you have three projects that share a common resource. You are concerned about how this resource can be allocated to the three projects.

  - *Extraction.* Filter or extract all high-level tasks of the template along with the tasks that involve the resource for each schedule. Combine the results from each schedule into a new schedule.
  - *Visualization.* Split the screen with a GANTT chart on the top and a graph or table showing the resource use on the bottom.

- *Analysis.* You can now adjust the schedule and move tasks in the GANTT chart. The impact on resource usage will be seen immediately on the bottom as the bar in the GANTT chart moves. The analysis can be conducted in a meeting with the project leaders using a projector for the PC image on a screen.
- *Actions.* Once you have an acceptable allocation and change, then the original schedules that use the resource can be modified to what was agreed to in the analysis.

- **Resolving issues across multiple projects.**
  The situation here is that you want to analyze and resolve one or more issue(s) that is/are involved with several projects.

  - *Extraction.* Filter all of the projects involved with the tasks that are directly impacted by the issues along with the following, dependent summary tasks. This will allow you to see the impact of changes to the tasks involving the issues. Combine the results into a new schedule.
  - *Visualization.* You might again employ a split screen. The GANTT chart for the new schedule can be on top; on the bottom is a resource table that shows the number of hours each resource is used per unit of time.
  - *Analysis.* As before, you can adjust the GANTT chart or change the tasks and determine the effect on resource consumption on the bottom.
  - *Actions.* The most likely action is that after considering several alternatives, you will find a way of allocation and division of tasks that resolves the issues with minimal schedule impact overall.

- **Analyzing dependencies between projects.**
  Assume that you are considering a number of projects with different types of dependencies.

  - *Extraction.* Extract all major milestones and summary tasks from the schedules along with the dependent tasks. Combine the results into a new schedule.
  - *Visualization.* Split the screen with a GANTT chart for the extracted information and a GANTT chart for one of the projects about which you are concerned on the bottom.
  - *Analysis.* You can change dates and dependencies of the tasks in either GANTT chart and see the effects in the other chart. Doing this allows you to assess the impact of slippage. You can also modify and add tasks to change the dependency and see what happens.
  - *Actions.* This analysis can be used to narrow the scope of the dependency. It can also be used to assign higher priorities to one project so as not to impact others.

Step 8: analyze projects in terms of the business vision, mission, and issues

Carrying out this step follows from the discussion in the preceding section.

Planning across multiple projects

The preceding steps prepare you to plan over the longer term. That is, with resources known and the templates established, you are prepared to create multiple projects for each project idea. You can then combine these projects into an overall project. This summary project contains both ongoing work and potential projects. This analysis is critical if your organization is contemplating adopting a new direction in technology. Examples of the impact on resources might involve data warehousing, client-server systems, electronic commerce, wholesale replacement of legacy systems, and intranet systems.

Managing resources across projects and normal work

This is one of the most critical issues in project management. For you have not only issues of resource allocation between projects in the portfolio, but also the critical conflicts between the non-project and project work by employees. It is easy to say that project work should get priority because of their contribution to change and benefit. However, you still have to keep the current systems and operations running. Thus, maintenance, operations, and enhancements can easily push aside the projects. It is the same in everyday life. Let's suppose that you want to learn dancing and make it a project. However, many times when you had dancing lessons scheduled, something got in the way. A child is sick or needs help with homework. You have to do extra work to meet a deadline on your job. This continues and you find after a month that your dancing skill has not advanced at all. Very frustrating, eh? It is the same in IT. Regardless of how IT managers emphasize the importance of projects, other things get in the way. That is why we take up a method for resource allocation on a dynamic basis later in this chapter.

Project selection alternatives

In the sections that follow we will consider in detail how to perform project selection. To prepare you for this, here we consider some alternatives for general project selection. This discussion applies to the new project ideas. Here are several potential rankings.

- *Business issues*. Projects are ranked based on their potential effect and amelioration to business issues. Think of this one as ranking based on *urgency*.
- *Contribution to vision*. Projects are rated based on their contribution to strategic direction of the firm. This rating is generating through the mapping of project ideas to the business mission and vision. This rating is called *strategic fit*. This is closely tied to a rating based on focusing on key business processes.
- *Tangible benefits*. You could sort the projects based on tangible benefits. This is not the same as the previous one since many projects result in short-term benefits, but contribute little to long-term goals. This rating can be termed *benefits*.

- *Issues.* Another rating is based on the issues in the project ideas. Projects with few issues, and hence lower risk, would be ranked highest. This might be favored by IT to reduce the chances of failure, but the projects selected here might not improve the business at all—they might help IT operationally. We can call this type of rating *IT risk.*
- *Resistance to change.* This is a very conservative approach in which you select projects for business units that are really supportive of change and not consider those that are resistant to change. However, while reducing risks, this rating will likely not advance the business.
- *Resource availability.* Projects are rating in terms of available resources in both IT and the business units to perform the project work. This rating can be called *resource availability.*
- *IT critical.* Some project ideas help fix pressing issues in IT related to software and infrastructure. The business benefits, but generally later. A rating based on this can be termed *IT urgency.* If a project is critical to IT, how do you sell management on it? By giving the impact on the business and systems if the project is not done.

You should prepare several of these alternative ratings so that management can do trade-offs between different projects. Often, we have seen the selection including top-rated projects in several categories.

Note that IT should generally adopt an attitude of *positive neutrality.* That is, IT is positive about doing the projects, but is neutral in selection. The selection of new projects belongs to the management of the organization with IT in an advisory role.

Setting priorities and the project portfolio

Several times a year, the management steering committee grapples with allocating resources: hardware, software, network, and personnel resources. For hardware, this includes not only what and how much will be acquired but also where it will be deployed. Staff resources that are being apportioned include operations and network support, systems analysts and designers, programmers, support staff, business unit staff, and contractor and consultant staff.

Types of projects

You will have many projects and will have to divide them by type. Here is a set of categories that has proven itself over time. Assume that you have a long-range strategic systems plan that has identified new project opportunities.

- *Operations support.* This is the daily work that keeps the software going. It includes backup, recovery, restart, and other programming activities. It also includes keeping the network and computers operational. Upgrades to operating systems and other related work are included here. This support is going to consume a great deal of resources.

- *Ongoing development projects.* Typically, there are some development projects that are continuing from the current year and will still be going a few months from the present time.
- *Architecture-related work.* This can include upgrades to hardware, system software, and the network. It can also include replacements. The work goes beyond installation. It includes testing, integration, documentation, and training.
- *Backlog of project requests.* From previous years there is typically a backlog of work that did not get attention last year. These items now present themselves.
- *Strategic systems plan action items.* These are project ideas from the long-range, strategic systems plan.
- *Maintenance and enhancement work.* Some of this work is often mandated by law or regulation. Maintenance is defined here as fixing problems and ensuring that the software continues to meet its requirements. Enhancements include the addition of new features and capabilities or the extension of capabilities.
- *New project requests.* These are new project ideas from divisions and the systems organization in addition to those proposed in the strategic systems plan. Some of these may be targets of opportunity.

Note that if you try to combine any of these, you could run into trouble since each area has its own criteria for evaluation. To free up resources you might want to determine if you can cut down the resources necessary for each area. Here are some comments by category:

- Could you ever reduce operations support? The answer is yes if you can simplify the architecture and modernize it.
- How can you control ongoing development resources? Determine how much of this is real development and whether sufficient progress is being made.
- How can you control architecture-related work? The best answer is through careful planning and staging of the work to be efficient. You might also get vendor resources.
- If you examine the backlog, you often find that the requirement or pressure for the project dissipated. The users were able to do something else.
- For the strategic plan elements you can take out the action items that do not require systems and technology resources. You thereby reduce the candidates exclusively to projects.
- For maintenance, go through each area and kill off the requests that lack benefits. The same applies to enhancements.
- For the other new project ideas, you really have to ask why these did not arise during planning.

Some comments on analyzing and handling project requests are as follows:

- The need for the project is important. A government reporting requirement, for example, may be dictated. This can be stated here. The need for other types of items must be based on the business process and not the organization. It is often in the improvement to the business process where the benefits will be.

- For resources required, please identify the extent of scarce systems staff time needed as well as other resources. This will identify conflict situations between resources later and assist in their resolution.
- The impact, if not approved, is a very good item to require. It encourages people to conceive of a backup plan. They also have to discuss what they do now and how they have gotten along so far without the project.
- Divide tangible and intangible benefits. Over the years people have become more insistent on hard, tangible benefits. Many technologies and projects promise a lot, but few truly deliver. However, you can also acknowledge that real results often fall short of goals and expectations. Tangible benefits focus on cost savings or avoidance as well as revenue generation. For example, groupware might seem fuzzy and intangible, yet it speeds up a project. Speeding up a project lowers its cost, producing tangible benefits. Increased quality, improved customer satisfaction, and reduced turnover of staff are tangible. Ease of use can result in training savings.

How the project will be managed refers to the role of the business divisions and information systems. This item is important due to the number of projects that lurch out of control after starting because no one stepped up and assumed responsibility. If information systems is to run all aspects of the project, then the business will not be involved. Lack of business involvement will likely doom the project.

After the initial review, classify project requests according to the categories covered earlier. All requests for new development or software acquisition as well as requests for enhancements and maintenance originate from business divisions. Operations support and architecture-related work come from information systems. Strategic systems planning project ideas are to be put forward by business units and not the planners. The business has to demonstrate support at this time. The exception here is the set of architectural projects that require the technical support of the information systems organization.

Before and after allocation

Without a proactive process, resources are typically consumed by operations support, maintenance and enhancements, current development, and a few new projects. You probably have observed this repeatedly in diverse organizations. If you consider what is actually performed over several years, you see that the mixture does not change very much. This is how an organization can spend vast sums in systems and get nothing in return.

In the new process, the project slate composition changes, but not radically. Why? Because operations support consumes so much resource. Use some of the techniques presented here to cut down maintenance and enhancement and some development. You would be able to do some architectural improvement and some strategic planning projects. By diverting some resources into architecture and the strategic plan, you work toward long-term benefits.

The criterion for evaluation is specific to each category.

- *Operations support.* The analysis begins with assessing whether the numbers are in line with the past. As an earlier suggestion indicated, you might go back to systems and ask what they could buy or do to reduce this by 10–20 percent. This then leaves room for emergency fixes and repairs—work that cannot be predicted.

- *Infrastructure support.* This includes hardware, system software, and network support. Here look for escalating costs and labor due to aging equipment and software. You might see if you could get competitive bids for some of this support.
- *Ongoing development projects.* The first criterion is to assess whether the business requirement that generated the project is still valid. This is necessary. Projects have gone to completion without anyone ever asking about whether the business needed them. The next criterion is to determine if these are on target with respect to schedule.
- *Architecture-related work.* The criterion here is to support the strategy in the planning process. However, there are many ways to do this. Should you spend all of the money this year? Or, should you hold some back for next year to take advantage of technological improvements? Usually it is best to stretch it out, if possible.
- *Backlog.* Much of the backlog can be dropped. Often, the systems group does not want to appear to be uncooperative so systems personnel politely tell the business unit that it is in the queue of work to be performed. The division goes away and opts for an alternative. Nothing is done. Members of the division become so mad that they don't tell systems to remove the division from the queue. Information systems, on the other hand, leaves it in the queue because excessive demand is impressive, making the information systems unit feel wanted.
- *Strategic planning projects.* While these plans originate from divisions, you still have to be willing to compromise. Will you compromise to get the best projects approved? You may end up backing high-priority project ideas in divisions with high levels of management support.
- *Maintenance and enhancement.* Here is where you get out the budget ax. Look for areas in which a business department has received dedicated support at a certain manpower loading for years. Also, search for work that was generated by individual deals between an IT manager and the supervisor of a user area without a review of real benefits.
- *New projects.* Rank these in terms of benefits. The new projects must be consistent with the framework of the plan and the architecture.

Each area has its own criteria. When you add them up, there is overcommitment in some areas, while other areas may have spare resources. This is the fodder for trade-offs. The next analysis step is to assess the projects between categories or consider the pool in total. Try more than one approach.

Allocation percentages

Consider specifying a percentage for each category that will provide limited support for new projects. Here is an example:

- Operations support: 20 percent
- Infrastructure support: 15 percent
- Ongoing development: 10 percent
- Architecture-related work: 7–8 percent

- Backlog: 5 percent
- Strategic planning projects: 5–8 percent
- Maintenance and enhancement: 25 percent
- New development: 10 percent

Are you surprised by these numbers? The proactive allocation leads to a gradual shift. Eventually, planning items diminish as does operations support and maintenance and enhancement. They are replaced by new development. Note that old systems and architecture are being addressed in these percentages. You are still performing substantial maintenance. After setting the percentages, apply them within each category.

Allocation based on fairness

Associate projects and work with business units. Assign a fixed percentage to enterprise-wide support (say 45 percent). Then allocate the remainder (55 percent) across the business divisions based on each division's importance to the business plan.

Allocation based on the strategic IT plan

Assign priorities based on the objectives and strategies within the strategic systems plan. The criterion might be alignment with the objectives.

Now review the results of each of the three. You can even create a table. The rows are the projects and the columns are the allocation methods. In the table place a yes or no as to whether the allocation method included the item. Create a fourth column that contains an average of the scores or ratings.

For the meeting of the steering committee, a potential agenda is as follows:

- *Introduction.* This section discusses the process followed.
- *Summary of the strategic systems plan.* This section provides perspective and a reference point for evaluation.
- *Summary of projects that made the first cut.* This section highlights those that clearly need to be supported. This agenda item ends with pie charts of the resources consumed and those still available.
- *Summary of dropped projects.* This discussion points to some of the projects that did not make the cut but are still viable candidates.
- *Discussion and setting of the slate.*

As a result of the meeting, you will have the slate along with some projects to which management specifically assigns high priority. Other projects will be waiting in the wings for resources.

A suggested outline of the project slate report is as follows:

- *Introduction.* Describe the process followed.
- *The project slate.* Identify each project in terms of description, schedule, project leader, costs, and benefits.
- *The projects that almost made the slate and that may be activated during the year if resources are available.* Again, provide description, costs, and benefits.

- *Summary of the state of systems and technology if all of the project slate items are completed.*

For this last item, try a scenario. That is, consider several business processes. Give the before and after workflow in the processes. This is also useful for highlighting the interdependence of the projects and plan action items.

Dynamic resource allocation

In planning and selecting projects to create the project portfolio and in managing the portfolio, resource allocation is key. We discussed resource allocation for projects and other work above in a strategic sense. However, as we pointed out, the conflicting demands for resources push and pull people constantly. If you do not take control of almost daily resource allocation, people may end up spending most of the time on non-project work. In part, this is due to the pressures and urgency of maintenance, operations, and so on. Also, there is a human tendency in many to not want to work on projects and do project work. How can this be since the project work is more interesting and challenging? Here are some reasons:

- People are often only aware of the risk and problems in doing project work. There is little of that in current work.
- They are paid the same for both project and non-project work so why do the extra work?
- Project work brings people under deadline and schedule pressure. Who needs this?

IT managers and project leaders, therefore, need to actively monitor what people are working on and keep emphasizing projects. In working with team members who have substantial non-project work, you have to stress the positive benefits of doing work on the project in terms of their skills. This is in addition to the importance of the project.

To ensure that projects receive adequate attention, IT managers and project leaders should carry out regular meetings where the activities of individual employees are discussed for the next period. Experience has shown that this is best done once a week toward the end of the week for the following week. At the meeting there will be a consensus on what these individuals will be working on the following week. This agreement will then help prevent a single manager from redirecting an employee during the next week.

Cases and examples

Astro Bank

Astro Bank is a leading consumer and commercial bank that operates in multiple states. The bank had relied on many old legacy systems. When it was decided to modernize these, management insisted that the same programmers doing maintenance also develop the client-server and distributed systems. The result was a disaster. Maintenance suffered and no new system resulted. The approach was abandoned and a new distributed systems group was established for the new development. The strategy initially was to develop new systems that employed the legacy systems for batch processing. After these new systems were developed, the legacy systems were to be replaced or modernized. At the start of the analysis, the two groups were not cooperating with each other. The legacy systems staff continued to do enhancements and failed to inform the distributed systems group of what they had done. The software on the distributed systems side blew up. The distributed systems staff in frustration began to build modules and functions into the new software that replicated the functions in the legacy system. It looked like another disaster coming down the track.

In the first step, information was gathered from each group separately. Each used different project management software, different methodologies, and entirely different management styles for resolving issues. Neither side really took advantage of lessons learned. Building the templates had to be conducted separately with each group (Step 2). A new resource list was created. Most tasks had to be edited into a common framework that was between the styles of the two groups. The interdependencies were difficult to establish because neither group had tasks that related to the other group due to a lack of communications (Step 3).

Issues were also a problem (Step 4). The distributed group provided a list of issues. The legacy group did not acknowledge these issues. The legacy group provided user requests for maintenance and enhancement. Additional interviews were required to solicit the information to build the issues. Several methods were used to group projects (Step 5): by business unit, by legacy system, by network, by issues, and by banking product. Each of these provided a different insight into the projects.

The analysis of the issues (Step 6) revealed that many issues were missing. This was reinforced from Step 3 when many new tasks of interdependence had to be defined. The new issues related to these tasks. A meeting of project managers was held as part of Step 7. The order of presentation was as follows:

- *Review of the revised schedules of each group.* This showed a common structure and introduced templates that crossed both groups.
- *Review of the issues from each group.* This revealed a common set of issues.
- *New tasks and issues.* These were presented along with the impact of what would have happened had these tasks and issues not been defined.
- *Priority list of issues.* This triggered a discussion of the issues that were faced by both groups.

It would have been asking too much for the two groups to cooperate immediately and fully. The cooperation built over time. The Astro Bank example will be followed up on in later chapters.

Questions

1. Astro Bank looks like a disaster, but these things are not uncommon. In a later chapter we cover change management and resistance to change. From the above what were signs of resistance to changing the old methods?

2. Most organizations have some old, legacy systems. Give some reasons why these are not modernized.
3. Suppose that you were at Astro and were assigned to map and analyze dependencies between three projects. How would you proceed?

Mapping to the PMBOK and PRINCE2

Both methodologies relate single projects to groups and the project portfolio. Both also address interfaces and interdependencies among projects. Neither, however, address portfolio project analysis.

Lessons learned

Managing an implementation of a major new system such as ERP (Enterprise Resource Planning), CRM (Customer Relationship Management), or SCM (Supply Chain Management) often means managing a set of related projects. There is a mini project slate in which you struggle to allocate people across subprojects as well as work with the dependencies between milestones and tasks across the subprojects. Here are some examples of dependencies for an E-Business implementation:

- Marketing needs to specify the discount structure for merchandise so that both IT and business departments can handle the discounts as soon as they are offered. The same applies to promotions.
- Existing procedures and policies within a department may have to be modified to be synchronized with those imposed by E-Business. Otherwise, the customers or suppliers on the less favorable side will begin complaining—giving rise to a crisis.
- The same people are needed in different subprojects because of their expertise.

The situation is even more complex when you move up to the overall organization. A major system implementation requires detailed knowledge of the company's business rules. Unfortunately, this information often rests in the minds of a few critical and senior employees. These people are required for normal work—just to keep the business going. How will you allocate their time between normal work and the systems subprojects? That is a challenge. In one case, the company dedicated the people to the new systems effort and the company experienced revenue loss and customer service complaints. In another, a firm gave priority to normal business. It took forever to implement the new system and then it did not work right. There must be a balance.

Guidelines

- Should you create multiple systems projects in a single business unit? Only if the projects are directed at the same goal. Otherwise, the projects can tear the business department apart by requiring extensive time and involvement by key business department staff.
- With success, a single project that is not finished can spawn other projects. This occurs because management sees success and wants to spread it around. It is a

natural reaction. The problem here is that these additional projects will likely require some of the key staff from the original project. The original project can be delayed and put in peril.

- Treating all projects the same can smother smaller projects. The approach here allows for smaller projects to be tracked within the template and issues as larger projects. There is no increased overhead in management or administration unless there is risk in a smaller project. Risk translates into more issues and a greater attention to the schedule. This is really what you want—the degree of attention and management effort depends on the risk, not on the size of the project.
- Related to the preceding guideline, you need to treat small projects as projects, since if they just exist as work, there is a lack of control.
- Try to avoid long-term resource allocation. Systems projects can change in terms of schedule quickly. Therefore, experience indicates that doing long-range allocation of scarce resources across projects is only useful for general estimation. Allocating far in advance can lead to inflexibility if you have to shift resources later. It makes sense to analyze and allocate resources for a month or two in advance. This can be done in a rolling mode where each week a new week is added.
- Establish customized data and formats for the project management software in advance. If you attempt to learn the details of the software at the same time you are gathering the information in the early steps mentioned previously, you will probably not do a good job with either. Learn the software and establish any customization up front.

Questions

1. Research the Web and find ten guidelines for managing the project portfolio.
2. Suppose that a company has divisions that operate autonomously. They do address similar customers and markets. Assume that each division has their own IT department and that each manages their own project portfolio. What are the benefits and drawbacks of this approach?
3. Suppose that you are a project leader and you find that a member of your team is not spending time on the project. Instead, he or she is putting out fires and doing maintenance on other systems. What actions could you take? How would you try to communicate with the line supervisor to whom the employee reports?
4. You are an IT manager and are working on resource allocation for the next quarter. There are several people who appear to be overcommitted in the allocation. What possible actions could you take?
5. Assume that a midsize company has 250 employees and an IT department of 3 people. Discuss how useful project portfolio management could be, even with limited resources?

What to do next

1. For each category of interdependence, identify several projects. Next, assess how these dependencies are currently being managed. This will indicate some of the benefits to managing the portfolio.

2. Collect the existing project plans and begin to build a resource list that can be employed by all of the projects. Then start to build high-level templates. To get support from project leaders, solicit feedback on an iterative basis as you go.
3. Perform a dry-run analysis to see what resources could be moved between projects. This will be a sensitive topic, so you present results in the aggregate. In other words, state that if projects were managed collectively, 10–15 percent of the resources could be reallocated. Don't name specific projects.

Summary

From a business perspective, systems projects are highly interdependent. From a systems perspective, it is necessary to divide these into single projects for purposes of management and accountability. It is a dilemma. To get your cake and eat it too requires you to impose standards on all projects so that you can perform analysis, trade-offs, and allocations across projects while at the same time preserve each project's own individuality and integrity. It is a delicate balancing act. However, experience shows that the benefits far outweigh the effort.

- Lessons learned can be applied across many projects, thereby improving work quality and performance.
- Resources can be shared among projects to obtain some economies of scale.
- Information systems can take advantage of new technology across multiple business processes and systems faster.
- Issues that once were submerged in single projects can be surfaced.
- The project management process is more consistent.
- Information on projects is shared among systems and business managers and staff, leading to greater cooperation.

Part two
Project planning

5
The project concept

Introduction

The first four chapters laid out a project management process and provided suggestions for managing the project portfolio. The detail now begins. Part two starts with the initial concept of a project and ends with the completion and approval of the project plan. From there we will move on to the management of the project and address specific types of systems and technology projects.

In the past someone would come up with an idea for a systems project. This quickly led to the development of a project plan. The budget and the schedule were then derived from the project plan. Systems projects are often notoriously vague when they are started. This fact, combined with the rapid development of a plan, can produce many problems later. Experience and lessons learned point to the benefits of hashing out the purpose, scope, and other factors in the project first—prior to developing the plan. If you wait until a plan is in place, there is so much detail that most managers will not question the plan—or the detail. There is also a political goal for the project concept—that of gaining understanding and support. From experience this has helped to dampen scope creep.

A project concept defines the purpose, scope, roles, benefits, issues, and framework for a project idea. The notion of developing a project concept has demonstrated a number of benefits, including the following:

- Management can perform trade-offs at a high-level relative to purpose and scope. Specifically, the extent to which process and architectural improvement will be part of the project can be set.
- The business unit roles and responsibilities can be defined. Whether the business unit will step up to these in the project can be validated.
- Related to the roles and responsibilities, the benefits of the project to the business can be roughly estimated. This can lead to a discussion of how to measure the benefits later.
- Because management and business units have an early role and involvement in setting objectives and scope, there is less likelihood of changes later in the project.
- Key interfaces with other systems and technology can be determined.
- It is less expensive economically and politically to address issues at this time than to wait until the project has started.

- Management gains an understanding of the issues and potential problems that will potentially have to be faced in the project early. These can be discussed rationally before the issues arise—an early warning system.
- It is far easier to understand a project concept than a detailed project plan. As such, the project plan demonstrates how the concept will be carried out.

There is an analogy between the life cycle of systems and this approach for projects. The project concept corresponds to the feasibility stage of a project. The development of the plan can be seen as requirements and design for the plan.

Developing a project concept is valuable for any project management process. The project concept allows you to do an organized analysis of the project idea in the process. It also helps you build management support prior to developing a detailed project plan. This chapter deals with the development of a project concept. After completing this step you will have management approval for the project team to be identified and the project plan to be developed.

What is in the project concept?

Here are the key ingredients:

- *Objectives.* The objectives of the project are set. Objectives here mean the impact on the business processes or technology base. Pinning down business impacts as opposed to just completion of the setup of a system will yield a better estimate of system benefits.
- *Scope.* What is in and what is out of the project? Experience reveals that although many can agree on the objectives of a project, much disagreement can arise as to scope. Considerable time will be spent here.
- *Roles of IT, business units, and vendors.* What activities in the project will each party be responsible for? Will they participate in evaluation, design, installation, training, and so on? Will they help manage the project? How will issues get resolved? How will the parties interact with each other?
- *Major milestones and task areas.* Using the template you can develop rough estimates of the work ahead and milestones that have to be met.
- *Benefits, schedule, and costs.* With the objectives, scope, milestones, and tasks, you can estimate the benefits, overall schedule, and costs. These will not be precise, but they will help management to understand what it will take. How the benefits will be verified should be discussed.
- *Initial issues.* What are known issues at this stage? There can be resource shortages, business policy questions, and resistance to the project, to mention a few. Identifying these issues at the start prepares everyone for the road ahead. If you use an issues database and checklist, then you can identify which issues are applicable to the project.
- *Success and change.* What is the definition of project success beyond getting the work done on time and within budget? What changes will result in both the business units and IT?

- *How will success, benefits, and change be measured?* It is nice to claim that a project can accomplish many things. It is another thing to say how this will be measured.
- *Impact if not done.* What will be the effects on the business and IT if the project is not done? Some projects may have a lot of benefits, but if they are not done, there is little impact. The answer to this question will be important when project selection comes up later. For example, if two projects had similar benefits, you would pick the one with the greatest urgency or impact if not done.

Do you just write down what comes to mind and go ahead? No, this is an opportunity to follow an organized approach and prepare some alternatives. Management input can then be sought as to what is most suitable. An interesting behavioral phenomenon occurs. Many systems people start with a narrow purpose and restricted scope. When the concept is completed, it often is more broad and includes more of the business activities as well as technological support than that of the original version. It is important that as many managers as possible be involved in reviewing and discussing the project concept. In that way you are more likely to gain consensus and have fewer problems later.

Conceiving of a project

This is a good time to be creative. Before you start nailing down the concept, you can consider a wide range of alternatives to address the situation. You may want to avoid doing a project and address the situation some other way. Each project stems from a combination of business and technical needs. Here are some potential alternative strategies.

- **Do nothing.**
  This is important because it indicates what will happen if the project is dropped. Or not selected. What will really happen if no project is done? Here are some detailed questions:

  - Will business units go out on their own to get other systems?
  - What will be the additional costs if the system and changes are not done?
  - What is the impact on the competitive position of the organization? How price competitive is the company without additional automation?
  - What are competitors doing?
  - Will the price or performance of the technology really improve by waiting?
  - If the company does wait, then when is the logical time to resurrect the project idea in the future?

- **Move work to another department.**
  Under this alternative, the work that the project targets moves to another department. The logic here is that the problems in the current situation stem from problems within the department where the work is being performed.

  - Which departments can handle the work?
  - What problems in the current process can be related directly to the people?
  - Are there training and morale problems that could be addressed by this change?

- **Outsource the work.**
  Instead of fixing the problems yourself, you can think about having an outside firm who is more familiar with the process do the work for you. This is typically considered for many support functions. Consider these questions:

  - Is there a competitive advantage in being able to market now that you are not doing the work yourself?
  - Is there internal, company-sensitive information that cannot be allowed to go outside?
  - Is there any special knowledge that the internal staff must have to do the work?
  - If the work were to be outsourced, what is your firm's dependence on the outsourcing firm?
  - What efficiencies does the outsourcing firm bring to the table that your organization lacks?
  - What might be the cost of outsourcing?

- **Change the business process, not the system.**
  With this alternative, the procedures of the business process are updated. Additional training in the business process can be done. Included here are short-term changes called Quick Wins discussed later in the book.

  - What is the current state of the business process? Are the problems related to systems and technology?
  - What is the staff turnover in the department?

- **Change the system, not the business process.**
  This is the narrow definition of the scope of a project. The key question is, "If you plug in a new system and keep the process the same, will there be any benefits?" It is possible that this can occur if the current business process is efficient. However, this is unlikely in most cases because people over time tend to build the procedures and handle exceptions around and through the system. If the new system did not address the changes and exceptions, then it might not be very effective.

- **Automate less.**
  Under this alternative, you consider removing some of the automated system from use and then simplifying what is left. Why is this a viable option? Because the business could have changed after the system was implemented. The old system does not fit well with the new process. Also, the new process may not be stable so that implementing a new system may yield more problems and no benefits.

- **Cut down on the number of staff involved in the business process.**
  The concept here is not to change any procedures or systems. Instead, you consider reducing the number of people involved in the work. This is a possibility if the overall workload dropped but the staff was not downsized.

- **Increase the number of staff members involved in the business process.**
  Under this alternative, people are added to the process. This might be a short-term solution if the project was not approved. Adding people to handle work is a traditional solution.

  - If you added more people, how long might it take for them to be effective?
  - What is the cost of the additional people, facilities, and support?

    – What additional systems support is required for the additional people?

    – What happens to the error rate and rework?

- **Split up work among departments.**

  The approach here is to make the existing business process disappear. Functions are divided and assigned to different departments. This strategy is employed when companies are merged and reorganized. The thinking behind it is that if several departments already do similar work, then some could take on additional work with minimal impact.

- **Change business policies only.**

  This alternative requires some discussion. Business policies are the basic rules for defining how the business unit will perform a business process. If you change policies, you can impact the workload dramatically. Suppose that your firm had the practice of issuing letters to new customers and you are considering a small project to automate the letter generation. What if you decided to not send out the letters because you could find no discernible benefit? This change of policy eliminates the need for a new system.

- **Change the business unit organization.**

  The concept here is that the current organization and management are getting in the way of the process being performed. If new management was put in place, then the performance of the business process might be improved.

Consider creating a table using the list in Figure 5.1.

- Alternative.
- Source of alternative. This is the idea chosen from the above list.
- Alignment with mission and vision.
- Assessment of urgency.
- Rough costs estimates.
- Rough estimate of elapsed time.
- Rough estimate of resources required.
- Potential impacts.
- Potential issues and risks.
- Potential benefits.
- Ability to measure and determine benefits.

Figure 5.1   Comparison of alternative project ideas

Considering these alternatives is a good idea because you can later explain to managers and the project team all of the various alternatives that were considered. You did not just plunge in and go for automation because you are familiar with information systems. Let's put it another way. If you don't consider these, management may ask you to do so later. This will harm your credibility and erode support for the project. Using this approach your credibility and that of the project is enhanced.

The approach for developing the concept is broken down into seven steps. Because client-server and other major examples are addressed later, several other examples will be considered here. One is the decision to upgrade PC software for office functions and electronic mail. This seemingly straightforward project can be a nightmare. The second project consists of implementing imaging for an insurance company, such as Beaumont Insurance.

Structured brainstorming

Here you could have meetings within IT and with business units to generate project ideas. This aids in decision-making. *Structured brainstorming* consists of methods that elicit project ideas by examining current work and problems. Its major benefits are the identification of new ideas and the gaining of common consensus.

Benefits of structured brainstorming include the following:

- Seeking ideas from different people will improve the coverage of analysis and will be more successful than doing alone or with only a few people.
- The method can open up a culture of collaboration—a key goal of the book. As such, it can pave the way for greater cooperation later.
- The technique prevents one or a few people from dominating the generation of ideas.
- It increases creative thoughts not only on the problems, but also on solutions. In a number of instances we found that some simple solutions were obtained that caused the project not to be done or considered.

Here are some guidelines for using structured brainstorming:

- At the start of the meeting, identify the objectives in terms of identifying project ideas along with some ideas for their scope.
- Each participant will participate in the meeting.
- The attendees are not allowed to criticize the ideas and comments of the others.
- Go around the table and ask each member for input. Skip no one.
- Repeat the process until the ideas are exhausted.
- As this is done, you can consolidate ideas and even eliminate some infeasible ones.
- Keep focused and don't get sidetracked into too much detail about one idea.

Two techniques for doing structured brainstorming are SWOT (Strengths, Weakness, Opportunities, and Threats) and PEST (Political, Economic, Social, and Technology). In SWOT you focus on the processes. For PEST you can look at more wide-ranging ideas. In PEST you could, for example, consider ideas that supported the company mission and vision.

TRIZ

TRIZ is the acronym of a set of collaborative problem-solving techniques. The translation of TRIZ is The Theory of Inventive Problem Solving. The TRIZ technique applies to situations where there are conflicting ideas about a process.

Using TRIZ a coordinator for the meeting asks each participant for principles to solve a problem such as a particular process problem. He or she also supports these and gives examples. The coordinator works with the group to uncover contradictions.

TRIZ provides more structure than free-style brainstorming since it focuses on getting down to the details of how potential solutions would work and what concepts the solutions are based upon. With TRIZ you identify conflicts early on. When we have used it, we found that you can rapidly get to the conflict over a business process in terms of (a) leaving it alone; (b) carrying out some minor changes; (c) undertaking a major project. Another benefit is with a more structured approach, you find that people will be less likely to concur on one solution too soon. In addition, the group can work through the impacts of implementing one of these three alternatives.

Step 1: define alternatives for the project objectives

A suggestion is that you begin with a very narrow systems objective. This might typically occur in the installation and completion of a system. Nothing is mentioned here about business impacts or change. In the two examples, this might be stated this way:

- *Example 1*: Upgrade the software and hardware for the employees' PCs.
- *Example 2*: Install and test the imaging hardware and software.

These are traditional, narrow systems goals reminiscent of past decades. Now look under the sheets. In the first example, the staff will be upset and disturbed because the software that they use most and are most familiar with is being replaced. Their productivity will be affected. How will all of these people be trained? How will their current files be converted to the new software? If there are letter and other word processing and spreadsheet templates, will these be recreated on the new software? Who can the employees call for help and questions? It is clear that the purpose must be expanded if you are to ensure success. If you don't do this, then some of the questions will not be addressed. They will fall through the cracks.

For the second example just installing imaging does not yield any business benefit. Forms have to programmed so that you can employ optical character recognition (OCR). The image software must link to the software applications and databases. Suppose, for example, that you have loan application processing and servicing in mind. Then you scan the loan application form and have the system fill a data entry screen with what it recognized. The system should route the entered application to someone who can determine the applicable rate and whether you will issue a policy. These steps constitute much more work than just installing hardware and software.

In each example the narrow objective is just the tip of the iceberg. It is the first phase of the project. It is not the project. Here are some expanded objectives.

- *Example 1*: Implement new end user software and ensure that it is in use.
- *Example 2*: Implement a complete image system that front-ends the existing application processing system.

These are better. They are more complete. Notice that there is much more to each objective. You want to keep the wording short. However, there are still problems with these statements. No expectation or benefit is identified. If you were a higher-level manager, you might ask, "Why should we spend the money to do this project?" As a project leader, wouldn't you want everyone to keep in mind why people on the team are doing all of this work? Therefore, you must further expand the objectives to include the major benefits. Doing this, you can define the revised objectives:

- *Example 1*: Implement new end user software to provide new capabilities and increase employee productivity.
- *Example 2*: Implement a complete front-end system to increase efficiency and improve management control.

A note on the second example. Increased efficiency comes through reduced data entry and ability to route the transactions between different employees. Management control is improved because the system can track each transaction to determine how long it took to complete and the time spent in various states.

In forming objectives, here are some guidelines:

- Ensure that the objective is sufficiently broad as to include the business role.
- Phase the objective in terms that the business managers and staff can comprehend.
- Include major benefits in the wording of the objective in business terms.
- Employ a standardized sentence structure starting with a verb and ending with the benefit.

What are the benefits of taking this approach? First, you provide a convenient way to list the various projects so that business managers understand them. Second, there is uniformity. Each new project idea has to clearly identify its benefits at the start. A third benefit is that by focusing on objectives in business terms, you are more likely to achieve benefits since the emphasis is on the business rather than implementing a system.

Scope management

You might think that managing scope arises first in the project plan. Not true. You want to have scope discussed as you discuss and analyze various project ideas. You are trying to determine the natural boundaries of project ideas so as to prevent later scope creep or expansion and major project changes.

To do this it is helpful to identify what would be needed for the project in terms of:

- Business organization;
- Business staff resources;
- IT resources;
- Business processes, procedures, and work;
- Methods and tools in both the business and IT;
- Facilities;
- Technology and infrastructure.

As you are doing this, you also want to determine things that are not within the scope.

Step 2: determine alternatives for the scope of the project

If you have the right objective, why is scope important? Scope determines what is in the project and what is out. Through the scope you will build the major headings of your project and template. Cut the scope and you cut the project. This is difficult for managers to see if they are looking at a task plan of 500 tasks or more.

A systems and technology project idea can be viewed in a number of dimensions: underlying technology, business unit involvement, extent of business process impact, extent of interfaces to existing systems, existing technology interfaces, impact on business policies, and impact on the business unit organization. These dimensions allow you to compare different scopes. In example 1, if the scope of the project was just the systems group, then you have the chart shown in Figure 5.2. This chart shows that there is virtually no business involvement or impact. If you expand the scope to match the revised objective that was developed, you obtain Figure 5.3. In these diagrams a scale of 0–3 is employed

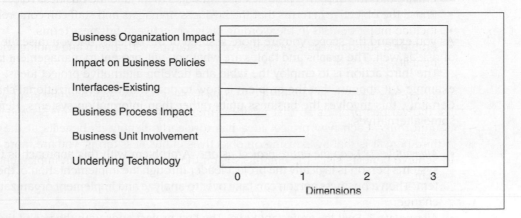

Figure 5.2   Restricted scope

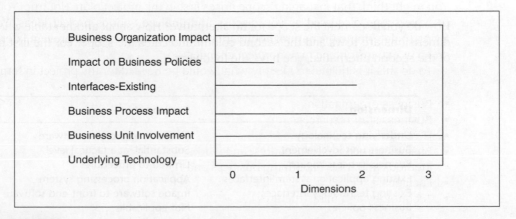

Figure 5.3   Expanded scope

Example 2 is more complex. It was already agreed that the business process is involved. There are additional questions related to scope. When you change the work flow in the data capture process, you impact data entry and servicing. Therefore, it is natural to consider changing the organization. Because the new system can automate the business rules for insurance application approval, you might want to change business policies to allow automatic approval if the application meets certain criteria.

The first action in working with scope is to define alternatives and graph them as was done earlier. The second action is to determine the impact of different scope alternatives. The following table is suggested, using your information for example 2.

Scope	Business impact	Project impact
Imaging technology only	Few likely benefits	Narrow project with little risk
Imaging, work flow, linkage	Some benefits	Manageable, but complex
Work flow, organization, policy, and so on	Assured benefits	Project becomes political

As you expand the scope, you are more assured of the benefits, but you raise the level of risk as well. The graphs and tables are what you will present to management later.

The third action is to employ the table and develop alternative project ideas. From example 2 it appears that the problem is how to deal with the organizational change. Certainly, this involves the business units rather than information systems. Here are some alternatives:

- *Alternative 1: Keep the entire project as one.* A problem with this approach is that a systems person is logically the project leader through the implementation of the system. Then a business person can take over to analyze and implement organizational change.
- *Alternative 2: Split the project into two.* The first project ends with the use of the system. The second project is a business project dealing with business policies and organization.

How do you document the scope for an alternative? How about another table where the dimensions are rows and the second column indicates the scope. For the first project of the second alternative, you have the following:

Dimension	Comment
Underlying technology	Network, application software
Business unit involvement	Substantial, at a tactical level
Business process impact	Limited to procedures
Existing application system interfaces	Application processing system
Existing technology interfaces	Image software to front-end software
Business policies	Not applicable
Business organization	Not applicable

How does an objective relate to scope? You can have the same objective for several alternative scopes. The scope has to fit the objective. Because the objective is general, there is room for several alternative scopes, as was done with example 2.

You can also prepare a spider or radar chart indicating different alternatives for scope. The dimensions for the chart are:

- Business processes. To what extent does the alternative involve the business process?
- Benefits. What are the business benefits that result with the scope of the alternative?
- Risk. What are the project risks with the scope of the alternative?
- Costs. What is the magnitude of the cost of the project with the scope of the alternative?
- Elapsed time and schedule. How long would the project take with the scope?
- Systems and technology. What is the degree of work and change required by the alternative?
- Organization. To what extent does the business unit have to be involved in the project to make it successful?
- Policies. To what extent must policies be addressed and changed with the scope?

You can now draw lines linking the appropriate levels for each dimension. This helps you trade-off between different alternatives. Experience shows that it is the scope where management input and discussion are most valuable.

Step 3: prepare alternative schedules, costs, and benefits

For several alternative purposes and scopes, you now will try to figure out costs and benefits by developing a general schedule. The temptation here is to plunge into detail. Don't succumb to this temptation. Remember that several alternatives are available.

The first action is to define a high-level list of tasks based on the narrowest scope. If a template is already available, then start with it. Otherwise, proceed from the top down and define the first level of tasks. Here is a cut for example 2.

1000   Define the detailed project plan.
2000   Define new work flow and process for data capture.
3000   Implement imaging hardware and software.
4000   Design and implemented the front-end system.
5000   Customize and interface imaging software to the front-end software.
6000   Implement interfaces to the legacy application system.
7000   Develop new procedures and train business unit staff.
8000   Implement new business process and system.

Some comments are appropriate here. First, each task is numbered so that it is easy to follow. Second, each task begins with a verb so as to indicate the action required. Third, note that the project ends with the new process in place. There are no policy or organization changes. To expand the scope to these, you can add these tasks:

9000   Analyze business policies and organization.
10000   Implement new organization and policies.

You now have two task lists at a very high level. Next, determine the dependencies between these tasks. This is your second action.

The third action is to identify resources for each task. Don't do this by name. Instead, indicate the type of person needed (for example, systems analyst or programmer) and the number required for each task. Later you will refine this by adding more tasks and more detailed resources.

The fourth action is to develop an estimate for how long each part will take. Be conservative. Base your estimate on previous project experience. Where you perceive risk, add more time. For example, you might think that task 9000 will take about a month. Don't kid yourself. It will take longer because human resources and management will have to determine which people will move where. Allow 3 months. The same is true for task 10000.

With the estimated schedule and resources, you can now perform the fifth action—estimate the cost of the project. Many people fail to identify certain types of costs. Be as complete as you can. If you require some people on a part-time basis, include them. If you need to test hardware and software, include a charge for the use or acquisition and use of this technology.

Step 4: define the role for the alternatives

The role of the business unit flows from the objectives, scope, and schedule you have created. The wider the scope, the more likely it is that business unit role will expand. If the scope grows to provide additional systems functions, then this expands too. Here you can develop another table. Here is a partial table for example 2.

Task area to be performed	Business unit doing work	Comments
Training of end users	Data entry and operations	Requires train the trainer
Development of procedures	Data entry	Needs guidance and support
Policies for automated approval	Management model	Must match organizational model

What can this table be used for? Develop a table for each alternative that you considered in Step 3. You are now in a position to discuss the impact of scope on benefits, schedule, and the business unit role. Expand the scope and you expand the role. Without this many managers opt for the wider scope. After all, it has greater benefits. However, the downside is the longer schedule and the expanded business unit role. Potential business unit roles include the following:

- Recurring training of employees in business unit procedures and systems use
- Training materials for the process and system
- Initial training in the new business process and procedures

- Operations procedures for both the process and systems
- Definition of the new business process and procedures
- Comparison of the new and existing process to get requirements and benefits
- Assessment of the benefits after the new process and system are put in place
- Participation in testing and conversion
- Analysis of the current business process and identification of issues in the process

Notice the order of this list. This is the order in which you should discuss the user role with the business. It gains commitment.

The same comments apply to both the IT and vendor roles in the project. As you define different alternatives, you can then assess how IT, business units, and vendors will interact and interface. If the business unit is unwilling or unable to assume the appropriate role, then this is a good time to stop work and not proceed with the project—because unless they are committed at the start, history in projects reveals that it is more difficult to get the commitment later.

Step 5: analyze the results of Steps 1–4 and determine the recommended project concept

In this step you will perform any further analysis of the work you have done. You may still have several alternative project concepts. It is in this step that you contact some of the managers and let them review the material to get their input on the scope of the project. Start with a discussion of the schedule and the business unit role. Once this is understood, move to what happens when the scope is expanded. Use their input and feedback to modify and update the tables and estimates.

Step 6: Identify Key Performance Indicators

You want to pay attention to what is driving the business. *Key Performance Indicators (KPI)* consists of defining the benefits from a project. This provides further insight into the scope of the project. KPIs are aligned to the objectives of the business. They are established by business units for the project in the project concept development. Defining KPIs will aid in making decisions during the life of the project. KPIs improve the likelihood of the acceptance of change by the business.

Key Performance Indicators relate to project costs, benefits, timelines, technology, and systems on the IT side. On the business side they relate to business process performance.

Step 7: identify initial issues.

In this step you can now identify issues that you know will appear. Here are some examples for example 2. These are organized by the chapter headings in Part four. Note that this is just a sample of more than 75 issues that were developed.

- **Business issues.**

  - Can OCR be effective if only a small number of forms are programmed (or, is this a situation in which automating 5 percent of the forms will give you 65 percent of the volume?)
  - How will exceptions in the work flow be handled?
  - Do other departments require access to the image?
  - Can the paper be destroyed after scanning?

- **Human resource issues.**

  - How long will it take for the programmers to come up to speed in programming the image software?
  - What will be the resistance of the business unit staff to the system?
  - How will job descriptions be developed?

- **Technical issues.**

  - What are the network requirements to support the routing of images? Can the current network support this workload with adequate response time?
  - Can the application software be modified to accommodate a link to the images?

- **Vendor and consultant issues.**

  - What support will the image vendor provide?
  - What support will the vendor of the insurance application software provide?
  - Are the tools provided by the different vendors compatible?

As a result of discussing issues, management gains a better understanding of the challenges that will have to be faced. The issue discussion may lead backward to revise earlier steps. In general, issues tend to bring people down to earth. There are less likely to be problems in management and user expectations later. Also, when some of the issues later emerge, then there is less surprise.

Step 8: obtain management feedback and commitment

In this step you seek agreement to develop the project plan and more detailed budget. Here management has the opportunity to view the project concept without massive pressure to get the project underway. Remember that you seek agreement on objectives and scope and the other items. The approval of the resources and detailed plan will come later.

Assume that you have already obtained some management feedback from the previous steps. What are the detailed goals here?

- The business unit management must commit to the project.
- Information systems management must support the project in terms of making resources available and juggling priorities to support interfaces, the network, and so on.
- Upper management must see the benefits and resources required.

Business unit commitment is revealed in the roles defined in Step 4. There is commitment from upper management in the unit as well as from middle-level managers and staff.

Here is a useful series of actions that you can take with respect to management presentations. The first step is to get information systems support for the project. You can use the issues that you have identified in the previous step to indicate the type of support that you require. If you fail here, then it may be because the information systems unit places a higher priority on other work. Management may feel the same way. The project concept is dead in the water.

Let's assume that you have passed this first hurdle. Turn to the business unit next. Approach the business unit managers that you have been in contact with and inform them that you desire to present the project concept to a wider audience in the business unit. You are attempting to reach the people in the departments that will be working with the new system. You want their support to buttress the support of their own management. They can also provide you with more details about benefits.

After you have lined up information systems and the business units, approach individual upper-level managers either directly or through intermediaries. When you come into a management meeting for support, introduce the project and then turn it over to the business unit manager first. The business unit manager can indicate the benefits and the business unit's commitment to the project. The information systems manager can follow indicating that the approach is feasible, doable, and can be supported.

Cases and examples

Astro Bank

The initial work started out badly. Recall that there were two systems groups. The distributed group plunged in and developed a project plan. It was too narrow. Not only did it leave out the legacy system tasks, but it neglected changes in business procedures, policies, and organization. The plan was rejected. The approach was to hold several planning sessions to determine the scope of the project. Most people agreed on the overall purpose. The problem initially was the scope. The application was an online servicing front- and back-end system to an installment lending legacy system. Some of the questions that arose were as follows:

- Will changes be made to the legacy system since the legacy systems team was going to have to do work to support the interfaces to the online system?
- Will the business unit do loan servicing at its branches as was the case? Or will servicing be centralized?
- Is the telephone system to be modernized to support both incoming and outgoing calls on a more automated basis? What are customers able to do for themselves?

Answers to these questions determine the extent of benefits. If the business process, organization, and telephone system are left intact, then there are few benefits. However, both systems groups felt uncomfortable about expanding the scope to these areas. A second meeting was conducted with these managers and the business unit responsible for installment lending. In this meeting the scope was expanded to include all of the elements mentioned.

With the scope settled, the responsibilities of the business unit were addressed. At the start of this discussion, the business managers indicated that they had no staff or time to spare. They wanted the systems groups to do documentation, testing, and training. It was pointed out that (1) this would delay the implementation by months and (2) the support provided by systems in these areas would not be business specific. Reluctantly, the business unit manager committed to the role.

At the next meeting, the purpose, scope, and roles were reviewed. Attention then drifted to the schedule and benefits. The business unit manager was reticent to sign up for specific benefits. To get down to details and resolve the issue, the outline of the new business process for servicing in a centralized mode was developed. This led to a comparison with the current process and the identification of the saved steps and labor. The business unit was assigned to then define the benefits.

When the schedule was presented, major problems erupted over sequencing of the project. Will the new system be implemented first? Will the telephone system be installed? Or can the staff and servicing be centralized? These were the most important questions after the scope. In the end it was agreed to centralize first. This might standardize procedures and allow for the organization to become stable. Then the telephone system is installed. Finally, with the organization and communications in place, the system can be implemented.

A later meeting was devoted to defining the initial list of issues. More than one hundred business, technical, and policy issues were defined. Some of the following issues were raised:

- What will happen to the staff in the branches?
- What access does the branch need to loan data if there were a central servicing area?
- What was the bank's policy on the role of the branch staff?
- Do any other business unit staff members require access to the new system beyond those in the servicing center?
- How will the transition at each stage be done?
- Who will serve as the project leaders?
- What will happen to the backlog of user requests for changes to the installment loan legacy system?

Note that if the scope had been narrowed to the system, most of these issues would disappear. The network would have had to be extended to hundreds of branches to support servicing.

Questions

1. What do you think would have happened if someone had just gone ahead with a project plan instead of this work on the project concept?
2. Let's assume that in the meetings with the business, no one had any radical ideas. They were confident with how they serviced loans. What steps could you take to get more participation?

3. This case discussed the sequencing of IT and business work. What if attention had been limited to IT? What would have been the impacts on the project?

Mapping to the PMBOK and PRINCE2

PMBOK treats the project concept as part of project planning. PRINCE2 differentiates the two. The project concept is addressed in the process of starting up a project. The detailed project planning is covered in initiating a project. In this regard, this chapter provides guidelines for starting up a project.

Lessons learned

The project concept is essential in almost all projects. Management typically sees E-Business implementation as an IT project. It is not. IT work is quite limited compared to the overall scope of the effort required. Some of the elements that have to be addressed typically are:

- Changes in marketing strategy and policies;
- Definition of sales, promotions, and discounts;
- Changes to existing business processes to make them synchronized with the systems;
- Organization change to support the change;
- Definition of new business processes to support the change.

Suppose, for example, that you are a retailer moving to the Web. You would have to handle orders, customer service, returns, refunds, discounts, billing, and other transactions differently to support E-Business in many cases. The techniques in the steps above turn out to be very valuable in determining the direction of implementation and the implementation strategy. Some additional comments are:

- By discussing alternative objectives, you can mesh the implementation with the overall strategy of the use of systems and technology for the firm.
- Through comparing alternatives for scope, you can see how much will have to be changed.
- The issues analysis paves the way for a more realistic assessment of schedule.

Guidelines

- When defining an objective, if the wording of the objective is too complex, then consider breaking it into several projects. For example, suppose your objective was, "Implement a client-server system and wide area network so as to improve your competitive position." You can simplify the objective by establishing the client-server system and the wide area network as separate projects.
- The objectives and the scope do not have to match. The key is that the objective be covered within the scope. The scope gives you room to work within, while the objective provides focus.

- When expanding the scope of the project idea, remember that often you will have to extend the scope in several dimensions to be consistent. For example, if you wish to include the manual steps of the business process in a project, then you are likely to want to include the other systems and PC-based tools used in the business unit.
- After defining potential issues in each of the preceding categories, you can rate them according to different criteria:
  - Importance to the project overall
  - Importance at the start of the project
  - Impact if the issue is not addressed
  - Organizations, technology, business process, policy, and so on involved in the issue.

- To show how important these issues are, select one issue of importance early in the project, develop alternative solutions for the issue, and then define the impacts on the project for each solution.

Questions

1. For what project ideas would you go directly into developing the project plan and avoiding the project concept work?
2. Suppose that you encounter a lot of hostility in a structured brainstorming session. How would you respond to this?
3. Next, suppose that there is a great deal of conflict among attendees in a brainstorming session. How could you deal with the conflicts?
4. Should you have project concepts formulated for just new projects? Or, should you also include existing projects? Under what conditions would the project concept be useful for current projects?
5. After the brainstorming sessions, you find that you have five good project ideas and several marginal ones. How do you communicate with IT and the business units about the marginal and rejected ideas? How would you respond to someone saying, "We really need this project and cannot understand why it was not considered a good idea?"

What to do next

1. For a creative exercise, consider looking around for a potential small project. Examine this potential project in terms of the alternatives defined in the chapter. Develop the table that was presented.
2. Take several projects and see if you can formulate the objectives of each project.
3. Consider one project that is not meeting its schedule. Define the purpose and scope as they were at the start of the project. Now do the same thing for the current state of the project.
4. For a project with which you are familiar, develop the scope in terms of the charts and tables identified in Step 2.

5. Drawing on the previous exercises, define the business unit involvement that is both possible and feasible. What types of resistance do you think that you might encounter?
6. Develop an initial list of issues in the categories defined earlier.

Summary

This chapter helped you to develop the concept of a project prior to developing a plan. Even if a new project management process that recognizes the project concept is not in place, it is very useful to think through the steps presented in this chapter. Doing so will solidify your support for the project. Another benefit is that a project concept provides a framework for developing the project plan later as well as for enlisting people to be on the project team. Developing the project concept can save you time and avoid issues later. The project concept allows management to put the objectives, scope, roles, and other elements into clear focus.

6
The right project leader

Introduction

With larger and more complex IT projects, companies face formidable challenges in attracting, managing, and supporting project leaders. Some of the questions they must answer include the following:

- How will new project leaders be found?
- Will there be a project office to direct all projects?
- What autonomy will a project leader have?
- How will project leaders be trained?
- How will we cope with project leader turnover?
- How will we deal with a shortage of project leaders when the projects must still continue?
- How will analysis be performed across projects?

These are but a few of the questions many firms have cited in surveys. The purpose of this chapter is to examine the role of the modern systems project leader. This is different from traditional approaches in that the role of the project leader in systems and technology projects is different today from what is was 10 years ago. Today, there are more issues involving business units, processes, and external factors in addition to new technology.

The scope of the chapter is wider than the traditional approach that concentrated on duties and gave too much attention to the mechanics of project planning. The duties of the project leader also change within the project as implementation is finally reached. For example, for some large projects, it may be useful to have a separate project leader for the implementation and rollout of a system to a large business unit.

To highlight the differences between traditional and modern, let's examine the traditional project manager. Individuals started out in information technology in a technical role. They might have been systems analysts. The systems manager might select one to be the manager of a small project. Preparation and training was limited. Often, people were just thrown into the situation. They might have been offered some training in project management. This training typically focused on project management concepts: GANTT, PERT, CPM, and so on. Each project manager was on his or her own. Project managers reported to the IT manager and resolved problems one-on-one with the manager. The traditional approach worked because projects were mostly independent of each other. The business unit had little dependence or involvement. Life was simpler. When a large project came along, the same method was used. This method of managing project leaders had a number of shortcomings that persist today. Look at the following list to see how many apply to your firm.

- There are no common schedules or approaches across projects because each manager is on his or her own—making it difficult to roll up data across projects.
- There is no sharing of information. Sharing of information might be seen as a sign of weakness.
- Only mechanical/technical training is available for project managers.
- There is a lack of coordination on solving problems among projects. Problems are solved one at a time on an *ad hoc* basis.
- There are no standard approaches for reporting on projects. Each project manager can determine how to report.
- Project managers use a different variety of software tools.
- No lessons are learned from projects.

What should you look for in a project leader?

Here is a list along with comments.

- *Problem-solving ability.* The most important attribute of a project leader is the ability to identify and solve problems. This capability in systems projects requires some technical knowledge, business knowledge, ability to work with people, and good analytical skills for evaluating problems. How do you detect this ability? Instead of asking someone about their achievements, ask what types of problems have they solved. After they mention some, then pose the following questions:

  - What were the symptoms versus the problems?
  - What alternatives did you consider in analyzing the problem?
  - What decisions were made about the problem?
  - What actions were taken from the decision?
  - How did it turn out?
  - If you had to do it all over again, what would you do differently?

- *Learning curve.* Does the person have a learning curve where lessons learned and experience are reflected in better work as a project manager? How do you test this? Ask how the project the person is managing now differs from the one that he or she managed for the first time?
- *Seeing a project through.* A person can be a genius, but project leaders must have the willingness and stamina to see a project through to the end. Try to determine if the person changed between projects. Don't ask why the person switched. Instead ask, "Will you describe both projects—the one that you left and the one you went to?"
- *Being able to work with others.* In the past, this meant being able to work with technical staff. This is still important, but as important are abilities to work with other

project leaders, line managers, and upper management. Here are some questions to test this:

- How did your recent projects interface to other projects? What issues arose between projects? How were these resolved?
- How do you foresee working with other project leaders? If you were assigned to help a junior project leader, what would you do?
- What is your approach for making presentations and communicating with line managers of business units? What kinds of contacts and what was the frequency of contact that occurred?
- What do you think are the most challenging aspects of managing highly productive technical staff?
- In what ways did you interface with upper management? How did you approach management to resolve issues?

- *Business experience.* In a modern organization, it is very important that a project leader have business experience. It would be helpful if the candidate has managed a line organization. Project leaders must be comfortable with business processes, personnel issues in line organizations, and managing business unit employees. This is at least as important as technical knowledge.
- *Technical experience.* This does not necessarily refer to programming or operations experience. You first have to ask how you would have the leader apply the knowledge. First, the leader would need to be able to understand and analyze problems. Second, he or she would participate in the project team by doing some of the work.
- *Project experience.* It is helpful to have a wide range of project experience, if possible. Here are some questions you might pose:

- What were the longest and shortest projects on which you worked? What were the differences between these projects?
- What was the most interesting project? What was the most boring project? Why?
- What were the most challenging issues that you faced?

- *Project management concepts and methodologies.* Project leader candidates should be familiar with at least three of the leading project management methodologies: the PMBOK, PRINCE2, and Agile. Certification in the method used by the firm may also be required.
- *Administrative abilities.* This can come further down on the list. Included are knowledge of project management software and other tools, as well as doing analysis, preparing budgets, and other similar work.

How do you find and select project managers?

Good project leaders are hard to find. One reason is that good, experienced project leaders are relatively scarce. Another reason is that while a number of people have certification and have been educated in project management, fewer have the in-depth experience dealing with multiple projects, resource allocation, dealing with complex issues.

Here are some guidelines for your search and evaluation:

- Keep a list of potential candidates—both internal and external. Consider people in business units as well as those within information technology.
- Delay appointing a project manager until the project concept is defined. This will give you more information about the project so as to pick the best candidate.
- Quiz the candidates based on the objectives, scope, and issues that surfaced in the development of the project concept.
- Create a table that compares candidates with areas of risk in the project. The rows are candidates and the columns are the areas of risk identified through issues in the project concept. In the table enter the numbers 1 through 5; the higher the score, the better you feel that the candidate can address the area of risk. You can also rate each area of risk on the same scale. If you now multiply the rating of the risk by the candidate's rating on that issue and then sum these, your total score should indicate how the candidate would be able to address the risks.

How should you interview project leader candidates? You could just go over their resume and experience. However, you can probably get more useful information if you focus in the interviews on the lessons learned from past projects that they would apply to future projects. You could ask, "What were three lessons learned from your last project?"

Another important subject to cover is their capabilities with respect to issues management. In addition to asking about issues in the past projects, you could pose several issues and see how they respond. Make sure you cover not only technical and business issues, but also political issues. It is important that project leaders be able to navigate the political minefield of organizations.

Once you have a list of candidates, then prepare a table such as the following. In the column labeled "Importance" put in a 1 through 5, where 1 is low and 5 is high. Rate each candidate on the same scale. Then you can multiply the rating for importance by the rating for the candidate to get a total score. In this example, candidate 1 is preferred with a higher score. Had administrative ability been highly rated and problem solving lower rated, the choice might have been candidate 2.

Attributes	Importance	Candidate 1	Candidate 2
Problem solving	5	5	2
Learning curve	4	4	2
Seeing project through	4	4	3
Work with others	4	4	5
Business experience	3	4	3
Technical experience	2	2	5
Project experience	3	3	3
Project methodology experience	3	1	3
Administrative abilities	1	2	5

What are the duties of a modern project leader?

Throughout the project the project leader is focused on:

- Managing the work toward the deadlines.
- Ensuring that the client or users are satisfied. This is often done through the management of issues. The fact is that if there are no significant issues, then the client or user will be satisfied. However, note that because of resistance to change, some people will never be satisfied.
- Management of the team.
- Communications with management, business units, team members, and vendors.

You might expect to see a list of duties here. In systems projects, this does not make much sense because the duties vary depending on the phase of the project. Let's define duties according to the following phases:

- *Initial project kick-off.* This is the period that begins with the appointment of the project leader and ends when the plan is approved, the team is approved, and the work has begun.
- *Preintegration phase.* This covers feasibility, analysis, design, software selection, and software development up to integration and testing. It also includes architecture and infrastructure work. It also includes work related to business processes.
- *Integration and implementation phase.* Covered here are integration, testing, business unit procedures, policies, training, conversion, and cut-over to the new system.
- *Postproject phase.* This includes closing out the project, gathering the lessons learned, and going on to the next project. However, note that lessons learned must be gathered along the way. If you wait to gather lessons learned at the end, people will have moved on to other work.

Now you can divide the duties into categories:

- *Major duties.* These are the mainstream responsibilities on which project leaders spend most of their time.
- *Administrative duties.* These are the overhead functions that are significant in supporting the project.
- *Background duties.* These are duties that the project leader will be doing in the background. Examples are performing work in the project and ensuring that methods and tools are being used properly.

Why are these categories used? If you are going to be an effective project leader, then you must manage your time and be very aware of priorities among tasks in these categories.

You can now build a table such as the one in Figure 6.1. The rows are the phases and the columns are the categories of duties. Each of the table entries can now be discussed.

Phase/Category	Major	Administrative	Background
Kick-off	Develop plan Assemble team Set methods and tools Begin work Resolve issues	Set up project files Establish communications tools	Collect information on other projects Collect information on team Coordinate with other projects
Preintegration	Resolve issues Monitor actual work and quality Perform marketing Interact with business and IT managers Resolve resource conflicts	Update project status Make presentations Analyze actual versus planned data Coordinate with business units Gather lessons learned	Perform work on project Track status of related projects Monitor resource assignments
Integration-implementation	Resolve issues Monitor actual work and quality Perform marketing Interact closely with business units Resolve resource conflicts	Coordinate with other projects Update project status Make presentations Analyze actual versus planned data Gather lessons learned	Perform work on project Track status of other projects
Postproject	Measure the benefits and impacts of the project Gather/organize lessons learned Support placing team members	Close out project files Prepare personnel evaluations Update project templates Update issues database Closeout presentation	Ensure team gets credit Prepare cost-benefit analysis Prepare issues analysis

Figure 6.1   Duties of a project leader by phase

- **Kick-off**
  Major.

  - Develop plan. Here you will develop the plan and gain management approval. It is assumed that the project concept has been developed. If it has not, then this would be an additional duty here. Included in developing the plan is the marketing of the plan as well.
  - Assemble team. This includes finding the team members, negotiating availability, providing motivation, and building a team atmosphere.
  - Set methods and tools. There are two areas here. One is the methods and tools for managing the project. The other consists of those methods and tools that pertain to doing the real work in the project itself. Included here is the training of the staff in the methods and tools. Here the project leader should apply the project management methodology of the firm.
  - Begin work. Work on tasks begins. It is here that the project leader builds a pattern of how work will be reviewed and how it will be coordinated as a team effort.
  - Resolve issues. The scope covers identification, analysis, decision-making, implementing actions from the decisions, and measuring the results of the actions and decisions.
  - Build communications with line managers and upper management for the project.
  - Assess and create ties with other related projects and work that impact your project.

  Administrative.

  - Set up project files. This includes all project setup: paper files, electronic files, databases for issues, actions, lessons learned, and so on.
  - Establish electronic communications tools. The project files must be established on the network. How electronic mail, groupware, the Internet, and other tools will be used is determined and implemented.

  Background.

  - Collect information on other projects. Your project does not exist in a vacuum. You must establish coordination, share project information, and collect information on other projects.
  - Coordinate with other project leaders. Get to know the other project leaders. Establish a working relationship with them.

- **Preintegration**
  Major.

  - Resolve issues. Same as above.
  - Monitor actual work and quality. You will have to monitor all work and determine tests of quality, completeness, and performance.
  - Perform marketing. This is a major duty because you must unceasingly work with upper management, business units, and other systems managers.

- Interact with business units and other systems managers. This is the detailed interaction on specific systems activities. In this phase, it tends to focus on the business process that is going to be supported by the new system.
- Resolve resource conflicts. Allocation of resources and follow-up are two major tasks here.

Administrative.

- Update project status.
- Make presentations on projects. This can include informal and formal presentations on issues, status, budget, and benefits.
- Compare budget to actual analysis.
- Coordinate with business units.

Background.

- Perform work on project. A project leader must do work in the project. Typically, this would be in the areas of systems analysis and design.
- Track status of related projects. You must determine the impact on your project of work and slippage in other projects.

- **Integration and implementation**
  Major.

- Resolve issues. Issues here tend to be very important because you are getting closer to going live with the system.
- Monitor actual work and quality. In this phase you are overseeing the work of the business unit staff as well as systems work in other projects.
- Perform marketing. Marketing here includes change control and ensuring involvement in the project.
- Interact closely with business units.
- Resolve resource conflicts.

Administrative.

- Coordinate with other projects. Coordination today often means joint scheduling of work in this phase.
- Update project status.
- Compare budget to actual analysis.
- Make presentations on project.

Background.

- Perform work on project.
- Track status of related projects.

- **Postimplementation**
  Major.

- Construct lessons learned. Although you are gathering lessons learned throughout the project, it is here that you have the time to put these together.
- Support placing project members. As the project leader, you owe it to the team members to help them migrate to other work.

- Measure the benefits of the project. You will develop statistics on the tangible benefits of the project.

Administrative.

- Close out project files.
- Prepare personnel evaluations.

Background.

- Ensure that team gets credit.
- Prepare cost-benefit analysis.

How do the duties shift during the life of the project?

Note that there are many similarities between the preintegration and integration phases. The tone is quite different, however. In the preintegration phase the emphasis is on internal development and work within the team. In the integration phase the focus moves outside to the business unit and other systems areas. These differences point to the potential benefit of having separate or multiple project leaders because the preimplementation phase of a large project can be quite different and place different demands as compared to the implementation phase. This is a telltale sign of why some projects can appear successful during development and then fail miserably in implementation.

How can you use this information? If you have a project concept, then you can assess where the risk is. Is it in the earlier work or implementation? The answer to this question can be employed in selecting a project leader.

What does a project leader need to know?

What do you need to know to be a project leader? It obviously depends on the nature of the project. Beyond general management skills, here are some examples:

- *Knowledge of the business process.* If the project is tied to a business process, then knowledge of how that process works, the exceptions, the policies, and the procedures can help.
- *Technical knowledge.* You should have some knowledge and at least limited experience with the systems and technology that are being employed in the project.
- *General project knowledge.* This is your background and knowledge of the projects in your organization. Included here is information on how the project management process works. Included here is your knowledge of the project management methodology and how to apply it.

Another area of expertise is conflict management. This can be triggered by some of the following:

- Poorly defined expectations;
- Changes that are made without consultation;

- *Ad hoc* planning and decision-making;
- Inadequate resources and their allocation;
- Vague objectives.

To prevent potential conflicts requires excellent communication skills as well as a constant push to involve people. That is one of the reasons why collaboration and communication are key themes in this book.

How do you become a project leader?

It is easy to be discouraged. Managers will tell you that they want experienced project leaders. Yet, if you can't get experience, then what do you do? Here are some suggestions:

- In a project team, volunteer to take on issues. Gain problem-solving experience.
- Volunteer to take notes and perform project analysis. This will give you experience in different areas.
- Create several accurate versions of your resume for line and project assignments. As you will see, these are quite different. The line resume gives attention to the business process and number of people managed. The project resume focuses on the benefits, size, and hurdles overcome in the project. It is more difficult to get a project leader job with a line-manager-oriented resume.
- Come up with some project ideas and submit these to a friendly manager. The risk here is that the idea may be given to someone else. Therefore, pick some subject that people would not be attracted to. Here is a good idea for you: Gather and organize lessons learned from various projects. This is a task that many do not care to do because it appears to be too mundane.
- Get familiar with the project management process in your organization. Learn about other existing projects.
- Collect information on issues. This may prove valuable later in a project.
- Take steps to learn at one project management methodology. Take classes and make an effort to obtain certification.

What is the role of a superproject leader?

In many situations there are several systems projects that are highly interrelated. How do you manage all of these if you have project leaders who are equals in each of the projects? Consider creating the role of the *superproject leader*. This is a person who oversees all of the projects in terms of dependencies and issues among the projects. The role does not include the detailed management of each project. That remains with the individual project leaders. Examples of superprojects are the implementation of an ERP (Enterprise Resource Planning) system, process improvement, and E-Business.

In more detail, here are some examples of duties:

- Perform analysis across projects in terms of resources and schedules.
- Identify and track issues that cross multiple projects.

- Conduct meetings among the individual project leaders to share information, resolve issues, and disseminate lessons learned.

What are the trade-offs here? Creating a superproject is probably a good idea if you have an application systems project linked closely to a technology infrastructure project. An example might be client-server applications with a wide area network deployment. On the positive side, you dedicate management resources to the projects as a group. This frees up management from involvement in the details. Issues among the projects tend to be resolved faster. Work quality may be better with more supervision. On the negative side, you incur the added cost. You also create problems when other projects, which are not in the group of projects, have to interface with a project in the group. Management can become too removed from the projects as well. Overall, is it a good idea? Experience indicates that a "superproject leader" concept should only be employed under exceptional circumstances when there are few dependencies with other projects not in the group.

In a superproject you divide up the project into large, but manageable subprojects. These subprojects can be based on responsibility, risk, or phase. In each subproject all of the responsibilities are discussed within the subproject.

How do the responsibilities of a manager of a small systems project differ from that of a large project?

Some might say that there are major structural differences. Experience indicates that much of the difference is a matter of degree. Issues are more frequent and important in larger projects. There are more people with whom you must coordinate and work. The technology can be more complex. There can be more interfaces.

Keep in mind one important factor—size is not as important as risk. You can have small projects with high risk and large projects that are routine. Another factor is time. If a project starts small, it can grow. If the work was begun without a project structure, then when this growth occurs, it becomes difficult to retrofit the work as a project. People on the team may feel that they are being penalized by having the bureaucracy of a project laid on top of them.

When should there be a project and project leader? From lessons learned, not every piece of work is or can be treated as a project. If you create too many projects, then you will spend much more time managing these projects and less attention will go toward minimizing risk. A guideline here is that work that involves multiple departments or key business processes should be treated as a project. If there is a short project within one department that impacts no other area, then it can be handled as work in the department with support from IT.

The responsibilities of the project leader for a small project then are the same as that of a large project. The goals are also the same: to minimize risk, to get the work done on time and within budget, and to ensure quality and performance. When you consider a large project, you want to consider the handling of multiple issues and interfaces at the same time. This will affect your selection of a project leader. However, it is not always true that junior project leaders are only suitable for small projects, because you can have large, routine projects that do not require extensive experience and expertise. An example might be deploying new versions of PC software across a large organization—a lot of work, but often with limited risk. The dominant factor is risk and the number, type, and severity of issues rather than size.

What is the role of the project coordinator?

The project coordinator and the project office concept have been described in previous chapters. In either case, the modern role centers on the goal of ensuring consistency and quality of project management across all projects. Duties to support this include the following:

- Train and provide support to individual project leaders.
- Develop and maintain project templates.
- Monitor the project information and state of the projects.
- Support the identification and resolution of issues.
- Maintain and disseminate lessons learned across the organization.
- Coordinate the sharing of project information and resource deconflicting among projects.
- Perform project "what if" analysis.
- Make presentations to management on specific issues, project status, and trends.
- Monitor the use of project management software tools and recommend upgrades whenever appropriate.

What are the role and suitability of the project management office?

Moving up from the individual coordinator, you can expand the role to the project office —the project management office (PMO). The PMO controls the processes, practices, use of methodologies, tools, and other activities related to project management across the organization. The group tends to consist of very experienced people in project management.

As such, it performs the same duties as the project coordinator—it is a matter of scale. Some questions to answer are these:

- What is the number of projects that you anticipate over the next 3–5 years?
- Is the information systems unit going to provide project management support to other parts of the company?
- Are the projects significant in terms of business impact? Do they cross multiple departments and divisions?

The reason for the first question is obvious. The second question addresses whether the information systems organization is going to provide support outside of narrow information technology projects. The third question addresses the extent of communications and exposure that information technology has.

The project office entails more overhead and expense. Moreover, it runs a greater risk of being bureaucratic. With a project coordinator you can rotate the job function among different people. The project coordinator role is also useful in bringing new people into project management. This is less true with the project office. The danger here is to create a clerical, mechanical, reporting nightmare. The offset is that if you answer the previous questions positively and with a large number of projects, then you are more likely to benefit from a project office.

Surveys indicate that only about one-third of PMOs is successful. One factor here is that since the function is overhead, it is a target for cost-cutting. In addition, the PMO often lacks upper management support.

Here are some guidelines in managing a project office:

- Rotate the staff frequently in and out of the project office.
- Review all reports and requirements placed on the project office to ensure that the workload is necessary, meaningful, and has value.
- Segment the roles of the project office (see the project coordinator list) among different people so that you have accountability.
- Insist on measurement of the project office in terms of how long issues and so on remain in the project office.
- Allow project managers to approach a specific manager if they are running into problems with the project office.

Can a project leader manage multiple projects?

This is essential. There are not enough good project leaders to go around. Furthermore, more of the IT projects are intertwined and interdependent. This may lead you to think that managing multiple projects is good. However, follow some guidelines and lessons learned.

- Make sure that the projects do not conflict with each other for resources. Otherwise, you will find that the project manager is setting priorities on his or her own. Management has less visibility and might have a different opinion of what can be done.
- The projects should not involve widely different technologies. This spreads the manager too thin. For example, you might not want a manager to handle an intranet project and a legacy system project in which there is no interface between the two.
- The projects should involve the same business units. Projects that involve different business units face several risks. First, the manager must interface with more managers and so will be spread thin. Second, there are probably additional projects that interface with the same managers. This can create confusion with the business unit managers.

Sources of failure of a project leader

From years of observing systems projects, the following factors can lead to failure by the project leader. Monitor yourself to ensure that you are not falling into any of these traps.

- *Dealing with issues as they arise.* This is a reactive mode and very dangerous in systems projects where there are many interdependencies. For example, if you make a decision on a client interface for a client-server system, it may have far-ranging impacts across all client-server applications. You must analyze issues in groups as opposed to individually.
- *Spending too much time in project administration.* This can cover many areas. You can spend too much time with management and not enough with the team. You can bury yourself in project management software. Your time is zero-sum; that is, when you spend it in administration, it detracts from the time in doing work and addressing issues.
- *Spending too much team contact time on status.* Project leaders who are not comfortable with the technology often retreat to hammering the team on project status. Look at the manager in the Dilbert cartoon strip.
- *Becoming obsessed with the schedule and percentage complete.* In these situations, status and progress take the front seat and quality and real performance are in the back. It is a problem because it just delays when problems will be addressed.
- *Micromanaging the project.* A technically oriented project manager may lean toward managing each detail of the project. One manager had all programmers submit code written during the week and reviewed it all on the weekend. It got programming results, but design and implementation issues were not addressed.
- *Failing to address outstanding issues.* Some managers work on the K of N reliability system. That is, if K out of the N issues are addressed, then they feel comfortable that they are on top of the situation. The problem really lies in the oldest outstanding and most severe issues. Not resolving these can have a major impact on the entire project.
- *Failing to get involved in the project work.* Even if you are not technically inclined, you can still perform some of the systems tasks related to analysis, design, testing, documentation, training, and so on. It is useful if the project leader works closely with the business unit staff. This shows that the manager is hands-on and gives the manager a better idea of what is happening in the business unit.
- *Tweaking the project plan or making too few changes.* On the one hand, you can drive people crazy by changing the project plan too frequently. On the other hand, you lose touch with reality if you don't change the plan to fit reality. The recommendation here is to make fewer, major changes to the schedule so as to be flexible and provide stability.
- *Getting carried away with the technology.* The project leader who falls into this trap gets enamored with new technology and diverts the attention of the team toward the technology. After a few episodes of this behavior, team performance can be affected.

Success for a project leader

Several suggestions for success in the project leader role have been given already. Here are some additional success factors:

- *Continue to learn and grow technically with the project.* Many project leaders let their technical knowledge and skills become obsolete. Don't let this happen to you.

- *Be in frequent informal communications with line and upper management.* This includes not only addressing problems and opportunities, but also communicating interesting project stories and status.
- *Know what is going on in the project at all times.* This includes what people are working on, what issues are active, the status of the project, and upcoming milestones. Be prepared to answer almost any question on a moment's notice.
- *Work with team members individually.* Although team communications and work are very important, much of systems work is individual. Take care to keep in touch with each person as an individual. Go to your team members' offices and chat casually on a regular basis.
- *Use the team to identify issues.* Perform much of the analysis of issues yourself. Allowing team members to suggest issues that can lead to problems or opportunities gives them a larger role in the project. It adds to their commitment. On the other hand, be very careful about delegating issues to team members. They may have too narrow a perspective and lack organization and political knowledge.
- *Project management is political—don't forget it.* Across all projects, managing projects is and has always been political. Remember that projects typically mean change. Change can be threatening and disruptive. There can be resistance. Groups and departments may fight for resources. These situations are just a few examples of how politics enters into project management.
- *Ability to adapt the project management methodology to a project.* The project leader should know not only the methodology, but also how to implement and use it in real-world projects.

How do you cope with the politics? Experience reveals that this is one of the biggest challenges of project management. It is closely tied in with the ability to solve problems. To solve a problem, you must market and implement a solution. Politics also means getting along with people that may detest you or the project. Because of shifting roles during the term of a project, you cannot afford to alienate or get people angry. If you win an argument, you may later lose the war. Consider the following examples:

- *Line managers.* These people may have little interest in the project. They see it as disruptive. They may fear technology. Work with them and especially their people through the project to gain their confidence.
- *Upper management.* Frequent, informal contact where you convey status, issue information, and lessons learned will get their interest in the project and support.
- *Systems managers.* Some may feel that you have a more interesting project. Others may resent the high priority that your project has because it robs them of their people.

How do you measure a project leader?

Here are some questions you might ask relate to a project leader.

- How much time is being spent on the major activities versus administrative activities? Too much time on administrative matters will detract from work.

- What is the age of the most severe unresolved issue in the project? If it is a long time, then the project leader may not be addressing the issues.
- Is the project leader aware of the exact current state of the project now?
- How often does the project leader communicate with upper management on the project on an informal basis?
- What is covered in project meetings? How long do the project meetings last?
- What is the turnover and mood of the project team? Do people on the team jump at the chance to work on other projects?
- What is the mixture of time spent on issues, communications, work in the project, and administration? The sequence here is probably the desirable ranking of priority.
- How does the project leader communicate with the team and departments?

Examples of project leaders

Project leader in manufacturing

One of the best and most capable project leaders encountered is in a high-technology manufacturing firm. He is one project leader among literally hundreds. Why does he stand out? He saw that there was a need to modernize the project management process across the company. He developed the concept and marketed it to management over the period of 18 months before it was accepted. He implemented the new process in about 35 percent of the company. It was very successful. It was build on many people accessing project information and updating their own schedules. Everyone can see each schedule. He also changed and salvaged the project office and changed it from a bureaucratic, controlling group into a proactive supportive group. His success was rewarded with another project involving international communications. What were his strengths?

- He demonstrated initiative and creativity and developed many of the detailed ideas on his own.
- He stuck through the rough early days of the project when there was a great deal of resistance.
- He was successfully able to work with everyone from technicians to upper management.

Did he have enemies? Was the atmosphere political? The answer to both questions was yes. He ended up spending over half of his time marketing and handling issues. Toward the end of the project, he spent less than 10 percent of his time completing project tasks due to the need to overcome resistance.

General systems project leader

This is a person who began work driving a taxicab in New York City. He was very street smart and savvy. He began in project management by learning it on his own while working in a bank. He then moved up to becoming a senior vice president. He also handled projects in insurance, manufacturing, and software development. He was very demanding, but very fair. He took no credit for anything and gave credit to the team. He built up tremendous loyalty among his staff. When he changed jobs, people clamored to follow him. His secret as a systems manager was to run all major and most minor work as projects. To him, everything became a project. He developed a sense of being able to detect risk.

Project leader in the Chilean mine collapse

On August 5, 2010, 33 miners were trapped underground due to a collapse at the San Jose mine in Chile. Rather than pursue a bureaucratic approach, the President of Chile reached out and selected an experienced mining manager and project leader, Andre Sougarret. He was faced with these initial issues.

- At that time, it was not known if the miners were alive.
- Or, where to find them.
- Never had such a deep rescue effort been made.
- There was tremendous pressure on to reach the men fast.
- He also knew that he would be blamed if the project failed.

When he arrived at the mine site, all he encountered was confusion and disorder—another issue. Seven different companies were attempting a rescue.

He later told how he assembled a team of experts and methodically worked the problem—his biggest challenge. He organized the project at the mine—involving fewer companies. From his previous experience, he avoided thinking about the state of the miners. That would just raise the stress level.

Probing the mine, it was found that the collapse began at a depth of 1000 feet. The center of the mine had collapsed with 700,000 tons of rock. He and the risk manager at his regular job determined that a new hole would have to be dug to reach a safe area where food, water, and other supplies had been placed.

The first drilling effort failed. Close to the miners, but not close enough. Tension mounted. In all three bore holes were drilled to reach the men. Each of these used different tools and managed as separate, but related subprojects. These supported his two technical and business goals of shortening the time to get the miners extracted and minimizing the risk. On October 9, one of these bore holes reached the miners. Now he knew the rest of the work was more routine. There was a lot to do including preparing the shaft for the rescue of the men and creating an escape capsule.

It was recommended to him that information provided to the miners be tightly controlled. He decided to avoid this and inform them of as much details as possible. This helped to calm the men.

There are several lessons learned here.

- The government empowered the project leader and got out of the way.
- He stayed calm during the entire project.
- He managed the project by managing issues.
- He coordinated the issues by focusing on the most urgent.

Cases and examples

Ratchet Aerospace

Ratchet Aerospace makes satellites for both government and private firms. Each satellite has 13 stages of manufacturing. The final stage is integration where the components are put together and the entire satellite is subjected to extensive testing involving complex test equipment and two test chambers. Management wanted to improve the project management process. As such, templates were constructed. A project management office was established. Standardized lists of issues were defined. A project management methodology was implemented. Project management software was provided with training and advisement to all project managers and supervisors. There was some improvement, but not that much. Management could not figure out what to do next.

In analyzing the situation attention turned from the methods and tools to the project leaders themselves. It was found that some had not had sufficient experience. Another issue was that the project leaders for each separate satellite worked independently and competed for staffing, testing, and facility resources. If management gave priority to satellite A, then the project leader for satellite B did not get the resources, but was still told to adhere to the schedule. The result was that the project leader for satellite B and those for other satellites would still attempt to take resources from the project leader for A.

The solution was to implement the following measures:

- Each junior project leader was paired with a senior one to transfer knowledge.
- A weekly resource allocation meeting was held among managers of line units and the project leaders. The rule was that no one could change the priorities for the following week once the priorities were set.
- Training in issues management, conflict resolution, negotiation, and collaboration was conducted.

As compared to the earlier cost of improving the project management process, the costs of these actions were insignificant. Improvements followed quickly. Productivity improved as was schedule and cost adherence to the plans. A key lesson learned here is that you have to give attention to all facets of project management if you are going to improve the project management process.

Questions

1. If the firm had carried out the project leader changes first, would that have been better? Or, would that have caused management not to implement the other project management changes?
2. There has been a great deal of attention given to the project leader. There has been much less attention to project leader interaction among themselves. Why do you think this has happened? What are the characteristics of modern projects that emphasize dealing with multiple project leaders?

3. In this case, the project leaders operated with substantial autonomy and independence. Under what conditions should there be more structure? Less structure?
4. Research the Web and find an example of a successful project leader in business, government, or politics. Try to find an interview. Then extract what they attribute to their success and what lessons learned they give.
5. Research the Web and find an example of a project failure and its project leader. Try to uncover some of the reasons for failure.
6. Discuss the advantages and disadvantages of being a project leader versus a business or IT manager or senior staff member.

Mapping to the PMBOK and PRINCE2

Both of the methodologies provide guidance on the roles, responsibilities, and duties of the project leader. PRINCE2 also gives these for the team leader, reporting to the project leader. In PRINCE2 the project leader is responsible for the day–to-day work on the project. In PMBOK the project leader role goes beyond this to the entire project.

Lessons learned

As was noted, many IT projects tend to be large and complex. Today, often ongoing work is required to keep the firm competitive. For these reasons, you should consider having two project leaders over the implementation overall. One should be business focused. The other can be IT focused. Why do you need two project leaders? One reason is that E-Business is so important that you cannot afford to not have backup. Second, you need a wide range of skills and knowledge. It is not likely in a big project that one person can handle it. Third, since it is a program, you will need to have someone continue the management of E-Business work after the initial implementation is completed.

Several other lessons learned are:

- You cannot underestimate the importance of project leaders being able to deal with political and other complex issues. That is why we rate "dealing with political issues" high on our list of desirable attributes.
- The project leader should know how to scale the project management methodology to fit the project. If you impose everything in a methodology on a small project, it will die.
- Give training sessions to the group of project leaders. Here you can propose issues and ask how they would address them. This will support the sharing and transfer of knowledge among them.

Guidelines

- Give credit to the team members. Never take credit yourself. You will get credit as management recognizes the project. Management first tends to recognize the work in the project. Then they consider the project itself. If you carry this off right, then you will be praised by the team members.

- Build a reputation for measured action. That is, perform a great deal of analysis on systems issues. Then when the decisions are made on the issues, put the supporting actions into place quickly and with determination. If you merely act without sufficient analysis, you will acquire a reputation as a shoot-from-the-hip gunslinger. If you analyze and decide, but fail to act, then you will be viewed as indecisive.
- Establish ties to multiple managers in upper management and business units. Don't rely on just one person. That person may change jobs during the project. Also, you will sell ideas to multiple managers. If you sell to one person, you are then relying on that one person to carry the day.
- Trade off youthful enthusiasm versus experience in selecting a project leader. Both have advantages. If you give this careful thought, it will help you to understand the project better.
- If you are project leader, be alert to the fact that you can be overused and abused. In some industries such as consulting, this can result in burnout. This is particularly true for project leaders who gain a reputation for being able to turn around a project. They continue to be assigned failing projects. What do you do if this happens to you? You must have the guts to jump ship. Keep your resume handy and look for new opportunities.
- Linked to the preceding point is that when you are hired by another firm as a project leader, people's perspectives of you will be fixed quickly. Your first actions as project leader will be watched closely. Be careful.

Questions

1. You are interviewing a project leader who has said he or she has a great deal of experience in the project management methodology used by your organization. How do you test his or her knowledge in the application of the methodology to a real project?
2. Assume you are a new junior project leader. What are some sources of knowledge on the Web that would help you improve your skills?
3. As a project leader one day you are hit with a surprise. A manager comes up to you and asks why your project is in trouble. What should you do? How do you respond?
4. As a junior project leader you have trouble communicating and working with senior project leaders. They don't want to take the time to talk to you. How can you approach them? A clue here is to admit lack of experience.
5. Search the Web to determine five reasons why project leaders run into trouble.

What to do next

1. In your organization, analyze how people become project leaders. Are the same people always selected? How do these people keep up their skills? Are there some common skills among the project leaders? For example, are they all good at problem solving?

2. Suppose that you want to be a project leader. Which projects do you think you can manage? It is important to analyze why you feel that certain projects are more suitable than others. This will tell you a lot about yourself.
3. For a project that you are involved with, what ties exist between the project leader and the business unit managers? How do you assess the communications with business units on the project? What issues can you trace to communications problems with the business units?

Summary

The best project leaders often got there by working successfully on a series of projects. They turned some around and successfully completed others. They may have had good luck, political support, and other things in their favor, but in the end it is often the hard work and perseverance that pulled them through. When you become a project leader, you must constantly measure yourself along the lines suggested in this chapter. Be your own worst critic.

7
Project human resource management

Introduction

A team in a systems and technology project is unlike standard teams in several respects. In a standard, traditional project, the team members often tend to stay on the team for the duration of the project. The scope of the project tends to be more stable and fixed. People on these projects do not have to perform non-project in many cases.

Systems and IT projects have a number of members who enter and leave the team after doing a relatively narrow range of work. Many IT staff members have their time spread among multiple projects as well as non-project work. Many team members have to do their normal business or IT work in maintenance, operations, and enhancement. Some of the non-project can be of an emergency nature so that they become unavailable to your project.

Managing teams in systems projects is more challenging due to the following factors:

- The team members are more in demand by other projects, as well as by companies who want to hire your people away.
- As new phases of the project begin, the requirements on the team change.
- Team members often have very different backgrounds and skills and approach their work differently.
- There is usually a mix of technical and business-oriented team members which can produce misunderstandings and conflicts.
- There are more opportunities to work on joint tasks as well as more parallel effort. The challenge for the project leader is to take advantage of this for the project.

Due to these factors, it is more difficult to manage the teams in such a fluid situation. Project leaders spend considerable time finding new members, releasing team members, and building teamwork—more than they do for standard projects.

Even with the differences, there is some common ground. Today, organizations and projects move to *empower* team members to define their work and how they would go about it. Team members are also held *more accountable* than those in systems projects 20 years ago. Motivation of team members and the building of team spirit are important for the core members of the team—the people who are going to be on the project for a long time.

Earlier, we recommended that you have small project teams. Even in large projects, consider establishing a small core team of no more than three to five people. These are individuals who are generalists and problem solvers and who can deal with issues in different phases of work across the project. The lessons learned for managing the core team resemble those learned from managing a traditional project team. Carry out much of your planning and problem solving with this team. Examples of core team members, in addition to the project leader, include the following:

- A systems analyst or designer who will support initial requirements through testing and implementation.
- Key programmers who will develop the software for the system and interface it to the existing internal software.
- Business unit staff. There are several roles here. One is a coordinator who acts to control changes, handle coordination, and arrange for resources from the business unit. This is a higher-level person. Another person will address lower-level tasks associated with requirements and the business process as well as training, testing, and documentation.
- A network or operations person. This person is responsible for overseeing the hardware and network as well as the non-application software.

These roles are most often filled by internal employees. However, a contractor or consultant may be most suited to some of these roles.

There are pros and cons for smaller and larger core teams. Smaller teams reflect the problem of getting good people. A small group is easier to manage and coordinate. There is less chance of having people around who are underutilized. However, if a member of a small core team leaves, there is a major gap to fill. If people in a small team cannot get along, then there can be more problems than in a larger team where you can attempt to isolate the problem. In some organizations, a larger team means more power for the project. This is less true today, but it still holds true to some extent.

Moving to the project team overall (called the general project team in what follows), you will find roles for many more people. They include bit parts, walk-on parts, and part-time parts in your project cast. Slightly different but consistent rules apply here. Examples of roles include the following:

- Network installation and testing;
- Hardware and system software installation and testing;
- Additional business unit staff to support testing, documentation, training, and so on;
- Other programmers who support the systems with which the new system is to interface;
- Operations staff to support testing and implement production;
- Contract programmers;
- Consultants;
- Business staff who are energetic and desire change;
- Business staff who have extensive experience and knowledge of business rules, shadow systems, and exceptions.

What are the responsibilities of team members?

Each project member has a responsibility to define the detailed tasks that will be needed to perform his or her work. The individual must define what methods and tools must be employed to do this work. Flexibility is desirable so that these will conform to the methods and tools endorsed by the organization. Each team member can establish his or her detailed tasks in the project plan on a network. Team members should be able to update their respective parts of the plan. In addition to supplying status information on the work, they can participate in reviewing other work in the project. These remarks apply to both the core and general project team.

The core team members have a wider range of responsibilities in the project. They identify issues as well as potential solutions to the project leader. They must take responsibility for investigating issues and proposing solutions. They act as an early warning system for any potential problems that arise outside of the project team. As people with general skills, they must be able to stand in for each other. If multiple business units are to be dealt with, then some members of the core team might be very involved in working with them. Core team members must review the project plan on their own to determine potential problems. This is valuable because they have different project and technology experience than the project leader. In some cases, core team members oversee the work of the part-time team members.

An important responsibility that is often overlooked is political. Team members should be encouraged to gather information pertaining to the project as they do their work and make contacts with management, vendors, and business units. They can act as external eyes and ears for the project. They can detect early signs about the progress and direction of the project. We have employed this approach for over 20 years and have found it extremely useful in that many potential problems and misunderstandings were uncovered and addressed so that they did not impact the project later. Another related step is to inform managers, business units, and vendors to feel free to express questions and concerns about the project to them. They often will not be able to answer them, but they can feed the information back to the project leader for action.

What skills do you require for the team—by phase?

Project start-up

Ask yourself here and at each step, "Where is the risk?" At the early stages of a project, the risk is in not getting the requirements and business transactions defined properly. The risk is also in underestimating what will be required in terms of infrastructure (such as hardware, network, or software). A recommendation is to ensure that the project is covered in terms of systems analysis. This will be helpful for developing requirements, technology sizing, and identifying what is required.

Preimplementation

Risk here can lie in development, interfaces, and guarding against changes in requirements. If the analysis performed at the start of the project is not complete, then additional business rules and exception transactions will now surface. These changes can have a severe impact on the schedule because they were unplanned. The core team must not only perform the work in this phase, but also monitor and ensure that the scope of the project does not begin to expand. Required here are technical skills related to analysis, design, and programming. In addition, the team must address issues that arise related to the business unit and respond quickly to any technical questions to avoid delays.

Implementation

During implementation, many of the technical skills continue to be required from preimplementation for support of integration and testing. Many new skills are needed. These relate to procedures for the business process and system, programming, testing, documentation, training materials, operations, and training. Once errors or problems surface, the expanded team must move to resolve these. If they cannot be handled through programming in the system, then there may be pressure to implement a workaround the system to cope with the exception.

Postimplementation

What is this doing here? The project is done and people more on, right? Too often, this is true. A better approach from experience is to include this as one more area of the project. In that way, IT can support change and measure benefits. Here is a political tip. Leave a few issues unresolved at the end. The new system is live, but these issues need to be addressed. This gives IT a reason or excuse to continue to be involved with the business unit. This work is carried out by IT and the business unit staff.

When should you form the team?

For the core team, identify people during the development of the project concept. These are the individuals who will be brought on board first. For the general project team, wait. If you form the team too early, you can run into problems. There may not be work for them to do. Morale will then suffer. If you bring on people before you have coalesced the core team, you risk disturbing what you are trying to accomplish with the core team. Err on the side of assigning people slightly late and then make up the small difference in the schedule. Call this just-in-time staffing or "lean" staffing. Note that in a traditional project you want to establish the team early. This has several drawbacks in modern technology-related projects. First, you really do not know who are the individuals most suited to the project. Second, if you get people too early, there may not be enough for them to do. Third, you may not have a sufficiently detailed understanding of the detailed work required.

Note that the general project team will never be completely formed because it is always in transition. Tasks for the part-time people tend to last at most several months.

As the work progresses, there will be overlap as people enter and leave the project team. Identify these part-time members according to the work that is to be done rather than trying to obtain specific individuals. Traditional project management often stressed getting people early. However, at the start of an IT project you may not have information on what you need and who the most suitable people are. Moreover, if you get people too early, they may not be productive on the project.

How do you get team members?

For the core team, you can rely on your experience and what you know about the project. You will have to negotiate with the managers in systems and the business units. Prepare a brief informal presentation about the project. It answers the following questions:

- What is the purpose and scope of the project?
- What is the role and importance of core team members?
- Why is the project important to the organization?
- If the project is not successful, what can happen in a business sense?
- If the project is successful, what are the benefits to core team members?
- How will their work be managed?
- What flexibility is there for them to return to their organization?
- Identify and discuss the other work that the team members still have to perform and suggest how resource allocation will be done.

This last question is important because you appeal to the team members' self-interest. Two things a project manager can provide are support and exposure. That is, you can give them opportunities to present the results of their analysis and work to management. A good project leader gives the core team and some of the part-time members this opportunity for recognition.

Interview potential team members

How do you interview potential team members? You could just look at their resumes, ask about their skills, and probe into their experience. Doing this will often elicit canned responses since they are ready for these questions. Here is another approach that has been useful many times. Ask about lessons learned from their previous work. For example, you could ask, "What are the five things that you learned from your last project?"

A second area to consider is issues. Ask what major issues they faced in their past work. How did they detect these? What decisions and actions did they take? What new issues surfaced in their last project that had not appeared before?

A third question is to ask them about their career goals. Ask what skills and knowledge they would acquire or improve upon. You can also have them take their resume and write down how it would be changed if they were on the project and the project was successful. Alternatively, you can wait to do this when they are on the team. This will give you an insight into their self-interest.

In IT, since many people have extensive non-project work, you must inquire as to what the work is. Also, ask about their work on other projects. You also want to probe into how they divide their time with projects. Try to find about their priorities and what work they consider urgent.

Will you get all of your first choices for the project team? Most likely you will not. A method here is to approach a manager and indicate your requirements, schedule, and minimal level of capabilities. Let the manager suggest several names. For the part-time team members you will have less political clout. Recognize this and live with it.

It is common for a project leader to seek the best and smartest people for a team. This approach has problems. These people are in high demand and will likely be less available or pulled from the team. Some of these people are difficult to manage. Moreover, in IT their work may not be easily maintainable. Instead, you might seek people who are qualified to do the work, but can function more in a team environment. For business units, project leaders often want the senior users—the King and Queen Bees. The rationale is that they have detailed knowledge of all of the business rules. Taking them on can exact a high cost and incur risk. They may not want change and attempt to derail the project. They may not really know the business rules. Taking them from a business unit may cripple the work in the department—thereby incurring the wrath and resentment of the supervisors and staff. From experience it is often better to involve more junior people who are supportive of change.

Should you use consultants?

While this is the subject of Chapter 12, we discuss this briefly here. IT has long been an employer of consultants and contract help. Unfortunately, however, organizations often decide on consultants on an *ad hoc*, one-event-at-a-time basis. Their use for individual tasks may make sense for control, but it also raises costs and can yield inconsistent results. This approach has a number of drawbacks:

- Use of consultants is uneven within IT causing the internal staff to become confused as to the role of consultants in projects.
- There are no ground rules for evaluating, selecting, and terminating consultants.
- Without an overall approach, the use of consultants, the choice of consultants, and other related factors are almost entirely based on political considerations.
- Why employ consultants? Here are some of the political and technical reasons:

  ○ You lack specific technical knowledge. You will use the consultant to provide this knowledge and train your people so that they can be self-sufficient.
  ○ If you use consultants, management may believe them more than internal staff. This is regrettable, but it does occur. Sometimes, you find that credibility is directly related to the hourly rate: the more you pay per hour, the more credible the consultant is to some managers.

- You require a consultant who knows the business and industry. This is increasingly common due to reengineering, E-Business, and client-server systems that fit with the business process.
- You are overcommitted to projects. Consultants can augment your staff. An example might be the use of consultants to do software maintenance.
- Due to various circumstances, you find that you are unable to attract and retain qualified people. Consultants provide a means to continue work.
- You are interested in saving money. Consultants are sometimes less expensive than employees when you factor in overhead and benefits. You also avoid a long-term commitment.

To establish an orderly approach for consulting, first develop a set of objectives for your projects and systems. After matching your staff to these objectives, you find that you want to consider consultants. What are some potential objectives for the consultants?

- Provide low-cost basic services related to information systems. This approach will likely result in few consultants because you will be operating in a maintenance mode. There will be little development.
- Establish major new systems and technology capabilities quickly. This objective will require more consulting because your current staff members cannot handle their current work along with this new work.
- Ensure flexibility in staffing. Here you might be ready for business mergers or acquisitions and you wish to retain flexibility to add people later. Therefore, you will use consultants to provide that flexibility.
- Concentrate your internal resources on only core systems activities and business processes. The overflow, so to speak, can go to consultants.
- Establish an approach for allocating consulting resources during the project.

When considering consultants, you must examine constraints or barriers. One is the company policy related to the use of consultants. What are specific rules and restrictions? Another is your budget—not just the total budget but how much you have set aside for outside services. A third constraint is the availability of consultants with the specific skills that your projects require. The project itself also plays a role. If the project involves company-sensitive information or will yield a system that provides competitive advantage, then even with signed legal agreements, you may be at risk of having the information and expertise move to a competitor.

Develop an overall strategy in line with the objectives you set. Here are some examples of strategies for consultant use:

- Employ consultants to maintain current systems so that the internal staff can develop new systems. This strategy sounds nice, but it may be difficult to pull off due to the system-specific knowledge associated with legacy systems.
- Apply the reverse of the first strategy—use consultants on new development and then migrate the current staff to the new systems later. This has the risk of lowering morale of the internal staff because the consultants will get all of the "interesting work".

- Augment project teams with only selected consultants where there are short-term needs. This can be dangerous because it can be open ended.
- Determine areas where you want to outsource certain systems activities on an ongoing basis. Examples might be PC training and hardware support.

How should you hire and direct consultants?

The biggest mistake people often make is to approach this backward. That is, they go out and find a consultant. Afterward, they define the assignment and work. A more organized method is to follow these steps:

- *Step 1*: Define your objectives and strategies with respect to consultants.
- *Step 2*: Identify the target functions, activities, or projects that consultants are suited to within the strategy of Step 1.
- *Step 3*: Develop requirements for the consultants in terms of a statement of work.
- *Step 4*: Define interview and evaluation criteria and identify members of the project team that will conduct the evaluation.
- *Step 5*: Identify and contact potential consultants.
- *Step 6*: Conduct the evaluation and selection.
- *Step 7*: Negotiate the terms of the agreement.

The statement of work describes the project, the role of the consultant, the specific tasks that the consultant is to perform, the end products expected from the consultant's effort, the schedule of the work, and the methods and tools that will be employed. This does not have to be formal. It can be developed as a series of lists. The statement of work provides focus and can help potential consultants explain their qualifications in terms of the work.

Gather the team members who will conduct the technical interviews in a meeting to discuss how they will perform the interviews and the questions they will ask. Particularly important is the validation of experience and capabilities. Encourage questions such as, "How would you address_._._._?" By providing situations in programming, analysis, and other areas, you can get the person to open up and provide you with more information. Team members can develop a list of questions in advance.

To find consultants, you can get referrals from friends and contacts. You can also search the Web and Internet for potential firms. Another source is magazine articles. What are the types of firms and their advantages and disadvantages? If you hire a large firm, then you have less control over the individuals who will be assigned to the project. You do get the benefit of gaining access to a wider pool of people. However, larger firms may carry a greater overhead and burden rate. This can put them out of your budget. Some firms and individuals are probably preferred for limited scope projects. You will obtain a lower cost and you can be assured that the people you interview will be the ones who actually do the work. However, if they leave the project, you may be at risk and may have to start all over again in finding someone. Because they lack backup, you probably will have to assign your staff to work with them closely.

In evaluating and selecting consultants, select at least two or three. This will give you backup in case a problem arises with the leading contender. In some projects, you may want to employ several firms. For example, if you were implementing local and wide area networks in several locations, you might pick a local firm in each city. If you were implementing many PCs in one location, you might also divide the work among several firms. This involves more coordination and management time, but often can give you a lower cost.

On a specific development project, there is some benefit in having several individuals from different companies. You are provided with different points of view. You also may be provided with better service because the individuals are competing for potential additional work later.

Virtual teams

A *virtual team* is a team that works together through electronic media such as e-mail, video conferencing, and so on. The team may never meet or may occasionally meet physically together. This is common in global projects. Some factors that give rise to virtual teams are as follows:

- Team members work in different locations and time zones.
- It is too costly to relocate team members.
- Team members have existing duties in their current locations.
- The project and the company do not require a single physical location. An example here is a small software development team.
- The work requires a great deal of creativity so that they are more productive in surrounding they are familiar with.

The technology that can be employed includes the following:

- E-mail
- Video conferencing
- Voice over Internet Protocol (VOIP) for voice conferencing
- Groupware for collaboration (e.g., Google Docs)
- Software to support live meetings and demonstrations (e.g., Microsoft Live Meeting and WebEx).

There may be no choice in global projects, but to use virtual teams. There are a number of benefits cited for virtual teams including higher productivity and lower costs. However, this can be offset by the following problems:

- There may not be a sense of real teamwork due to separation.
- Team members cannot really get "close" to each other.
- Staff in remote locations can be pulled off for other work by local management.
- Virtual teams require a great deal of self-discipline.
- It is often difficult to discuss sensitive issues and even lessons learned remotely.

From experience, we have the following recommendations in the use of virtual teams.

- Have regular face-to-face, in-person meetings especially during requirements, integration, and testing.
- The project leader should not rely on virtual meetings and teams, but should travel to the locations where team members are.

Team dynamics

At the start of a project, the project leader must build team spirit—people on the team work together on their own without direction from the project leader. You must set the stage by discussing the following aspects of the project with each person individually:

- The purpose of the project and why the person's role is important;
- The scope of the project and how the individual will fit within it;
- Why the person is on the team;
- What you expect of the individual;
- What he or she will get out of being on the project;
- How you will support the individual and provide for training and tools;
- How you want team members to work together; give examples;
- The individual's role in project management with respect to status and issues;
- What you want to do for the individual.

Ask if the person has any concerns. From experience, be able to respond to the following questions:

- If the project is changed or cancelled, what will happen to us?
- Will the right tools be available for development?
- What are the major risks in the project?
- What is the current status of the project?

In terms of benefits to a team member, here are some possibilities:

- Implement new technologies and gain new skills;
- Add a successful project to your resume;
- Have the opportunity to work with new people and gain contacts;
- Help by the project leader in advancing your career after the project has been completed.

After this, you can hold a team meeting and go over the following:

- Review the purpose, scope, and project concept with the team.
- Reiterate roles of each team member and what is expected of each one.
- Identify how you expect the team members to draw upon each other.
- Identify how project meetings will be conducted and held.

- Review the benefits of the project to each member of the team from each individual's perspective.
- Identify potential issues in the project so as to minimize the likelihood of surprises.
- Go over the politics of the project. Indicate where and what form of resistance to change will likely occur.
- Indicate the role of management in the project and what issues they may raise.
- Address how the team will deal with scope creep and changing requirements.

Sharing team members between projects

In modern projects, you will be increasingly sharing members of the project team with other projects and the line organization. What are your goals? You want the person available to your project for the specific tasks for which he or she has signed up. To ask for additional time and effort is probably unrealistic if the person is in demand. Here are some guidelines on resource sharing:

- Negotiate availability with the line manager or other project leaders at the start.
- Indicate the tasks that you must have their involvement in and the general schedule.
- Establish a process for notifying the manager in advance as to when the person's services will be required.
- Indicate that you will monitor the work and release the team member as soon as possible and that you will provide informal status information.

Common team problems

Note that some specific team issues are addressed in Chapter 21 on Human Resource Issues. In a technology project, it is possible for the team to become locked into a specific method, tool, or approach. This is not unusual because the team is living so close to the work under pressure. Here the project leader can play a unique role. The project leader is often the only one in the team who can take a wider perspective and sit back and ask some basic questions such as "Is there a better way to organize the work?" "Should assignments be changed?" "Should the project approach be altered in a major way?"

You can assume that the people on the team will talk about the project with individuals in their line organizations. This is natural and you cannot control it. However, this tendency opens the potential for damage. If the wrong impression of the project leaks out, then you, as the project leader, will have to spend hours turning the situation around. What do you do? At the start of the project, address communications outside of the team. Indicate that if anyone has a problem or issue, you want to know about it first. Point out the potential damage to the project and team if disinformation is disseminated. Follow this up during the project by visiting each team member and asking what is on his or her mind. What concerns do the team members have? Do this in every meeting.

You may be forced through politics or circumstance to take someone onto the team that you feel is not qualified or has some problem. You can attempt to fight it, but that can be counterproductive. The person will find out how you feel and that will cast a pall on the project. If you are thinking that this situation will occur, then define some initial small tasks that you can monitor. Let those team members who you are concerned about perform these tasks until they prove themselves or fail. Then you have grounds to replace them. This method will also minimize the impact on the project.

Team members may not get along with each other. Over half of the projects that the authors have been involved with have had this problem. Expect it, because many technical people have their own opinions and methods of doing things. What do you do if this happens? Attack specific questions and disagreements as issues. If the underlying problem is severe, then consider getting the people involved in a room for a meeting. Indicate that you have observed communication problems, that this is to be expected, and that you expect them to behave like adults and discuss issues openly. Don't insist that they get along.

Technology projects burn people out. These projects have tight deadlines and other pressures. You cannot run a project as a non-stop "death march". This can kill the project. Instead, plan when the team will have to perform on a superhuman scale. Plan also for periods of slack. Much of the pressure in projects is generated by the project leader or manager. If you are asked to speed up a project, ask what is behind the request. What are the business reasons and benefits from the acceleration? Remind a manager that this can only work for a short time. The pressure will have to ease up. If you fail to follow these recommendations, then you will lose control of the project, the people will become burned out, and the overall project may fail or slip even more.

Much project work is routine and seemingly boring. For example, many program-mers don't like to do testing and integration. They prefer development. Recognize that this can happen. Plan ahead to monitor the work during this period more closely. You definitely want to show interest in their work at this time.

In many small team systems projects, you are dependent on one or two people for many critical tasks. Sometimes, in response, a project leader will ride these people and drive them nuts because the leader feels that these team members are so critical. A more laid-back approach may yield better results. Indicate to them that they are critical. Ask if you can provide any help or extra assistance. If they decline, they should still feel better because you showed that you cared about their welfare.

Problems can arise when new technology is adopted in a project. The team members may not know what is expected of them with respect to the technology. They may feel that there is even more pressure because they have just acquired the added task of learning the technology, although the overall schedule remained the same. What do you do? Before the technology is deployed, indicate the impact on the schedule. Explain what is expected of team members in reference to the technology. Discuss how you will provide for training and support. Have several people learn the technology and teach others. Do not immerse everyone in it. That will destroy productivity. Establish someone on the team as an expert or at least someone that the team members can go to with questions.

Systems projects have many interdependent tasks between people. This can lead to problems if someone waits for another person to finish a task before he or she can work. Head this up during project planning by defining each hand-off and how the individuals can continue to work while waiting for the results of the predecessor task.

Management seeks to change the direction of the project and even the composition of the team in the middle of the project. How do you react? You should never have gotten into this position in the first place. When the project is approved, point out the potential impact of change then. Reinforce it through the early phases of the project prior to implementation. Once you reach implementation, then the momentum will likely keep the project going. Next, have some early milestones and implementation that shows success. Management will be less willing to make changes. Third, ensure that there are sufficient milestones along the way that can help buffer the project from change. Also, build support for the project through the business units and indicate to them that there is always the threat of change and stopping the project.

Managing teams

The project leader is responsible for building and maintaining a team culture on the project. Lessons learned show that in systems and technology projects this is very important. The culture determines how people will share information, bring up issues, and resolve issues among themselves. Team culture also impacts the extent of cooperation. These are critical success factors in the project, especially because almost all modern projects involve substantial integration within systems and with business units. What is the project culture? Here are some attributes:

- How team members work with the project leader. This includes how they bring up issues, how they report status, and how they share information with the project leader.
- How team members work together. In addition to performing work, this encompasses how team members work together on issues with and without the project leader.
- How team members perform their own individual work. Included here are the sharing of lessons learned, the organization and approach to work, documentation, and how one's work is passed onto others in the team or external to the team.
- How the team deals with crises. This seems to be unpredictable, but in modern systems organizations you will find the same crises occurring again and again.

How do you build and sustain the culture? Here are some guidelines:

- Establish some basic rules at the start. Define each person's role with respect to the team as a whole. Give examples of interaction.
- Reinforce the need for cooperation by singling out examples of cooperation throughout the project. The problem is that many project leaders give accolades to individual achievement, which reinforces the importance of individual work over teamwork. Alternatively, some project leaders give general praise to the team. This is so vague that it appears meaningless and has little impact.

- Simulate some crises to the team in a meeting. An example might be to propose a major change in requirements. Have the team attempt to deal with this hypothetical crisis. This will build teamwork and will also get the team ready for a crisis when it occurs.
- The project leader should meet with not only the individuals and the team as a whole but also with groups of several people on specific areas of the project. The project leader must sustain the team in subgroups.

Motivating team members

There is both positive and negative team motivation. In positive motivation you will work hard to be supportive and understanding of the individual team members. This means more time spent with them. At the start, you need to follow our guidelines for understanding the goals and aspirations of the team member. You have to be sensitive to their other work beyond your project. You want to build their self-esteem. You should seek out their opinions and get them involved in the investigation of issues as well as sharing lessons learned. In this way, you demonstrate that you value their contributions. Remember as the project leader to take no credit, but give the credit to the team.

In negative motivation, a manager attempts to instill fear in the team members. There are actually several places in a project where this is a good approach. When the project concept is being reviewed, you want to stress the impacts if the project is not done. This raises the fear of management if the project is not done. Another place is with business unit employees who are resisting the project and change. Here you would stress the negative impact on them if the current situation remains and the project is stopped. This fear can be used to overcome the fear of change.

Team member rewards

Let's go through a list of potential rewards for team members and see how they apply.

- Basic salary. Here the project leader can recommend to the employee's supervisor action to reward work performance. However, this is not guaranteed. So the project leader should not lead the employee into thinking a raise is in the future.
- Overtime. This is sometimes possible. The problem in IT projects is the counting of this and who gets what since many people on the team may be putting in overtime. There also may be budget limitations.
- Compensating time off. This is more common. Here during a calmer period in the project, the team members get some time off to compensate for the additional time spent earlier.
- Bonuses. We will explore this in the next section, but here we note it can lead to trouble and discord among the team. Usually, only the person with the biggest bonus is happy.
- Pay tied to performance. In IT this is difficult to measure.

- Payment by results. This usually applies to consultants and vendors. Even then there could be problems about the results.
- Recognition. This is always good in projects.
- Additional training in methods and tools. This is part of job enrichment to prepare the employee for later work.
- Job transfer or rotation. In IT it is difficult to carry this out given the unique skill sets required and the knowledge and skills of the employee.
- Teamwork. This can raise morale and is one of the basic themes of the book. In a team you don't let your team members down.
- Empowerment. This has been employed in the development of the project plan where the team members define their detailed tasks and update them.

How do you keep team members?

Team members can lose interest in your project. They may have competing demands from other projects. Assuming that you do not want to keep them through financial means, here are some suggestions. Involve team members in identifying and resolving technical issues. The greater the involvement up to a point, the more they become committed to the project. If you over-involve them, then they can get turned off by the politics.

A basic lesson learned in project management is that many team members detest the overhead and bureaucracy of project management methods. They hate the endless status meetings. They don't like being hassled about issues. Consciously attempt to minimize the hassle factor. In meetings, focus only on issues and work. Reserve status and updates of plans for short one-on-one meetings. Minimize the amount of paperwork that you require of team members. The project leader keeps the administrative side of the project away from the team. Complaining about this to the team can impact morale.

Another thing people resent is being kept in the dark. Many technical people don't like surprises. For example, let's suppose that you expect management to request that the project be speeded up. You can wait until management makes the announcement and then pass it on, but people can be really angry about this. On the other hand, you can alert team members to the possibility. Then you can ask them to plan their work for this contingency and see what they can come up with on their own. Later, if management makes the decision to speed up the work, the effect is reduced.

A commonsense suggestion is to show interest in the team's work. Don't just ask for status. Instead, have members describe it in more detail to you while you visit their offices. Ask them if they need any help or resources.

How do you discharge and replace team members?

What if you have removed someone from the project? You can assist people who have done their work well by helping them in transitioning back to their organizations or to other projects. For people who presented problems, then work to find them their next homes or projects first. If you confront them and indicate that they will be leaving, they may do damage to the team and project during the time between your announcement and their actual leaving. When someone does leave, announce this in a project meeting with everyone present. Indicate the person's achievements, new position, and how his or her role will be filled.

You have several choices with respect to replacement. You can move to replace someone immediately. This is the common method, but it has several shortcomings. First, it assumes that the new person has exactly the same skills and similar technical knowledge of the person who departed. This is almost never possible in systems and technology. Second, you are missing an opportunity to reformulate the project. Third, you are not giving the new person an opportunity to put his or her stamp and organization on the work. Many programmers, for example, resent being thrust into some situation where they must inherit someone else's work.

A better method of replacement is to leave the position open and start recruiting. When you have narrowed the field down to two or three people, then go back, look at the plan, and determine how you may change the plan and schedule to take best advantage of each person's skills. In systems projects a major personnel selection criterion, in addition to skills and knowledge, is how an applicant fits within the project. Each finalist can be interviewed by key members of the team. After the interviews, answer the following questions:

- What does the person add to the project that is not there now?
- In what areas are there gaps or holes if this person is brought on board the project?
- How would this person get along and interact with the project team and the culture in the project?

Cases and examples

Astro Bank

The management of the project teams for both the legacy and new systems started badly. Separate project teams were established for each. No roles, responsibilities, or rules were established. The project leader assumed that everyone had previous project experience and knew what to do.

The projects began to deteriorate. The new system project team had never worked together before. Many were junior people who lacked project management experience. The work was not getting organized. The team just started in and began on tasks. The legacy system team was the reverse. Team members had operated in a bureaucratic project management mode for years. However, the projects were merely maintenance, operations support, and minor enhancements. Their approach was ill-suited to development and major interface work. They treated the new work like the old. Their project meetings were almost social occasions.

The project leader faced change or failure. The first step was to impose project management similar to that described above on the new team. Members of this team were the least resistant and most accepting of organization. Once this process was in place, it was time to turn to the legacy system team members. There were two alternatives. The project leader could attempt to invade their existing culture in their organization. This was seen to be very risky and would run into management as well as staff resistance and dissension. The project could afford neither. The alternative was to involve the legacy system team members as individuals within the new system project team. This was the first step. Over time, the project leader then carved out a subproject for the legacy system team and ran the group under the same rules as the new systems project team. Meetings were held in the offices of the new systems development area—away from the legacy system staff.

Questions

1. We have seen the same behavior again and again around the world—teams often work poorly together. Given that many team members have had limited project experience, this is not a surprise. If you were going to carry out projects in a company, what steps would you take at the start of the project to improve teamwork and team communications?
2. Following up on the preceding question, how could you detect a project team was experiencing communications problems?
3. Legacy system support is often a major issue in organizations. Given changing technology and business conditions there will always be legacy systems. There is just not enough resources to keep current with the latest technology. Nor is there usually a business reason to do so if the current systems meet business requirements. It has been said that IT staff who support legacy systems have rather different attributes than those for new system development. What differences do you think there are between these two groups? Discuss how you could migrate IT staff from maintenance of old systems to new work. Identify the barriers to accomplishing this transition.

Mapping to the PMBOK and PRINCE2

The PMBOK

Chapter 9 of the PMBOK is concerned with project human resource management. There are four parts:

- Develop human resource plan. Included here are the identification of team members and the definition of roles and responsibilities. Project skills are determined along with reporting relationships. This is covered in both Chapter 5 on the project concept and Chapter 8 on project planning.
- Acquire the project team. This includes the negotiation with managers to get the team members. Team assignments are made. Resource calendars are set. In IT projects many if not most team members are split between other projects, your project, and non-project work. Therefore, it is critical that you negotiate the

priorities of a person's work as well as the extent of their availability to the project by time period.

- Develop the project team. Inputs in the step are the staff assignments, the project plan, and resource calendars. Team member skills and knowledge are built up and then their performance is assessed. Keys to team building in IT projects are as follows: joint tasks and shared work; the gathering and using of lessons learned; participation in issues investigation and management.
- Manage the project team. This includes all of the activities in managing a group of people. One area discussed is conflict management. In IT projects team members can get very emotional about their methods and tools, for example. As project leader you want to get down to the detailed level—underneath the emotion. Do the same with business unit staff who can get passionate about transactions and their work.

PRINCE2

PRINCE2 has several levels. There is the project leader. Reporting to the project leader are team leaders. This allows the creation of team plans or subprojects for each team. Teamwork is also addressed through work products and communications.

Lessons learned

The guidelines and approach in this chapter apply to almost all IT as well as many general projects. The projects greatly benefit from having many users involved at different times. Also, as work progresses, different skills and knowledge are required. Critical business users are important to the success of the project because of their knowledge of business rules. For IT staff it also applies because most of the IT have other systems duties and responsibilities. While it is nice to consider assigning people to such an important project full time, it is impossible to ignore or drop work that keeps the core systems and technology operational.

A critical success factor in IT projects is resource allocation. A regular method is necessary to dynamically allocate IT, business staff, and consultants. Consider doing this on a weekly basis in a meeting with business and IT managers.

Another lesson learned is that you need to make the team aware of the politics of the project. Since all IT projects result in change, there is likely to be resistance to the change and project. The argument that this distracts the team from the work is not valid. If they are kept in the dark, when they encounter political stuff, they will often not understand it and be unprepared. This can cause major problems in the project. Here is an example. A government agency in the Middle East wanted to implement a new accounting system. This was favored by the director, the head of finance and accounting and IT. You would think the project would be a slam dunk. Not true. The accounting group consisted of long-serving King Bees who did not want change. When the new system was presented, they said nothing. They were told by management that a new system was needed because the programmer for old system could no longer maintain it. Later, they took the programmer who was a European and got him intoxicated. He admitted that he could indeed continue to support the old system. This came back to management and work on the new system stopped. Our work consisted in turning this around by getting support of the more junior King Bees. The other employees then followed.

Guidelines

- In most projects you seek to have as many business users involved as you can. Why? Because the people involved will be supportive of change later.
- Have team members fill in detailed tasks under your summary tasks. Involve the team in hands-on updating of their schedules. These actions will increase their level of awareness and commitment to the project.
- Make all issues and project plans available to project team members at all times. If you attempt to hide or make it difficult to get information, it will only create doubt and mistrust.
- Consider dividing the project team in both the preimplementation and implementation phases into subteams. The use of subteams does not necessarily add bureaucracy to the project, if done informally. Each subteam can focus on a major milestone. This makes it easier to manage the subteam as opposed to individuals. Another benefit is that you can organize and monitor discussions and interfaces between the subteams.
- Keep in touch with the line managers who supplied team members to you. Remember that the only other communications are word-of-mouth, second-hand information, and what the team member provides to them in the way of feedback. This can be disorganized and lead to the wrong impression. Keep in regular touch with all line managers by providing them with informal status and issue updates. This will keep them interested and provide a context for understanding other information that they receive.
- If you have a choice between a highly experienced person and a junior person for the project, whom would you choose? Conventional wisdom might be to select the experienced person. This is correct for highly technical work. However, many tasks in a systems project do not require this skill level. Seriously consider a junior person who is willing to learn.
- Institute an apprenticeship method; that is, pair junior people up with senior people on some tasks. The senior person may resist on the grounds of productivity. However, make it clear at the start of the project that this is part of cooperation. Indicate what your expectations are for the apprenticeship and what each role is. The junior person must perform specific tasks and cannot just be a part of a two-person subteam.
- Team communications can be taken to extremes. If some of the people have worked together before on different projects, they may socialize too much. Therefore, it is important to keep project meetings focused on technical and business issues. Otherwise, the conversation can drift off into discussions of the past.
- When the project adopts a new method, tool, or technology, anticipate resistance and even some hostility. Some programmers and analysts resent having to learn

something new when they feel that what they have used for years still works. This had been behind the failure of many "structured" techniques in the past.

- If a team member is faced with many tasks, it is natural for the person to work on the easy tasks to show early progress. This attitude is reinforced if the project leader keeps emphasizing progress. For most systems projects, it is better for the person to work on the more difficult tasks that carry risk and uncertainty.
- A project leader works side by side with the project team members. This is more than just sitting in on meetings and providing feedback. By participating in the work of the project, the project leader builds respect from the team.
- If the roles and work processes within the team are not defined and enforced, then the team will not know what to do. They will start inventing new methods. These can then become habits that are difficult to break.
- At the start of specific tasks, have the team members discuss how they would assess quality and perform testing. Delaying this discussion until the work is done can negatively impact the schedule. The person who did the work may become defensive then as well. At the start of the task, there is not the sense of ownership of work, so the discussion can be more open.
- Assign each detailed task in the project plan to one person. This will ensure accountability.
- Encourage and collect lessons learned during the project. Don't wait until the end. Ask, "What have we learned in the last week?" Ask this question regularly. The project leader can maintain this information.

Questions

1. Let's assume that you have interviewed two potential team members for one position on the project. How would you select the most suitable based on: their existing work, skills, knowledge, and understanding of the business.
2. A team member is about to leave the team. What steps could you take to ensure that there is transfer of knowledge to the team.
3. It is natural that team members have disagreements. How can you detect when these differences begin to have an effect on the project.
4. Suppose there is a junior team member on the team who is largely ignored by the other senior team members. What steps could you take to achieve greater teamwork and cooperation?
5. A team member is about to exit the project. He or she has said some negative things about the project in the past that were untrue. You suspect that this person will criticize the project after leaving. What steps can you take to mitigate this potential issue?

What to do next

1. In your recent projects, were the roles and responsibilities of team members clearly identified? If not, what was the impact of this lack of definition?

2. Build the following table for several projects that you have observed or in which you participated. This will help you to determine some successful and less than successful methods.

3. Conduct the following survey of a project. In this list 1 is low and 5 is very high.

What was the turnover of staff in the team?	1 2 3 4 5
What percentage of meeting time was spent in getting status versus discussing issues?	1 2 3 4 5
What level of orientation was given to new members of the team?	1 2 3 4 5
What was the level of participation of the team members in defining their own work and tasks?	1 2 3 4 5
What was the level of participation of the team in project management activities?	1 2 3 4 5
What was the level of involvement of team members in presentations before management?	1 2 3 4 5
What was the extent of information provided by the project leader to the team on management communications?	1 2 3 4 5

4. What was the level of cooperation between team members?　　1 2 3 4 5

Summary

Managing systems and technology project teams is often more complex than that of standard projects. There are more interfaces and the need for a greater degree of cooperation. The resources on the project team are often required by other projects. New methods and tools as well as new technology products are constantly emerging. The best approach in team management is a mix of formal and informal methods. Formal methods include defining roles and responsibilities, establishing rules in the project, monitoring cooperation, and ensuring participation. Informal methods include working with the team members individually and in small groups as well as sharing information.

8
Developing the project plan

Introduction

In traditional project management, you developed the project plan when you defined the project concept. However, this is too early and locks in the project too soon. Using the method here, the project concept has been approved by management and is ready for support with the detail of the project plan. Many think of a project plan as a dry list of tasks with resources and schedules. For systems projects it is much more. It is a political document that can assist you in communicating with business units and gain support for the project. Ask yourself how a business manager can understand a technology project with no technical knowledge—through the project leader, the project concept, and the project plan.

Another misconception is that the plan consists of only the schedule and costs. It is much more. What and how information will be managed are part of the plan and approach. These are significant because in systems projects you desire to have greater standardization across projects as discussed earlier.

The goals in developing the plan include the following:

- Determine how the information relating to the project will be managed.
- Define the project plan itself.
- Develop budget estimates.
- Identify roles and responsibilities.
- Determine costs.
- Link the plan with those of other projects and work.
- Assess issues and risk in the plan.
- Market and sell the plan to management, the project team, and the business units.

Notice that the scope includes marketing and sales. You can develop the most wonderful plan, but if you lack backing and support, you and the plan lose.

Financial analysis methods for projects

This section covers the most commonly used measurements to analyze and assess costs and benefits— cost-benefit analysis. Note that in each of these different numbers or percentages can be obtained by using alternative financial inputs. For example, in the first one you could use gross profit or net income. Thus, even though the formulae seem straightforward, in practice there is variation. Thus, it is important to clearly understand the meaning of the terms that are used in the various calculations.

For IT projects, it is easier to determine the costs of a project than the financial benefits. For IT projects the benefits are often quantified in terms of reduced cost of an improved business process. But what about infrastructure projects? For these the financial benefits are spread throughout many systems. In such cases, it is often useful to consider the costs that were avoided due to modernization of infrastructure and systems. This was frequently done when IT groups responded to the Y2K problem.

Return on Investment

Simply put, *Return on Investment* (ROI) is the net money gained or lost divided by the amount of money invested. ROI can also be called Rate of Return (ROR) or rate of profit. The net money gained or lost is the difference between the financial benefits of a project and the cost of the project. As such, ROI is a percentage. Obviously, you want the percentage to be positive—the more positive, the better.

Let's take an example. Suppose a project costs US$100,000. The estimated benefits are US$150,000 over a 3-year period (US$50,000 per year). The difference between the benefits and costs is US$50,000 over the 3 years. Dividing the 50,000 by the cost of 100,000 gives an ROI of 50 percent. In real life, benefits could change over time so that you would have to consider each time period. With inflation, future benefits are worth less in current dollars or currency so the benefits would have to be adjusted for this.

ROI is one of the most popular measures for doing cost-benefit analysis for different projects. In doing comparative analysis, it is important that the time horizon considered is the same for all of the projects considered.

Net Present Value

The value of money changes due to inflation and deflation. These factors act to change the interest rate on money. *Net Present Value* (NPV) is the amount of money that you would need to invest to earn a certain amount of money over a determined time period. In our example, the project costs US$100,000. After 3 years, the benefits total US$150,000. We first calculate the present value of the project. This is defined as follows:

$$\frac{\text{Future value}}{(1 + 1)^{**}N}$$

Here I is the interest rate and N is the number of years. Suppose that the interest rate (I) is 10 percent. In our example, the present value is US$112,697 (US$150,000/1.331). Think of it this way. Suppose you wanted to have US$1 at the end of 3 years. At 10 percent, you would have to invest US$0.91 to obtain US$1 in 1 year. For 3 years, you would have to invest US$0.75. The process of these calculations is referred to as *discounted cash flow* since it discounts future monies based on the interest rate. The NPV is determined by subtracting the cost of the project from the present value of the benefits to get US$12,697.

Internal Rate of Return

The *Internal Rate of Return* (IRR) is the interest rate that is required to make the NPV zero. This is used to compare projects that have very different costs over the life of the project. Some IT projects such as infrastructure have their expenses and costs at the start in acquiring facilities, hardware, software, and network components. Later costs are for installation, testing, and so on and are labor based. On the other hand, a large development project will have substantial costs spread out over a longer period.

In our example, you would have to solve the following equation for R—the internal rate of return. The cash flow in the initial period is US$100,000 and so is negative. The IRR is over 10 percent.

$$0 = \frac{-\$100,000 + \$50,000}{(1+R)} + \frac{\$50,000}{(1+R)^{**}2} + \frac{\$50,000}{(1+R)^{**}3}$$

Payback period

The *payback period* is the time required to recover the cost of a project through the benefits achieved. In our example, the project benefits are US$50,000 per year and the project cost is US$100,000. So it will take 2 years to recover the cost of the project. The payback period is 2 years. You can adjust for different periods. For example, if you had determined some Quick Win changes to a business process and that the benefits would be realized in a month, then you can use a month as the time period.

Accounting Rate of Return

The *Accounting Rate of Return* (ARR) is the ratio of the annual net benefit of a project divided by the cost of the project. In our example, the annual benefit is US$50,000. The cost of the project is $100,000. The ARR is 50 percent ($50,000/100,000).

Profitability Index

The *Profitability Index* is the ratio of NPV and the cost of the project.

Note that some of these measures are dependent future interest rates that are impacted by inflation or deflation. All of the methods require a quantitative, accurate measurement of future benefits by time period. Under certain conditions different measures would produce different rankings of projects. For example, if there was substantial inflation, then those that delivered faster and greater benefits would be favored under IRR and NPV while a different ranking might result for the payback period.

Network diagrams, PERT charts, and GANTT charts

There are several types of charts and diagrams used in project management. A GANTT chart was originated by Henry Gantt in the early 1900s. It is a bar chart in which the rows are the tasks and milestones of the project. The horizontal axis is time. For each task, you draw a bar from the start date of the task to the end date. Milestones are shown often by a diamond or box symbol. Dependencies between tasks can be shown by dotted lines.

PERT is an acronym for Program Evaluation and Review Technique. A PERT or network chart shows tasks as circles or boxes. Lines are drawn between the boxes or circles to indicate dependencies. The chart is read from left to right. The horizontal axis is time. Additional task information can be included in the box such as resources.

Here are some tips from experience. We tend not to use network and PERT charts. Why? Because in IT projects they can reinforce sequential thinking. We most often use different forms of GANTT charts. These are absolutely critical in showing the critical path in the project as well as tasks with issues and risks, and so on.

The *critical path* in a project plan consists of the group of tasks such that if any task in the critical path is delayed, the project is delayed. This is widely used, but it has a problem. In this definition, you can see that there is no inclusion of issues or risks. What commonly happens is this. Management and the project leader focus on the critical path. Then some task off of the critical path experiences issues that result in delays. The critical path changes. Management and the project leader are caught off guard. Therefore, often, it is more important to pay attention to tasks and milestones with issues—that is where the risks lie.

What information must be managed?

Beyond the plan and schedule, and the work, you must define the method for coordinating issues, lessons learned, and action items to resolve the issues. All of this must be integrated with the project plan. How can this information be related?

- Once an issue has been identified it must be related to the specific tasks in the schedule to which it applies. Otherwise, how do you determine the impact of not resolving an issue on the schedule? In turn, you must be able to move from the tasks to the list of issues.
- After a decision has been reached on one or more issues, actions must be taken to resolve the issues and implement the decisions. These are to be tracked. The actions may involve changes to the plan. It is useful to indicate in the revised plan why and when these changes occurred.
- If you have built up a body of lessons learned, then the challenge is to employ them. Lessons learned must be related to the tasks in the same way as issues were.

Implementing these in the context of project templates creates greater standardization and supports more effective project analysis.

What methods and tools will be employed for project management?

Two sets of methods and tools are used in a systems project: one for project management and one for the work in the project. Areas for project management are as follows:

- Team communications;
- Issue tracking and information through issues databases;
- Lessons learned information through lessons learned databases;
- Project plan information;
- Project documents;
- Integrated project information (all of the above in one place).

Note that the issues and lessons learned databases are defined in Chapter 12 on Project Risk Management. A tool is the software package that you will employ for an area. A method consists of the procedures for carrying out the coordination and task. It is best if the methods and tools are in place at the start of the project. In that way, you can build habits of use early. If you wait for a crisis, then the lack of methods will probably aggravate the situation.

The following tools are appropriate for each area:

Category	Tool
Team communications	Electronic mail, groupware
Issue tracking	Network-based database management system, groupware
Lessons learned	Network-based database management system, groupware
Project plan information	Network-based project management software
Project documentation	Files on network server
Integrated project information	Groupware

Many project management software packages allow customizing of fields associated with each task. Here are some examples of the use of text fields:

- Person responsible for the task. This may be different than the resources used in the task. It supports accountability and aids in tracking (text field).
- Indicator of whether the task has high risk. The task is then management critical. This allows you to filter on only the high-risk tasks (flag—yes/no field).
- Issues related to the task (text field). This supports the linkage to the issues database.
- Lessons learned related to the task (text field). This is useful for linking with the lessons learned database.
- Related tasks in other projects (text field).
- Date task added. This is important for later analysis (date field).
- Reason task was added (e.g., rework or revised estimate). This helps in your budget versus actual and planned versus actual analysis (text field).

- Organization unit responsible (text field).
- Indicator of whether the task is in the template (flag field). This is useful for extracting a summary of the schedule for the template.
- Requirement that generated the task (text field). This field allows for tracking the additional work generated by the requirement—very useful in tracking the impact of changing or new requirements.

The project leader is responsible for establishing the initial data in each category on the network server for the project. This information can then be presented to the project team as it is employed during the project. Build a list of realistic situations or scenarios. For each compose a small plan and use playscript to clearly show each role in the method. Playscript is the technique whereby paper is divided by a vertical line into two columns. In the left column is the person or entity (computer) that is performing the step. The right column contains the detailed actions that are performed in that step. By doing this, team members will realize what specific tasks are expected of them. Using this organized approach, you seek as few areas of ambiguity and uncertainty as possible.

What methods and tools will be used directly in the project?

The methods and tools to be employed in the project depend, of course, on the nature of the project. Here is a potential list of areas in which methods should be identified. Note that these are identified for all projects to ensure consistency.

- Network
- Setup of software on a server
- Monitoring of software use
- Monitoring of network performance
- Troubleshooting
- Security management
- Antivirus controls
- Software development
- Languages and compilers
- Editors
- Debuggers
- Translators
- Object libraries
- Configuration management

Once you have identified the tools, you might think that you have finished. You are really just getting started. Here are some additional tasks for you:

- Determine the goals and expectations for each tool.
- Define methods for how each tool is to be employed.
- Identify contact points for methods and tools.

- Document methods and make them available on the network along with lessons learned and guidelines.
- Define how gaps between tools are to be filled.
- Establish rules for monitoring method and tool use.
- Define the parameters required to support the tools.

You will want to present these to the project team. Experience suggests that you give an overview for all areas. Then zoom in on those that will be employed in the next 3 months. Hold a similar meeting every few months.

Templates and the Work Breakdown Structure

A *Work Breakdown Structure* or WBS was originally defined as a complete list of tasks to be used by all projects. This turned out to be unworkable often because some tasks were ambiguous and the tasks were not project-specific. It is since been updated to be the division of project work and end products into smaller and smaller components.

A WBS has value in that it specifies a task and milestone structure. However, that is all in terms of the information. The goal of the book for you is cumulative improvement. That is, over time your project management capabilities increase and the projects you manage have a greater chance of success. To do this you would like project structures to be more complete and have more information.

What additional information would you like to include? Here is a list.

- General task dependencies. If you have a standard structure, you can, from experience, identify dependencies between these general tasks. This can cut down the effort in developing the project plan.
- Linking lessons learned to the tasks and milestones. This is very important. Suppose we gave you a book of lessons learned and told you that for the work you are doing now, there are six great lessons learned that you could use. You would have to go through the entire book to find them. Not realistic. You must link lessons learned to something so that you get ready access to the lessons learned related to the specific work.
- Linking issues to the tasks and milestones. We have stated that while each project has its own problems and issues, the reality is that at a general level the same issues apply to the same tasks at a high level. The differences lie in the details of the project. So why not link the issues to the tasks and milestones? That will get you started faster on project planning since you will have issues that were commonly encountered on similar projects.

A *project template* consists of high-level tasks and milestones along with related issues and lessons learned along with dependencies. General resource types can be added to tasks as well. Examples are analyst, programmer, business unit staff, and so on.

Even though an IT department can work on hundreds of projects over years, there are only a small number of possible templates. Figure 8.1 gives a list of potential templates. Over the years, we have found that this list covers almost all IT projects.

- Project concept and definition
- Project requirements
- System design
- Programming and unit testing
- Integration
- Testing
- Quick Wins—changes to business processes that require little time with little cost
- Change management
- Data conversion
- Training
- System acceptance and turnover
- System and process measurements
- Software maintenance
- Software enhancements
- Network planning
- Network implementation
- Network upgrades
- Infrastructure procurement
- Software outsourcing procurement
- Software development procurement
- Consulting procurement
- Facility upgrades
- Security measure implementation
- Quality reviews and quality assurance

| **Figure 8.1** | Potential IT project template areas |

Note that for many projects, such as system development, you would employ a group of these smaller templates to obtain a general system development template. This modular approach helps to ensure consistency.

How templates, issues, lessons learned, and the plan link

Templates, issues, lessons learned, and the project plans all relate to each other to achieve cumulative improvement. Look at the diagram below in Figure 8.2. Let's walk through it. The template is used to generate the plan. Estimating tasks and doing work in the project can use the lessons learned that are linked to the template. Individual issues are linked to the tasks in the plan using the linkage between issues and template tasks and milestones. As you solve the issues, you may be able to extract more lessons learned. This, combined with experience, allows you to improve the template—resulting in cumulative improvement for templates. Over time the database of issues stabilizes. The lessons learned improve. Moreover, with improvements in templates, issues, and lessons learned, the project plans improve—more cumulative improvement.

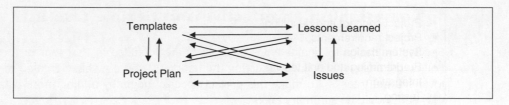

Figure 8.2   Relationship between project components

How should you develop project templates?

How do you develop these templates? If you start with blank sheets of paper, it will take forever. It is far easier to use the existing project plans and extract high-level tasks and milestones as a starting point. Then you refine these later through experience.

The template includes resources, tasks, general resources assigned to tasks, and dependencies between tasks. Templates allow you to analyze multiple projects and to prepare summary analysis reports for management. Without a template you will have to compose a summary schedule by hand from the disparate schedules. There are the following additional benefits of templates.

- Building, using, and maintaining templates give project leaders and others the chance to participate in the improvement of the project management process.
- Using a template to start with saves time.
- Junior project leaders can take advantage of experience through the lessons learned and the templates.
- Using a template can improve credibility of IT to the business unit or client.

To construct a template, follow these steps:

- *Step 1*: Create a general resource list. It will include general resources such as job titles (such as senior programmer or systems analyst) as well as detailed resources (specific people and equipment). This resource list will be employed by both the templates and the detailed project plans and act as a resource pool.
- *Step 2*: Create a task list for the template in a top-down manner. Don't get down to individual tasks, as that is done in the creation of the specific plan.
- *Step 3*: Establish dependencies between the tasks in Step 2. These are simple tail-to-head dependencies.
- *Step 4*: Associate general resources from Step 1 to the tasks developed in Step 2.
- *Step 5*: Link lessons learned to the tasks in the template.

Retrofitting an existing schedule to a template is covered later. To turn a template into a schedule for a specific project, you will add the detailed dates, tasks, and durations, and make the resources specific.

How do you establish an effective and flexible task list?

Specific examples for major types of projects are included in Part four of the book. Follow the suggestions in constructing the template. You now have created the high-level summary tasks. To make this project specific, begin by adding more detail, but they still should be summary tasks.

It is assumed that the team has been identified. If not, then you will have to complete these steps yourself.

- *Step 1*: Identify task areas for each team member. In your plan, you can use the text field for the person responsible to indicate this.
- *Step 2*: With a summary schedule, sit down with each person and review the plan. Have each participant attempt to create detailed tasks and dependencies.
- *Step 3*: Review what each person does and refine it.
- *Step 4*: Collect what each person does and standardize the wording and abbreviations of the tasks.
- *Step 5*: Assign other resources to the tasks.
- *Step 6*: Establish linkages with other projects.
- *Step 7*: Fill in the durations and dates.

Look carefully at these steps. Note that the team members prepare detailed tasks and dependencies without dates and durations. This allows you and the team to focus on the work and verify the task details along with identifying potential problems and issues. You can also discuss methods and tools to be employed in the work. At these meetings you can discuss doing more work in parallel. This will help break down sequential thinking. If you discuss here the durations and dates of the work, they will get the most attention. Moreover, if you have had these meetings, the team members are better able to give more accurate estimates of durations and dates.

How should you assign resources?

With the task list and general resources, you can replace general resources by specific resources. For example, the resource "systems analyst" could be replaced by the person's name. You can also assign specific resources to each detailed task. Systems projects usually have only a few key resources for each task. Don't include resources that are commonly available as this will just create more work for you.

How do you relate areas of risk to the plan?

Recall that risk management relates to the management of issues. You first begin with the issues associated with template tasks and milestones. In addition, each team member identifies tasks he or she feels have substantial risk. The risk can relate to the technical nature of the work, the team member's level of knowledge and experience, uncertainty about what is involved in the task, and relationship to other work. Indicate risk in the appropriate text field of the plan. You are now in a position to assess risk by relating known issues to tasks with high risk.

You may encounter three potential situations here: (1) If you have an issue with no related tasks, then the task list is not complete. (2) If the issue relates to tasks that are not yet labeled as risky, then consider relabeling. (3) If you have high-risk tasks with no issue, then you are missing issues. This analysis helps make the plan more complete and integrated.

This method is different than putting in contingencies. Some people pat their task durations to be safe. If you do that, you hide the risk and issues. The schedule will also be too long and unacceptable. It is better to identify issues associated with the tasks that you cannot estimate and, if necessary, add additional tasks that relate to the contingency. Hopefully, these tasks will never have to be performed.

How should you establish dates and durations?

Have team members estimate durations of all detailed tasks. If the estimate exceeds ten business days, then define even more detailed tasks. If the tasks are all constrained to begin as soon as possible, then there will be few dates to enter. Dates will be set by dependencies, the start date of the project, and durations. For flexibility in planning, maintain the scheduling constraint "as soon as possible". If you fix the dates for a task or change the constraint to "as late as possible", "must start by", "must end by", and so on, then you lose flexibility. You will often get error messages because some tasks will have negative slack.

What happens if you have trouble estimating durations? Chop up the task into smaller parts. Then if you still cannot do the estimation, identify the subtask that you cannot estimate. Why can't you estimate it? The reason is an issue that you can add to the issues database. Work on the issue with others to define an estimate. It is positive that you define these issues early. Don't succumb to the temptation to just put down some estimate!

It is possible that the schedule produced will not be acceptable. The end date will be beyond that defined in the project concept. What do you do? Go back to team members and first review the detailed tasks for the next 3–4 months and make adjustments here. Next, move to future tasks. Test the durations and dependencies to try and move the dates in. Remember that you, as the project leader, are being tested by the team members. If you give in to their estimates of durations too easily, then you have just established a pattern where you can be pushed around. You will have more problems later. Here are some additional tips on compressing the schedule. See if you can do more work in parallel. This may require you to divide up tasks into subtasks. Another suggestion is to work on the issues behind the tasks that have risk. This is better than trying to compress tasks that have no risk.

Here are some additional tips for dealing with team members:

- Probe the reasons behind their estimates. You want to get at their assumptions.
- Try to break up the task into subtasks. See if these can be performed in parallel.
- Do what-if analysis in their presence to determine the impact of changes.

If you assign joint tasks to two team members with one in charge, you will receive multiple inputs as you develop the schedule. In addition, you have a backup if one person becomes unavailable.

How should you link projects?

To just say that two projects are linked is almost useless. You cannot perform any analysis. Carry out the following activities to establish linkage:

- Link projects at the detailed task level as well as at the summary level using the project management software. This is possible because all of the plans are on the network server.
- Identify the individuals on each project team that will be responsible for interfaces between the two projects.
- Identify a list of potential interface issues.
- Establish an interface method for coping with issues with the managers of the related projects.

Linking is possible using project management software such as Microsoft Project. The best linking occurs if the templates follow a similar structure.

How do you create the project budget?

With a schedule defined, you can work on estimating the budget. Experience for systems and technology projects tends to favor an approach where you start from the areas that are the most defined and have the least risk and then proceed to the areas where there is greater uncertainty. If you consider a typical project, it is composed of hardware, network, software, and personnel costs related to development and implementation. Some people make a big deal out of hardware cost estimation. This is typically based on the sizing of the hardware required. However, hardware takes up a smaller percentage of a project budget each year and is one of the most certain costs. The network has greater uncertainty because there may be unknown problems in implementation and additional network software that was not known at the start of the project. Software packages can be estimated more easily in terms of cost. The problem here is that you might miss some elements of software. The greatest uncertainty and risk lie in personnel time and effort.

Here are some guidelines in estimation:

- *Hardware.* Estimate hardware first. In terms of end-user hardware, allow for a fully configured system and more workstations or PCs than you require to allow for change. Lessons learned indicate that people from the business unit will underestimate their hardware needs. Then when they see the system, they change or increase their requirements. Perhaps, make the end-user hardware an item separate from the project budget.

With respect to the server hardware, this depends on the specific company and situation. In the past, underestimation has been due to not including history data for online access, databases for *ad hoc* inquiry and reporting, and data warehousing type applications. In terms of labor associated with hardware, ensure that you have covered testing and installation.

- *Network*. For cabling connect up the reasonable maximum number of locations. This is because the greatest single cost factor is the labor involved in installation rather than the cable itself. To have the installers return and cable additional offices can be very expensive.

  Network hardware and embedded network software are straightforward if you have one or only a few vendors. In your budgeting, allow for the hardware to be fully featured, even if you actually order less. If you are adding a new application on top of an existing network, then consider adding money for hardware upgrades due to the increased workload.

  The network management, diagnostic, and control software is more complex because it may operate on host hardware and may involve additional staff. Try to place a limit on the budget amount by setting criteria for turnover to production and operations as well as on the labor effort in installation.

- *Software*. The system software is easiest to estimate and include. Utilities are often underestimated in that people miss some of the software required. Talk to the vendors as well as other software users to determine what software they have acquired. Even if you do not elect to purchase it now, put it in the budget. Next, try to apportion the software cost between ongoing operations and the project. It is not really fair for the project to pick up operational and maintenance costs.

  For software tools such as development environments, database management, fourth-generation languages, and so on, some of the leading factors in underestimation are as follows (1) not including all of the necessary modules, (2) not allowing for sufficient training in the software, and (3) failure to include consulting by the vendor to get you started.

  The preceding remarks apply to software packages. Additional factors here are the customization required of the application software to fit specific business requirements and the design, programming, and testing of interfaces with other software. Solicit vendor estimates as well as experience from existing users of the software package. With major integrated software packages, you can seriously underestimate the costs.

- *Staffing*. With the schedule and resources identified, you can determine the people and their costs. Then you can add overhead. For contractors you can solicit specific bids for task areas. If this sounds so straightforward, then why does it go wrong? What happens is that requirements or technology change(s). The schedule then slips. Once the schedule slips, the labor costs go up. The costs are a trailing indicator of the problem. The core of the issue is how to protect the project from change. If there are changes, then an allowance has been made for changing both the schedule and the budget. Estimation gets a bum rap here because somehow people are expected to see into the future. However, there is no extrasensory perception for software development yet.

What if you do a good job estimating and end up with a number that is too large to be acceptable? What should you do? Do you arbitrarily cut the number to fit someone's plan? The answer is no. Try to move some of the costs out of the project and into the business unit or other areas of systems. The project budget may look big to information systems, but it typically is much less significant to the business units—and, after all, they are ones who are going to benefit from the new system and technology. For PCs and the network, you can argue that these items will eventually be required by the business unit to complete its standard tasks, not including the new system. The new system represents an incremental application on the network and hardware.

Some of the common mistakes people make are as follows:

- They fail to include sufficient hardware for development, test, and production environments. These should be three separate environments. Otherwise, you are likely to have incomplete testing and quality assurance.
- There is software missing. When you acquire a substantial Fourth Generation Language, for example, there are many additional components and utilities that you should get. Validate the software components.
- If the project is going to go for a year, then you should allow for upgrading to new versions. Many people only put in the initial purchase or acquisition cost.

Moving on to staffing, go to the project template and the estimate of the plan. In Microsoft Project and other software project management tools, you can obtain a "Resource Usage" view of the data. Here the rows are the resources and tasks and the columns are time periods. The entries in the table constitute the number of hours that the resources work during that period on the tasks. Export this table to a spreadsheet. There you can apply money to the resources. Don't use this as is. Follow these guidelines in doing the analysis.

- Allow for additional resources that are not included in the plan. After all, the plan is not a detailed budget entity. Rather, it is a management one. If you attempt to make any project plan totally accurate in resource allocation for each and every small resource, you will not have enough time to update the schedule. It will be too unwieldy to use.
- For consultants and contractors you should allow for start-up and termination.
- Remember that the project plan is for work in the project. There are also support tasks that have to be included in the resource estimates.
- A rule of thumb is to take the total number of hours in a given period such as a month and then apply an average cost. This will give a ballpark starting number to start with.

How do you determine benefits?

Benefits were discussed earlier in general. Here as part of the plan you are going to define these in more concrete terms. Here are some guidelines on benefits.

- Create a table of both tangible and intangible common project benefits. The first column is the benefit. The second column has the tangible benefit. Obviously, tangible benefits are repeated. For intangible benefits, you would list tangible ones in the second column. For example, ease of use is intangible. However, it leads to the following more tangible benefits: less training time and cost, lower error rates, and improved customer service. By using a table you provide for more standardized benefit analysis.

- Insist that all benefits be tangible. Management has heard enough fuzzy benefits.
- Insist that the business units develop the benefits with your help. They should stand up before management and present these. If you are a consultant or in IT, you are just not credible because you do not know the business and, more importantly, you cannot make them come true.
- Determine how the benefits will be achieved.
- Pin down how the benefits will be measured. This is best done by measuring the business processes that are impacted before and after implementation.
- Benefits should be revenue- or cost-oriented. Any cost reductions should be supported by how labor will be cut or reallocated.

These are tough guidelines, but are essential for credibility and support. Figure 8.3 presents a table of commonly cited benefits. The left side is the benefit and the right side consists of the corresponding benefits.

There are additional benefits beyond those mentioned above. These consist of the costs you avoided if the project was not done. This is very useful in justifying

Benefit	Tangible Benefit
Cost savings	Same
Ease of use	Reduced training costs; reduced rework
Fewer errors	Reduced labor and rework
Increased volume of work with the same resources	Reduced labor costs
Higher productivity	See item above
Improved quality	Reduced rework
Improved customer service	Increased sales; more repeat business
Elimination of exceptions	Higher productivity
Elimination of shadow systems	Higher productivity
Improved management information on work	Reduced costs
Less dependence on King/Queen Bees	Improved morale and productivity
Reduced employee turnover	Reduced training costs; higher quality work
Improved flexibility and agility	Improved productivity
Improved morale	Reduced turnover; higher productivity

Figure 8.3 Common project benefits

infrastructure requirements. The costs are the impacts on IT and the organization if the modernization is not done or the legacy system is not replaced. How do you measure the costs that you avoided by carrying out a project? You should measure deterioration of the business process and work when you gather requirements by comparing the situation and transactions today with that of a year or more ago. Then you can project the rate of deterioration. People often underestimate the true benefits of a project because they do not include the deterioration that was prevented.

The benefits are owned and determined as well as supported by business units. When you are doing this, you should perform these two actions:

- Identify the potential impacts if the project is not done. This includes not only the impact of problems in the business processes now, it also includes estimated future deterioration of the work. This can be estimated from past deterioration by comparing processes last year and now.
- Determine how benefits will be measured at the end of work and implementation of changes in the work. See Chapter 15 for measurements of business processes. Consult also Chapter 10 on change management.

How do you perform cost-benefit analysis?

Well, you have the costs and benefits. Now it is time to put them together. At the start of this chapter a number of alternative financial measurements were given for doing cost-benefit analysis. You would employ the one(s) endorsed by your organization. Here is a useful political approach for doing this. You validate the costs mostly within IT management. The benefits are owned and determined as well as supported by business units. When you have done the cost-benefit analysis, review it within IT. Then have someone from finance or accounting review the analysis. After this review it with the business units. If the business unit managers start to back slide, then indicate that you did not develop the benefits. Also, indicate that you are like the manager of a road repair crew. Repairing one stretch of road is just like repairing another. You demonstrate positive indifference. The business unit may want IT to own the project so that they are not accountable for the benefits. You must, by all means, prevent this. You can also raise the fear of not changing their work by pointing out the process deterioration as well as system maintenance and operations increased cost and potential lack of people to support older systems.

How should you establish multiple projects?

Most of the techniques presented for single projects apply to multiple projects as well. Here are some additional guidelines:

- Build high-level tasks for all projects first.
- Establish dependencies between projects at this high level.
- Identify common issues and associate them with appropriate tasks.

It is important for the line and project managers involved to build their plans in a collaborative, shared information environment. Otherwise, it will be more difficult to resolve issues. Information hiding at the start of the project can really hurt later and result in more political games and maneuvering.

How do you establish a baseline plan?

Most project management software allows for multiple sets of start and finish dates for each task. When you are working on setting up the plan, you are typically working with one set of dates—scheduled dates. You can save these into another set of dates and then make changes to see what happens to the schedule for what-if analysis. The software allows you to set the baseline plan dates. This typically means that the scheduled dates are saved as planned or baseline dates. This is referred to as setting the plan. Later during the project you will enter tasks as complete and make changes. These will be saved from the scheduled dates into the actual dates.

How can you take advantage of the other dates in systems projects? Some examples from lessons learned are the following:

- *Customer or business unit dates*. These may be separate or in addition to the project manager dates.
- *Modifications to baseline*. Due to issues, resource reallocation, and so on, a major schedule change may be necessary. You can still keep the baseline dates by saving them into another set of dates. Then you can establish the new baseline plan. The original baseline plan is then not lost and can be employed for later analysis.

You must retain any significant change to the agreed upon schedule due to requirements changes, external factors, and so on. You can then track and present the history of the project. Most software allows you to show three sets of dates in the bars of the GANTT chart. For example, in Microsoft Project, you can store many different start and finish dates. If you run out of these, then you can save the schedule to retain the older dates.

How do you market and negotiate for the plan?

Let's consider each audience you are attempting to reach. Your objective and approach will be different for each.

- **IT and upper management.**
  The plan must mesh with the project concept. If there are major differences in dates and budgets, then you will have to redo the concept to fit the plan and market it prior to presenting the plan.

  Now put yourself in management's shoes. What do you ask about a plan? Here are some examples:

  - The project concept identified initial ideas about risks. What has the project plan done to minimize the risk?

–   What resources does the plan require? Are these available? Will these demands affect other current work?

–   Are interdependencies among projects clearly identified? How will they be managed?

How do you sell the plan to management? Review the project concept and highlight how you have addressed risk. Next, discuss how the plan and project will be managed in terms of the business unit role and interfaces with other projects. Another area to discuss is resource management—how will the team be coordinated and managed? You can use fear by emphasizing what will happen in the business work if the project is not done.

- **Project team.**

You will succeed in marketing to the project team if team members participate in the updating of the plan and in project management as well as in giving support for the schedule dates. You fail if all that you achieve is their understanding.

Go over the plan with all members of the core team and major part-time team members individually. Review their tasks and dates. Have them identify risks and more detailed tasks for their work. After doing this, gather the team together and present the plan along the lines of management presentation discussed earlier.

- **Business units.**

There are specific marketing objectives here. The plan reinforces and defines the role of the business unit. You want the unit to acknowledge and accept this role. The business unit must see what responsibilities their employees will have and how important they are to the project. Third, you want people in the business unit to understand that the plan can help in communications and in resolving issues.

Visit the business unit managers and review the project concept. Present the plan at a summary level. Don't bury them in detail. With this overview show them what tasks their staff will be performing, when this will occur, and the importance of the work. How do you indicate importance? One way is to show how slippage will occur if the tasks are not performed on time. Another is to explain the impact of lack of task completion. Another technique is to use the fear factor as was mentioned for management. How will the work deteriorate over time without the project?

Many project management books end here. However, you must set the stage for addressing questions and issues with them later on. From lessons learned and the initial issues identified in the project concept, discuss some of the likely issues that will be faced. This can naturally lead to a discussion of the issue resolution process and how the plan and issues will be updated. Return to the issues and select one. Go through the process of issue analysis and resolution. An example of an issue is what will occur if the person assigned to the project is no longer available.

How do you fix an existing schedule?

Here is a step-by-step repair process:

- *Step 1*: Review the resources assigned to tasks and establish a standard list. This means that you will gather all resources across schedules and compose a standard list. Then you will edit the list of resources in each schedule to conform—thereby ensuring compatibility.

- *Step 2*: Establish the highest level summary tasks in the schedule. Create a top-level summary schedule of fewer than 20 summary tasks.
- *Step 3*: At each level introduce dependencies between tasks. At each level insert dependencies that are tail to head.
- *Step 4*: Move down in the level of detail to lower summary tasks. Keep adding more detail, and then add dependencies at that level.
- *Step 5*: When you have fixed the detailed tasks, add the resources from the resource list to the detailed tasks. You should assign no more than three to four resources per task at the detailed level.
- *Step 6*: Enter dates and durations of the detailed tasks. These will normally be the scheduled start dates and durations for the detailed tasks.

Cases and examples

Electronic commerce

Let's give an example of a template for electronic commerce. Once a company embarks on electronic commerce, it is likely to have several electronic commerce projects for individual transactions, justifying the creation of a template. Key areas of the project relate to business partners, interfaces to legacy and other host systems, and controls.

1000	Project management
2000	Business partner relationships
3000	Business and process analysis
4000	Technology support
5000	Host/legacy system interfaces
6000	Security, firewall, and network access
7000	Software development and implementation
8000	Electronic commerce controls and security
9000	Technical integration and testing
10000	Process changes and procedures
11000	Marketing changes and support

Note that the areas have been employed to define the project structure by highlighting integration and marketing. Who might be involved in the project? Beyond IT you have the business units including marketing.

If you were already doing electronic commerce, you would probably have already completed a small project to define strategy, costs, benefits, assessment of competition and Web sites, and overall schedule as well as technical direction. This standardization can then be employed across other electronic commerce projects.

Questions

1. It would seem that electronic commerce would not require marketing internally within the organization. Why do business units and employees resist electronic commerce in their departments?

2. What are the differences between electronic commerce projects and standard internal projects?
3. E-Business between customer firms and their suppliers got off to a rocky start. Yet, the benefits to both customers and suppliers are obvious. Why is it difficult to initiate projects between suppliers and customer firms?

Mapping to the PMBOK and PRINCE2

The project plan is addressed in Chapter 3 of the PMBOK. Additional information is contained in Chapter 4 (Project Integration Management) on developing the project charter. Chapter 5 deals with Scope Management and gives useful ideas for defining the scope and WBS. Project Time Management (Chapter 6) provides information on defining activities, estimation of durations, and schedule development. Project Cost Management (Chapter 7) discusses the preparation of the budget.

PRINCE2 provides a compatible approach to PMBOK for project planning. PRINCE2 divides up the project concept and planning while PMBOK addresses the concept as part of the project plan effort. PRINCE2 offers less detail on specific methods that are covered in PMBOK.

Lessons learned

Building a project plan requires a great deal of collaborative effort. Estimating the hardware, network, and software is easier than the business side. Here are some guidelines.

- Make sure that you include a test environment for the software. Software projects require you to be thorough in quality assurance. In one company there were several errors that were undetected. The software was put into production. Someone found out that they could order and receive merchandise free by combining promotions and discounts. This was posted in a chat room. Within a week, the firm had unknowingly given away over two million dollars in merchandise!
- Use external information as a start in estimating benefits. This will give the areas of benefits for implementation.
- Be sure to include the benefits of changed internal business processes as a result of the project. Give attention to process deterioration. In many cases, this is where the real benefits that are tangible will be initially received.

Guidelines

- Keep task descriptions simple and use a standard set of abbreviations (e.g., Rev for review). Number all tasks for easier reference later. Keep task descriptions short (25–35 characters) so that you can still have the GANTT chart on one piece of paper.
- Set the fonts to be 12 pitch. This is standard and easier to read than smaller fonts.

- Review all task descriptions. Split tasks that are complex sentences.
- Each task should begin with an action verb (define, develop, review, collect, design, and so forth). Milestones indicate what is to be completed (such as prototype completed or tested). This ensures consistency and differentiates between tasks and milestones. Another tip—create a standardized list of action verbs.
- If a team member has never done task planning before, work with them to define tasks and get started. Your goal is to have people be able not only to work alone, but also to work together. If you don't do this, you could be locked into the old mold where the project leader gathers the status information and becomes a clerk.
- To market the idea of a template, develop a strawman template and have people review and comment on it.
- Make sure that you develop the plan areas with the business unit staff as well as internal systems team members. Begin to have them enter tasks into the project management software.
- Number all tasks and milestones. This makes it easier to discuss the plan. Often, the wording in tasks has political implications. Numbering can help get around this.

Questions

1. The overall method of developing the schedule supports that of PMBOK and PRINCE2. Using the Web, research how project plans are developed using Agile or the Critical Chain method. Discuss how the methods discussed in this chapter can be applied.
2. Suppose that in estimating tasks, you did the work yourself as project leader with some input from the team. What are the advantages and disadvantages of this approach versus the one presented in this chapter?
3. You are asked to review a project plan. How would you relate the plan to the project concept?
4. You have finished the project plan and are about to present it to management and the business units. What questions do you think they would most likely pose to you?
5. You are interviewing potential members of your project team. What could you do to make the project interesting and appealing to them? What are the benefits of this approach as compared to having management tell them they must work on the project?

What to do next

1. Collect several project plans and review the task structure for the plans. Answer the following questions for each plan:

   - Are the high level, summary tasks consistent in the schedule?
   - Does the project cover all of the areas of risk?
   - Is the level of detail consistent across the schedule?
   - How have updates and changes been made to the schedule?
   - Is it easy to find specific tasks or do many have the same names?

- If you had an issue in the project, then could you find the associated and affected tasks?
- Has a baseline schedule be set?
- Is the wording of the tasks consistent?

2. Move up from single to multiple projects. Answer the following questions.

- How easy or difficult is it to create an overall project plan that combines several project plans?
- What inconsistencies and problems have to be fixed first before you can combine the projects?
- Is it easy to find issues that cross projects?

3. Assuming that you were going to build project templates, how many and what different templates would have to be constructed? What types of resistance would you encounter?

Summary

Developing the project plan is a political process in which you reinforce how people work together, what they can expect, what is expected of them, and their commitment to the project. If you miss this opportunity, then you will face an uphill battle in establishing methods later.

By empowering the team, the project leader can spend more time on issues and on doing project work. The team members can think on a larger scale about how to do their work and the impact of what they do on the overall schedule as opposed to just focusing on immediate tasks. This collective approach also fosters more joint work among team members.

Part three
Project execution

9
Effective project tracking and coordination

Introduction

In the past much of the emphasis in managing a project was directed toward updating and analyzing the schedule. Today, in systems projects it is a different situation. Updating and analyzing are still important, but these are trailing activities. Problems and issues have already surfaced by this time. It may be too late if you wait until slippage occurs to prevent problems.

Adopt a more proactive approach in managing projects. A primary duty of the project manager is to identify, analyze, and resolve project issues. An issue can be a problem or opportunity. If you address issues, then you can reduce risk and increase the chance of project success. This is such an important activity that the chapters in Part four address more than 60 specific issues in different areas. Alternatively, if you let issues linger and concentrate on project accounting, you jeopardize the project.

A second part of being proactive is to participate in some of the project work and to review work quality. This can extend across several projects. If multiple, related projects are not managed together, it is possible that each project can be successful, but together there is failure through lack of coordination.

It is necessary to define your goal in managing and completing projects. Traditionally, systems projects were successful if they were completed on time and within budget. Today, this is unacceptable. You must achieve the benefits from implementation and completion of the project. This is asking for more, but is consistent with the earlier discussion of the project concept. Failure then lies in not only not completing the project, but also in not achieving the benefits. In response, you can say that getting the benefits is not the responsibility of the systems group. This is true and points to the need for a sufficiently wide scope to accommodate process change and improvement. You want the tasks of measurement and implementation of process change to be included in the project plan and performed by the business unit. This will result in a longer project time line. Another impact of this definition is that business unit management and staff will be more heavily involved in the project.

Earned Value Analysis

Earned Value Analysis (EVA) consists of methods that measure work in an ongoing project in terms of cost, value, and other parameters. The roots of EVA go back to the early 1900s to work by Frank and Lillian Gilbreth. They formulated the concept of earned time. The method became standardized by the US Department of Defense in the 1960s. It then expanded into private enterprise and other areas of government. Through EVA you can combine measuring scope, schedule, and cost. As such, it can provide a warning of future project problems. EVA has been employed to communicate progress, deal with scope creep, and keep a team focused on critical milestones and work.

In EVA there are three concepts:

- Budgeted Time for Work Scheduled (BCWS). This is the budgeted amount of work cost plus the effort required to be done in a specific period of time. It answers the question, "How much work should have been done so far in the project?"
- Actual Cost for Work Performed (ACWP). This is the cost of the work done within a given time interval. This answers, "How much money has been spent so far in the project?"
- Budgeted Cost for Work Performed (BCWP). This is the cost budgeted for completed work added to that budgeted work to be completed in a given time period. This answers the question, "What is the value work accomplished so far?" This is also called EV.

Other related definitions are:

- Planned Value (PV). This is the authorized cost assigned to the work.
- Actual Cost (AC). This is the total cost incurred for a specific group of tasks or work.

From these you can compute both schedule and cost variances. These are as follows:

- Schedule variance (SV). This is the mathematical difference between EV and PV or EV-PV. This measures schedule performance.
- Cost variance (CV). This is the difference between EV and actual costs AC expressed as EV-AC. This measures cost performance.

From these you can derive the following:

- Schedule performance index (SPI). This is used to measure actual versus planned progress in work. It is the ratio of EV to PV expressed as EV/PV.
- Cost performance index (CPI). This is employed to measure actual versus planned costs of work in progress and is the ratio of EV to AC. This is expressed as EV/AC.
- Cost variance percentage. This is the ratio of cost variance to EV or BCWP. It is expressed as CV/BCWP.
- Schedule variance percent. This is the ratio of schedule variance to BCWS. It is expressed as SV/BCWS.

Firms working for governments are often required to calculate and report on these measurements. Most of the major project management software packages, such as Microsoft Project, calculate these and more from the schedule and plan data. In order to get these measurements, it is required that resources be assigned to all tasks. To obtain the cost ratios and measures, you have to enter the costs of the resources.

If you just had the planned cost, actual cost, cost variance, start date, and schedule variance, then you would know if the project started on time, how much it would be late, and the extent to which it is over budget. However, these are not sensitive to the details of the schedule and cost in specific time intervals. That is why you want to use the other measures.

In the previous chapter, we related issues to tasks. Doing this allows us to compute the following:

- The number of hours of work completed that had issues and risk.
- The actual cost of the work completed that had issues and risk.
- The remaining hours of work in progress and to be done that has issues and risks.
- The remaining costs of the current and remaining work with issues and risks.

You can obtain this information by filtering on the schedule with the flag indicating yes as well as either completed or future and current work.

With these you can compute the following:

- The percentage of remaining and current work with issues to total work.
- The percentage of past work completed with issues to the total work.
- The percentage of the cost of remaining and current work with issues to total project cost.
- The percentage of the cost of past work with issues and risks to the total project cost.

The preceding measures can also be obtained by filtering on issues and risk for the tasks.

The value of deriving these measures related to issues and risk is evident. First, it reveals the progress that the project is making on issues and risk in the past. Second, it foretells what lies ahead with the work in terms of issues and risks. For the past 10 years, we have implemented these issue and risk-related measures in project reporting.

How do you identify and manage issues?

A project leader must constantly be looking for potential issues—both problems and opportunities that can impact a project. Issues can surface internally from team members or externally from other projects or groups, business units, vendors, and management. That is a good reason why a good project manager spends much of his or her time communicating with these entities. The last thing you want is to be caught off guard by a nasty telephone call, memo, or e-mail message.

Once you have detected something, you have to understand it. Is it a symptom of an existing, known issue? Is it new? Here are some questions to ask. A symptom is an effect of an issue.

- Is it a symptom or an issue? If you fix it and there remains a problem, then it is an issue. If it is a symptom, create a statement of the underlying issue.
- Is it related to an existing issue? If so, is it another symptom? Does it expand the issue? Can it be treated separately?
- What are other symptoms and potential causes of the issue?
- What are the impacts of the issue on the project? On other projects? On the organization?
- What is the priority of the issue?
- What happens if the issue is not addressed?
- What are related issues?
- Who will analyze the issue?
- What will be the analysis approach?

Let's give an example. Suppose that a team member tells you that the business unit wants to change requirements. There is a tendency to run over to the business unit and determine if it is true and what the new requirement is. You can see how the requirement can be addressed. This knee-jerk reaction is often counterproductive. You risk being "nickel and dimed" in changes. Instead, treat the issue through analysis.

Turning to analysis, first, determine the status of work in the project. This will provide you with perspective later when you meet with the business unit. Second, assess relations and communications between the team and the business unit. Why didn't this change surface before? Why does it appear now? Next, plan for contact with the business unit. Push for a review of all requirements as well as project status. This will put you in a proactive position as opposed to being on the defensive.

In the meeting with the business unit, relate each and every change to the business process. Get the tangible benefits out on the table. Test what happens if the change is either not made or made through manual procedures. If the change remains real, then you have a bona fide issue on your hands that you can address.

Establish an issues database as was discussed earlier. Update the database with new information on a regular basis (at least once or twice per week). Using this database you can now move to group-related issues. Seek to solve multiple issues with one set of decisions and actions. Return to the example. Let's assume that there are additional issues related to the business issue and commitment. For example, suppose that the business unit is not actively participating in the project to the extent originally agreed. Because you are dealing with requirements already, it is natural to include these as well. There is the potential for a trade-off here—you support the new requirement; in return, the business unit provides more support to the project.

How do you measure open issues?

At any time you have a number of open issues that vary in priority, impact and age and you can create a graph where the horizontal axis is time and the vertical axis is the number of open issues. The chart tracks the number of open issues by age for different priorities and in total. The curves have been smoothed. This chart is normal and desirable because it is logical that most of the open issues have been discovered recently.

You can produce another chart that is more serious. The horizontal axis is now for aging. The furthest point on the right is current time. The far left is the project start date. The vertical axis is the number of open issues based on the date that they became active. You could construct several lines on the chart. One could represent all of the issues. Another could represent those for internal issues. A third could represent those for external issues. This could reveal that the lingering issues that have not been addressed for a long time are external. These older issues fester and can seriously impact the project. Look at the changing requirements example. Suppose the decision is deferred. Then if the final decision is made to implement the requirement, much of the project work may have to be redone.

What general issues analysis do you perform?

Let's sit back and consider how you should analyze issues overall. Start with these basic data elements.

- Issue number
- Status
- Type
- Date discovered
- Date resolved

These simple data elements can give you the basis for many comparative graphs. Here are some examples.

- Total number of issues at point in time. What is the trend in the total?
- Total number of issues by type. What is the trend in business, technology, external, and process issues?
- All issues by date discovered—number of issues by discovery date. Are more issues being uncovered later in the project?
- All issues by date discovered and type—number of issue by discovery date for a specific type. Are more issues of the specific type being uncovered?
- Average time to close issues by date of discover. Is there a trend as to how long it is taking to resolve issues?
- Average time to close issues by type and by date of discovery. Is there a trend as to how long it takes to close issues of a certain type?

How do you measure the work in a systems and technology project?

It starts with collecting information on status. If the project team has been updating its part of the schedule and issues, then you can start with a review of this information.

If collaborative scheduling is not in place, you have to determine status manually. Don't fall into the trap of holding a project meeting to determine status. Instead, meet with each person in his or her office, if possible. Plan ahead for the sequencing of the meetings with team members. Start with the team members who are working on tasks with the greatest risk. This is probably where you can do the most good.

Here are some guidelines for individual one-on-one meetings:

- Ask how the work is going and what issues or problems the team members have run into. This gets them to open up to you in their own words.
- Translate what they say into the impact on the tasks they are working on. Have them review what you did. This is more effective than just handing them a list of tasks and asking them to check off what is complete.
- For each task that is completed, plan on how you will review it for quality.
- Now go down the list of open issues and determine which are impacting their work. Examples might be availability of resources or waiting for other team members to complete their work.
- During this meeting, ascertain whether they are communicating with other team members on their own, or are they working alone? If they are working alone, plan ahead for a small meeting to get them together with other team members.
- Ask what resources or help they need for current and near-term future tasks. Volunteer to get them help.
- Don't ask what percent complete their current task is. This is a very ineffective question in software and technology projects. Instead, ask them what is left to do in the task. This focuses on getting it done as opposed to how much they have done.
- When addressing future tasks, ask them to define the work in detail. This will help flesh out the detailed schedule. Of course, it is better if they maintain their own tasks because they can be self-sufficient and more involved in project management.

You can review work at several levels—just like child's homework. You can take their word for it. You can ask to see it, but you don't review it. Or you can have the work reviewed. Time doesn't permit a full review of every end product. Moreover, in systems projects a number of milestones are almost self-evaluating. That is, the work is immediately put to use and tested. Other milestones might not be critical at the time. Several criteria are applied for picking which milestones or end products to evaluate:

- *The most important milestones.* This is traditional project management. It makes sense if you can know which are the most important. However, if people know that they are important, they will consciously do well on these.
- *The milestones that have the greatest risk.* These are the ones on which much later work depends. It is recommended that you use risk as the main criterion for selecting milestones for review. In some cases, risk and importance lead to the same milestones.

How will you evaluate a significant milestone? Employ an approach that uses several people from the team. You want to use the review to build the team dynamics. Have each person involved in the review develop a list of questions ahead of time, then ask how they want to do the review. The purpose is to encourage a proactive, positive review process.

What do you do after a meeting? Don't wait until you talk to the entire team. If specific actions are necessary, such as follow-up on procurement or installation, get on this right away. Report back to the team member. Part of your job as project leader is to identify and address issues.

After you have determined status, update the issues database first. Then go to the project plan and schedule. Here are some guidelines for updating the schedule:

- Mark all of the tasks that are complete first. Don't use percent complete for detailed tasks.
- Insert more detailed tasks for current and future work based on the information that the team members provided. Insert the date that the task was created in a text field within the project management software. Use some symbol to indicate that it is a new task.
- Mark the tasks that are now started.
- Associate the issues with the tasks for traceability.

Do all of this with a copy of the schedule. Now filter or extract out the tasks for each person for the last month and a future month. Have each person on the team review what you have done. Make any corrections and changes to the schedule. Update the schedule. This will become the new actual schedule. This is the manual version of the process. In collaborative scheduling, each person performs the update steps listed.

What are some of the problems that you can face in the review of work?

- *The work is behind schedule.* Reasons for this are (1) the original estimate was too optimistic (2) the resources were not available to do the work, and (3) the scope of the task was not understood properly.
- *The quality of the work is not acceptable or complete.* This can be due to a misunderstanding of the task. Another reason is that the person doing the work lacks specific training. That is why it is urged that each person define his or her own tasks.

What do you do? Some people might just extend the schedule. Don't do this. Create an issue and follow up. If the person doesn't appear to be making progress, volunteer to get help. Many people try hard and because of ego or some other reason don't want to admit problems. Don't blame them. Get them help. This is especially true when you have a mix of junior and senior programmers and analysts. Encourage the senior team members to help the junior team members. Emphasize to the senior staff that part of their job in the project is to mentor and help the junior members.

To handle these situations you should create new tasks. Tasks are created for unplanned work and for the extra work required for a task. With each new task, you can enter the date the task was created along with the reason for the creating and addition of the tasks. This supports later analysis and traceability for slippage in the plan.

How do you analyze a project?

You now have updated the schedule. You can produce several of the standard graphs and reports, or you can produce an updated GANTT chart that shows actual versus planned results. However, before you do this, perform an analysis of the schedule. Here are some specific steps for analyzing the schedule:

- Look at the number of outstanding issues and plot a graph such as that presented earlier.
- Examine the oldest outstanding major open issues. Why are these still open? Start doing research to determine what is going on. What can you do to resolve these issues?
- With the update you probably have added more detailed tasks. The schedule probably has now been extended. Don't leave this as is. Look at the future tasks and find those that are likely to require more detail. This will help you see how bad the situation might become.
- Look at the future tasks by person and determine which have high risk. Label these in a field in the project management software.
- Filter the schedule by extracting those future tasks with high risk. Has the number and extent of risk grown? Are the tasks with risk on or near to impacting the mathematical critical path? Here you are working with the management critical path.
- Now you can copy the current schedule and create a model of what the future might hold. Adjust the task durations based on the previous analysis steps. This will probably be scary because it will extend the schedule even further in the future.
- Review the list of issues and compare it to the future tasks that have high risk. There are several possibilities here. For tasks that are risky with identified issues, assign these issues high priority. For tasks that have risk but with no issues, you must attempt to identify the issues that lead to the risk. You can consult the team members who will be working on these tasks in the future.

Do you realize what you are doing in this analysis? First, you are being proactive in addressing issues with current tasks. Second, just like team members who prepare for the future tasks, you are preparing for the tasks that have high risk. You are attempting to identify and address issues in these tasks so that the risk can be reduced. It is a myth that you have to wait until the task starts before you define the issue. Don't wait that long.

At this point in your analysis you have several schedules. You have the updated current schedule with the additional tasks and revised estimates from the project team. In addition, you have the baseline or plan schedule. Remember this is the one that management sees as official. You have also created a third schedule based on future estimates. It makes sense to put these together in a GANTT chart. However, the baseline has less detail than the current schedule which, in turn, has less detail than the "future" schedule. How do you put these together? Summarize each schedule to the same tasks. That is, roll up the tasks to the summary level. The summary level is the same for all three schedules. In some project management software packages, you can now combine these schedules so that each summary task has three sets of start and finish dates in the GANTT chart. An alternative approach is to create a new summary schedule and copy and paste the actual, planned, and future dates into the new schedule. Three sets of dates is normally the maximum number that can be shown on a GANTT chart clearly.

The GANTT chart can now be employed to do further analysis. You can answer the following questions:

- What is the impact of the current information on the current status of the project? If there is little or no change, then no action is required. If there has been a major change in the schedule, then proceed to the next question.
- What is the estimated effect of current knowledge on the future schedule? This will indicate whether there is major slippage in the future.

There are now several cases to consider. If both the current and future do not change the scheduled completion, then no immediate action is needed except for the actions identified earlier. If the current schedule is okay and the future schedule shows slippage, then you must take several actions. First, you must follow up on the issues related to future tasks to reduce risk and possibly improve dates. Second, alert management informally of the potential for slippage and explain what you are going to do.

In the third case, the current schedule shows slippage but the future schedule shows either improvement or the same slippage. What you do here depends on the degree of slippage. If it is severe, then you may want to follow the steps in the last case below. If it is not severe, then you can report that to the management along with the actions you are taking.

In the fourth case, there is slippage in both the current and future schedules. Now you must do more analysis of the issues to verify that your estimates of the future are correct based on your current information. If they are or when they are, you can proceed with considering alternatives. Do this analysis prior to any management presentation. Here are some analysis steps to consider:

- Can the structure of the project be changed to have more tasks performed in parallel? This what-if analysis can be performed with your future schedule. Save it before you start. Save the revised schedule with the structure change.
- Go to the list of open issues. See which ones impact the schedule. Revise the future schedule based on the structure change in the preceding step with changes to show the effects of early and favorable outcomes of issues. Save this schedule separately as "Issues".
- What happens if more non-personnel resources were added? This might include additional hardware or software. In other words, what happens if you throw money at the project? Do this analysis with a copy of the schedule with the structure changes. Save this schedule as "Resources".

- What happens if you add more people or add more time from current staff on the project? The personnel can be either employees or contract people such as contract programmers or consultants. Save this schedule as "Personnel".

You now have four different models of the future. For each of these schedule versions, prepare an estimate of the budget impact so that you have a budget-versus-actual analysis. These can now be discussed with management.

This analysis takes considerable time. How often do you do this? It is recommended that at most you do this once every few weeks or month. Otherwise, you will spend all of your time doing this analysis. How can you reduce the time for this analysis? Be very organized in your files and work habits. Here are some guidelines and lessons learned:

- Do the schedule update at a different time from the analysis. Updating is mechanical. Analysis is not. Doing them together will also take too much dedicated time and requires different attitudes.
- Organize your computer files so that the updated and baseline schedule are on the network. The additional files you have created are on your hard disk. For each schedule you create, document the assumptions and changes that have been made. Otherwise, you will not be able to remember all of them and will have to reconstruct your work—very time consuming.
- Print out each GANTT chart and label it. Put these charts in paper files along with labels as to assumptions and dates.
- Summarize your analysis results in bullets organized as follows:

  - Assumptions
  - How the schedule changed
  - Impact of schedule change
  - Feasibility of making the changes

If you are considering changing the schedule after meeting with management, make sure that you include future changes as well as changes based on current information. The goal in systems projects is to have as *few major changes to a schedule as possible.* Managers will question what you are doing if you keep changing the schedule and running to them with problems. Having constantly changing schedules will likely disturb the project team. Team members will question the direction of the project.

How do you perform budget versus actual analysis?

You can start with the EVA discussed at the start of this chapter. You can track the expenditures for equipment, the network, and software in standard ways. For labor analysis, you would follow the same approach in planning. You would generate the "Resource Usage" view of the data of the project. This would then be exported to a spreadsheet. There you can compare it to the same information for the baseline plan. Once you find discrepancies, then you can zero in on the tasks that created the differences. You can also perform EVA measurements.

How do you track multiple projects?

What do you do differently with multiple projects? Begin with analysis of the schedule for each project. If you have project leaders for these projects, have them perform the preceding analysis. Work with them individually to review their work. Identify problem areas and issues for each project. Work on the issues that cross multiple projects and prioritize the issues across projects. An example of an issue might be the need for specific programming software tools. Another example is the need for additional design or programming resources, which have the same area of expertise. This will move you up to the level of perspective across multiple projects. For each common issue do the following:

- Formulate a general version of the issue that will apply to each project.
- Define what will happen to all projects if the issue is not resolved, and do this by showing the impact of slippage on the schedules.
- Define potential solutions for the issue and show how these could impact the schedule.
- Estimate the cost and benefit of the potential solutions.
- Determine how you and the project leaders will control and manage the solution to ensure a result.

Now download the project schedules that the project leaders have developed from the network onto your PC. Filter or extract the tasks from each schedule that are currently active or that occur in the next month or two. Combine these extracted schedules into a single schedule. You can now see the resource requirements across each schedule. This only works if the project leaders use the same set of names for resources (e.g., they use the same resource pool), they follow the same general template forms, and they have assigned resources to tasks. You can now perform your own what-if analysis to see what happens if you reallocate resources. As you make changes that appear to improve the schedule, make notes as to the changes that were required.

With this analysis in hand, the next action is to gather the project leaders in a meeting and see how resources can be shared across the projects more effectively. Use a PC attached to a video projector so that you can, as a group, do the same what-if analysis. Here you can show them the problems in the individual schedules with specific resources. You can indicate the changes and see the reaction of the project leaders. You can employ the same approach to see the impact of issue resolution and solutions. There are several goals in carrying out this exercise. First, you are attempting to share resources across the projects so as to improve the schedules. Second, you are trying to get the project leaders to work together more closely in a collaborative mode.

How do you deal with project changes?

There are a number of sources for project change. These and some examples are listed in Figure 9.1.

- Government regulations

  - A new law or policy goes into effect—impacting the project.

- Management

  - There is managerial turnover. This normally would affect long-term projects.
  - Management changes the direction of the organization. This is an infrequent event.
  - Management wants to expand the scope of the project. This is common and should be anticipated.

- Vendor or supplier

  - The supplier discontinues the technology or product. Usually, you get forewarned so this is rare.

- Business units and processes

  - Business units, once understanding the requirements, now want changes.
  - Business units want to have the project address more transactions and work. This is another example of scope creep.
  - There is turnover in the management of the business unit. If you base the requirements on the actual, detailed work, this should have minimal impact on the project.

Figure 9.1   Sources and examples of project change

Here are some comments. Just because a new law goes into effect, don't rush in and make changes. Any law requires interpretation. Based on the interpretation, changes may be needed. It can take months for the interpretation to be clear. Thus, many times you put off the change and carry it out as a separate project after the original project.

Much has been written on scope creep and expansion. If you follow the guidelines below, experience shows that much of the scope expansion can be prevented.

Here are some observations about changes in projects.

- If the project is critical to the business, it will be less likely to have requests made for changes. Why? Because management and the business units realize the importance and urgency of the project. Only the most essential changes will be considered—those that are part of the minimum requirements to complete the project.
- Conversely, if the project is not critical, managers and business unit staff will suggest changes since they do not perceive a major impact resulting from delay.
- The longer the project life span, the more changes will be made.
- Some change requests are political. A new manager wants to put his/her mark on the project. Another example is that people who don't want process change or the project may suggest changes to delay the project and eventual change. If they are successful, the project may die. This happens more frequently than you think. More comments on this are contained in Chapter 10 on change management.

In the past, requirements were signed off for a project. They were considered frozen. This has, over the years, often proven to be unrealistic. The Agile method of development, for example, allows for requirement changes later in the project. Some of the factors behind project change were given in Figure 9.1.

Changes don't have to be negative. There may be features or capabilities that can and should be added to the requirements that have real, substantial value. Use the guidelines below to treat them the same way as the ones mentioned above.

What should your goal be with respect to managing project change? Well, you don't want to disrupt the project. But, on the other hand, you don't want to deliver a system or end a project with something with a lot of problems and shortcomings. In between, you can see that the goal is "To implement project change based on the urgency and importance of the need for change."

This goal sounds very general. It is. Let's see how to support the goal with guidelines. Here are some that have proven themselves over and over again during the past 20 years.

- Point out to management, business units, the team, and vendors that project change is possible as long as the following questions are answered:

  ○ What is the desired change?
  ○ What are the benefits of the change?
  ○ Can the change wait until the end of the project?
  ○ What is the degree of urgency of the change?
  ○ What if the change is not made? What will happen in the work and process?
  ○ What else is there? If there is one change request, there may likely be many more. Get them all out on the table.
  ○ How did they get along without this change in the current work?
  ○ Why wasn't the content of the change request discovered and included in the requirements for the project?
  ○ How would the benefits and impacts of the change be validated?
  ○ What is the justification of and factors behind the change?
  ○ Is the change request supported by the organization?

The common change request covers often only the first two points. This encourages people to make change requests psychologically since there is little work in preparation of the request and no downside. By including the other questions, you force the person to really think things through.

- Consider change requests in batches. If you deal with each change request one at a time, the project may really suffer. It could suffer death by a thousand cuts—each cut being a change.
- In considering project changes, you should answer the question, "What work will not be done if the resources are directed toward the changes?"
- When reviewing a group of changes, indicate the impact on the budget, schedule, and resources. Discuss the impact of delays and additional work on the business processes that will be altered by the project. Do this within IT first. Then with the business unit. Then with management. Then back to the business unit.
- Enforce the first point throughout the project. Seek out potential changes to avoid unpleasant surprises.

Politically, this works. Why? Because of what the person requesting the change must produce in terms of evidence. It can be daunting and intimidating. Here is an aside comment. We mention political and social factors in every chapter of the book. Why? Because projects result in change. Change alters jobs, careers, and work.

Many people are comfortable with what they have and do now. They may see no need for change. If you ignore the politics, you put the project in jeopardy. It is more likely to fail. Maybe, you think that politics should not be considered, but it cannot be avoided. Therefore, we provide tips and guidelines on how to take advantage of politics for the benefit of the organization, IT, and the project.

How do you cope with a project crisis?

The preceding discussion will work for most situations. However, in rare occasions there is a true crisis. Action is required quickly. There is little time for analysis. A crisis typically occurs because either a new issue arose or because an existing issue reached critical mass. Many people have a tendency to panic and jump at a solution that involves throwing money at the problem. Don't fall into this trap.

If you encounter a crisis, think about a series of changes that can be made to resources, the schedule, personnel, system requirements, business requirements, the business unit role, and so on. Don't restrict yourself. This is your chance to get a number of things in the project and across multiple projects fixed at one time. Use the crisis as an opportunity. Dealing with the crisis means going through the same steps that were discussed earlier.

How can you employ lessons learned effectively?

"Lessons learned" is a popular phrase. As mentioned earlier, it is now more formally part of "knowledge management". Whatever its name, there are several challenges in using lessons learned effectively. How will lessons learned be identified? How will they be retained? How will they be applied to the project? What will be the follow-up to see if they did any good? The first two questions were addressed in previous chapters. Here it is assumed that there is a body of lessons learned. To apply these lessons to a project, you must apply them to specific tasks. This is not as easy as it sounds. Start by associating each lesson learned with tasks in the project template and then in the plan. With these lessons learned, you are now in a position to apply the information. Get the analysts and programmers together and discuss each lesson learned that applies to the task. Have them as a group indicate how they might apply the information and what they expect in terms of benefit. Some people may be resistant to changing their methods. They are free to propose alternatives and argue for them. Either way, the methods and tools used in the project are discussed openly between junior and senior team members. This serves to educate the junior members. It also leads to measuring the benefit and effect of the lesson learned later.

As work is performed, you should gather the lessons learned regularly—each week. Don't wait for a milestone. Of course, you can gather more when a milestone is reviewed. Before a phase of work begins, you and the project team can go over not only issues, but also lessons learned on how to do the work and the applicable use of the methods and tools.

Cases and examples

Beaumont Insurance

Beaumont Insurance had two groupings of development and enhancement projects. Rather than manage each project separately, it was decided to group these. A group leader was appointed for each. The responsibilities of the group leader included the following:

- Identifying and addressing issues across multiple projects;
- Gathering and sharing lessons learned among the projects;
- Sharing resources among projects.

The project leaders were still held accountable for the project milestones given their resources. At first there was resistance from both project leaders and team members. Project leaders felt that their roles were diminished. The group project or superproject leader continually had to reinforce the role of the project leader. This took time to establish a habitual pattern of behavior.

The team members felt that this was an unnecessary layer of management. A useful response was to show how the superproject leader can gain access to management and to resources more readily than could individual project leaders.

What were the benefits of grouping the projects? There was more sharing of resources in the areas of testing, network support, analysis, and data management across the projects. In the past, some projects finished early and others late. With the superproject approach, projects tended to finish on time more often. There were also fewer surprises for management in terms of issues. It was found that about 20 percent of the issues were shared by at least three projects. The fear of additional overhead vanished when it became obvious that the superproject leader performed different roles from the project leaders. Another benefit was that the business unit could contact one manager to address a specific problem. Technology experience and selection was more open across multiple projects. This was particularly valuable in sharing client-server and intranet experience.

Questions

1. Discuss the advantages and disadvantages of having a group project leader over multiple projects versus single project with no group leader?
2. When project work is moving along as planned, there seem to be fewer issues and no resistance to change. Yet, when management attempts to make changes in the management of the projects, resistance is often encountered. What types of

resistance do you think management would encounter if they changed the project management structure in the middle of projects?

3. In this example management initially failed to convey a sense of urgency for the change. What are the advantages and disadvantages of stressing urgency versus the benefits of change?

Mapping to the PMBOK and PRINCE2

As expected, both methodologies employ similar methods for tracking and managing projects. PMBOK contains more details on specific methods. For example, in PMBOK, EVA is treated in Chapter 7 on Project Cost Management. Schedule control is discussed in Chapter 6 on Project Time Management. Scope control is part of Chapter 5 (Project Scope Management). Control is also addressed in Chapters 8–12.

PRINCE2 addresses project tracking and control generally—not specific to IT projects. The discussion is more general than that of PMBOK.

Lessons learned

Project tracking can be very demanding. Here are some specific comments.

- Management will ask for many presentations since they view the projects as important. You must be ready with organized and canned presentations at all times. You do not have time to customize each presentation.
- The issues tracking and graphs discussed earlier are valuable in project management since they provide management and business units as well as the team with an assessment of what is going on and where attention is needed.
- Using a common issues database allows you to determine the effect of single and multiple issues across the projects.

Guidelines

- At the start of the project, take some time to explain to the team members how you will be managing issues, reporting status, and working with them. Many people assume that team members automatically know what will happen. This is not true because this is usually the first time that this particular group of people have worked together.
- Eliminate any project meetings that involve status. Devote project meetings to technical issues, lessons learned, and how methods and tools will be used in the project. This will reduce the overhead and perceived overhead of project management on the team. It will also reinforce the team's view that you can care about results and not the project management process.

- Actively pursue informal communications with several managers. This includes several business unit managers as well as the managers in information systems. This will broaden the base of support for the project.
- If you are managing multiple projects, manage them at several levels. On the general level, focus on the issues that cross the projects. At the detailed level, plunge into a project with the project leader and get involved in the detail. Do this on a consistent basis so that the team will not think that you are pushing aside the project leader. Indicate to the project leader that you want to use a hands-on management style. Attend project meetings unannounced.
- Foster an atmosphere of applying lessons learned across different projects. This can be accomplished at several levels. One is the technical sharing of information among programmers or analysts. Another is between project leaders. Consider having regular lessons learned sessions among project leaders.
- In management presentations on issues have managers or senior staff from the business unit there to emphasize the impact on the business unit if the issue is not addressed, as well as to support early resolution.

Questions

1. If Microsoft Project or some other project management software is available, review the documentation on how EVA is calculated and how you can generate reports on these measurements.
2. Define a situation in which the EVA statistics are fine, but that those measurements dealing with issues and risk indicate problems.
3. Discuss the importance of using body language and voice in gathering information on project status.
4. Suppose that you were managing a team at a remote location. Discuss how you would gather status information from them on a regular basis.
5. In your personal life, identify three issues or problems that have been unresolved for some time. These could relate to relationships with family members, for example. What has been the impact of not resolving the issues? Why haven't they been resolved?

What to do next

1. Review how your current projects are reported to management. Address the following questions:

   - How are issues associated with projects and schedules?
   - What analysis is performed across multiple projects?
   - How are resources allocated across multiple projects?

2. What is the process followed for reviewing milestones? When is a milestone considered sufficiently important for measurement of quality? What constitutes acceptable quality? How are the results of milestone reviews disseminated and followed up on?

Summary

Managing an ongoing project is much more than doing work in the project and calculating and reporting status. In a systems project, you must be proactive by looking ahead to the future and identifying and addressing issues that raise the risk of the associated tasks. Don't wait until an issue surfaces on its own. This results in an unpleasant surprise. Work of the project leader includes constant efforts to build the "team" as a team. This is especially important in systems and technology projects where much of the work is perceived as an individual effort. You must build the team so that you raise the level of the junior team members and reinforce the value and self-esteem of the senior team members.

10
Implementation of project results—project change management

Introduction

In the past you would not have found this chapter in a project management book. It used to be that IT would carry out analysis and design and then implement a system. Then people would move on to other work. The situation has changed for a number of reasons.

- The implementation of the systems requires more process change that must be undertaken along the software. Examples are Enterprise Resource Planning (ERP), Supply Chain Management (SCM), and Customer Relationship Management (CRM) systems.
- Business unit staff are often neither familiar with process improvement or change, nor are they often willing to make changes on their own.
- Much of the project management expertise in organizations lies in IT. Since the change must be organized as a project, IT must be involved.

This trend has been borne out in the updates to the project management methodologies. For example, in PRINCE2 change management is explicitly addressed.

Stepping back a moment you can see that change management, project management, and process improvement are closely tied together.

- You would not do a project without getting benefits. Benefits require change and often process improvement.
- Process improvement entails change and, to be effective, should be managed as a project.
- Change management often involves business processes and also should be undertaken as a project.

Incorporating change management into project management affects a project from data collection on the current work past the implementation of the new system.

Spreading change management out through many chapters can be confusing and not give you the whole picture. Hence we devote a separate chapter to the topic. In this chapter we first give some of the background for change management. Then we progress through the project life cycle and examine change management techniques as they apply to IT-related projects.

Change management

Change management consists of structured methods to migrate organizations, processes, and individuals from their current situation to a desired or planned situation. A central part of change management is the process to empower employees and organizations to accept and support changes in their business activities. Change does not sell itself. Thus, another ingredient in change management is marketing along with communications. Skills often have to be enhanced and upgraded to meet the requirements of the altered environment.

To be effective, change management in projects must be included in the project concept (Chapter 5). Here it enters in the form of potential issues. Examples include the following:

- The department staff members who will be involved in the new system are very senior and may resist change.
- The business processes involved in the project have not changed in a very long time. Hence, there is a great deal of inertia.
- Past attempts with projects and change in these departments have failed so that people feel that this will likely be another failure.
- The new system provides a great deal of new and valuable information for management. However, for the employees it means not only change, but also more work—for the same pay.

Wait a minute. If management wants the project and the change, then the employees will go along with the project. Sounds logical. But it is not necessarily true. Employees may say they support change, but under the covers, they resist it. Here are some of the factors that the project must overcome.

- Senior employees see a loss of their informal power and influence. Junior people may become better as users of the new system.
- Employees and people in general are comfortable with their current situations unless shown that change is needed.
- Some people just fear change.
- Change can upset the management structure because some systems empower the employees. The supervisory roles are altered.

What is the potential downside? The project could itself be resisted and it may fail. The project may result in the system being implemented. However, it either may not be used at all, or not be exploited in terms of its full capabilities. In either case, the benefits that were expected and planned for are not realized.

Here is the basic approach.

- You first find the areas that have the greatest potential benefit through change. This is often determined by management. However, in generating project ideas, we have found that it is very useful to look into the key business processes from a change view as opposed to only a systems view.
- You collect information on the current work. This resembles requirements gathering, but as you will see, it is wider ranging.
- You develop a strategy or roadmap for change. Changes should be phased in groups.
- While the project progresses, you implement Quick Wins or simpler changes that pave the way for the long-term change brought about by the new system.
- More changes are introduced toward the end and after the conclusion of the project.

This last point can affect the scope. If you accept the traditional scope of an IT project, it ends when the system is installed, up and running, and accepted. However, just because the business unit managers accepted the system does not mean that change will occur to take full advantage of the system. Thus, the life span of a project should be extended to include the changes after implementation.

Process deterioration

Everything we have deteriorates over time—bodies, houses, cars, and so on. So it should not be surprising that business processes deteriorate over time. What forms does the deterioration take?

- The existing system cannot handle some new types of transactions. This creates more exceptions. Workarounds to the current system expand.
- The department staff improvise and create informal internal systems (called *shadow systems*). This creates more complexity and further reduces productivity. Moreover, the department becomes dependent upon the employees who support the shadow systems.
- Personnel turnover in the departments occurs. The employees lack the experience with the process resulting in more rework.
- Business policies and procedures can change. However, neither the current system nor the current practices in the departments change or keep up.

What are reasons for deterioration? Here is a list from experience.

- Senior business users (referred to as King and Queen Bees) continue to resist change and attempt to either sabotage the new process or warp it back to the way it was.
- New business employees are often hired in to replace departing staff one at a time. There is no time, money, or value seen by business unit management in formally training one person in the process. Instead, they are often placed under the wings of a King or Queen Bee. The King or Queen Bee can exploit the situation and exert power over them.

- The nature, volume, and other characteristics of the work change. Interface with other departments changes.
- There can be managerial or supervisory changes. The new managers may want the work done in a way that they were familiar with in their previous positions.

Figure 10.1 gives a checklist related to deterioration. In this list management awareness indicates the importance attributed by management to deterioration. In another item the role of process coordinator is identified. A *process coordinator* is someone who is tasked with measuring the business processes and recommending actions to fix the problems.

- Management awareness of the importance of deterioration;
- Continued use of measurements of business processes;
- Methods used to detect deterioration;
- Number and type of problems related to deterioration detected;
- The use of a process coordinator;
- Impact of deterioration;
- Average time to respond to deterioration;
- Effectiveness of the responses to the deterioration.

Figure 10.1   List to assess response to deterioration

Process deterioration is almost inevitable except for full automation in the case of E-Business. Otherwise, you cannot stop it any more than you can stop aging. You just have to accept and deal with it. That is why it is valuable to return once a year to departments after implementation to assess the deterioration and take countermeasures.

Determine areas for change

Almost every organization has literally hundreds of business processes. It is entirely infeasible to examine all of these. So you must choose which ones to examine. There are several possible criteria, including the following:

- The processes that are in the most trouble. They have the most known problems and complaints. This approach can fix some of the problems, but, overall, the processes are not moved ahead.
- The processes that are managed by the loudest managers. They tend to get a lot of attention. These processes may have the least justification for change.
- The processes that tie most closely to the mission, vision, and objectives of the organization. This is positive, but it may not lead to immediate benefits.
- The processes that are supported by very weak and old systems. This approach is IT based and has merit, except that the old systems may still support the processes and departments adequately.

- The processes that a competitor is modernizing. This is relatively frequent since companies must maintain their competitive edge and position.
- A new system or type of system (such as ERP, E-Business, CRM, or SCM) comes out in the form of several new products. This then creates the opportunity for change driven by external technology.
- You could ask the question, "What if this process is not changed? What will be the impact on the business?" The approach represents urgency. This is not the same as one with the most problems. You can have a lot of problems, but they are not urgent.

All of these surface and to some extent each has validity. Experience suggests that you select several of these and propose different groups or slates of processes for potential review. These can then be presented to management and the business units for their input and decisions. This is a proactive approach to define the processes for work. A reactive approach occurs when some business unit manager pushes for a project in his or her area. Management and IT then react. These processes may neither be the most important, nor the most in need of help.

From experience we have seen that the winning approach is often the last one. However, whichever approach is applied or selected, you have a group of processes to examine.

Data collection on current work

Here we focus on data collection from a change management perspective. What are goals of data collection? You might answer "To collect data." This is partially correct in change management. You start with the basic assumption that people are relatively content doing their work on a daily basis and see no need for change. Therefore, the purposes of the data collection on the business process are as follows:

- Collect information on the process.
- Identify the players. Who are the King and Queen Bees? What role do they have with respect to other employees?
- Through data collection, you can start to identify the individual who are for change and those who are more reticent and resistant to change.
- Determine problems exist in the current work.

Note that in standard IT systems analysis all business users tend to be treated as equals. Such is not the case in reality. In the real world there will be people who know the problems and make their concerns known. Others will be more non-committal. Often, it is the junior business users who favor change. Why? They are frequently suppressed by the senior King and Queen Bees.

This last one has to precede the gathering of requirements. For data collection is similar to drug and alcohol addiction. The person has to admit that they have a problem before they are willing to change. Your political objective is to find these problems first. After you find the problems, then you work with the business employees to ascertain the impacts of the problems on their work. This has two benefits. First, they admit that there are problems in the work. Second, through the impacts, they see how bad they are. It is best if you can do this at the transaction level. You would create the table. Another purpose is to solicit from them ideas on what has worked before and what they think could work to solve the problem. This approach is politically beneficial since it shows that the project is aligned to the actual people doing the work and not just management—further getting support for change.

Transaction: _____

Step	Who	What is Done	Problems	Impacts

You can then roll tables for the transactions up to obtain the following summary table. Here the second and third columns are summaries from the detailed tables. You can have frequency and volume as the fourth column and comments as the last column.

Transaction	Problems	Impacts	Frequency/Volume	Comments

Beware that a number of problems may have nothing to do with IT or systems. Should you do the common thing and say, "We would like to help you on this, but it is not in the scope of the project." If you say this, you likely turn off the users. They mentioned problems and you showed little interest. This could contribute to dooming the project. Instead, embrace the problems and include them in the tables. Look, if you can fix these with little effort, you can gain allies for change and support for the new system.

These inexpensive and rapid changes will be called *Quick Wins*. Here are some examples of Quick Wins or Quick Hits.

- Procedure changes;
- Retraining of staff in the process;
- Knowledge sharing among business employees on how best to do the work;
- Minor policy changes;
- Minor changes to the current system;
- Minor changes to staffing assignments;
- Minor changes to facilities.

The use of Quick Wins has a number of benefits, including the following:

- You test the waters for potential resistance or acceptance of change. This can help later when you implement the system.
- You get benefits for the project right away instead of waiting for the system to be implemented.
- You show the business users that you are really trying to help.
- You might want to eliminate and/or simplify requirements for the system implementation—thereby speeding up the project.

As an example, we managed several times the implementation of ERP systems. In doing these projects, we followed the approach in this chapter. Business rules were simplified so that the system implementation timeline was reduced and improved. We gained support for change and a willingness to participate in change.

As you are doing this, you can also gather requirements and business rules.

Can you do all of the transactions? No, of course not. Focus on the common and frequent ones. We have found that using a table approach leads to more rapid understanding and support from the business staff.

How do you collect the information? Usually, most books indicate from interviews. But using tips from news reporters, you want to include observations of the work. You might even want to be trained in the work and then ask questions about the transactions. This will often elicit more accurate information than formal interviews.

How to collect the information

In systems analysis, the collection, organization, and analysis of the data is performed by the IT staff member. This doesn't work for change management. In change management terms, the person who does this owns it. You really don't want IT to own this. It belongs to the business unit. They need to do the work coordinated and helped by IT staff. There is another reason for doing this. If someone outside of a department such as a consultant or an IT staff member performs the work, it will take a lot longer. Why? Because they have to get familiar with the terminology used in the department, the detailed processes, and so on. The business unit staff have lived every business day.

How should a team be organized? First, the team should be small—three or four people. The IT staff should coordinate the team and act as a resource. If the leader of the team is from the business unit that does the process work, they may think everything is fine. There will be no problems or new ideas. A better idea is to have the team leader be someone from another department—preferably a person from a department that often has problems with that department. If, for example, you were going to review accounting processes, you might find someone in sales or marketing. One or two team members should be from other departments. The last team member is from the department operating the process. Even here be careful. If you pick a senior King or Queen Bee and the team starts looking for problems, they may get defensive and freeze up. Therefore, a good idea is to find a less senior department member who will more likely support change. Does this sound too political? Well, remember change is political.

Now let's turn to the methods that the team will use. Since they are very familiar with the work, they can plunge right in. At the first meeting they can start identifying problems. Ah, but remembering politics, it is best to label as "opportunities". For each opportunity, they can briefly estimate the following:

- Description of the opportunity;
- Impact if the opportunity is not followed up on;
- Potential actions that could be taken;
- Resources and effort required;
- Importance or urgency of the opportunity to the departments;
- Elapsed time to implement actions on the opportunity.

Our experience is that this can be done in a few weeks. The people can usually do this while still doing most of their regular work. Morale often rises even though there are a number of opportunities. Why? Because they feel that they can finally get in and fix some long-standing problems.

Move ahead in time and assume that there are 30 opportunities. It is not possible to do all of these. In addition, some will take too long or require too much in money and/or resources. So you have to be selective. For Quick Wins the key factors to consider are time and effort, and impact if not done (urgency). IT cannot determine which are the best ones. Why not have the decision-making and recommendations on rankings be done by the team? They could vote on both of these. Here are two lists. The one in Figure 10.2 applies to benefit and importance. The other list in Figure 10.3 gives factors related to the ease of implementation. Of course, the elements in the lists will depend on the type of organization and department.

The team could rate each opportunity on a scale of 1–5 (1 – low; 5 – high). For ease of implementation the rating of 5 is the easiest to implement while a rating of 1 is the lowest. The coordinator of the team will now work with the team to arrive at a consensus score. Each could then be averaged so that each opportunity has two values—one for benefit and one for ease of implementation. You can then develop the chart as shown in Figure 10.4. Note that there are five opportunities shown here—5, 8,

---

- Customer relationships
- Product selection
- Channel contribution
- Vendor relationships
- Accountability and direction
- Organization
- Morale and work environment
- Revenue contribution
- Cost reduction contribution
- Improvement in processes
- Systems and technology

Figure 10.2 List of benefits for opportunities

- Expense to implement
- Time to implement
- Cultural resistance
- Manager and staff resistance
- Technology complexity
- Effect of other projects and work
- Effect on other projects and work
- Dependence on other work
- Competitive for resources
- Ease in measuring results
- Compatibility with the organization

Figure 10.3   List of factors related to ease of implementation

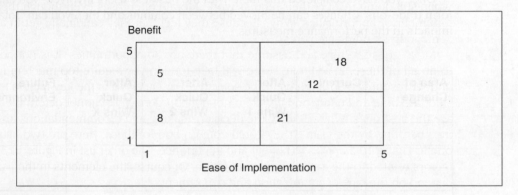

Figure 10.4   Chart of benefit versus ease of implementation

12, 18, and 21. Here opportunity 8 has low value and is not easy to implement so it is dropped. Opportunity 5 is dropped since it is also difficult to implement. Opportunity 21 is easier to implement, but has limited value so it is dropped. We would go with opportunities 12 and 18.

This approach is appealing for several reasons. It is relatively simple to apply. Another benefit is that management can first look at the chart and then probe members of the team for the reasons behind their votes and ratings. Who presents the results to business unit managers? The team members, not IT.

Your change implementation strategy

You have now identified problems and their impacts along with requirements. You also have collected ideas for potential solutions to the problems. The tendency is often to plunge in and start to solve these. However, this can lead to disorganized change. Moreover, some of the changes may later be undone by the new system. Instead, you want to map out how to phase in the changes.

This step is to create a change implementation strategy or roadmap for change. The structure for this table is shown in Figure 10.5. The first set of rows consists of areas of change. This could include not only IT, but also facilities, training, procedures, staffing, and so on. The second column is the current situations. The other columns except for the last one are for the waves of Quick Win changes that will be implemented. The Quick Wins are implemented in groups to avoid disruption to work. The last column is for the future environment after the system has been implemented. You would enter the specific Quick Wins in the appropriate phase of change and area of change. For the current situation you would enter the impacts of the problems in the areas. In the last column the entries are changes from implementing the new system and changing the process. At the bottom of the table are performance measures. These include costs, benefits, risks, and time. The table entries are the impacts for the total of the changes in the areas for the specific column.

Once you have completed this table with the business users involved, you can perform trade-offs. Changes can be moved between columns and then you can "total" the impacts in the performance measures.

Area of Change	Current	After Quick Wins 1	After Quick Wins 2	After Quick Wins X	Future Environment
Performance Measures					
Cost					
Benefits					
Risk					
Time					

Figure 10.5 Structure of the change implementation strategy

Note that in traditional systems projects, this table would consist of three columns: area, current, and future. The rows of areas of change would be one—IT. This reveals how much more comprehensive change management can make in the project. Bigger scope is traded off against a higher likelihood of success.

What are the benefits of the implementation strategy? First, the employees see the roadmap for change. There will be fewer surprises. Second, using the table helps as a communications tool with the management. Third, if change is successful, you can move forward more of the later Quick Wins.

Implement Quick Wins

Following the change implementation strategy, you make the first series of Quick Win changes. What next? Do not even think of implementing the new wave of changes. Instead, you should measure the results of what has been changed. How do you do this? Have the business employees do it. Then they own it. They move to embrace change. Start with individual transactions and have them do a comparison of old and new. Include here the following:

- How the problems in the old process were addressed;
- How the impacts of the problems were mitigated;
- What benefits were achieved through the change;
- What surprises did they encounter in the changes.

You use this information to not only plan for the future waves of change, you also can use the information as input to the project overall. For example, let's suppose that the Quick Wins generate 80 percent of the benefits of the new system, but at a cost of only 2 percent. Then you might want to do what we have done a number of times. Stop the project since the incremental benefits are not justified by the high cost of the project. What if someone says then that, "We didn't have to do the project in the first place." This is dead wrong. If it had not been for the project, there would have been no change and no benefit.

On the other hand, suppose after waves of Quick Wins, the effort expended was 30 percent of the project cost, but resulted in only 5 percent of the benefits. This could indicate that there is much more resistance than you thought. Also, it could indicate that the project is really much more complex than was planned. In either case, you want to use this information to update the project plan. In extreme cases, you may want to kill the project. Better now than later after all of the expenses.

Implement change upon project completion

Now you are ready to implement the system. Using change management, you would roll out the new system along with changes in policies and procedures, staffing, supervision, workflow, and other factors. Some might say then you cannot determine the true benefits of the system since there are all of these other changes. Not so. The goal of the project is to fix or improve the business situation and process. These other changes are part of the project. The system change and implementation is just but one major component of change.

Recurring change management

Why do we need this section? The project finished and the staff moved on to other work. However, remember that the process, even the new process, begins to deteriorate over time. Therefore, we recommend that you revisit the business process each year to measure it. Use the measurements in Chapter 15 on business processes as a start.

How do you conduct the measurements? Follow a similar course of action that was laid out in the initial data collection. What things are you likely to uncover? Here are some examples from experience.

- New exceptions to the work that surfaced after implementation;
- Substantial staff turnover so that many people did not experience the earlier change and project;
- Additional shadow systems;
- Parts of the process could have reverted back to the old ways due to King and Queen Bees;
- A sense of staff complacency with the new process.

By using the measurements, you can identify new Quick Wins. No, you will not want to implement another new system. However, you could add enhancements to address some of the problems that surfaced.

Although this seems at variance with the standard life cycle of a project, it is really not. By carrying out measurements on a regular basis, you show the business employees that you care. The reviews and additional actions prevent further decay of the process. The key benefit is that this approach improves the business process and work on a cumulative basis. Another benefit is that the business unit employees will realize that importance is given to keeping the business process current with the work. They will be more motivated to continue to support the change.

Cases and examples

Astro Bank

The management of the bank wanted to modernize the system for credit card collections. The project was begun focusing on gathering requirements. When they visited bank branches, they discovered that there were many non-IT problems related to policies, workflow, and procedures. Unfortunately, they ignored these and concentrated on systems. After a great deal of effort and money, a pilot system was deployed for testing. It failed almost immediately because the system did not address the other problems. The project was stopped. Several months later the project was restarted under management pressure. The second time an outside team was brought in and initiated Quick Wins. This led to reduced requirements and eventual success for the new system. As an aside, the new system actually had fewer capabilities than the pilot. Why? Because the Quick Wins mitigated the need for some of the features of the new system.

Questions

1. Why do you think management at Astro paid little attention to the need to consider change management and focus, instead, on IT solutions?

2. Looking back at the history of project management, change management only recently became a concern in IT projects. Discuss some reasons for this.
3. People have attacked the use of Quick Wins or Quick Hits as being temporary and subject to being undone later. How would you respond to this statement?

Arcadia health services

Management had attended marketing seminars by several firms which offered systems to automate patient records. This has been a long-standing dream that only now is becoming reality. In this case it was too soon. IT told management this, but stated that the project should be done anyhow. Why? Because the processes could be improved with or without a new patient records system. The solution was to implement Quick Wins under the project. The project was then stopped as the systems available were too limited.

Questions

1. Assume that you were the IT manager here, how would you expose management to new technologies in a more orderly way?
2. Let's suppose that your group has been very successful with Quick Wins with five departments. A sixth department approaches you to do the same with their processes. They just want some Quick Wins. How do you respond?
3. Assume that you have identified a set of policy and procedure changes for a business process. These will deliver immediate benefit. However, they will later be changed when the new system is installed. Discuss whether you should implement these Quick Wins? Assuming that you go ahead, how would you transition and market changing these again later?

Mapping to the PMBOK and PRINCE2

Both methodologies have similar approaches for change control in a project. PRINCE2 gives more attention to change management than PMBOK. However, for both change management at the end of a project would be considered as one area of the project plan. Thus, all of the techniques in each methodology would apply.

Lessons learned

IT staff are often not oriented toward Quick Wins. Instead, they often assume that the way to fix a process is through IT work. While it is true that systems work will be less prone to deterioration, the IT staff should still be aware and gain some experience in discovering short-term Quick Wins. Try to conduct two exercises with them. The first is to find Quick Wins in processes within IT. The second is to find Quick Wins in a department with whom IT is on good terms.

The problem of getting lasting change is not new. It is as old as civilization. More recently, in the 1920s time and motion studies and industrial engineering defined methods for improving how people did their work. In manufacturing, for example, the detailed ways that workers used tools were examined. Improvements were defined. Changes were implemented by training and motivating the workers. The engineers thought they were successful and moved on to the next department. What happened when they revisited the workers months later? They found that the work had reverted to the old practices. Why did this occur? One reason was that the engineers looked into the work and not the politics of change. They assumed that there would be no resistance since the changes they designed were so logical. Another reason is that they did not consider the drive for productivity. When the workers used the new methods, their work slowed down. Managers told them to speed it up. So they reverted back to the faster, older method. One lesson learned here is that management has to allow time for efficiency to build up after the changes are implemented.

Why not do just Quick Wins? Why go to the effort and expense of an IT project? The answer to these questions is that automation is more stable than manual methods which are subject to the human factors in a department. The lesson learned here is that Quick Wins are often best done in conjunction with an IT project. Here are some other observations:

- You need a project to get sufficient, organized attention to the work. This is preferable to *ad hoc* changes which later can prove to either not work or encounter resistance.
- IT can act as a catalyst for change. IT can overcome the inertia in departments built up over years of work.

Guidelines

Most of the IT staff should receive training in change management and process improvement. We don't mean formal, in-depth training in a method such as Six Sigma. Rather, we want the IT staff to:

- Search for problems in the current business process.
- Be aware of political factors in IT projects.
- Understand that they are likely to encounter resistance to change even when management enthusiastically endorses the IT project.
- Be able to coordinate the identification and implementation of Quick Wins.
- Be able to use the Quick Wins to adjust the requirements for the project.
- Understand the importance of measurement of the work after the project is completed.
- Understand process deterioration and be able to look for signs of it.

Suppose that you wanted to go into a department, analyze the work, and coordinate some Quick Wins. Sounds like a good idea, right? Wrong. You will likely run into resistance. People will almost immediately question the need for change and complain to their managers. The work will stop. A better approach which we have used many times is to start an IT project. People are used to IT projects. They are not surprised. Under the covers of the IT project you start identifying problems in the work, impacts, and Quick Wins. These Quick Wins are implemented and the project ends. Does this seem like a dirty trick? Not really. It is just another political way to achieve change and improvement.

Questions

1. Try the Quick Wins approach on yourself. Look at your apartment or house and see if you can make some improvements without spending a lot of time or money. Examples might be cleaning things up or moving furniture.
2. You can also apply change management to managing your time. Write down how you spend your time. Next, identify things that you wish you could do if you had an extra hour a day. This provides motivation for change. Now examine tasks that you can combine and things that you do that can be eliminated.
3. Research the Web to find an example wherein a new system was implemented, but the benefits failed to be realized. Determine reasons for the lack of benefits in terms of the absence of change.
4. Here is a good discussion question. It seems evident that you must get change from a project in order to reap benefits. So why is it that IT for many years stayed away from change management?
5. Sit back and look at how you spend your time and money now as compared to a year ago. If you have problems remembering what you did a year ago, then you should begin to keep a log of what you do. This can just be a short list. It can be done once a month. Compare last year and today and see if you can detect deterioration—lost time and wasted money.

What to do next

1. Revisit a business process that was affected by a recent IT project. See if you can detect: (1) deterioration of the process; (2) change and benefits that were projected.
2. Consider using the potential for deterioration as one criterion in evaluating potential new projects.
3. Go to a friendly department and work with the staff to understand how the work is performed. See if you can get them to identify potential problems and impacts. Then see if you can get them to define potential solutions.

Summary

In traditional IT thinking, this chapter and the ideas presented herein would seem to be beyond the scope of the project. This is not the case. The goal of any IT project is change. Otherwise, there is little reason to expend the time, money, and resources to stay in the same place. As we have seen, change management can make the IT part of the work simpler by reducing requirements. Change management can also generate more support for lasting change since the employees are more involved in the process of change in the project.

11
Project communications management

Introduction

Everyone communicates all of the time. So why do we need formal project communications management? Here are some reasons:

- If you do not plan the message that you are going to convey, there can be misinterpretation. In everyday life, this can easily be corrected. It is not true in politics, projects, or business.
- The wrong communications can trigger hostility or resistance, making the project leader's job more difficult.
- Team members communicate with business units often during a project. The team member may respond to a requirement request affirmatively without thinking. This can create many problems later for the project leader if what was requested is not feasible or within the scope of the project.

In this chapter, we first cover some basic ground rules for communications and present guidelines. Communications can be informal or formal. We cover this next. The next part of the chapter deals with management, team, and vendor communications. This is followed by a discussion of guidelines for specific types of presentations. The last part of the discussion provides guidance for body language and tone of voice. It is very important that you can "read" people's words and gestures. It is also important that you work on your own body language and tone of voice.

Communicating a message

In communicating a message, you first get an idea. Then you give structure to the thought. The next step is to place the message formally into grammar and structure. On the receiving end, the receiver first perceives the grammar and structure. This is followed by the perception of the idea. The final step is that the receiver understands the message. Here is a fundamental rule:

If the message fails in any way, it is the fault of the sender.

In this section a detailed approach is given for preparing and sending a message. If you apply these to all of your communications, then you would get little done. You have to decide on whether to use these guidelines based on the importance and urgency of the message.

In communicating you have to make some strategic decisions.

- Format. Choices can include: e-mail, call, visit, and so on.
- General length. Long messages can be ignored. Messages that are terse and too short may convey the wrong meaning.
- Method and organization. This concerns how you will unify and put the message together. Do you start with a problem and move to a potential solution, or should you start with the impact of the problem?
- Direction. Where will you begin and end your message?
- Your attitude toward the receiver. This will affect the style of the presentation of the message. Remember that your attitude conveys as much as the message.
- Personal impression. What do you want the receiver to think of you after reading the message?

You are now prepared to make tactical decision regarding the communication. Here are the key areas:

- Evidence. What data and information will be shown as evidence in the message?
- Specific length. You have to allot the space or time to specific parts of the message.
- Tone. This links to the attitude toward the receiver and personal impression you want to leave. The tone tells the receiver what you think of him/her.
- Diction and jargon. You have to decide what vocabulary you will employ. For business people you want to avoid IT jargon, for example.
- Attitude toward the topic of the message. What is your feeling toward the topic? Enthusiasm and indifference are two possibilities here.

How do you determine if the message was received? In verbal communications you receive a response in words, but also you can read signs in their body language and tone of voice.

How do you choose the medium for communications?

Today you have a wide variety of choices for the medium of the message. Our two best mediums are as follows:

- Face-to-face. This is probably the best medium since you get the message, the tone of voice, and body language.
- Voice mail. At least here you can convey the message through tone of voice.

Another political advantage of face-to-face is that there is no record of the conversation until it is being secretly or openly taped.

Turning to the written mediums, the most common mediums are as follows:

- E-mail. People are often flooded with e-mail. It is so convenient. While you cannot restrict it, you can provide guidelines to the team on what is appropriate. Give some examples of bad e-mails as well. Also, make sure that they run the spell checker!
- Internal memoranda. This is the classic form of written communication. With e-mail and other electronic messaging systems, it is dropped way off in use. That should tell that you message might more likely be read if it is in this medium.
- Telephone conferencing. Often, for communicating with groups in remote locations, this is the cheapest and easiest to use instead of video conferencing.
- Video conferencing. The important thing here is to have all locations organized so that the conference can be effective and avoid diversions. A good video conference requires more planning than you think in terms of telephone and e-mail. Video conferencing is useful for technical discussions and lessons learned.
- Instant messaging. Most instant messaging is personal. People want to stay in touch and networked. In projects the messages are often complex and carry nuances and political ramifications. You probably need more characters than instant messaging allows. Of course, if something is urgent and you cannot reach the person by telephone, then this is one is a useful alternative.
- Blogs. Be careful here. You should assume that everyone in the world will read your blog. While you can display your knowledge and experience, you can also turn off people and make mistakes. Blogging requires the same kinds of planning as other message mediums.
- Short text messages. Not really very useful in project management. Also, not everyone uses twitter—they do use telephones and e-mail.

Informal versus formal communications

Informal communications includes personal contact, telephone, e-mail, and so on. Formal communications includes presentations, reports, and written correspondence. From experience, it is useful to keep most communications informal. Restrict the formal presentations to the ones discussed in later sections. However, you should require yourself to make a decision on which type to use—just as you do with the medium.

Informal does not mean unplanned. Informal communications have a greater need for planning since without it the wrong message may be conveyed. Misunderstanding can occur. Without planning you may also show the other person that you did not prepare well. This could mean, to them, that you (1) do not see the communication as important, or (2) that you do not hold them in esteem. Either way—you lose.

Management communications

Meet informally with your manager each week or every other week to give status. This can be done early in the morning in a one-on-one informal setting. A formal meeting is not necessary. What do you discuss?

- Communicate the status of the project(s) in terms of budget and schedule.
- Raise a flag that there are specific issues that must be addressed at some point in the future. Indicate the impact of the issue on the schedules. However, also point out that you are considering several alternative solutions that will be presented to them.

This informal communication can pave the way for considering the issues later in more formal settings. The approach also gives managers a comfort level about the project. They might suggest some actions or remark on some possible changes. All of this goes toward getting them to participate in the project at a management level. Another point is that the manager is less likely to contact you if you maintain steady contact.

Team communications

When you are gathering information on the status of their work or issues, you should go to their office or workspace and meet face-to-face. The body language and voice will likely tell you more about status than their words. Gather status ahead of the project meeting and then summarize the status at the start of the meeting.

In earlier times, people shared offices as there was no such thing as a cubicle. To encourage team communications, consider having team members share the same office space. They can have desks around the sides of a cubicle and a round table in the middle to share ideas. This approach is often in Agile system development.

If people do work in separate cubicles or offices, then you need to take steps to get them to share knowledge with each other. That is the purpose of having project meetings devoted entirely to lessons learned.

Vendor communications

In managing a vendor or multiple vendor relationship, you want to give the greatest attention at the start of work to communications management. This will head off many problems later and make it unnecessary to implement formal communications in the middle of a project.

You want to cover all written and verbal communications between any vendor employees and any employee of your organization. Here is a list of items to address in no particular order:

- How progress information will be conveyed if there are few issues;
- How progress will be conveyed if there are many issues or there is a crisis;
- How issues that are identified will be communicated;
- How knowledge and lessons learned will be handed over;
- How the investigation of issues will be communicated;
- How decisions and actions will be communicated;
- How information on methods, tools, and data will be conveyed;

- How change requests will be conveyed;
- How decisions on change requests will be addressed;
- How staffing changes will be communicated;
- How questions and answers related to business processes, business rules, and requirements will be transferred;
- How to validate that information was received and received correctly.

In discussing these, you want to cover the medium of communication that is preferred along with outlines for each of these if they are available. The outlines reveal what is to be contained in the messages.

In addition, you should provide examples of some common communication problems and simulate with the vendor(s) how communications would work. Here are some examples.

- The vendor suggests using a new method or tool to the organization.
- The vendor uncovers a new problem or issue.
- The customer organization encounters a new issue.
- The vendor staff have technical questions.
- The vendor staff have questions related to business processes.
- Management at the customer organization wants to change the project scope.
- The vendor wants to change work assignments of their people;
- The vendor needs more time to do the work;
- The customer organization encounters problems during testing and integration.

Doing these things consumes a lot of time. However, this is a time well-spent. It will provide structure for all later communications. There will be little or no *ad hoc* communications that can result in surprises and be disruptive to both the work and the customer–vendor relationship.

During the project, you start to notice that either team members or managers are violating the guidelines established at the beginning. Or, that the vendor managers or staff do the same. Don't let it slide. Go back and have the information conveyed in the previously agreed upon structure.

How do you present the project concept?

In this and the following sections we discuss the most common presentations you will likely make for single or multiple projects. Outlines and guidelines are presented. Think of the outlines as templates. These should be standardized across all projects. Why? Go back to the start of the chapter and you see that the receiver of the message first has to perceive the structure of the message presentation. Then the receiver or audience moves to the content of the message. If there is a common structure by presentation type, then the audience gets to the message easier and more quickly. If a variety of outlines or templates are employed by different project leaders, then the audience must first struggle to understand the structure. This takes their time away from the message. Your message is more likely to be misunderstood.

Recall the contents of the project concept from Chapter 5. One way you could present this to management or business units is to use the following outline:

- Background of the project idea;
- The project idea and purpose;
- How the concept was developed;
- Alternative ideas that were considered;
- Details of the project concept.

This might work well in a technical presentation, but it is deadly here. This presentation is marketing and sales oriented. You want a decision of approval so that the plan can be developed and team assembled. The above outline fails since it includes no action items. It also fails because the audience is likely to get bored and turned off in the middle. It may come across as you sell your analysis skills.

Here is a better outline that has been employed many times.

- Purpose of the project. Cut down or out the description. The audience should be aware of this already.
- Impact if the project is not done. This goes to the heart of the matter. What happens if the project is not done?
- Benefits and how they will be validated.
- Cost elements.
- Schedule.
- Potential issues. This is a tool in the presentation to lower expectations to a more realistic level for the project as well as showing what may lie in the future.
- Action items to be taken. Make sure that most of these don't involve money. Asking people for money only may just fuel resistance. By making many actions oriented to doing project planning, data collection, and analysis, you reduce the tension and gain more support.

How do you explain and sell the project plan?

If you did not do the project concept presentation, then you should not present the plan in a dry manner. Instead, present the project concept as discussed above. You can hand out the plan during or at the end of the meeting.

If you did earlier present the project concept, then start with a summary of it to bring people back up to speed. Don't assume they will remember some meeting a few months ago. With that out of the way, you want to show how the project plan supports the project concept. If you start discussing detailed tasks, you will turn them off. Instead, present a high level GANTT chart in which the emphasis is on critical milestones. Then turn to the issues. Go into several of the ones that are likely to occur early in the project as well as a few toward the end. This will prepare them for the issues when they arise. You can then move onto other elements of the project plan including costs, benefits, roles and responsibilities, and other factors. This does not cover all of the items covered in some of the project management methodologies, but your time and their attention span are very limited. Since this is also a marketing presentation, you want to close the presentation with action items involving the first set of tasks and milestones.

Many people think that the marketing and presentation of the project plan is a one-time event. Experience reveals that this is not the case. As a phase of the work in the project is wrapping up, you will probably want to present the plan for the next phase in detail as well as the remaining work on the project.

How do you provide project status?

Systems and technology projects are a challenge for management to understand and grapple with. Many managers lack a technical background. Even if one manager has a technical background, others will not. What can you do? How do you convey information on technical projects to non-technical people? From experience, the use of a standardized one-page form for reporting on each individual project, regardless of size, is a good approach. The areas to cover include the following:

- *Title, purpose, scope, leader, and date.* It is important to always reinforce the purpose and scope of a project because the elapsed time of the project may be long. Management must be kept aware of any changes in requirements to the project.
- *Budget versus actual.* This is a chart that plots the cumulative actual costs of the project as well as planned costs. An example is given in the form.
- *Summary GANTT chart.* This highlights the baseline and actual schedule on the same chart.
- *Key active issues.* This area lists the major open issues that remain unresolved along with their impact if not resolved.
- *Major accomplishments.* This is a list of the major achievements and milestones since the last report.
- *Upcoming milestones.* This lists what achievements and milestones you anticipate in the period.
- *Performance statistics.* This includes: age of the oldest outstanding issues, percent of work remaining with issues and risk, mix of open issues by type, percent complete, and amount of work completed with issues.

At a glance managers can see what is going on with the project. Their eyes will be drawn to the quantitative data first (budget vs. actual and GANTT). Then they will see the issues. This will aid in making them more aware of the issues to be handled. They can analyse the impact of the issues on the work through the mapping of issues to tasks. They can also see the progress that is being made.

What do you do with multiple projects? Well, you already have provided the individual project information. For status you want to show the benefits and impact of the projects as being greater than the sum of the parts.

If the projects have similar structure, then you can develop the following table. This shows the projects listed as rows. The columns are the high-level milestones. The table shows the estimated completion date or code for completion.

Projects	Analysis	Design
Web server development	C	March 31
Data warehouse	February 15	May 5

This is an easy way for management to track milestones.

You can also show common issues by using the following table. The rows are issues and the columns are projects. This table highlights the impact of the issue on the project. A dashed line or blank can be used if the issue has no effect on the project.

	Projects	
Issue	Project 1	Project 2
Issue 1		
Issue 2		

This table shows how the projects link together through the same issues. It will help you in gaining management support for resolving the issue.

A third table shows how projects share common resources. The rows are resources and the columns are projects. The table entry is the quantity and the type of resource being used by the projects. This table helps to show how you are trying to share resources across projects for synergy.

	Projects	
Resources	Project 1	Project 2
Resource 1		
Resource 2		

How do you present issues and risks?

Analyzing issues and the schedule that have been covered. You have information ready to go to management. How do you present it in a manner that will yield support for your proposed actions? Here is an outline of an approach that works:

- Summary of status of project(s);
- Issue(s) to be addressed;
- Impact on the project(s) and business unit if the issue is not addressed;
- Benefit to the project, business unit, and organization if the issue is resolved;
- Alternative approaches for resolution;
- Recommended decision, follow-up actions, and timing.

If this looks like the outline of a television commercial, it is not by chance. Note that nowhere is the technical side discussed. You first get to the issue and its impact. This is like someone with a headache. Next, show the benefits of having a solution. The ad shows how the person feels and looks better with the treatment. You want to show that you did your homework and have considered several alternatives.

Some guidelines are appropriate here. When discussing the impact of the issue, focus on the business side of the impact in terms of delays and effect on business costs. If you consider only the project, the effect will be diminished. The same applies to benefits. With respect to alternatives, consider the following:

- Do nothing. That is, take no action that requires money or slippage. What happens to the schedule? This is the case of restructuring the schedule.
- Throw money at the project. This is the alternative of applying non-personnel resources to the project.
- Apply additional resources to the project.

The decision you recommend will need follow-up actions. These might include reassignment of staff, procuring hardware or software, or getting a consultant or contractor. Have these actions ready to go. You want to be able to act on the decision immediately after the decision has been approved. You don't want to have to come back to management for approval. Keep in mind that there will be a tendency to delay a decision that requires more resources. Managers may not want to take the risk to make a decision. This is countered by the impact of the issue if not resolved.

For multiple projects, you may wish to focus on common issues and resources. Here are some examples:

- A combined GANTT chart that shows the use of a specific resource across several projects.
- A combined GANTT chart that shows the impact as well as resolution of an issue on the projects.

What if the project is now to be changed due to requirements, resources, or some other issue? What do you do? After the presentation to and approval by management, you are now ready to implement the actions and inform the project team or the project leaders. Here are some steps to take:

- Prepare all paperwork related to acquisition of resources immediately, and get it started through the system.
- Prepare a new schedule with the new dates, milestones, tasks, and so on.
- Update the list of issues with what has been decided.

You are now ready to present your plan to the team or group of project leaders. A lesson learned here is to review it first with each manager or team member one-on-one. This will allow them to ask questions and punch holes in what you have done. Then you can present it to the group. Here is an outline of your presentation:

- Summarize the issues and what was being addressed.
- Highlight the impacts again of not getting a solution.

- Present the new schedule, which gives the audience an overall view of the situation.
- Define the specific actions that will be taken and discuss how they impact the audience as well as the schedule.
- Indicate how the actions will be followed up in terms of measurement and actions.
- Just passing out a new schedule does not cut it. You must indicate how you will determine if the actions worked.

How do you deal with a project that should be terminated?

We discuss project termination here because communications are the critical component of termination. Why? Because of the political ramifications and the danger of the "blame game" or scapegoating. In actual work we avoid the term "termination" due to its implications. Instead of terminating a project, often the best approach is to reassign resources and put the project to sleep. Later, it can be restarted if there is a need and there are resources available. By putting a project to sleep, its visibility is diminished. What do you say if people ask, "What happened to the project?" Answer, "Other work had higher priority. We may get back to the project later." This approach is political and should not sound strange. After all, at home everyone starts projects but then stops them because of more urgent and compelling work. Later, you go back and pick up where you left off. One of the authors had a home project to use cement blocks to terrace a hill behind his house. This was a big project. In the end over 1400 blocks were placed. Project work was done during spare time on weekends. The entire project took over 9 months. If it had been given the highest priority, it could have been done in a few weeks. Most of the time the project was asleep.

Sleeping projects are politically useful. There is no blame. People understand urgency. When you wake up a sleeping project, you already have management approval so it can be restarted easier than a new project. Another political benefit is that the wakened project can deal with changed requirements that surfaced during the sleeping period.

A project can run into serious trouble for some or all of the following reasons:

- The number of open, major issues keeps expanding. The key issues do not get resolved.
- Resources are pulled from the project for urgent work. This makes it impossible to finish the project.
- The business conditions or processes changed, negating the need for the project.
- Money runs out.
- Management changes direction and priorities.

How do you proceed to put a project to sleep? The main focus for the team should be on their future work on other projects. This alleviates fear. Another feeling that must be addressed is that the team may feel that their time was wasted. If the project followed our guidelines to include Quick Wins in the business work, then these are milestones that delivered benefits and tangible results. They would not likely have been carried out if there had been no project. Another thing to emphasis is the knowledge and skills they gained through lessons learned and dealing with project issues.

Now suppose that you have to give a presentation of the project to management. This may seem to be a very difficult piece of work. You may get the blame. Should you try and avoid giving this presentation? No. By giving the presentation, you present a view of the project that can be adopted by management. Moreover, you can demonstrate an orderly phase down the work to avoid problems and disruption.

Here is an outline of the project termination and put-to-sleep presentation.

- Revisit the project concept with an emphasis on business need and impact if not done.
- Summarize the work progress to date.
- Highlight the accomplishments and benefits to date including the Quick Wins. This is the business benefit.
- Briefly discuss the lessons learned and experience from dealing with issues. These are the management and technical benefits.
- Cover in a non-political way the changes that have transpired since the project was started.
- Discuss the impact on the business if the project is put to sleep.
- Cover the reassignment of team members to new work.
- Present the plan for termination in an orderly manner.

Should you expect to make this presentation often? No. Of course not. However, you should be ready and have an approach. We developed this method and then applied it not just to kill projects, but also when a project required major change to meet new business requirements. When we have assumed the role of the IT manager, we have commonly terminated 30 percent or more of the current projects. Why? To free up resources for more urgent work. Because of the lack of progress and issues.

How do you give project results?

The previous section is useful, but also has a negative tone. Let's go positive now. You have the project completed. The world is great and you are going to present the project results to management. Here is a common outline for this type of presentation.

- Original purpose of the project;
- How the project was accomplished;
- Summary of the costs;
- Summary of the schedule;
- Benefits of the project.

At first glance, this looks OK, but it has a number of problems. How were the benefits validated? What change in the business occurred? Does the business unit buy into these benefits? Another problem is that management is not really interested in how the project was accomplished—most of the time they are interested in results.

Who should give this presentation? Not the project leader for the entire presentation. The leader of the presentation should come from the business unit that got the benefits. The business unit is far more credible than the project leader with management.

To address these and other issues, here is another template used many times. Who presents each point is given.

- Business purpose of the project—business
- Summary of the problems in the work—business
- Example transaction done in the old way—business
- Example transaction done after the project—business
- Benefits of the project in business terms—business
- How the benefits were validated—business
- Summary of costs, schedules, issues—presented by the project leader
- Lessons learned from the project—business.

There are a number of advantages of this template. One is the tone, and thrust of the presentation is from the business. They are the stakeholders and owners of the project as well as the business work. Another is that by summarizing the old problems, the audience can see why the project was important. A third point is the use of examples. This is widely used on television—before and after examples. An example demonstrates both the change and difference in the work, as well as the tangible benefits. Not only are benefits covered, but also how they were measured and validated. The lessons learned are given to show that experience has been gathered and will be used on later work and projects to make improvements.

Guidelines for body language and voice

Studies show that body language and tone of voice convey about 90 percent of your message. The rest is the actual words that are spoken or read. Space limitations do not allow for a complete discussion of these. Here we will concentrate on guidelines for specific attitudes. When considering body language and voice, there are several factors to consider:

- The context of the communications. This includes the setting, nature of relationships between the parties communicating, expectations, and time of day.
- Non-verbal messages should be grouped in clusters—not single signs.
- How the voice, words, and body language align and combine. This is called "congruence".
- The variation of meaning in different cultures.
- Knowledge from previous contacts. You would use your past contact experience as a guide to evaluate what is going on now.

You should apply these to meetings, interviews, reviews of work, and presentations. How should you apply and use these guidelines? Start with yourself. Look in the mirror and give a presentation. Another parallel action is to be more aware of body language and tone of voice in meetings. Write down what you are observing and then review. Note that these are general guidelines. You would probably not take any action without further thought or investigation. However, the guidelines could tip you off to a problem or issue very early.

- *Defeat and frustration*. A lowered head is a negative signal that communicates acceptance of defeat. Running fingers through hair can mean that someone is frustrated. Other signs are narrowing eyes with the eyebrows brought together, mouth turned down at the corners with the chin pulled up. People who feel insulted, caught-out, or threatened will likely break eye contact. Tapping or drumming fingers communicates impatience or frustration.
- *Dishonesty*. A false smile will often only engage the lips, and will be fairly symmetrical or larger on the left side. Lowering the eyes is a sign of submission, fear, or guilt. The person may have little or no body movement. People will sometimes "freeze", not quite facing the other person, and will move as little as possible during the lie. Alternatively, some people will fight this by being overly dramatic, moving the body much more than normal to try and "sell" the lie. Nervous movement will attract our attention especially when we are not used in seeing those movements during conversation with someone we know. They can also exhibit front-back movement of the body, either in a sitting or standing position. The sudden change of position may also indicate lying or untruthfulness. For example, if someone is sitting cross-legged, but when replying to our question changes his or her feet position. The process of lying even for the professionals causes inconvenience. So the body does not feel convenient, and thus changing positions is a very telling sign that someone is lying. For example, unconscious movements of the hands or feet, such as shaking the legs, shaking hands on the table, tight squeezing of the hands, and pressing the thighs together. Another sign of dishonesty is if the person is sitting and turns the feet in another direction from the other person.
- *Indifference*. Handshakes that are weak with lack of energy used by passive or apathetic people. Another sign is if they extend one leg over the arm of a chair they're sitting on. When they do this, it may also mean that they are apathetic, disinterested, or unconcerned. A backward lean while seated could indicate that the person is cocky, arrogant, lazy, or apathetic. Sitting or leaning back, and not facing the subject who is speaking can show an apathetic attitude.
- *Confidence*. Looking directly into another person's eyes without staring signifies self-assurance. A person may push their shoulders back to demonstrate their power and signify that they don't fear attack. Positioning hands behind the back shows that someone is relaxed and comfortable; though it can also be used on purpose to convey a message of power and confidence. Walking briskly with an upright posture shows confidence. The wider a person's feet are positioned from each other, the more dominant and powerful they feel. Sitting with legs open, apart means that a person is comfortable and is feeling secure in their surroundings. The "figure-of-four cross" occurs when one ankle is placed on top of the other legs' knee, with the top leg's knee pointing sideways; this signals confidence and power.
- *Resistance*. Someone may touch or slightly rub their nose if they are doubtful about what is being said or if they are rejecting an idea. People often pinch the bridge

of their nose and close their eyes when making a negative evaluation. A person with folded or crossed arms is placing a barrier between themselves and their surroundings; indicating that they're not happy with what is being said or done. Open arms, particularly when combined with showing palms, can imply acceptance. Crossed legs can be either a negative, defensive position or a relaxed, comfortable one; it depends on how tense a person's leg muscles are.

- *Trustworthy*. A genuine smile engages the whole face (including the eyes) and is usually larger on the right side. Upward facing palms signify that a person's defenses are down and that they're speaking sincerely with an open heart. Open palms occasionally touching the chest imply honesty. Leaning of the torso towards an individual can send differing signals based on accompanying gestures, no matter how small. Combining a forward lean with a smile offers the impression of warmth and sincerity.
- *Interested*. A tilted head symbolizes interest in someone or something. The occasional nod from a listener to a speaker is a positive message; it's an indication that they are listening and are interested. People place their hand on their cheek when they're thinking or evaluating. A widening or brightening of a person's eyes shows an increased interest in a situation or conversation.
- *Bored*. Too much nodding implies that a listener has lost interest, is not really listening, and is simply nodding to be polite. A person who consistently looks around them is bored with a situation/conversation. Fiddling with objects such as pens, pencils, or keys can be a sign of nervousness or anxiety. Alternatively, it may be done as a result of boredom or impatience. A slightly kicking or bouncing foot when sitting with crossed legs suggests boredom or impatience.
- *Hostility*. Projecting the chin towards another person demonstrates defiance or aggression. Running fingers through hair can mean that someone is frustrated. Projecting the chin towards another person demonstrates defiance or aggression. If the side of the mouth is raised in a sneer or smirk, it may mean contempt. Lowered eyebrows, wrinkled forehead, and tensed eyelids and lips could imply anger. Staring is interpreted as aggression and implies that a person feels dominant and powerful. Sizing up a person by looking at them from head to toe is associated with assessing them as a potential threat. A pulled back chest with forward curled shoulders is a defensive position taken by people who want others to know that they are no threat to them. Finger pointing is interpreted as either a sign of assertiveness or a sign of aggression. Standing with hands on hips expresses either readiness or aggression.

Now here are some guidelines relating to your voice.

- Vary the pitch of your voice. Avoid the dreaded monotone by raising and lowering your voice to emphasize or de-emphasize certain points of what you are saying.
- Employ a soft volume. Nobody wants to be yelled at, so speak just a little softer that you normally would, especially when talking to someone who is physically close to you.
- Adopt a relaxed tone. If there is tension in your throat or chest, your voice will sound hoarse and forced, almost as if you have laryngitis. Relax your upper body,

including your shoulders, neck, and abdominal muscles, and your voice will sound more gentle and pleasant.

- Pause before emphasizing an important word or concept. Doing that will make you punch out what comes next to show the audience this is important.
- Speed up your rate to show excitement. Speeding up will invariably make the tone of voice more urgent and compelling.
- View in your mind the message you are telling. This will translate into your vocal quality. That is why a person who retells a story of an event that just happened will tell it with more excitement in the voice because the picture of the event is still fresh in his or her mind. Train yourself to relive the story as you tell it and you will see a difference in your tone of voice.
- Define a place in your speech that might be considered a "wow" factor for the audience. When you get to that point, the audience will think, "Wow! I did not realize that!" If you can anticipate that point in the speech, you will be more likely to put punch into the tone of voice as you speak and your content will impact your audience with greater effect.
- Include vivid facial expression or bigger gestures when you get to an emotional or dramatic part of your presentation. More expressive body movement will often be reflected in the tone of your voice.
- Include dialogue in your speech. Narrating a conversation will cause you to vary speaking rate and volume to accommodate the different characters in your story so that your tone of voice will be more expressive.
- Make sure you are breathing from the diaphragm. Many people are shallow breathers. This can cause the voice to sound strident.
- Drink lots of water to keep the voice sounding pleasant all day long. The ordinary person uses up a quart of water an hour. When you talk all day long on the phone, it is important to keep the vocal cords lubricated.
- Sit up straight. Posture does affect breathing.
- Use gestures to make your voice sound energetic. It is especially important to use gestures when you are tired. They will give your voice additional power and will help you to emphasize words or phrases to get your point across.
- You automatically warm up the tone of your voice when you smile. Your audience will notice the difference. Keep a mirror on your desk and notice if you are smiling while talking.
- If your voice is particularly high or low, exercise the range of your voice by doing a sliding scale. You can also expand the range of your voice by singing.
- Record your voice and play it back. Would this be a voice that says, "I care?"

Cases and examples

Sycamore University

One of the authors assumed management of IT at Sycamore. Previously, there had been four different IT managers in 2 years. Projects were in a mess. Communications was all *ad hoc*. While we gave much of our attention to the organization, business units, and projects, as much work was put into structuring communications. Just a few of the communications problems were as follows:

- Business unit staff made *ad hoc* requests of programmers and other IT staff.
- Each presentation was prepared from scratch by employees without outlines or templates.
- The number of meetings in IT was very excessive. It seemed that a meeting was going on all of the time. This affects work output substantially. As an example, if eight people are in a one-hour meeting, you lose a day's worth of work.

A first step was to implement more structured communications within IT. To deal with the excessive meetings, one of the conference rooms was turned into cubicles. Employees had to report how much of their time was spent in meetings. This made them aware of the amount of time consumed by the meetings. In addition, the request for use of a conference room had to be accompanied by a statement of purpose and what was likely to result. Meetings dropped off dramatically. Productivity rose.

Dealing with business units was more complex. One-on-one meetings were held with the business unit and department managers who were the worst offenders of direct IT staff contact. Rather than insisting on change and directing change, a more effective approach was to demonstrate the impact of excessive communications and avoid IT managers. To measure the extent of contact, progress reports prepared for business unit managers listed each direct contact out of channels. This fixed the problem.

Questions

1. What if the communications problems had not been addressed systematically but instead had been treated one at a time as they arose; what would have been the impact on IT and the business units?
2. Some business unit managers had grown used to direct contact with IT staff. It had become a habit. When the new structure was put in place, several of the managers resisted? How would you respond to this resistance?
3. Some of the technical staff in IT lacked communication and writing skills. In addition to providing training, what other steps could you take to improve these skills?

Mapping to the PMBOK and PRINCE2

The PMBOK

The PMBOK devotes Chapter 10 to project communications management. There are five parts considered:

- Identify stakeholders. As part of identification the goals of the stakeholders are defined along with their relative power and interest. These were discussed also in Chapters 5, 8, and 9 in this book. It is important that you identify not only high-level stakeholders, but also business employees who are heavily involved in the business processes affected by the project.

- Plan communications. Here a communications approach is determined. This has been discussed at length in this chapter.
- Distribute information. This part covers the choice of media, presentation techniques, style of writing, and facilitation techniques. It is difficult to find a balance between providing too little and too much information. If too little is provided, the audience can feel frustrated. If there is too much, the audience can get confused and take no action. Answer the question, "What is the minimum amount of information needed?" This will head off going into excessive technical details, for example.
- Manage stakeholder expectations. After identification and project work starting, you have to manage expectations. One way to dampen expectations is through issues management. Here issues discussions help prevent and deter the raising of expectations. We discussed other techniques relative to scope in Chapter 5.
- Report performance. This is the process of gathering and distributing project performance information. Project tracking and reporting were covered in Chapter 9. What information is provided on project status is critical. For example, if you just provide budget and schedule performance information, the audience may get the impression that everything is fine. Also, these are relatively boring figures. By including issues information, you raise their level of interest. Moreover, they will get a more complete view of the project status.

PRINCE2

Communications are addressed in many parts of PRINCE2 during each phase of the project. Particular attention is given to the communications management strategy. This contains the means and frequency of communication within and outside of the project. It includes: communications procedures, tools and methods, records, reporting, timing, and roles and responsibilities. Quality criteria are also provided. This includes identification of stakeholders, communication standards, formality, and frequency of communications.

Lessons learned

Project meetings can cover very sensitive topics and issues. Misunderstanding sometimes occurs as a result of errors in the meeting minutes. It is no surprise that for years as project leaders we have taken the notes at the meetings and distributed them. You should consider doing the same.

Earlier in the book it was recommended that project meetings should cover lessons learned and issues. Let's expand on this. Often, there is a tendency to make decisions on issues after they have been discussed. This is natural in that team members and people in general like closure. Making decisions on issues unless they are urgent can result in the following problems:

- The wrong decision or actions are decided upon. These then have to be undone later. The result is wasted effort and a lack of credibility.

- There is insufficient information available to make the decision.
- Emotional factors can enter easily into the discussions affecting the decision.

So, most often, in meetings you should seek inputs from the team and discuss these. Unless, there is a true emergency or urgency, the decision can be put off. To make the team comfortable you should point out this approach at the first project meeting.

A useful expense for a project is to have the team attend a short class on body language and voice. Why? Because the team members will interact with business units, management, and vendors. You want them to be better prepared. We have done in every IT group and every project we have managed. In foreign countries, you would bring in a local instructor. The instruction should include simulations and conversations where the team members demonstrate what they have learned. In later one-on-one and project meetings, you should have team members cover both body language and voice.

In some presentations, the speaker indicates at the start that questions will be taken at the end of the presentation. Avoid this. Take questions any time. Yes, it can interrupt the presentation and there is a danger of being sidetracked. However, there are more benefits to doing it this way. First, the audience will be more involved and interested. Second, they will not get frustrated if they have to wait until the end. Third, you can get an opportunity to demonstrate your knowledge, expertise, and enthusiasm.

Here are several lessons learned for presentations. Presenters of formal presentations are often told to keep the number of words on a slide to a minimum. This can later lead to misunderstandings about the meaning of the slide. This is particularly true for the people who could not attend the presentation. Make sure each bulleted point expresses a complete thought.

Another idea is to dry run the presentation with the project team first. One benefit is that they feel more involved in the project. Second, they understand what the project leader is presenting so that they will be better prepared if business unit staff or managers ask questions about the presentation. Some business managers we know make it a point to ask team members about the presentations. Why? To see how much the project leader communicates with his or her team.

A third political lesson learned is to make one-on-one presentations to individual managers. By doing this you get them involved. Questions get addressed before the meeting. A rule of thumb is to do this for at least half of the audience up to, say, five or six people. This will also head off surprise questions. Another benefit is that you present the slides tailored to their interests and perspectives.

Guidelines

As a project leader you should emphasize the types and volume of communications that are useful and appropriate. Don't discuss political or sensitive issues through written correspondence. Such things cannot only be distracting, but also damaging to the project and team members. If you find that the volume of messages among the team grows too much, then step in. Communications is essential and critical, but too much of it takes time and effort away from work. It is also distracting.

Many project leaders want to be able to instantly communicate with team members all of the time. This can be distracting. Moreover, some project leader start to communicate excessively. In some projects we turned around, the former project leader had distracted the team members from their work too much. Another tip—suggest that they don't leave their cell phones on all of the time. They can become interrupt-driven—another distraction from work. If there is a deadline pressure, encourage them to not answer calls, but to let them go to voice mail. They can then check their messages every half an hour or so. Again, a project leader cannot enforce these as rules, but can suggest them as guidelines.

On e-mail, the project leader and team should not respond instantly to each e-mail. They may not send the appropriate response. Messages need to be planned. Unless some mail is truly urgent, it can wait for an hour or so. If you show you are always available, you may convey the impression that either you are not interested in what you are doing, or that what you are doing is not that important. Studies have shown that many recipients discard e-mail based on the title of the message. Thus, you should and your team should carefully phrase the title of the message. If it is too general or vague, or if it does not appear to affect the interests of the receiver, it will more likely be dumped. When people open an e-mail, the system typically displays a few lines. The reader then scrolls down to read the rest of the message. Make sure that your message is conveyed at the start of the e-mail.

In most books and courses, you are taught that you must gain approval of the concept before starting the project plan. You can't start work on the project until the project plan is approved. This sequential approach can delay the project due to the time for review and approval. Here is a political guideline. While you are doing the project concept, start work on the plan so that you can either refer or show management that there is momentum gathering. You can do the same with the project plan. Here some analysis could be performed. In process improvement as well as IT-focused projects, you can determine some Quick Wins. This will gain more support for the project and, again, show momentum.

Questions

1. Taking the discussion of body language and voice, research the Web to find additional guidelines. Apply the guidelines in this chapter and others you gather to your classes, family members, and others. You want to increase your awareness of body language and voice and be able to rapidly interpret this information.
2. Before you give any presentation, give it in front of a mirror. Video tape yourself. For telephone calls, record the conversation and review your own voice. Save these. Then review them several months later to see if there has been an improvement.
3. Assess your own communications by keeping a log of how many times you have to repeat or clarify an earlier message. This will help you improve your future communications.
4. Select one day and apply the steps in planning and decision-making for all of your telephone calls and e-mails. This will take time, but you will instill in your mind the steps so that your communications will be more effective.

5. When you are preparing for job interviews, here are some steps to take. Interview yourself or have a friend do it in front of a mirror before your first interview. If you have had much interviewing experience, then you should select the first two to three firms for being interviewed as the ones that will not likely hire you. Why do this? It can be depressing. Not at all. You are using these interviews to gain experience and skill for the later interviews that really count. You might practice your interview skills by applying for part-time work as well.

What to do next

1. Review your current project and evaluate communications with the team and management. What issues arose? What was the impact of the problems? Develop guidelines for communications that you can implement for the remainder of the project term.
2. Review how progress is reported and communicated for multiple projects and even the project portfolio. Is there a standard structure being used by all.
3. Once you have identified communications problems, propose the use of templates for all formal presentation.

Summary

Of all of the chapters in this book, communications management is one that should rank as among the most important. Don't wait until the end of the class or the end of the project to use this material. Start immediately—if not sooner. Once you feel that you are communicating more effectively, then you will gain more self-confidence and self-assurance. Remember that your communications skills can always be improved. Never become complacent. As with the major theme of this book, strive for cumulative improvement.

12
Project risk management

Introduction

Let's first examine the risks in a project and the issues behind these that give rise to the risks. As was stated earlier, the term "risk" has many different meanings. So it is appropriate that we begin with some definitions.

- An *issue* is a potential or actual problem or opportunity in a project. Part five of the book addresses many commonly encountered issues in IT projects.
- Project *risk* is the impact of the issue on the project and the organization.

These are related since the issue is the cause and the risk is the effect. Thus, when dealing with risk, we must address issues. That will be how we get at the risks, which can be fuzzy.

Mathematically, risk is the multiplication product of the likelihood of an event occurring and the exposure or loss if the event occurs. Let's examine each of these. The likelihood of an event occurring is the likelihood that substantial or significant issues will surface. A significant issue is one that if not treated will have a major impact on the project schedule and/or cost. The exposure or loss is reduced if we have taken steps to minimize losses. These steps include handling issues.

Let's take an example outside of IT. Suppose that you live in a house in the hills surrounded by brush. The risk is fire damage. The issues include the following: too much brush around the house, a wooden roof that can catch fire easily, and the lack of a sprinkler system for the roof and yards around the house. To reduce the likelihood of the fire, you would clear the brush, put on a flame retardant roof, and install a sprinkler system. Now turn to exposure. To reduce loss, you could buy a fireproof safe for critical papers. You could store things in a more secure location off of the property. You could make copies of documents, photos, and videos and store originals off-site. That will reduce the loss of replacing these things if fire should occur.

It is the same in IT projects. If you identify potential issues in a project at the start, you are better prepared to deal with the issues if and when they arise. You can also take preventative steps to ensure that the issue never arises. By doing this you effectively reduce the likelihood of a problem since you are prepared. You also reduce exposure through the preparation. Some issues are almost certain to appear. These include, as examples, the following:

- Changes in requirements and scope of work.
- Unexpected loss of team members due to illness, other work, and other factors.
- High management expectations.
- Resistance to change.

Each project is unique. However, many, if not most, are, in general, the same.

If you have a systematic and organized approach to manage issues, there will be fewer lingering issues that create havoc later in the project. You address the issues that are the most urgent in terms of their impact on the project and organization in a timely manner. These actions serve to reduce exposure to risk. Taken all together the approach minimizes risk.

Keep in mind that you never eliminate all issues. Thus, you cannot eliminate project risks. It is the same with your life. You cannot eliminate all risks from driving a car unless you stop driving. Then you encounter other risks and issues related to walking, riding on an airplane, train, subway, or bus.

The organization of this chapter is as follows. The next section defines a proven and effective approach to risk and issues management. This is followed by sections that address specific areas of project risk management in more detail. Note that this discussion partially overlaps materials in Chapters 5, 8, and 9. We have a separate chapter on project risk management due to its importance across the project portfolio.

Risk can arise most often from something negative—one or more problems. However, it can also arise out of a positive opportunity. For example, you want to exploit some new technology. This involves risks due to lack of expertise. Thus, issues include both problems and opportunities.

Issues and risks relate to lessons learned. As you deal with and resolve an issue, you gain experience. From the experience you can add and refine the lessons learned. In reverse, you use the lessons learned to help investigate issues. By linking issues and lessons learned, you will find that the lessons learned are more accessible. Also, some people view issues in a negative way. Lessons learned are positive and so offset the negative feelings.

Since many issues are recurring and lessons learned can be applied to multiple projects, it is a good idea to establish databases for both. There are several interrelated databases for each.

Some comments on the preparation of these databases are appropriate. If time is limited, you could employ spreadsheets. You could also start with a limited number of data elements. Of the tables related to issues, the general one and the project issue database are the most important and a minimum to get started. On the lessons learned databases, these could come later. However, you want to give structure to lessons learned in order to achieve cumulative improvement in project performance.

These databases are maintained by the project management coordinator or, in some organizations, the Project Management Office (PMO). This is discussed more in the next section in Step 1. The first database is general (see Figure 12.1). Issues are mapped to each other in Figure 12.2 and to lessons learned in Figure 12.3.

- Issue identifier
- Issue title
- Issue description. This should be a paragraph that defines the issue in detail so it will not be confused with others.
- Type of issue. This would be chosen from a list including software, hardware, network, management, vendor, business process, business user, and so on.
- Date the issue was created. This is also the date the issue was entered in the database.
- Who created the issue. This can be a good source of more detail.
- General impact if the issue is not addressed.
- Importance of the issue on a scale of 1–5 (1—low, 5—high).
- Reason for rating of importance.
- How to prevent the issue.
- How to detect the issue.
- Potential decisions for the issue.
- Potential actions for the issue.

Potential areas or types of issues include the following:

- Management;
- Business units in general;
- Business employees;
- Business processes;
- Vendors;
- Technology infrastructure;
- Application systems;
- Hardware;
- Network;
- Security;
- System development;
- Software packages;
- Maintenance;
- Operations;
- Enhancements;
- Government regulations and rules;
- Marketplace and competition.

Figure 12.1   General issues and risk database elements

- Issue identifier-from
- Issue identifier-to
- Relationship between issues
- Comments on relationship

Figure 12.2   Issues mapped to issues

- Issue identifier
- Lesson learned identifier
- How the lesson learned applies to the issue
- Comments on the relationship

Figure 12.3   Issues mapped to lessons learned database elements

The database in Figure 12.4 can be employed to generate tables and reports of issues across multiple projects and the project portfolio. The data elements in Figure 12.5 support the tracking of issues.

- Project identifier
- Issue identifier
- Status of the issue in the project (open, closed, potential, inactive, or combined)
- As of date for the status of the issue
- Date the issue was identified for the project
- Who applied the issue to the project
- Importance or urgency of issue to project on a scale of 1–5 (1—low, 5—high)
- Reason for importance. This is statement of the impact on the project if the issue is not resolved
- Who the issue is assigned to
- Decisions made about the issue
- Reasons for decisions
- Actions taken on the issue
- Comments on the issue vis-a-vis the project

Figure 12.4   Project-specific issues and risk database elements

- Project identifier
- Issue identifier
- Date of entry
- Who entered the data
- Action taken
- Results achieved
- Comments

Figure 12.5   Project-specific issue tracking database elements

Figures 12.6–12.8 address lessons learned. The first two should be read only access except for the project manager coordinator. The third is open to anyone for inputs.

- Lesson learned identifier
- Area of the lesson learned
- Title of the lesson learned
- Content of the lesson learned
- Guidelines in implementing the lesson learned
- Anticipated results from using the lesson learned
- Definition of success in using the lesson learned
- Importance rating for the lesson learned on a scale of 1–5 (1—low, 5—high)
- Reason for importance rating
- Date the lesson learned was created
- Who created the lesson learned
- Comments

Potential areas of lessons learned include the following:

- Project concept
- Project requirements
- Project management
- Development
- Testing
- Integration
- Business process change
- Business units
- Management
- Vendor relations
- Documentation
- Quick Wins
- Change

Figure 12.6   General lessons learned database elements

- Lesson learned identifier
- Project template identifier
- Tasks in template identifier
- How lesson learned applies
- Comments

Figure 12.7   Lessons learned mapping to project template tasks

- Lesson learned identifier
- Date of update
- Who provided the update
- Guidelines and comments
- Suggested action

Figure 12.8   Update activity log for lessons learned database elements

What is an effective risk management approach?

This section contains a proven seven-step approach to establish issues and risk management. As you read this, you might wonder how you can sell this to busy managers. Here are the benefits to stress:

- Project leaders. They will be able to gain help in identifying and resolving issues due to the analysis and the databases. Issues will be more standardized so that there should be less time and fewer misunderstandings in explaining and dealing with the issues.
- Project team members. They become more aware of issues and so will start to surface more to their respective project leaders and supervisors.
- IT management and general management. They will see quantitatively how issues are impacting projects and where decisions are needed.
- Business unit managers and employees. They can view the importance of resolving issues and questions in a timely manner since they see the schedule impact of the issues through the work tasks and milestones they impact.
- Vendors. This approach applies to vendor management. Shared issues are employed. Through the analysis and statistics, a project leader can apply pressure on a vendor to resolve an issue.

Step 1: designate a coordinator for issues and lessons learned

In most organizations this need not be a full-time job. A better approach is to assign the role to a project leader. Every 6 months thereafter you can rotate the role between different project leaders. This will give all of the project leaders experience with issues analysis. Here are the responsibilities of the coordinator:

- Gather issues and lessons learned from project leaders and team members.
- Update and maintain the issues and lessons learned databases.
- Provide support in the development of project concepts to identify potential issues.
- Support and review the mapping of issues to tasks in the project plans.
- Provide advice on dealing with specific issues.
- Review progress reports on issues and recommend actions.
- Perform issues and risk analysis across multiple projects and the project portfolio.

Since templates and work breakdown structures are related to issues and lessons learned, you might add the following duties to the role:

- Maintain and update project templates and the work breakdown structures.
- Provide templates and work breakdown structures to project leaders.
- Provide advice to project leaders on tasks and milestones.

Some organizations have an existing PMO. In these instances, the activities listed above would fall under its role and responsibilities.

Step 2: collect issues and lessons learned from current and past projects

Don't wait for new projects to come along to get started on this. Start identifying issues and lessons learned from recent and currently active projects. How do you do this? Get the project leaders together in a meeting and create with them a list of issues. In this way, you will not only get a list of issues, but also you will come to know which issues are shared by multiple projects. We did this for a logistics firm in Singapore. There were four IT groups that operated separately to serve customers in different Asian countries. There had been little communication between the groups. Each had felt that they had individual issues. The meeting revealed that they shared most of the same issues. The differences lay in the countries, customers, and individual project characteristics. Figure 12.9 gives a list of the issues uncovered in two 3 hour sessions.

Customer-related issues

- Appropriate subject matter expert
- Available resources are too limited
- Customers are slow to respond to questions
- The customer team members are not open to change
- The customer team members do not know the quality of the data
- The customer team members are not qualified and are too junior
- The customer does not use the fields they have correctly
- The customer does not agree to bring down the system for work
- The customer does not sign off
- There is a lack of understanding of business rules
- There is a big surprise when you demonstrate work
- Insufficient customer resources are available
- There is a lack of information on their current system
- There are language translation problems
- There is lack of their understanding of the business
- There are too many requirement changes
- The wrong assumptions were made
- Senior customer users resist change
- There are billing disputes for additional work
- Customer staff assigned to the project are too busy to participate
- Customer staff disagree with each other
- The customer lacks standardized procedures
- Upper management in the customer firm has conflicts with their own staff
- There is a lack of agreement on the schedule of work
- Business staff put pressure on to get immediate results
- There is a lack of tracking of issues
- There is insufficient time to generate test data

Management-related issues

- There is staff turnover in their IT or business units
- There are language communication issues

Figure 12.9 Sample list of initial issues

- Outstanding issues and problems are not treated as high priority
- Customer management has unrealistic expectations
- The customer does not adequately fund the project work
- The customer assigns the wrong people
- Management does not give the project priority
- Delays in related projects delay the work
- There is no follow-up by the customer management after decisions have been made
- There is significant management change in the customer organization

Project management-related issues

- There is too much detail in the plan
- The customer and our team keep different plans
- The purpose of the project was not clear from the start
- The facilities of the project are not conducive to work
- The tasks are more sequential than planned
- The scope of the project is expanding
- People and management are resistant to changing the plan
- The project scope is not clear
- There is no organized approach to deal with contingencies

Technical-related issues

- There is too much rework in the project
- Data to be converted is not current
- Excessive manual data entry is required
- The old system lacks documentation
- There are too few people with detailed knowledge of the old system
- Some of the source code of the old system is lacking
- There is a lack of understanding of best practices
- The range of test data is insufficient
- Program modules do not function properly
- The test environment does not realistically represent the production setting
- There is poor sample data
- The quality of work is an issue

Vendor-related issues

The firm employs outside programmers. Here are some of the related issues.

- The vendor misunderstands requirements
- The quality of vendor work is poor
- The vendor does not follow standard methods
- The vendor fails to follow up on issues and problems
- The vendor does not meet the schedule and frequently requests more time
- There is miscommunication between the vendor manager and their own staff

Figure 12.9   (Continued)

- A vendor who will do the work for the desired price cannot be found The vendor went out of business before the work was finished
- The vendor contract is unworkable
- The vendor does not share information with internal employees
- The vendor is not willing to work on joint tasks with internal employees
- The vendor staff turnover is too high
- The vendor uses different methods or tools than we do

Figure 12.9   (Continued)

It is important that the project leaders and IT supervisors participate in a joint approach. If the coordinator or PMO staff does this one-on-one, there will be no discussion of the issues between different managers. If it is carried out in a meeting format, then they will collaborate, share information, and arrive at consensus on the definition of an issue.

Once you have held several meetings, then you can circulate the list. Feel free to add issues from this book, the Web, or other sources. You should end up with 80–150 issues. Don't try to be exhaustive.

When you look at the list, you can see that most of the issues are external to the project and fall into the areas of the customer, management, and the vendor. This came as a surprise to the project leaders in the meeting who had previously thought that most issues were technical or project related. They began to understand why their projects were frequently in trouble and that it took too long to resolve issues. Why? Most of the issues were outside of the project and so outside of their control. A final comment here. It has been 3 years since this list was developed. Since that time only five new issues have emerged. These were technical.

Step 3: establish the issues and lessons learned databases

This step follows the earlier discussion that defined the databases. This step does not mean just data entry. You want to start identifying the importance, preventive steps, means of detection, potential decisions, and possible actions. You can ask, "What can happen if you don't address the issue?" The answer will help get a handle on urgency and impact if not addressed.

Here are some tips on how to do this step. Circulate groups of issues to each project leader. Ask them to comment on the items in the preceding paragraph. Then conduct meetings to review groups of issues by areas such as those listed after Figure 12.1. You will have gaps. People will only have limited time. You can fill in more later.

Step 4: map issues and risks to tasks in current projects

With the issues and risks in hand, you can associate these to tasks in the project plans. The reason for doing this is to highlight which issues have the greatest urgency. Another reason is to make the project leader and team more aware of issues.

To perform this step, you could just hand project leaders a list of issues and their descriptions and ask them to do the mapping and hand this back to you. A bad idea. Project leaders have too much to do and this could waste time. A better method is to go to one project leader who is senior and do the mapping with them. If they have limited time, you could come with a candidate or "strawman" mapping for them to review and correct. When you do this, you can then identify missing tasks and issues that can be put in the plans and the issues lists.

Next, go to a junior project leader and follow the same approach. What is the benefit of this two-step method? You can start to see some of the areas where additional collaboration and training are needed. You would proceed to distribute to the other project leaders the following:

- Directions and suggestions;
- List of issues and their descriptions;
- Several sample project plans with the mapping.

How do you incorporate the mapping into the project plan? In Microsoft Project and other project management software, you can add customized data elements. For Microsoft Project, you would use three data elements. One is a flag field such as FLAG1 to indicate whether or not the task has one or more applicable issues. The second is a text field, such as TEXT1, that would contain the issue numbers. The third field is for lessons learned. You could use a text field, such as TEXT2, for lessons learned. Here the contents would be the numbers of the applicable lessons learned to that task.

Frequently, when we have coordinated this step with project leaders, we have found the following problems:

- The plans for each project differ in structure and level of detail. In some cases, it is impossible to assign issues to tasks because the tasks are so general. This then leads to creating more detailed tasks in the plans.
- There are valid issues for a project, but there are no tasks that apply to these issues. This leads to adding tasks.
- There are tasks that have issues, but the issues are not in the list. This leads to adding more issues.

This was discussed in Chapter 8. By mapping the tasks and issues to each other, you can validate the completeness of both the tasks and the issues.

Step 5: implement issues and risk reporting as part of project reporting

With the completion of the above steps, the project leaders are able to report on issues and risks as part of the regular project reporting process. At a minimum, they should produce the following:

- A GANTT chart that shows the tasks with issues differently than those without issues. In Microsoft Project this can be accomplished by using the Palette feature to show tasks that have the flag for issues as "yes" in a different color or shading than detailed tasks without issues. The purpose of this is to show management the criticality of the issues relative to the schedule.

- Earned risk. This was defined in Chapter 9 and is one way to show progress on work with issues.
- Percentage of remaining work with issues. Each task has resources assigned to it. Thus, you can use the project management software to obtain a spreadsheet or table of resource usage for tasks that have issues (again, in Microsoft Project you would filter the tasks by the flag for issues). You can then use this with the resource usage table for all tasks to obtain the percentage of remaining work with issues. This is very informative on the future of the project. Even if the current work is going well, if there are many issues ahead so that most of the work has issues, you know that the project needs more attention and may run into big trouble.
- Age of the oldest outstanding issue. Each issue in a project has a date when it became open or active. Using this you can easily obtain the age of the issue—how long it has been active. Lingering, unresolved issues are one of the biggest causes of project failure.
- Open and potential issues by type. Here you would take each category and give the number of open and potential issues in the project in two separate tables or charts. The use of a spider chart or radar chart is effective here. While only the number of issues is used, it can reveal how many are external to the project and, thus, likely to cause more problems and grief for the project. If there was available time, then you could use the project management software to give the number of hours for each type of issue.

To implement this approach, go to one project leader and produce the above information with them. Then distribute it as a sample to other project leaders in a meeting. During the meeting, the project leader you worked with can discuss how easy it was to do when the previous steps were carried out.

Don't stop there. You should go to management with the sample. Take them through each chart one-on-one with each manager so that they can see what they will be getting. Here you can give tips on how to use the information. You should suggest that the project leaders do the same with the business unit managers with whom they coordinate their projects with. What is the benefit of doing this? It can be to put pressure on management to help resolve open issues and help prevent potential issues. The numbers and charts are far more compelling than pleading with management for help with just words.

Step 6: perform and institute analysis of issues and risk for single projects

The specific analysis that can be carried out for one project is covered later in the chapter. Here we cover how the analysis is done. You would start with at least three projects of different types. Examples might be system development, enhancements, and technology infrastructure. With these examples, you can walk through the charts pointing out how they can be used as a tool for focusing attention.

A project leader often goes to a manager to get help with an issue. If the project leader just mentions the issue, it is now insufficient. The manager can insist on seeing the tasks in the project plan to which the issue applies. This will make both the project leader and manager have consensus on the urgency of an issue and its risks.

Step 7: perform and institute analysis of issues and risk across multiple projects and the project portfolio

The detailed analysis of multiple projects and the project portfolio are discussed in a later section. Here we discuss how to go about this and the benefits of the analysis. Note that while you can perform the analysis here across the entire project portfolio, in IT it is often more logical to group projects according to type, business unit, customer, or vendor. If you group by business unit or vendor, you can apply more pressure on each of these to resolve issues that are affecting multiple, rather than single, projects.

Once you have the project information with standardized issues mapped to tasks, it is possible to combine project plans using the project management software. Here is an example. You would filter all projects by a specific issue and time period. Doing this you would get all tasks across a group or all projects that share that issue. This can help the consistent resolution of the issue by getting all of the project leaders together to show them the joint impact and shared issue. This facilitates collaboration among project leaders.

For management you can demonstrate how past issues affected the schedules and plans of multiple projects. Here you could filter the project plans by a time range as well as by issues suppressing the detailed tasks with no issues.

Another useful chart for multiple projects is to create the following GANTT charts.

- All summary tasks, milestones, and detailed tasks with open issues. This and the next one is derived by filtering on these items. This chart can show management which issues and projects require the most attention now.
- All summary tasks, milestones, and detailed tasks with potential issues. This chart reveals to management where their attention will be required in the future.

There are a number of benefits to upper management, business units, IT, project leaders, and team members. Here is a list of benefits that have been achieved in past work.

How do you resolve issues?

As we have pointed out, you should not rush out and try to solve every issue. Issues are like fruit and vegetable farming. You have to wait until the issue is ripe. What is ripe? In issues and risk management, this is urgency. Urgency is the impact of the issue and risk on the project if it is not resolved. By waiting you gain more information on the issue. You can find out if it is the issue or a symptom of a larger problem.

When communicating on issues, you might take this approach used many times.

- You first alert the manager to an upcoming potential issue. No input or action is required. You are providing information.
- When the issue becomes open or active, you inform the manager. Again, no action is needed.

- As the issue becomes more pressing and urgent, inform them of alternative decisions. Include here the options of doing nothing, solving the problem without money or resources, and applying more money and resources. Depending on urgency, you would not press for a decision, but instead arrange for a later meeting to get a decision and actions on the issue and risk.

In this method the visibility of the issue rises gradually to management. If the issue is resolved without the involvement of the manager, you can report this too.

One benefit of this approach is that the manager is not surprised about the issue. Surprises here are very unpleasant and can damage the interpersonal relationship between the manager and project leader. It can happen that some other manager brings up the issue to your manager first. Then the manager is surprised and comes to you. Not good. You may not be prepared to respond. Better that you get to the manager first.

Many people do the investigation themselves. In projects this is not a good idea. You should seek input from all of the affected people or as many as possible. As we have said, project meetings are the way to discuss issues. You discuss not only facets of the issue and potential solutions. You also cover urgency and the impact if the issue is not resolved and lingers.

When discussing an issue, often people discuss the possible decisions. Decisions, however, are often general and vague. From experience, it is better to discuss potential actions that would make sense for the issue. These are more tangible and detailed. From the actions, you can then back into the decisions.

Once a decision has been made and the actions determined, you just explain these to the affected managers and staff, right? Wrong. Many issues are political and require finesse and planning in how to explain and sell the decision and actions. Often, the best way to sell a controversial decision is to show that it is the least of all evils in that the alternative decisions that are possible result in bad consequences. A guideline is then:

How the decision and actions are presented and conveyed can be as important as the actual decision and actions.

How do you analyze potential issues at the start of the project?

You have several project concepts and plans to evaluate. Or, you may be in the process of a go-no-go decision for several projects. Here is some of the analysis that the issues and risk management approach above can support.

- Filter and combine project plans based on potential issues and summary tasks. This will reveal the spread of issues across the schedule.
- Create a spider or radar chart in which each dimension is a type of issue. The scale is the number of issues by type. This will reveal the comparative distribution of issues by type between projects. One project may be faced with mainly internal issues,

thereby having less risk. Another may have a preponderance of external issues—thereby having much more risk.

For a single project, you could produce the following charts.

- The percentage of work by time period that has potential issues across the life of the project. This is an important chart. The horizontal axis is time and the vertical axis is the number of hours. Each time period, say a month, has two horizontal lines. One, the upper one, is the total number of hours of work in the period. The other, the lower one, is the total number of hours of work with potential issues.
- The same spider chart as described above, but for one project. Here the dimensions are specific types of issues in terms of total hours of tasks with that type of issue. If you see that there are many external issues and problems that can potentially cause trouble, then you might want to adjust the scope of the project to reduce the potential issues and their impact.

How do you analyze issues during project work?

We have discussed issue reporting. The analysis of an issue is unique to the issue. You should not rush to resolve issues. First, rank the issues that are open in terms of urgency. Urgency is the impact on the project and organization if the issue is not addressed. Second, rank the issues in terms of importance. Importance would be the impact on the tasks in general and not time specific. Of course, this is somewhat subjective, but it is valuable in giving perspective on multiple open issues. You would then concentrate on the issues that are urgent with special attention to the ones of greatest importance.

Try to address issues in groups. If you need management involvement, then giving them one issue at a time could result in them having a lack of confidence in your abilities as a project leader. Moreover, if you provide management with, say, three issues, they may not make decisions on all, but you are likely to come away with help on some of the issues. When you are discussing an issue or group of issues, focus on the impact of inaction to learn more about the issues as well as on potential actions. This can then lead to decisions.

How do you analyze issues across multiple projects?

Think of the issues and project plans as relational databases in which you can slice and dice the information in many different ways. Here are some examples of multiple project analysis.

- One or several issues across multiple projects. Discussed earlier, this can show commonality of the issue across projects—leading to less overall decision-making effort and supporting consistency in both decisions and actions.
- Issues impacting a specific business unit.
- Issues related to a specific system or technology.
- Issues related to a specific vendor.

There is real benefit in considering issues across projects. As has been mentioned, there is consistency in decisions and actions. Second, doing this analysis requires coordination and information sharing among project leaders. This can lead to greater collaboration in other areas of the projects.

Cases and examples

Sycamore University

Earlier in the book, it was mentioned that IT management had suffered a high turnover rate. Each project leader supported a different area of administration: student services, accounting and finance, materials management, and so on. There was no organized structure for addressing issues and risks. The project leaders believed that since their projects served different business units with different systems, there was little need for information sharing.

To turn this around, several meetings were held with project leaders for the purpose of identifying their issues. At first, they could not agree on what constituted an issue. After this was overcome, a list of 55 issues was defined. For each issue, every project leader to whom the issue applied was determined. This resulted in a table of issues versus projects and business units. This achieved one goal—the project leaders agreed that they shared the same issues. The battle was not over. They still disagreed on possible decisions and actions. Moreover, several project leaders did not pay sufficient attention to urgency. Overall, it took an elapsed time of several months to establish an issues management process across all projects.

Questions

1. What do you think was the impact of the problems with issues management and communications on IT and the business units?
2. Why do you think project leaders and people in general fail to voluntarily share information on issues with each other?
3. What resistance would have occurred if an issues management approach had been imposed on the project leaders by IT management?

Mapping to the PMBOK and PRINCE2

The PMBOK

The PMBOK has six sections in Chapter 11 on project risk management. These are as follows:

- Plan risk management.
- Identify risks.
- Perform Qualitative risk analysis.
- Perform Quantitative risk analysis.
- Plan risk responses.
- Monitor and control risks.

PRINCE2

One of the key themes of PRINCE2 is risk. All of the seven processes map to risk and issues. An issue report is defined that contains the data elements identified in the issues database for projects. There is a risk management strategy that describes the risk management techniques and standards to be applied along with responsibilities. The document also includes procedures, tools and techniques, timing of risk-related activities, roles and responsibilities, risk categories, early warning indicators, risk response categories, and proximity. Proximity here relates to the degree of urgency of the risk.

Lessons learned

Issues and risk management are linked. Some of the methodologies treat them separately. Experience has shown that this can lead to some confusion. What is an issue and what is a risk? That is the reason the attention has been given to issues that give rise to the risks. Otherwise, risks could be treated as serious issues. But then there is another problem. What is "serious?" Another fuzzy term.

It is logical to assign probabilities of a problem occurring. Experience shows that while you could use lessons learned and knowledge from past projects to try and estimate risk probabilities, it is difficult to do. Why? Because assigning a probability depends heavily on the details of the particular project. At any given time you often do not have sufficient information to estimate probabilities of events. Thus, it is easier often to get at urgency and importance. The importance of an issue can be seen by the effect on the project if the issue is not solved. Tasks are delayed and costs mount. Urgency is addressed by determining the impact of doing nothing about the issue.

Guidelines

In setting up an issues management approach start small with a few projects. Then expand it. In the Sycamore case, time and urgency did not allow for this approach. It would have been better to have examples from several project leaders at the start, but this would have taken more time.

Another point is to define what constitutes a significant issue. Here you struggle with the word "significant". From experience, a decent measure of this word is in the following sentence. An issue is significant if it could have a substantial impact on the schedule, work, cost, and quality of the project. This is subjective still. That is actually good. Because then you have to have project leaders collaborate to discuss importance, thereby building more communications.

In the chapter on project management communications (Chapter 11), it was strongly recommended that project meetings be devoted to discussions of issues and lessons learned. Status of the project work is summarized at the start by the project leader. Over the years, this approach has served to improve communications among team members. Moving up a level, the IT manager or any manager of a group of project leaders should adopt the same approach. Don't attempt to resolve issues at meetings. You are seeking ideas and information.

Questions

1. In your personal life, answer the following questions:

   How do you identify issues?
   Have you often been surprised when an issue appeared—seemingly from nowhere?
   How do you prioritize your active issues?
   Do you track your performance on issues?
   Do the same issues arise again and again?
   What is the oldest outstanding issue you have? Why hasn't it been addressed?

2. Using the Web, identify several alternative approaches for solving problems. Apply these to several of the issues in this chapter or in Part five of the book.
3. Using question 1 above, for several issues define their impacts and risks. How would you estimate the probability of a potential issue arising?
4. In your personal life compare and contrast addressing issues and problems one at a time versus in groups. What are the advantages and drawbacks of using the group approach?
5. It can be frustrating to have an issue linger as open and active for some time. However, many times people solve issues in their lives too soon and then suffer unintended consequences. Here is an example. Every time a child has a cold, the parents rush to the doctor for antibiotic treatment. The colds go away so the parents think the method works. Then the child gets a serious disease. However, antibiotics don't work well, because the germs have developed an immunity. Give some other examples of the problems that can occur if you treat an issue too soon.

What to do next

1. Evaluate the effectiveness of issues and risk management in a current or recent project. To do this, consider not only the material in this chapter, but also the score cards in Chapter 15.
2. Assess the extent to which information is shared on issues and risks in your organization. Identify potential improvements along with the barriers to implementing these improvements.
3. Looking back at your experience and career, have you found that you are better able to cope with and address issues than you were several years before. Do you gather lessons learned from issues and reuse them later?

Summary

Risk and issues management are key parts of both PMBOK and PRINCE2. Rightly so. Too much attention in the past was paid to planning and tracking work. However, it is in issues and risk management that a project leader demonstrates real capability.

13

Project quality management

Introduction

Project quality management deals with quality processes and procedures across the project portfolio. At the project level, project quality management covers the project management, project work, and project end products. *Quality* in IT projects usually refers to the extent to which the system and work meet the requirements of the project. The International Organization for Standardization (ISO) is one organization that specifies quality requirements. Other organizations include the Institute of Electrical and Electronics Engineers (IEEE) and the American National Standards Institute (ANSI). There are also associations directly concerned with quality. One is the American Society for Quality.

There are also a number of methodologies related to quality. Some examples are Total Quality Management (TQM), continuous improvement, and Six Sigma. Two related concepts are verification and validation (V & V). *Verification* consists of meetings and reviews of documents, computer code, requirements, and plans. Tools that support verification include the following: checklists, structured walkthroughs, and inspection. *Validation* occurs following verification and involves actual testing of the system. Space does not permit a more detailed review of the literature or methods.

In IT, *software quality assurance* (QA) consists of the methods, tools, and measurements necessary to ensure software quality. What constitutes acceptable quality for software? Here are some attributes.

- The software is relatively error or bug free. For even moderately complex systems it is impossible and unreasonable to perform all possible tests.
- The software meets the requirements developed in the project.
- The software code is readable and capable of being maintained and enhanced.

The Capability Maturity Model (CMM) specifies five levels of process maturity that determine effectiveness in delivering quality software. CMM was developed by the Software Engineering Institute (SEI) at Carnegie-Mellon University with support from the US Department of Defense. Briefly, the levels are as follows:

- Level 1—lack of any order in projects. Project successes are not often repeated since there is a lack of structure and lessons learned.

- Level 2—project management is in place along with requirements and configuration management.
- Level 3—there are standard software development and maintenance processes in place across the organization.
- Level 4—standardized measurements and metrics are employed to track projects and work ensuring a high degree of quality.
- Level 5—having reached Level 4, the final level is effective continuous improvement.

Very few organizations reach levels 4 and 5. But isn't quality important? Yes, of course. However, there are trade-offs in terms of the schedules, budgets, and resources. Management also sets priorities for IT processes. To achieve higher levels requires more personnel, money, and time.

There are also many versions of a Project Management Maturity Model. While these versions differ in detail, they generally follow the Capability Maturity Model. There are five levels, defined as follows:

- Level 1—there is little or no formal project management methodology. Each project is treated separately.
- Level 2—guidelines are in place. Experience is gathered so that success in projects can be repeated.
- Level 3—there is a project management methodology in place that is applied to most projects.
- Level 4—a standardized project management approach is applied to all project.
- Level 5—continuous improvement so as to optimize project management.

Comments can be here that are similar to the ones made for the CMM. Levels 4 and 5 apply to all projects of any size and shape. This requires more resources than are normally available. Level 3 is probably the most reasonable level for an organization to work toward given schedules, budget, and resource levels.

This chapter will first give attention to the quality of the project management process. Then we will turn to quality at the project level. Included here is a discussion of the various types of software testing.

The importance of quality

Many people talk about the importance of achieving high quality in IT. However, it is often the fear factor that propels management to emphasize quality. One example was the management response to the Y2K problem. Billions of dollars were poured into IT to ensure that the systems would still be operational. Here are some of the effects and impacts of poor quality:

- The online software fails during working hours. This can totally disrupt the business processes. Haven't you attempted to access a bank Web site and been given the message that the system is not available?
- Software bugs or errors can cause large-scale financial losses.
- Software bugs can allow a security breach of a system.

Over the years we have collected a number of examples of impacts. Here are just a few.

- In 2009 a large school district implemented a major system without adequate testing. Student had no schedules at the start of the year. Grades were lost. Parents were in an uproar.
- In the same year a major insurance firm was prohibited by the government from selling certain types of policies due to widespread complaints of overcharging, benefit cancellations, and other problems.
- The air traffic control system in the United States is very old. At least once a year there are software problems that bring down part of the system. This has resulted in many cancelled and delayed flights.
- A number of firms have reported financial losses for the quarter or year. In their reports the reason given was software problems and malfunctions.
- At a major airport, the baggage control system was upgraded, but the upgrade was not fully tested. The system failed. Bags were "lost" for weeks.
- Many thousands of medical devices had to be recalled to fix the software. The software would not indicate when power being received by the devices was too low.
- Each year there are thousands and even hundreds of thousands of vehicles recalled to fix software bugs.

These are only a few of hundreds of cases. Not only are customer relations damaged, but profits and revenue suffer as well. Then there are the many lawsuits that follow the problems.

Quality of the project management process

Chapter 3 addressed the project management process. The project management process included the following elements:

- Project management methodology;
- Project strategy;
- How project ideas were generated;
- The use of the project concept to expand on the idea;
- The development of the project plan using work breakdown structures or templates;
- An approach for project review and approval;
- How project reporting and tracking will be done;
- The process of closing or terminating a project.

At first, it seems that assessing quality of these items would be difficult. Our experience says otherwise. One thing to always review is to see what differences exist in how large versus small projects are treated. Let's examine each of the above in terms of a quality review.

Project management methodology

It is easy to determine if an organization has adopted or developed a project management methodology. It is more difficult to determine if it is being used properly and effectively. To check for quality here you could address the following questions:

- Is there a staff member or several members to support the methodology? Project management methodologies are no different than those in other areas or fields. You have to train new employees in the methodology. You have to retrain and update employees. And you have to answer and provide guidance.
- A methodology tells you what to do. It does not tell you how to do it. Are guidelines available for how to use the detailed steps in the methodology? If there are no guidelines, then there is a danger that each project will implement the steps individually. This could mitigate the value of the methodology.
- Does upper management fully support the methodology? This is critical to provide credibility for its use.
- How are small projects treated in terms of the methodology? This was discussed in Chapter 2. If some projects are treated as exceptions and do not have to follow the methodology, then what is the cut-off point between those projects that do use it and those that do not. Is it based on size, issues, importance, or cost? It should probably be based on issues since the issues lead to risk. Size is a poor measure since some large projects are very routine and have few issues.
- Are there attempts to get around using the methodology? Take the previous question. In one organization we observed that people divided up projects so that each project piece fell under the cut-off point. The organization paid lip service to the methodology, but it was never really used.
- How is the use of the methodology enforced? A state can pass a law for punishment for some criminal acts. However, if these are not enforced, then the laws are meaningless. In the United States and elsewhere there are many laws on the books that are not enforced. They have been forgotten. It is the same with a methodology. If there is no enforcement, then it will not be used much, if at all.

Project strategy

Every organization has some approach for doing projects. Here are some questions to ask:

- Does the organization have a stated strategy for projects? If not, then work is often performed *ad hoc*. This would be an organization in Level 1 of the Capability Maturity Model.
- If there is a stated strategy, is it really followed? In several instances, we found strategies to be fine. However, what was actually done was entirely different and counterproductive.
- Does the organization attempt to measure progress in improvement as a result of the project strategy? Doing this helps IT and projects politically.

How project ideas were generated

This was discussed in Chapter 3. Here are the quality questions:

- Are most of the project ideas generated proactively or reactively? Proactive project ideas are those where managers and staff actively seek out new project ideas. These are often more successful than ones where IT is put in a reactive mode with a project request. Then resources have to be diverted. Management controls and time change.
- Do most project ideas come from a few business units? We have this happen frequently. One reason is that the managers and employees know more about IT and systems. Other groups that have less knowledge or desire request little or nothing except for enhancements to the current systems. Project ideas should address areas and processes of the business that are business critical. In the first instance, some of the groups that request IT projects have processes that are marginal to overall performance.
- What is done with the discarded ideas? Are they retained to be considered again or dropped? You never want to drop an idea since it could be beneficial later.
- Are project ideas considered in groups on, say, a quarterly basis? Or, are they considered as they arise—one at a time? The first approach is preferred since it allows management and IT to perform comparative trade-offs.

The use of the project concept to expand on the idea

In Chapter 5 development and benefits of the project concept were discussed. The project concept fleshes out the project idea but does not include a project plan. Questions to pose in this area are as follows:

- Is the project concept, or an equivalent, employed? If not, then work begins on the project plan after an idea is initially reviewed. This can result in misunderstandings since the project plan will be too detailed for managers to do higher level trade-offs. Also, you could waste a lot of time preparing plans for project ideas that are never approved.
- Do the project concepts include a number of potential problems and issues that have surfaced in previous work and projects? This would be accomplished by having a list or database of issues. Individuals preparing a project concept would then first consult the list and pull some of the known issues out to be included in the project concept. Then they could add more issues that apply to the specific project idea.
- Are there changes between the original version of the project concept and the one that gets approved? It is seldom the case that there are not changes due to management wanting to put their mark on the project, changing ideas about requirements, and so on. The absence of changes may indicate a lack of management interest and involvement.

The development of the project plan using work breakdown structures or templates

In Chapter 8 we addressed project planning using templates. The benefits of a WBS or template include reduced time in planning, more complete project plans, and more consistent plans to allow multiple project and portfolio management and analysis. If these are not used, then you have to test completeness, logic, and other character-istics. This consumes more time. Of course, you could say that each project is unique. However, at the highest level groups of projects in the same area have the same sum-mary tasks. For example, you may be acquiring three different software packages. Each is different from the others. However, the high-level tasks and milestones are the same.

An approach for project review and approval

Now let's move to the review and selection of projects from the ideas, concepts, and plans. The reference here is also to Chapter 8. Here are some questions to ask:

- Is there a formal approach for review and approval?
- Are projects reviewed and approved in groups at regular intervals?
- How many projects were approved outside of the regular review process? If there are more than a very few of these, then the entire review and approval process is in jeopardy since people will then tend to advance project concepts outside of the review process.

Remember the following basic rule.

It is not just the projects you did that count, it is also the projects you avoided doing that are important.

Why is this useful and valid? Because you could waste a lot of time, money, and resources in marginal projects. These things could have been applied to better, more useful projects.

How project reporting and tracking will be done

Project reporting and tracking were addressed in Chapter 9. Here are some quality-related questions to answer.

- Is there a formal project reporting process across all projects? Or, is each project's project reporting approach determined separately? If it is the latter, then there could be problems since management is getting progress drip by drip across projects. It is more difficult to do multiple and portfolio project analysis.
- If a project runs into trouble with several or many severe issues, does the project reporting process change? Is there a formal line over which the modified reporting

process takes over? There should at least two levels of project reporting. This will aid in demonstrating the urgency of the issues associated with projects in trouble.

- Is project reporting both formal and informally formal? What does this mean? Formal project reporting consists of supplying information on project progress in a structured manner. Informal reporting formally means that you supply information verbally in an organized, structured way. We make reference here to Chapter 11 on project communications.
- Does the project progress information contain information on the progress and status of open and closed issues? As we stated many times, issues are the predecessor cause for going over budget and over schedule. Issues are the cause of project risk. By presenting information on issues with progress, you achieve several benefits. First, you act to prevent and suppress changes in scope of the project since the presence of issues discourages making more changes that create more issues. Second, progress is not just defined in terms of work performed. This is the technical progress. The management progress is expressed in terms of issues management.

The process of closing or terminating a project

In many cases, projects end and the team members and leaders move on. Here are some questions related to closure and termination.

- Does the organization celebrate the end of a project and the benefits? Why is this important? First, it helps to sustain the change in the work. Second, celebration provides a means to demonstrate support for improvement. This will help future projects and change efforts.
- What happens when a project is terminated? Does it just get pushed under the rug? Are lessons learned gathered and used? Too often no one gives attention to terminated projects. They are an embarrassment. Yet, if you want to avoid future problems with projects, you want to gather lessons learned.

General project management process questions

Now step back and look at the project management process as a whole. Ask the following questions:

- How much non-project work is going on? How much of this consists of small projects? Why isn't this work managed as a project? It takes effort and overhead to set up plans, get approvals, and so on. The project is quick so why go through this—just do it. This might work many times. However, there are instances where these non-projects suddenly have issues, get management attention, and become nightmares. We are not suggesting that every little task be a project. We do recommend, however, that you systematically evaluate this work to see if it should be a project.
- An exceptional project is defined here as one that does not follow the accepted project management process. How many projects are exceptions? What was the

basis for the decision on making a project an exception? One common answer is expediency. "We need to just get the work done and so don't have time for all of the paperwork."

Quality of requirements

There are standard testing methods for software, hardware, and network systems. Requirements are more difficult to test. It is common to say that "Requirements must be clear, complete, detailed, attainable, and testable." But what does this mean? What is clear? You can read a paragraph and understand the words, but do you have the meaning and implication of what is written? Experience shows that if you ever attempted to gather complete, really complete, requirements, the project would never advance beyond this stage. How do you know if requirements are attainable? What if there is no budget for a software package and there are no internal staff available for implementation? Then even though the requirements are reasonable, they are not attainable.

A better goal for requirements is this.

Determine the minimum requirements to achieve the greatest change and benefit.

Why is this preferable to all requirements? This goal helps to focus on the critical work performed in the business departments and excludes marginal work unless it is important or needed by the critical requirements.

What do requirements specify in an IT project? Because this is a book on project management and not system development, our attention will be confined to transactions, data, business rules, and the user interface. There is obviously much more in terms of security, backup, recovery, restart, hardware and network requirements, availability, and so on.

The requirements define specific transactions and processing along with the related business rules. But if you were to identify and analyze all possible transactions in many departments, there would be hundreds. In an average bank branch, there are over 200 possible transactions. Requirements should cover the most common and standard transactions. For the rest that are exceptions, you would pick and choose based on impact if not addressed, importance, and contribution to the benefits of the project.

How do you test this part of the requirements? IT staff are not in a good position to do this since they do not work in the business unit. Therefore, testing and verification must be performed by the business unit. In many projects, there is one user or business staff member who reviews the transactions. This can result in problems. It is unlikely that one person will be aware of all of the business rules. Moreover, this one user faces tremendous pressure to approve the requirements so that further work can be performed. A better idea is to have several, and we mean several, different teams of business users review and simulate the transactions. One good way to do this in a concrete manner is to compare the old and new transactions side by side. This will not only test the requirement, but also provide insight into the benefits of the new system. Using this approach, your requirements will not be complete because you did not address the myriad of exceptions. How do you handle this? Make the scope of the project at the start limited to those transactions that provide the greatest benefit and have the greatest importance. In banking automation, attention was focused on teller, loan, note, and new account operations. These constitute the bulk of the work in a bank branch. Safe deposit accounting and sign in were often dealt with later as a distinct small project.

Requirements also include the user interface and the data. You can simulate in meetings with the same user teams using the user interface through paper designs and layouts of screens. The testing here would focus on whether the transactions could be processed as well as the efficiency in using the user interface. For data you would want to compare the data in the current process and system with the new one. Typically, some data elements may appear to be the same with the same names, but in the new system they will have a different meaning. Additionally, there are new data elements. How will the new data elements be captured? How will migration of the existing data to the new system be accomplished?

Quality of work

In IT it is difficult to measure the work while it is going on. You can progress reports, but unless you review partial documents, programs, test results, and so on, you cannot measure for quality directly. Time pressure and the range of work usually prevent direct measurements. So this section will identify some indirect measurements that have proven to be indicative of the work and its quality.

Here are some indirect areas that you should probe.

- Communications among team members. Here you could casually walk around and see how people interact. You can observe what happens in project meetings. Since the project meetings focus on issues and lessons learned rather than status, you will observe a great deal of interaction.
- How methods and tools are being used. Guidelines and tips on methods and tools used in the project will be covered in the lessons learned meetings.
- Whether lessons learned are being applied and gathered. First, they should be gathered as the work is done—not after the project since it is too late to be useful to the project. Second, for each part of the work before it starts, the use of past experience and lessons learned should be discussed.
- Body language and voice in one-on-one contact. Using the guidelines in Chapter 11, you can surmise a lot of information.
- How issues are being addressed. If an issue is put off even if it has substantial impact on the project, then this is a sign that work may not be going well. People may be avoiding the issue, because they do not want their work affected.
- What other work the team members are doing outside of the project. As project leader this should be a matter of great interest. When you ask what else they are working on, you can use body language and tone of voice to detect their enthusiasm

relative to their other work. You should also state why you want to know. You want to know because of the potential impact on their availability to do work on the project.

- In Chapters 8 and 9, it was strongly recommended that team members both define and update their detailed tasks—as often as twice a week. The updating will reveal slipped tasks and extra work. These tasks can indicate quality problems. Work of high quality should not require rework.

Information gathered from these areas is useful in determining:

- Status of work based on team member updates.
- Whether people are covering up problems and issues.
- How well the team members get along with each other.
- Whether technical issues are being addressed.

Quality of end products

End products include documents, programs, and test results. These are mentioned in general since the exact end products will depend on the details of the project. Now you do not have time to evaluate all milestones and end products. In Chapter 9 it was indicated that you should center your attention on those that have issues and risks.

In reviewing a milestone in an IT project, what are some of the problems you could find that relate to quality? Here are some frequently encountered.

- The requirement was misunderstood in development.
- A requirement is missing in development or implementation.
- The approach taken to meet a requirement is too complex.
- The end product is too difficult to maintain after implementation.
- The method or tool was not properly employed.
- The work was not adequately tested.
- There are gaps in the documentation. People often document the easy parts in detail and they may gloss over the parts that are more complex or with which they have less experience.
- The documentation is vague or unclear.
- Team members added additional features, material, or capabilities that will result in later extra work with marginal benefit.

Now let's suppose that you have a milestone due at the end of the month. Do you wait until the deadline to think about how to review the milestone? No. You should plan ahead for the review. In planning you first set the goals for the review. Then you plan on how to carry out the review.

You should identify potential problems that could arise if there are quality problems in the end products. This could mean additional work and rework. You should point these out at the start of a work review meeting. That will give an aura of seriousness in the review.

The goals typically might include the following:

- The work was carried out using the methods and tools properly.
- The work covers what was planned when it was initiated. It is complete.
- The work results can be easily understood for later work.
- The work results are maintainable and capable of later change.

Much has been written on reviews in addition to the discussion in Chapter 9. Here are some additional guidelines. In all of this, pay attention to body language and tone of voice as per Chapter 11.

- Have the team members discuss how they went about the work first.
- The team members can then identify problems they encountered and how they were addressed.
- The team members can cover how they used past experience in their work.
- Having discussed the "how" of the work, they can move on to the milestone. Rather than have a general presentation, they should first state the requirements of features that had to be incorporated in the work. They then cover how each requirement or feature was addressed in the end product.

This indirect approach is often sufficient for most end products. If the end product is critical and has many issues, then you have to probe into the work end product using structured walkthroughs or other methods.

The trade-off between quality and value

There is a trade-off in manufacturing between quality and value. For example, if you seek an error rate of one in 100,000 units, then the work and cost will be higher than if you aim at a rate of one in 1000. The consumer may not be able to tell the difference. Moreover, the consumer may not be willing to pay for the higher quality product so it has less value.

It is similar in IT. You could perform exhaustive analysis of milestones and work. This would result in high quality, but the schedule would suffer. Costs might rise excessively. Projects have actually been cancelled when this occurred even though the work was of very high quality.

Many years ago an IT supervisor of programmers would have the programmers provide their programs and code each week. The supervisor spent all weekend doing detailed line-by-line reviews. Quality was excellent. Later, however, in the project the supervisor could not keep up. Programmers waited for the review results. Productivity declined. The schedule suffered. Costs rose. There were two results. The supervisor suffered a nervous breakdown. Second, the supervisor was replaced. You can chalk this up to the law of unintended consequences due to an obsession with quality.

Software testing

There are too many different types of testing to cover them all. Here we highlight some of the most common first. Then we discuss the test plan and approach to testing.

- Black box testing. Testing is based on requirements and functions without any knowledge of the internal system design.
- White box testing. Here your test is based on knowledge of the internal code. This is much more time consuming, but does lead to more complete testing.
- Unit testing. Programmers finish coding. They then test the individual programs. This is called "unit testing".
- Integration testing. These are tests that stress combined parts of the system such as the user interface or batch updating of databases.
- System testing. This is testing of the entire system based on the overall requirements.
- End-to-end testing. This is a category of system testing that tests in a real-world environment.
- Regression testing. During testing, problems are found and fixed. Then retesting is required. This is regression testing.
- Acceptance testing. This is testing performed by the users according to their specifications using simulated or actual transactions.
- Load testing. This is testing of the system under stress. For example, banks connect one computer to their ATM system and feed a tremendous volume of work at the ATM system to see if the system can with stand the load.
- Usability testing. This is testing to assess the ease of use from an end-user view. This tests the clarity and completeness of the user interface.
- Recovery testing. This tests how the system recovers from failures and crashes.
- Security testing. This tests whether the system can withstand penetration attempts.
- Comparative testing. Here software is tested against competing software products. This could be employed in evaluating alternative software packages.
- Alpha testing. This is done by software development firms such as Microsoft, Oracle, SAP, and so on. This testing is performed by testers acting as end users. In alpha testing some minor changes to the design may still be allowed.
- Beta testing. Here the system is complete as is testing. End users now test the final system.

Instead of human beings doing testing, software development firms employ automated test data generators. These provide a stream of transactions for testing, thereby increasing coverage of testing and reducing the time.

Let's now consider the planning for the testing. During the gathering of requirements, specific transactions are identified along with their business rules. The test plan will identify the types of transactions that will be tested. These can be either online or batch updating. The requirements specify backup, recovery, and restore needs. The test plan should include these for testing. The test plan is a technical document that governs the testing through to completion of the project. The test plan should contain the following:

- Description of the new system
- Objectives of the testing
- Scope of the testing
- Approach to testing functions, what is included and excluded

  o Functional testing
  o Testing of interfaces
  o Acceptance testing

- Testing process
- Test phases

  o Integration testing
  o Operational acceptance

- Schedule for testing
- Roles and responsibilities of management, IT, vendors, and testing team
- Issues and assumptions for the testing

How do you trade-off the schedule and quality given limited resources?

Let's suppose that you have very limited resources along with substantial pressure on the timeline or schedule of a project. Yet, you and the team members want to do high-quality work. This should be addressed at the start of a project before the problem arises.

Here is a proven approach. For each of the major milestones in the project, answer the following questions

- What is the minimum level of acceptable quality?
- How will we verify that this has been met?
- What are the signs of problems during the work?

This approach has several benefits. First, it makes the team more aware of quality in specific terms rather than generalities. Second, it will help in planning for end product and work reviews later. Third, you can encourage team members to come forward with problems rather than hiding them. We have even given away free lunches and dinners to team members who presented the most problems. This is in direct contrast to a management style where the project leader does not encourage people to be forthcoming with problems. Better to know about problems and issues early—before they arise than to be surprised later.

Cases and examples

Sycamore University

Having had four directors of IT in less than 2 years, you can assume, rightly so, that the project management process was at Level 1 on both the Capability Maturity Model and Project Management Maturity Model. Business units lacked any confidence that IT could deliver on new projects. Maintenance and enhancement work ruled. Even though we knew how bad the situation was, we decided to measure almost all activities in terms of quality using the techniques discussed earlier in the chapter. Why do this extra work? One reason was to have benchmarks so that comparisons could be drawn to show improvement. Another reason was political. We wanted the IT staff, IT supervisors, upper management, and business units to vent their frustrations and realize the state of the situation. After improvements then, no one could say it was better before.

The measurements showed where the changes that had the highest priority needed to be done. Communications was improved. Also, attention was paid to the project management process. All existing projects and project requests were put on hold. The most critical processes were identified. In a university or college, these are typically admissions, student records, financial aid, accounting, payroll, and fund raising. Project ideas were generated for these followed by project concepts. The other main area of attention was infrastructure. Here more project ideas and concepts were generated. With these legacy systems it was not surprising that there was substantial resistance. For example, business units were reluctant to allow students, employees, and administrators to have online access to the systems in any way. We responded by indicating the impact of not doing anything. This worked and projects were started.

Another part of the quality push was to focus on the key business processes. Many of these were badly documented. There were many exceptions. King and Queen Bees (senior business users) ruled. We started to work with junior users on making Quick Win changes to processes. Politically, this diverted attention from the systems projects.

Questions

1. Why were not these changes and approach carried out before? Other managers had only focused on IT projects.
2. Why do you think that so little attention was paid to measurement and quality before?
3. This example reveals the benefit of parallel efforts. What are advantages and disadvantages of taking a parallel versus sequential approach to improvements?

Mapping to the PMBOK and PRINCE2

The PMBOK

Chapter 8 of the PMBOK addresses project quality management. There are three sections in this chapter.

- Plan quality. Here quality requirements and standards are specified. End products here include a quality management plan, metrics for quality, checklists, and a process improvement plan.
- Perform quality assurance. Quality of work and end products is determined here. The end products include measurement reports, plan updates, and change requests. Rather than wait until you have a milestone or end product to review, you should assess project quality using the methods described earlier to correct problems while the work is in progress.
- Perform quality control. Similar comments to quality assurance apply here.

PRINCE2

PRINCE2 defines "project assurance". This relates to the quality of project management. Examples of project assurance tasks carried out by Project Board overseeing the project include the following:

- Review the business case for the project.
- Verify that the project approach is technically correct and in line with company strategy.
- Confirm that the Quality Management Strategy meets required standards.
- Ensure that all risks and issues have been identified along with responsibilities and potential responses.
- Advise the project leader on people suitable to review work.
- Act as independent reviewers in project quality reviews.

In PRINCE2 key quality responsibilities are laid out in the Quality Management Strategy. The strategy defines the quality techniques and standards to be applied along with responsibilities. The document that deals with the strategy contains sections on quality planning, quality control including metrics and templates, and quality assurance methods. Quality standards are defined as the tasks are assigned.

Lessons learned

Often, IT staff will ask users for their requirements. Users often respond with what they do now and how they do it. If these become requirements, then there is a danger that the new system will closely resemble the old. There will be little change except improved, more modern software. Benefits will be greatly reduced. When someone describes what and how they do a piece of work, ask, "Why do you do it that way? Can it be eliminated? Can it be simplified?" Answers here could point to some Quick Wins that eliminate work and reduce the requirements.

Too much attention is paid in a project to schedule and costs versus quality. Quality is often assumed since you assume you have qualified, experienced people working with well-defined requirements for the work, right? Wrong. People take short cuts due to schedule pressure and the pressure of their other work. The project leader should always emphasize quality by focusing on the *minimum acceptable level of quality*.

Guidelines

- In implementing any part of your project management process, clearly give the rules and method for making any exceptions. If this is not done, many project leaders may try to make their project an exception.
- Keep a repository of requirements documents and presentations. Store the project plans, issues, and results of the project with the requirements. Encourage, not require, that project leaders review some of these before they start gathering requirements.

Questions

1. Research the Web to find two examples where system failed due to internal errors or bugs. For each discuss the impacts of the problems on the organizations.
2. A major argument for using software packages is that they have been more thoroughly tested than if you develop an equivalent application. Discuss potential problems that can be encountered if you select the software package approach.
3. Software reusability occurs when programmers are encouraged and rewarded for reusing working code as opposed to writing new code. Discuss how you could encourage programmers to reuse their existing code and those of others.
4. Let's assume that you wanted to test the requirements developed during the project. Using the discussion in this chapter, discuss how you would deal with requirements that failed the tests.
5. Assume that the system has been successfully installed and is in use. Problems start to come up that indicate errors in the programming. What alternative actions should you consider?

What to do next

1. A major source of problems is caused by the lack of testing of software changes after maintenance or enhancement work. What procedures do you have in place regarding testing of maintenance and enhancements? What problems have occurred recently? Were the procedures revised or updated?
2. An argument has been made for outside people to test requirements since the business units are too close to the work. Discuss the advantages and disadvantages of this approach. What work would be required for an outside vendor to come up to speed to do this testing?
3. Some firms have very low ratings in terms of the Capability Maturity Model. Yet, they are very successful financially and operationally. Discuss the shortcomings of this model and other similar models.

Summary

Quality measurement is both direct and indirect. Direct measurements result from testing. Indirect measurements can be detected based on issues, problems, change requests, and other similar situations. These indirect measurements are often easier to carry out. These can often point you to the areas that require detailed testing and analysis.

Politically, it is difficult to sell testing since to some it appears as overhead. To get the proper attention to testing, you should use the fear factor. What are the consequences of problems that are undetected, but later surface during operations?

Finally, note that quality is closely related to measurements. To assess quality of management you must measure decisions, resource allocation, and actions. As you read Chapter 15 on measurement, you will note many of the measures relate to quality of the work and management.

14

Project procurement management

Introduction

Outsourcing is the use of external resources to meet specific needs of an organization. It is thousands of years old. For example, the Romans used mercenary troops to defend their borders. Some contend that this contributed to the fall of the Roman Empire since these mercenaries, having been trained and gained experience, turned on the Romans. Misgivings about outsourcing were cited by Machiavelli in *The Prince* (see Appendix 2). Individuals and families outsource cleaning, gardening, tutoring their children, car maintenance, household repairs, painting, remodeling, and other activities.

IT companies, in general, have a long history of outsourcing for goods and services. In the early days of computers, firms paid vendors to perform their data processing. The firm provided the data to the vendor and got in return reports and other output. These firms were called "service bureaus". Another early example was time sharing services. Firms could not afford and did not have the expertise to support online systems. So they were provided and supported by time sharing firms. Recently, cloud computing has emerged. In cloud computing a firm depends on a vendor for software applications, hardware, staffing, and network support through the Internet.

Firms today rely on outside help for:

- Complete processing of business applications such as sales, accounting, and so on.
- Network services and management.
- PC support, installation, and maintenance.
- Hardware and facilities support and maintenance.
- Security systems and processes.
- Contract system development.
- Contract programming.
- Process improvement and change management services.
- Project management services.
- Help desk and user support.
- Training and documentation.
- Systems planning.

Outsourcing can be performed locally at the firm's location or overseas thousands of miles away. The use of outsourcing has grown dramatically as shown by the rise of software firms in India and China.

Procurement management for projects includes the following:

- All steps required to purchase or acquire goods and services;
- Results needed by a project produced by an outside firm;
- Contract negotiation and management;
- Change control related to the work and contract;
- Addressing any issues in the services or goods.

Outsourcing and contracting

What is a contract? It is a legally binding agreement between the customer organization and one or more vendors that is enforceable by law or through binding arbitration. Contracts can be written or oral. However, we will restrict attention to written contracts. Oral or verbal contracts are difficult to enforce and can lead to major problems and disputes.

There are several types of contracts that have to be considered:

- Fixed cost contract. Here the contract will specify a fixed cost for the goods or services. This has the advantage of knowing how much the procurement will cost. This type of contract is used for goods. For services it works best if the requirements are well-defined. If the requirements are fuzzy or there are unknowns or uncertainty, then fixed price is only suited for the first phases of work.
- Cost plus a fixed fee. This type of contract is often used for services wherein a firm charges by the hour or day. The fee includes the contractor's overhead and profit.

There are variations in each of these due to a variety of factors. One is fixed price subject to changes in economic costs or currency fluctuations. Another is fixed price with incentives for early completion of work. A third variation is a cost reimbursement contract. Another variation is the time and material contract used for outside work in which the requirements are not well-defined.

Think of procurement management in four stages. The first is planning. This includes the following:

- Determine what services and goods are to be procured.
- Define and document the requirements.
- Review the requirements with management, IT, and relevant business units and gain approval;
- Develop a plan for procurement and implementation of goods and services;
- Define acceptable levels of vendor service and product performance;
- Identify potential service or goods providers.

The second starts from the first and proceeds through the agreement or contract. Specific activities include the following:

- Prepare a document of requirements (often called a Statement of Work—SOW) for circulation to potential service providers. This is often called an RFP (Request for Proposal) or RFQ (Request for Quotation). If you are just seeking information from vendors, you would distribute an RFI (Request for Information). This will not solicit a firm proposal, but will show potential vendors your general needs as well as providing you with detailed information on their products and services.
- Set up a proposal evaluation process and team to review proposals.
- Receive and evaluate proposals.
- Identify the winning bidder along with an alternate. Why two vendors? You want to have a backup if the negotiations with the leading vendor fail. In that way, you may be able to avoid repeating the entire process again.
- Conduct negotiations with the vendors.
- Enter into a contract with the selected vendor.

These are just examples. Obviously, the process, criteria, and so on are defined by the organization and its needs. Government procurements have to follow very explicit rules.

The contract terms usually include the following:

- Statement of Work and deliverable items.
- Cost and pricing.
- Schedule that is planned.
- How performance is measured and reported.
- The process for identifying and resolving problems and issues.
- The specific roles and responsibilities of the customer firm and the vendor.
- Where the work will be performed.
- The methods and tools that will be used in work performance.
- The time span over which work will be performed.
- Terms of payment.
- Penalties for non-performance.
- Resources and facilities the customer and vendor will provide.
- Place of delivery of services and/or goods and how they will be installed.
- Review and acceptance terms and approach.
- How progress will be reported.
- Support of products provided.
- Limitations on liability.
- Warranties and guarantees.
- Insurance limits required along with bonding for work.
- How changes will be handled.
- How disputes will be addressed and how termination will be done.

Now assuming you have a contract, it is time to implement the contract terms. The specific steps are determined by the type of goods or services to be provided. For software, consulting, and other types, the steps include the following:

- Establish a joint team from the firm and vendor to transition and plan for the work.

- Create a process for dealing with issues and changes, staffing, status reporting, payments, work reviews, methods and tools to be employed, work quality, and other factors.
- Dry run the process by simulating problems, changes, and so on with the vendor. This will ensure that there is a detailed joint understanding and agreement.
- Begin the work.

The above also applies to teaming agreements. *Teaming agreements* are agreements between two or more organizations to partner or joint venture in developing some new product or service. Project management is conducted jointly among the partners.

Advantages of outsourcing

Let's start with a family. Why do they outsource? Here are some benefits and reasons.

- They lack the skills and expertise to do the work (e.g., car repair).
- They don't have the time to do it themselves due to work and other commitments (e.g., cleaning and gardening).
- They lack the knowledge and time to do it (e.g., tutoring the kids or teaching them music or dancing).

Companies outsource process and IT-related work for similar reasons. These are as follows:

- They see a process as second to their main activities. If they did the work themselves, they would have to divert resources.
- They do not want involvement in specific IT activities or may not perceive IT as a critical function.
- They lack internal expertise and it would take too long to acquire it.
- Management does not want to make necessary cuts to staff so they outsource it and turn over the problem. This is an expensive way to solve an internal problem.
- They have a great fear of failure and so want to rely on vendors with proven experience and a successful track record.
- They need to implement new capabilities rapidly. Doing it internally would take too long.
- They do not want to build IT up in remote or satellite locations.

Given the reasons, it is not difficult to determine the potential benefits which include the following:

- Lower potential cost;
- Faster implementation of capabilities;
- Stable support;
- Access to new skills and knowledge;
- Greater reliability by dependence on a large vendor;
- They can devote more attention to activities that are viewed as more business-critical;
- Access to new technologies.

Problems with outsourcing

So why is there not even more outsourcing? One answer is that a firm sees IT as a strategic weapon in the market. An example is Wal-Mart which builds most of their own software applications.

Another reason is that they do not want to be overly dependent on one or several vendors. If there are vendor problems or if the vendor disappears or goes bankrupt, then the company is faced with a crisis.

The vendor staff may learn about your business practices, marketing, and operations. Their employees could leave and work for a competitor. If there is no clause protecting client information and business knowledge, then the firm could propose work to a competitor. In any event the vendor learns a great deal about your business that can be employed later.

When you outsource, you find that your internal capabilities are diminished. You are dependent on the vendor. This even happens in a house where the family depends on a gardener to program a sprinkler system. If there is a power outage or a need to change watering times, then the family has to call the gardener in.

Expected cost savings may not materialize or evaporate. In some instances, firms outsource for a fixed cost to have specific services. However, the costs grow as business units and users ask for more capabilities. If there was an internal IT group providing the services, then there would be priorities due to limited resources. The business units may think that the vendor has many more resources so the only barrier they see is money.

Still another problem with outsourcing is that the vendor may, in turn, outsource your work to yet another vendor. Why would a vendor do this? They have too much work. They want to make more money by using cheaper labor. In one case, a major retailer outsourced cleaning of their stores. The vendor then outsourced to another firm that used illegal aliens. The government found out about this and levied heavy fines on the retailing firm even though the retailing firm's management had no knowledge of what was going on! This has to be prevented through the contract wherein it is specified that either only vendor employees can do the work or any outsourcing by the vendor must meet with your review and approval.

Frequently, outsourcing is used to exploit new technologies. The current IT staff then maintains the existing infrastructure and systems. This is a bad idea since it can reduce internal morale. The employees feel that they are being left behind. A better approach is outsource the maintenance and support of the old technologies and have the employees learn and use the new technologies. Why is this not widely adopted? Because it is less expensive in the short term to use the employees for maintenance since it reduces the transfer of knowledge workload.

Outsourcing then is a trade-off. The critical success factors in outsourcing include the following:

- The firm has to carefully select the activities to be outsourced.
- The firm needs to have clear requirements and performance criteria.
- A long-term view is needed rather than getting short-term results. You have to think about the implications of outsourcing years out in the future.
- Careful planning and implementation is essential.

- Sufficient resources have to be available to manage the outsourcing vendor and work.
- Management has to be able to make tough decisions regarding change of scope of work.
- Management has to be willing to terminate an outsourcing agreement based on performance measurements.

Service Level Agreements

A Service Level Agreement (SLA) is an agreement between a provider of services and a customer firm. The agreement can be part of a legal contract. Or, it could be informal and separate from the contract. What does an SLA contain?

- What services to be provided;
- Priorities for work;
- How problems will be handled;
- Disaster recovery, backup, and restoration of service;
- Roles and responsibilities of both parties;
- Guarantees and warranties;
- Responsibilities of the customer;
- Options for support;
- Types of content and data types supported;
- Termination.

Note the first bullet starts with "what" not "how". The "how" is left to the provider. Each area of service has specific levels of service to be provided. Since there are many types of SLAs for different services, an SLA could include the following: availability, performance, operation, reliability, security, billing, and other measures and activities. The level of service indicates the minimum level of acceptable performance along with a target level of performance. This might be an average level of service. SLAs can include penalties if the service levels are not met.

SLAs are not restricted to services provided by external parties. They can include services provided internally by IT or some other department to business units.

There are major benefits and some drawbacks to SLAs. One benefit is that what constitutes acceptable performance is often not clearly spelled out in the legal contracts. This can lead to both technical and management problems. Lawsuits can result and the work is cancelled. Another benefit is that the quality of service can be measured. In fact, by having measurements specified in the SLA, much more attention is given to performance than might otherwise be the case.

Internal SLAs have similar benefits. In addition, a company can measure the internal IT performance and compare it with what could be obtained through outsourcing. One drawback of an internal SLA is that the development of the agreement can take substantial time and money. Another is that if there are performance problems, there is no legal recourse such as a formal contract. It can be argued that if you manage issues with business units, the SLA is redundant. Another drawback is that the SLA development and monitoring not only consumes resources, but it also raises tensions between business units and IT. If the internal IT group uses SLAs, then there is a tendency to focus on service levels. This is not necessarily the same as improving business performance. IT's attention should be centered on business performance improvement. If the SLAs contribute to this, fine. Otherwise, it can be act as an obstacle.

How do you implement SLAs for an IT group? One is to determine whether an SLA is needed on an *ad hoc* basis. Here each project and work request is evaluated in terms of urgency and importance. A second approach is to have an SLA with each business unit. Then projects affecting these business units need to adhere to the SLA. A third approach is to apply SLAs on a project–by-project basis. This is probably more useful in that the SLA is customized to fit the project.

Here are some examples of performance measurements that could be in an SLA for a call center.

- Percentage of calls that are dropped while waiting to be answered.
- Average time to answer a call.
- Percentage of calls answered in a specific time period.
- Percentage of calls that are answered and handled without referral or callback.
- Average time to handle a specific task.

Let's turn to another example—cloud computing. In cloud computing a firm relies on an external service provider that supports multiple customers with the same hardware, software, human, and network resources. A key benefit is that the customer gets access to the shared resources without having to set up, operate, and maintain all of the software, hardware, network, and so on. SLAs are essential in cloud computing since the customer is so reliant on the service provider for critical business work. While cloud computing is relatively new, it really had its base in the 1950s and 1960s when customer firms did not have their own IT operation, but instead used a service bureau to meet their computing needs.

Here are the key steps in setting up an SLA:

- Step 1: Both the customer and the supplier should gather information about each other in preparation for not only decision-making, but also negotiations. For example, the service provider should determine if they can supply the needed type of service. On the customer side, there is a requirement to clearly (emphasize this work, clearly) identify the services required, priorities, and service levels need.
- Step 2: The customer and the service provider should have a number of meetings to discuss services, performance, and related terms of the SLA. This step is critical so that both are on the same page. There needs to be a common understanding of these before the effort begins on the SLA and the contract.
- Step 3: The customer and the service provider need to cover their working relationship. This includes responsibilities, transition of work and data, issues management, and conflict resolution. Why not do this during the formal negotiations? It may then be too late that they find irreconcilable differences.
- Step 4: Develop the terms and conditions of the SLA. This only results in a draft agreement.

- Step 5: You must gain agreement within the customer organization—not just at upper management levels, but also at business and IT management levels. Managers have to understand the implications of what they are getting into. Life will be very different as they are going to be very, very dependent on an outside firm over which they have limited influence and control. This will likely generate questions and require more negotiations.
- Step 6: Conduct final negotiations and enter into the agreement.
- Step 7: Both sides must immediately devote sufficient resources to effect an orderly, timely, and non-disruptive transition. Some of the work involves setting up procedures, measurement systems, reporting methods, training, and communicating with employees of the customer firm.

The next sections provide more detailed guidelines for each step in the procurement process.

Gather requirements for outsourcing

The first step here is to identify the candidate for outsourcing. Earlier, a list was presented of potential outsourcing activities. Some criteria for selecting the activity for outsourcing are as follows:

- Risk and exposure if a vendor runs into trouble. This would negate considering outsourcing critical business processes.
- The likelihood that the vendor has the required knowledge and skills for the work.
- The extent to which you are willing to depend on an external firm with its own agenda.
- The interdependence between activities. In some cases, you cannot outsource one activity without including others that are highly related.
- The potential impact if the vendor fails to perform adequately.
- The extent to which the activity includes critical business knowledge.

Having decided on the activity, you should measure it and determine if there are problems that need to be addressed before it is outsourced. You want to take steps to clean up the work or systems prior to outsourcing. This will reduce the overall cost and time as well as giving you more precise requirements and knowledge of what will be outsourced.

Here is a list of potential cleanup activities:

- You can make minor changes to the existing systems.
- Employees could be retrained so that their work is more productive and standardized.
- Procedures and policies can be reviewed and updated. Exceptions can be eliminated.
- The facilities and work layout could be changed.
- Work assignments could be altered.

Doing work in these areas can reduce the cost of outsourcing. In some cases, after the cleanup the work was so efficient that the outsourcing push was stopped.

While this is going on, you can identify potential vendors and gather information about the vendor, their products, services, and track record of performance. To speed things up, you want to do this in parallel to the cleanup.

A third parallel activity is to develop requirements. Requirements here are not only for the services or work to be performed, but also how performance will be measured, how the outsourcing work will be started, how the outsourcing vendor will be managed and tracked, and the procedures for issues management.

Carry out requisition and proposal solicitation

You have the requirements and have identified vendors. What next? You will prepare an SOW that will be distributed to vendors. It will be included in the RFPs or RFQs. It should include the following items:

- Objectives of the outsourcing.
- Requirements for the outsourcing work.
- Skills and knowledge required of the vendor.
- Methods and tools to be used in the work.
- Request for a standard boilerplate contract.
- Schedule for the work.
- Transition approach that will be used after contract signing.
- Project plan that will be employed jointly by the vendor and firm.
- Issues management and resolution approach.
- Measurement techniques and standards of performance.
- Technology and systems used in work performance.
- Evaluation method and criteria that will be employed in evaluating the proposals.
- References to be provided by the vendor for future contact during the evaluation.

How do you conduct the procurement? In addition to submitting the SOW to vendors, you may elect to hold a bidders' conference. Here the organization presents the requirements, evaluation approach, and other information relevant to the contract. At this conference, vendors can ask questions for clarification. Questions could involve the availability of internal staff, how the process works, existing documentation, and so on. Vendors are then allowed to submit questions in writing. After these are addressed, the answers are submitted to all vendors.

Undertake proposal evaluation and selection

You have to have a framework for evaluating the proposals. Often, a list of criteria for evaluation is devised. For each criterion a relative weight is assigned. When the proposals are received, they are evaluated individually by each member of the evaluation team. Meetings are held to gain consensus on the scores for each criterion. Then a total score is calculated for each vendor proposal. Examples of weights and criteria might include the following:

- Previous experience in the same industry;
- Software features and capabilities;
- Quality of the people proposed for the work;
- Price quoted in the proposal;
- Qualifications of the firm;
- Whether or not the vendor is a small business or minority firm.

These are just examples. Obviously, the process, criteria, and so on are defined by the organization and its needs. Government procurements have to follow very explicit rules. Another task after the receipt of the proposals is to have legal staff review the standard contract of the vendor for any problems or issues.

During the evaluation, you will likely contact existing or past customers of a vendor. If you ask questions such as "Were you satisfied with the vendor's performance?", you are likely to get vague and general answers. Most customers will not admit they made the wrong choice, because then they look bad. It is better to ask indirect questions such as follows:

- What surprises arose during the work?
- What are some of the lessons learned they acquired from the experience?
- If they could make changes to the past, what might some of them be?
- Did they work with the same vendor staff and managers throughout the work?
- What was their process for tracking performance and handling problems?

Answers to these and similar questions cannot only provide insight into vendor performance, but also give you some ideas to help hone your evaluation and management of outsourcing vendors.

Now advance in time and assume you have done the evaluation. Do you now select the vendor? No. The next step is to conduct vendor interviews. In these the firm presents the structure of the meeting. The vendor makes a short presentation summarizing its proposal and its capabilities. The remainder of the time is for the evaluation team to pose questions to the vendor. Examples of questions could include the following:

- How would they address specific issues?
- What is their approach to the transfer of knowledge and skills in case there is staff turnover?
- How do they propose to communicate with the firm?
- What project management techniques do they employ?
- How do they address work change requests?
- What methods and tools will be used? What is their level of experience in these?
- What is their experience with other firms in the same or similar industries?
- What lessons learned were gained from their last assignments?
- In doing similar work before, what issues and problems typically arose?
- How do they track their projects and work?

In most cases, you will want to select a winner and backup. This will allow you to have flexibility during negotiations and have a fallback approach. This also gives you a political advantage in that the winning vendor is fully aware that there is a backup vendor if negotiations fail.

Conduct contract negotiation

Negotiations are an art unto themselves. The basis for any negotiation is that you want some things from them and they, in turn, want some things from you. You can consider negotiation as being in several stages. The first stage is preparation. You have to have a clear idea about how you will present your points as well as which items you must have and what you would like to have.

Prior to negotiation there is an exchange of information. The vendor has the SOW, answers to questions generated by the bidders' meeting, and the results of the meeting with the firm. The company has the proposal and the results of their research and evaluation as well as the results from the meeting with the vendor.

The third stage is that of bargaining or negotiating. Typically, you have the standard boilerplate contract from the vendor. You could turn this over to lawyers. However, they often do not have the IT knowledge as well as detailed knowledge of the requirements. One way to begin the discussion is to focus on the work. This then leads into work tracking, measurements, and management. In addition to costs, you can negotiate on the schedule, the management, and the other aspects of work already mentioned. It is helpful if you have people involved who have negotiated successfully in the past. After all, the vendor has negotiated many times before and has greater experience than your people do.

Let's take a personal example. A husband and wife friend of the author went to Asia. While he worked, she shopped for two sweaters. She had never negotiated or haggled before. She negotiated on the price she would pay in the United States rather than the going price in Asia. She came back with two sweaters that cost $30 each and felt happy. Her husband took her back shopping the next day to demonstrate negotiations. When asked the price the vendor said "$50.00 each". He responded with $12. The vendor went down in price. He repeated the same price. They settled on a price of $15 for one sweater. Then the husband asked what was the price for two sweaters. The vendor said $15. The husband said $10. They settled at $12 each. You should work on negotiating skills.

Establish the initial working vendor relationship

OK. The contract negotiation is over. The contract is signed. Now what? Where do you start? You want to get going fast since the clock is ticking. Do the following tasks in parallel.

- Establish the method for communicating status, work questions, issues, and knowledge.

- Create a joint detailed project plan.
- Conduct orientation and mini-training sessions of vendor staff so that they gain familiarity with the work.
- Identify the issues in the transition of the work.
- Cover how, where, and what work will be done initially.
- Determine the detailed work tracking and measurement methods.

Now let's turn to the initial work. The first work tasks in any outsourcing relationship are extremely important. First, they show the level of involvement by both sides. Second, by carefully reviewing their end products of work, you show what you expect of quality and how you will perform reviews. Third, from the start begin to identify and deal with issues. The issues at the start should be minor, but they are important. Why? Because you use this experience to establish the method for resolving future, more major issues.

Manage vendor work and relationships

For managing work and/or services you will be using the SLA as the base. Here are some guidelines for managing vendor work after the initial period of work.

- In reviewing vendor work direct your attention to issues. Unless these are addressed, budget and schedule problems will surface.
- Conduct both unannounced and announced visits to the vendor site. In a case in Singapore we recommended this approach to a project leader who was managing staff in another Southeast Asian country. They had told her that everything was going well. The problems came out when she made an unannounced visit.
- Conduct quality of work reviews separate from performance reviews. If you combine these, then the attention will mostly fall on performance.
- Review in detail any requests for additional work by the vendor. Ask the following questions:

  ○ Why did this request come up now?
  ○ What is behind the request?
  ○ What if the request is not addressed? What are the impacts on the business?
  ○ What are the tangible benefits of results from addressing the request? How would they be verified?

- Conduct technical sessions in which knowledge is transferred to the internal staff. Inform the staff ahead of time that they might have to take over the work or the system. This will increase their level of interest.
- On issues management you want to focus on not only problems with the current work, but also future issues related to implementation or other services.
- When you measure the impact of vendor problems and non-performance, give special attention to the impact of the problems on business processes. This may help provide leverage with the vendor.

Dealing with multiple vendors

Let's suppose that you have several vendors on the same project. You can assume that there will be problems in how the vendors get along with each other. After all, they see their main relationship with the customer who pays them. To give this importance, set up a separate, but related project consisting of tasks that involve multiple vendors. This would include, for example, testing and integration. By managing it as a separate project, you give sufficient attention to the interfaces among the vendors. Issues management would carry over to this joint project. For issues that involve more than one vendor, have separate issues meetings with the vendors involved.

Cases and examples

Beaumont insurance

In one of their lines of business, the business unit relied totally on one vendor for key software for application processing and claims. Insurance regulations changed and the business unit submitted new requirements to the vendor. The changes had to be made by January of the year 20XX. The vendor then promised to deliver new software by September of the preceding year. The business unit accepted the answer and waited. And waited. By August the business unit was contacting the vendor every day. In late August when they called, they were told that the number had been disconnected. The new software was never delivered. The firm declared bankruptcy. The business unit now operated in a panic and crisis mode. A product from another vendor was found. However, the new software was installed in May of the year 20XX. What did the business unit do until May? They had to hire staff to process the work manually. Costs soared. Revenue dropped as they were unable to handle a large volume of applications. Business managers were sacked and terminated.

In another business unit, there was a call center for customers. It was very inefficient and staff turnover was high. Management thought it was a good candidate for outsourcing. Fortunately, this was stopped. Instead, the cleanup work of the process and work was performed as discussed earlier in this chapter. Procedures were improved and the system was enhanced. Turnover dropped and the efficiency and productivity rose. The activity was then outsourced. Had the business unit outsourced before cleanup, the cost would have been much higher and taken longer.

Questions:

1. What should the business unit have done to more closely monitor the vendor?
2. How could the problems have been foreseen and detected?
3. At what point should they have lined up an alternate vendor?

Sycamore University

At Sycamore the IT group provides a Web hosting service to faculty, students, student groups, and administrators. This was set up to achieve economies of scale and uniformity of standards as well as improve productivity of users. The SLA contains the following:

- What is to be delivered and supported? This includes course delivery as well as document sharing.
- Hours of operation and available times for support availability.
- Operating systems, browsers, and other software supported.
- Attempt to resolve issues and problems within 2 hours after initial contact.
- Security practices and policies to be followed.
- Updates to supported material.
- Online documentation to help users.
- Guidelines for users in terms of space.
- User registration.
- Support for domain names.

SLAs also include things that are not covered. In this instance, these include the following: customized programming and development, content and information architecture, and support on any non-standardized platforms. Note that this is an internal SLA and so does not have some of the formal parts that an external SLA would have.

Questions:

1. If the SLA had been with an external firm, what additional items would have been required for the use of an outside vendor?
2. Why do you think the IT group thought that an internal SLA was necessary? Include political reasons in your discussion.
3. Thinking of IT in general, what areas of internal IT are suited to SLAs?

Mapping to the PMBOK and PRINCE2

The PMBOK

Chapter 12 of the PMBOK deals with project procurement management. There are four parts:

- Plan procurements. Here some of the things considered include the following: requirements, risks, schedule, costs, performance, internal assets, and environmental factors. The end products are the procurement plan, SOW, selection criteria for vendors. Organizations experienced in IT procurements have little problems here since they have done it many times. The problems arise in organizations with little experience. Here is what can happen in such situations. A vendor displays their system to the organization. They get excited and want it. They rush into the contract without following the steps in this section. Later, they find the system does not meet their requirements. Or, that the vendor does not perform as advertised.

- Conduct procurements. A step-by-step approach is defined that is analogous to the methods in this chapter. As was stated earlier, large organizations and government agencies have strict procurement procedures. The problems arise during procurement at smaller firms or where the amount of money is small. Then sole sourcing can occur in which one vendor is given a contract without competitive bidding. A vendor could make an artificially low-cost estimate for initial work in the anticipation of adding to the cost later. This indicates the need for tight controls on procurement related to IT and strong requirements for sole source justification.
- Administer procurements. This section deals with managing the vendor work as well as dealing with change requests. IT projects and outsourcing often have a significant number of changes due to increased knowledge of the project and changing or more detailed requirements. You should anticipate in any outsourcing arrangement that changes will arise. Guidelines for dealing with changes were addressed in this chapter and Chapter 9.
- Close procurements. This section deals with closing out the contract and gathering lessons learned. The only significant difference here with this chapter is that we recommend gathering and using lessons learned as the work is being performed.

PRINCE2

In PRINCE2 there is not a separate section on procurement. Referring back to Chapter 2, procurement is included in the business case in terms of justification, lessons learned, focus on end products, and customization to suit the project. In terms of themes in PRINCE2 the business case, plans, change management, and progress apply to procurement. Two processes apply to procurement: project initiation and managing product delivery.

Lessons learned

If you are a vendor and are attending a bidders' conference, sit in the back of the room so you can observe everyone. Second, let everyone else ask questions. Third, be cautious in asking questions unless you feel they have not been asked or are urgent. Why? You don't want to show your ignorance. The customer will take note of dumb questions.

Another lesson learned is that IT staff are oriented toward technical work. You should improve their communications skills along the lines of Chapter 11. Here they can improve their body language and tone of voice in dealing with vendors. Another step is to make the IT staff aware of the politics involved in outsourcing.

One problem that sometimes occurs is that the vendor will go over the head of IT to upper management. IT may not even know this occurred. What should IT do? To prevent the problem, point this out at the start as a potential issue. Indicate that if this happens, there will be no winner. Alert upper management that this may happen. Give examples of what information the vendor may convey. This will also help. Another guideline is to have regular communications with management.

Guidelines

When you are in an outsourcing relationship, have separate meetings on schedules, work, and issues. Experience shows that if these are combined in one meeting, there can be a lack of focus. Moreover, issues may get insufficient attention. Another guideline on meetings is to vary the frequency of the issues meetings based on their urgency and importance.

If you are going to transfer knowledge to the vendor, make sure that you give the information to the people who will be doing the actual work. If you go through an intermediary, there can be problems. Requirements and features may be misunderstood and then miscommunicated to the vendor staff. Vendor staff ask questions through the intermediary so that you get garbled or partial questions. These things can lead to extensive rework and extra work. In two cases, they resulted in failed projects.

If you hear nothing from the vendor for a substantial time, don't assume everything is fine. Assume the worst. They are working on tasks for other customers. There has been staff turnover at the vendor site. They have run into a major problem and do not want to admit it. As we said earlier, stay in regular contact.

Before you start using SLAs internally, think through the consequences as we have discussed. Having an SLA could make relations with certain user groups worse. They would focus on the SLA and not on the actual work and its quality. Some IT managers have even used SLAs to narrow the range of their accountability. If it is not in the SLA, then it is not their problem. This is the political side of internal SLAs.

Questions

1. Search the Web and find an example of project failure when an SLA was in place.
2. Identify potential problems if you have to replace a vendor for non-performance with another vendor.
3. Select a particular IT activity and discuss the pros and cons of outsourcing.
4. What if you are in negotiations with a specific vendor and the situation deteriorates. You are forced with the decision of whether to salvage the negotiations or to begin new negotiations with the backup vendor. How do you decide what to do?
5. A vendor has performing their work well. Milestones are of good quality. The schedule has been met. They are about to turn over the software. Discuss alternatives for software maintenance.

What to do next

1. Review your current outsourcing arrangements. Are there standard measures of performance employed across all contracts? Or, is measurement performed on a case-by-case basis?
2. How successful was your firm in negotiating with vendors? Did you always use the standard contract provided with the vendor?

3. Look at the issues that surfaced in recent outsourcing arrangements. What do they have in common? Perhaps, you should generate and distribute a list of commonly encountered issues for future outsourcing.
4. Suppose that you have a vendor on which you are very dependent. What would be the backup plan if their service level deteriorated? What would be needed to be able to do the work internally.

Summary

There is no way to avoid some outsourcing at home or in IT-related work. It is just a fact of life. Therefore, procurement management should be treated in a standard, formal manner and not just *ad hoc* approaches for each outsourcing effort. Key to outsourcing is to have negotiating and communications skills. These are critical not only during negotiation of the original contract, but also for issues management and changes to the contract.

If you are going to be an effective project leader, you also must be able to manage vendor-supported projects. This can take the form of having a vendor staff member on your team. Alternatively, it could mean that you have to manage a project that is being done thousands of miles away by a vendor.

15
Measuring projects and project management

Introduction

When you ask many managers if they think that measurement is important, they would respond in the affirmative. Yet, in many organizations, there is a lack of measurement—at both the project level and the project management overall level. There is often a great deal of analysis performed to justify a project, but then at the end there is much less interest, drive, and energy in measuring whether the project did actually deliver the results. People move on to other things. The business continues to function, so things must have turned out all right, correct? The answer is that they don't know. It is the same with many books on project management which give the standard measures of progress, but fail to address more comprehensive measurement at the end.

From our experience as both consultants and managers, we have learned the real value to measurement and its importance. That is why we have included an entire chapter on measurements. Why does someone conduct measurements? One reason is to see what is going on. A second reason is to gather lessons learned that will help in future work and projects. A third reason is to better identify and select projects. Remember the goal of the book is for you to attain cumulative improvement. To do this you have to know where and in what state you are in now and have been.

In this chapter there are over 15 sets of measurements for different aspects of projects, multiple projects, and management. For each there is an extensive list of potential measurements. Can you use all or most of them? Of course not. There is just not enough time and energy. We suggest that you should use some of these and then expand their use. Another guideline is that you want to interpret and use the measurements for your current and future work. Therein lies their ultimate value. Let's take an example from everyday life. A man goes to the doctor who measures weight, blood pressure, and so on. The doctor tells the patient that he weighs too much and has a blood pressure reading that is too high. The guy leaves the doctor's office and just goes on about his life. He changes nothing. Later, not to the doctor's surprise, he gets very ill with diabetes and other diseases. What happened? He did not act on the measurements.

Why performance measures fail

Let's examine some of the reasons why performance measurements fail. Nineteen commonly encountered reasons appear in Figure 15.1.

Management selects measurements that are too subjective. You really want a mixture of subjective and objective measurements.

Management implements too many measurements at the same time. Doing the measurements and using them can slow down the work and project.

The purpose of the measurements is not clear or stated. This can result in a lack of motivation to carry out the measurements.

There is no one who is identified to provide ongoing coordination. Measurements in such situations are done *ad hoc* and often too late for effective actions.

- Measurements are collected but not used. People lose faith in doing measurements. "Why do it if nothing happens?"
- Management jumps at initial measurement data to the wrong conclusions. This can cause a change of direction in a project and lead to eventual failure.
- There are no previous measurements with which to compare. You are given a number, say 8. But you are not told what is acceptable performance. So the value of the 8 is unclear.
- Some people attempt to slant the performance measurements. This happens all of the time in politics. Organizations are political. Managers have their own agendas so this point is not surprising at all.
- There is a lack of statistical or analytical skills in the people analyzing the data. In one firm we worked with, the manager insisted on many measurements. However, there was no one qualified to do the analysis and set up a database for future use.
- Performance data is collected but is used incorrectly. This can be due to misinterpretation and lack of familiarity with the type of project being undertaken.
- There is no database to retain performance data. Projects are measured separately and individually. There can be little cross and multiple project analysis without some use of a database of measurements.
- Once performance data problems are noted, there is no corrective action.
- Performance measures are perceived as too subjective and political. As a result, people do not trust them and ignore them. There is no effective action.
- One manager pushes performance measures to the exclusion of other things such as the milestone reviews.
- Too much effort goes into measurement. This reduces the amount of effort available to manage and do the work.
- Too much detailed measurement data is collected. Most of the time people measure too little. This is the other side of the coin where much of the data is not used.
- Data is collected at the wrong time. An example is to identify the benefits immediately at the conclusion of a project. However, change in the organization may take time. Reversion and resistance to change may occur. Benefits which looked good may evaporate.
- Performance measurement is linked to a specific management action (e.g., to change the organization).

Figure 15.1 Common reasons for failure of project performance measurement

> - Too many people are involved in measurements. This can consume too much time of managers and staff.
> - There is a lack of structure to the way data is collected. This can result in erroneous data about a project. The effect may be to divert the project manager from managing to dealing with the measurements.

Figure 15.1 (Continued)

Critical success factors for measurements

Over the years we have identified these 11 critical success factors in measurement.

- Select specific measures that address key management questions. Examples might be the benefits of projects, issues that lead to project delays and overruns, and selected business processes.
- Define and simulate how the data collection and analysis process will work. This is useful since it not only prepares for the measurement, but also gains credibility for the measurements.
- Identify the approach for staffing for performance measures on an ongoing basis. This does not mean hiring someone full time for this, but it does mean that management should have a rotational staffing plan.
- Develop a database for performance measurement to serve as a repository for later analysis.
- Define the charts, graphs, reports, and so on that will be used for analysis ahead of time. This prepares the organization for what they will see. When you see a chart, you first try to understand its structure and then its meaning. This action cuts out the first part.
- Carefully explain to employees the purpose of performance measurement, how the data will be used. This is intended to remove any fear and gain participation.
- Link any improvements and change to the measurement to show the importance of measurement. Measurements need to be reinforced to avoid becoming *ad hoc* in a response to a crisis.
- Estimate the effort required for measurement before selecting performance measures.
- Identify initial measurements that will lead to Quick Hits and results. This will give credibility and support to the measurements.
- Implement measurement awareness training or orientation.
- Avoid the Heisenberg Principle which is that what you are observing changes when you measure it. This applies to measuring work in progress.

Implementation of measurements

There are too many measures to implement at one time. Here are some possible strategies to use in planning your measurements.

- Strategy one

  Concentrate on general measures
  Projects, processes, IT, and so on.

- Strategy two

  Concentrate on single project measures
  Project work, project selection, project termination, and so on.

Another part of implementation is to plan your data collection. Here are some questions to answer:

- Can the data be generated automatically?
- What is the effort required to collect the data?
- How will the data be stored?
- How will the data be used?
- What errors and problems can arise from data collection?
- How will the data be analyzed?
- Who will coordinate the performance measurement process?

The next sections present score cards or measurements for many areas of IT, projects, and processes. Note that there are too many items for you to measure. We did this by intent so that you could be selective in which to employ. Additionally, some measurements are recurring and some are used once. Note that there is some overlap in the lists since one item may be relevant to more than one list.

IT scorecard

The IT scorecard is given in Figure 15.2.

- Number of IT employees.
- Number of employees.
- Ratio of IT employees to total employees.
- Percentage of projects generated proactively. Proactive here means that the project idea was generated at lower levels of the organization and not by management. The higher the percentage, the more involved the employees are.
- Percentage of resources dedicated to projects. Projects are the most frequent approach to gain long-term improvement. Thus, it is better to have a higher than lower percentage. You can apply this to your own life in that the more time you spend on projects, the less you spend on maintenance and so your life and career will more likely advance.
- Average duration of projects. We have said that projects with a duration of over 1 year have a higher likelihood of failure.
- Percentage of projects that yield real benefits. This should be high, but often is not due to lack of measurement after the project is completed.
- Percentage of projects completed on time.

Figure 15.2   The IT scorecard

- Percentage of projects completed within budget.
- Percentage of total resource hours on projects that produced tangible benefits. This is important in that the organization should turn intangible benefits into tangible ones.
- Percentage of project ideas turned down. This should be substantial since it would reflect the presence of many new ideas. If the percentage is zero or very low, then there may be a lack of new project ideas.
- Common issues across projects. This indicates that the organization is tracking issues across projects.
- Use of templates.
- Turnover of IT employees.
- Transfer of knowledge from vendors. This is hard to measure directly. Instead, you could measure the number of problems with vendors due to lack of information.
- Common plans with vendors.
- Common issues database with vendors.
- Average time to resolve issues for IT.
- Average time to resolve issues by vendors.
- Templates for presentations. As was shown in Chapter 11, the use of templates here can save time and lead to faster understanding.
- Meetings for issues and lessons learned.
- Milestone and documentation evaluation method. Is there a standardized approach to selecting and evaluating milestones and documents for review?
- Requirements checklists.
- Process measurement and score cards.
- Process plans. There are too many processes for doing this totally. However, there should be process plans in place for the top 10 or so processes.
- Coordination role for issues, lessons learned, and templates. How are these maintained, updated, and deployed?

Figure 15.2   (Continued)

Project management scorecard

This list applies to the project management process used by the organization (Figure 15.3).

- Do you have an established, proven project management method in place?
- Does the method address small projects? An important question is how an organization addresses small projects. Part of this is what is the dividing line between a small and a large project.
- How does the method address issues and risk?
- When is a project called a project versus being treated as normal work?
- Are lessons learned gathered as the project work is being done or at the end of the project?

Figure 15.3   The project management scorecard

- Do you measure the percent of project work with risk?
- Is there multiple project analysis in place (project portfolio analysis)?
- How are resources allocated across projects?
- How is experience employed to improve project planning?
- Are lessons learned employed to discuss how to do the next phase of a project?
- How are resources diverted from non-project work to projects and vice versa?
- How is non-project work controlled?
- How are new project ideas generated? Proactively or reactively?
- Are project templates employed or does the project planning start from the scratch for each project?
- How do project leaders work together?
- How are issues that are common across projects handled?
- Do team members get involved in defining tasks?
- How are junior project leaders given experience and help?
- Are vendors required to share issues with the project team?
- How is knowledge transferred from vendors?

Figure 15.3 (Continued)

The project scorecard

This list can be employed throughout the life of a project (Figure 15.4). It links closely with Chapter 12.

- Number of open issues by type
- Number of issues by type
- Total number of issues
- Total number of open issues
- Percentage of issues unresolved
- Average time to resolve an issue by type
- Average time to resolve an issue
- Percentage of issues not controllable in the project
- Percentage of open issues not controllable in the project
- Percentage of milestones in the future
- Percentage of milestones in the future with risk and issues
- Age of oldest outstanding issue
- Percentage of future tasks with risk and issues
- Percentage of tasks with risk and issues
- Percentage of manpower hours with risk
- Percentage of future manpower hours ahead with risk and issues
- Existence of baseline schedule
- Use of project file
- Are issues associated with the individual tasks in the plan?

Figure 15.4 The project scorecard

> - Was the plan created from template?
> - Are resources assigned to tasks?
> - Are tasks defined by team members?
> - Are tasks updated by team members?
> - Is there an issues database for the project
> - Are lessons learned captured during project work?
> - Number of people in the team—full time versus part time
> - Turnover of team members
> - Number of people in the team by area
> - Budget versus actual costs
> - Schedule performance
> - Percentage of milestones achieved on time
> - User involvement. This could be measured by the extent of the project work performed by uses.
> - What is the average time required to reach a decision on an issue? This may seem difficult to estimate so you could, instead, consider the age of the unresolved issues.

Figure 15.4   (Continued)

Project selection scorecard

The project selection scorecard is given in Figure 15.5. This topic is covered in Chapters 3 and 4.

> - Number of project ideas in total. Hopefully, this is a substantial number.
> - Number of project ideas that were proactively generated. These include project ideas by employees to improve work and processes.
> - Number of project ideas that were reactively generated. These are ideas generated by a crisis or issue and would not have arisen naturally. Examples are the Y2K projects as well as projects required due to government regulation.
> - Percentage of project ideas approved.
> - Mix of approved projects by levels of issues and risk, size, benefits, and alignment to the mission of the organization.
> - Percentage of project ideas that result in true tangible benefits.
> - Source of project ideas. This is the percent of project ideas that are as follows:
>
>   Generated by management
>   Generated by process improvement
>   Generated by business requests
>   Generated by infrastructure need
>   Generated by competitive pressure
>
> - Percentage of project ideas rejected or put into the project backlog.
> - Number of project ideas that result in long-term projects.
> - Whether benefits are really measured.
> - The types of financial measurements used.

Figure 15.5   The project selection scorecard

Issues management scorecard

The issues management scorecard is given in Figure 15.6. This list corresponds to Chapter 12.

- Is there a common list of issues across all projects?
- Is each project idea evaluated in terms of issues?
- Are issues common to several projects treated at the same time?
- Are issues of different types treated separately?
- Are recurring issues recognized?
- Is the aging of unresolved issues tracked?
- Are management decisions based on the future of projects based upon unresolved issues?
- Are issues reported on as part of project reporting?
- Are issues examined by status, type, and impact?
- How many issues have been uncovered so far?
- How many new issues have been uncovered in the past year?
- Are issues discussed in project meetings?

Figure 15.6 The issues management scorecard

Methods and tools scorecard

The methods and tools scorecard is given in Figure 15.7. This list refers to the discussion of methods and tools in Chapter 8.

- Is there a formal list of approved methods and tools?
- Does this list cover the methods and tools actually in use?
- Is there a formal method for identifying, evaluating, and selecting new methods and tools?
- Is there a process for reviewing the use of the current methods and tools?
- Have the gaps been identified for methods and tools?
- Have the methods been mapped to the tools?
- Is the effectiveness of specific methods and/or tools measured?
- Are lessons learned gathered in the use of methods and tools?
- Are lessons learned employed when methods and tools are used?
- How is information related to methods and tools shared?
- How are specific methods and tools identified for elimination? How is the elimination carried out?

Figure 15.7 The methods and tools scorecard

Project work scorecard

The project work scorecard is given in Figure 15.8. This list refers to Chapter 9.

- Percentage of tasks that are assigned to one person. This should be low to support teamwork.
- Percentage of tasks that last longer than 2 weeks. This should be low to aid in tracking of work.
- Percentage of tasks that go beyond their estimated time.
- Percentage of tasks that have been added since the initial plan was approved.
- Percentage of hours of tasks assigned to one person.
- Percentage of hours of detailed tasks that are longer than 2 weeks.
- Percentage of hours of tasks that go beyond their estimated time.
- Percentage of vendor work that is not jointly carried out with employees. If this is very low, then there may be knowledge transfer problems.
- Percentage of business unit work that is not joint with other employees. A high percentage might indicate an overreliance on one person.
- Percentage of work that does not result in reviewable milestones.
- Percentage of tasks covered by formal methods and tools.
- Number of methods without tools used in the project.
- Number of gaps in methods and tools used in the project.
- Number of methods and tools without an expert.
- Is there an evaluation method for methods and tools?
- Are new methods and tools systematically evaluated?
- Are there measures for method and tool effectiveness?

Figure 15.8   The project work scorecard

Business mission and vision scorecard

The business mission and vision scorecard is given in Figure 15.9. This refers to the discussion of business mission and vision in Chapter 4.

- Is there a defined business mission and vision?
- Have IT objectives been mapped to the business mission and vision?
- Have business processes been mapped to the business mission and vision to set priorities for work?
- Are project ideas mapped to the business mission and vision?
- Is the alignment to the business mission and vision employed in the selection of projects and the setting of the project slate?
- After a project has been completed, is the change resulting from the project related to the business mission and vision?

Figure 15.9   The business vision and mission scorecard

Business unit scorecard

The business unit scorecard is given in Figure 15.10. This list refers to materials in Chapters 5, 7, 8, and 10.

- Number of different users overall in the project. This is useful since the greater the number of users that are involved in the project, the greater the user support for change and the project.
- Number of users now on the team.
- Percentage of team members that are users. This will depend on the phase of work, but especially during execution, this should be substantial.
- Total number of user-related issues. Since user issues are external to the project, this is an important measure.
- Number of user-related open issues.
- Percentage of open issues that are user related.
- Percentage of issues that are user related.
- Average time for users to resolve an issue.
- Age of the oldest outstanding user issue.
- Number of future tasks assigned to user.
- Percentage of future tasks assigned to user.
- Percentage of future effort assigned to user.
- User task schedule performance.
- Number of requirement change requests from users.
- Percentage of user requirement change requests approved and implemented.
- Quality of user work. This is subjective so that it is sometimes more useful to surprises and the number of issues resulting from work by the business unit staff.
- Relationship of users in team to other users. This is political. If all you have are junior users, then you are more likely to run into resistance to change since the senior users were not made part of the team.
- Percentage of user tasks that are joint with IT. This helps the transfer of knowledge of the business to the IT staff and the understanding of the work and what is required by the business.
- Percentage of user tasks that are joint with vendors. These are tasks without IT involvement. Such tasks can lead to misunderstandings.
- Percentage of user tasks involving more than one person. You want this to be high since otherwise you are overly dependent on one person.
- Knowledge level of users in project about their business processes. You can measure this by the number of surprises and issues that arise from the user work.
- Number of surprises from data supplied by users. This can be especially nasty and lead to major rework.

Figure 15.10 The business unit scorecard

Business process scorecard

The business process scorecard is given in Figure 15.11.

- Number of people directly involved in the process by department.
- Total number of people involved in the process.
- Turnover of employees by department.
- Turnover of employees involved in the process. A high number has advantages and disadvantages. On the negative side, the users lack history and knowledge of the process. On the positive side, they are less likely to resist change.
- Facilities used by process. There could be facilities issues such as lack of space, heat, and so on that impact the work as much or more than those addressed by the project.
- Systems provided. This could include the age of the systems, the amount of enhancement work, and the outstanding backlog of work.
- Costs of the process in terms of the following:

  - Total cost
  - Total personnel cost
  - Total IT costs

- Volume of work performed.
- Frequency of transactions.
- Number of reported problems by type.
- Average time to perform a transaction.
- Mix of work performed.
- Extent of rework.
- Percentage of work in exceptions.
- Percentage of work in workarounds. Recall a workaround occurs when someone bypasses the system to do the work.
- Percentage of work in shadow systems. A shadow system is work performed using a non-IT-supported process or system. Examples might be formulas and spreadsheets.
- Number of exceptions. Exceptions disrupt normal work so that the more they exist, the lower the productivity.
- Number of shadow systems.
- Number of workarounds.
- Quality and completeness of training. You can measure this indirectly by the amount of time senior employees and supervisors spend helping more junior staff.
- Employee skills. You could measure this indirectly by the number of complaints and problems.
- Quality and completeness of procedures. You can get at this by assessing the extent of informal procedures.
- Relevance of policies. Are the policies in the department followed in the work? This can be reflected in the number of exceptions.
- Extent of collaborative work in department. Collaboration works not only in IT, but also in business departments.
- Reliance on key people for the process. This sounds subjective but you could measure average seniority of employees and get a distribution of their department longevity.
- Volume of work per employee.
- Number of problems per unit of volume.

Figure 15.11   The business process scorecard

- Cost and revenue measurements:

  - IT cost/total cost
  - Employee cost/total cost
  - Cost per transaction
  - Revenue of process
  - Profit of process
  - Revenue per transaction

Figure 15.11 (Continued)

Resource allocation scorecard

The resource allocation scorecard is given in Figure 15.12. This list refers to materials in Chapter 4.

- Is there a proactive periodic resource allocation? Resource allocation that is reactive to events can lead to disruption and lower productivity.
- How are resources allocated across projects?
- How is non-project work controlled and reduced?
- Are there management measures to control or reduce non-project work?
- Is resource allocation followed up in terms of performance?
- Are there any penalties if resources do not perform as allocated?
- Are project leaders rewarded for releasing resources?
- How are resource allocations, that are changed, handled?

Figure 15.12 The resource allocation scorecard

Multiple projects scorecard

The multiple projects scorecard is given in Figure 15.13. This list refers to materials in Chapter 4.

- Are benefits of completed projects measured?
- What projects could have been done instead of what was done?
- How could the resources be applied differently?
- Were users held accountable for benefits?
- Can the method for project selection deal with small projects?
- What is the impact of project selection upon non-project work?
- Does the project methodology require the users to take actions or just do approvals?
- Are there checklists and guidelines to make the work in the projects more consistent?

Figure 15.13 The scorecard for multiple projects

- How are resources assigned across multiple projects?
- What is the spread or allocation of projects across business units?
- How are infrastructure projects justified?
- Is there any measurement of the processes after the project has been completed to detect reversion and deterioration?
- How are projects across departments addressed?
- How are projects across multiple departments managed?

Figure 15.13   (Continued)

Benefits scorecard

The benefits scorecard is given in Figure 15.14. This list applies to multiple chapters including Chapters 5 and 8.

- What is the condition of process before the project?
- What is the condition of process after the project?
- Reduced staffing.
- Reduced time in clerical work.
- Reduced rework.
- Reduced training time.
- Existence of formal procedures that are actually used.
- Existence of guidelines in how to do the work. Procedures are the "what" while guidelines are the "how." The "how" is just as important as the "what".
- Reliance upon King/Queen bees. This should be reduced.
- Teamwork among users. This should increase due to sharing of guidelines and lessons learned.
- Sharing of lessons learned among users.
- Extent of collaboration with other departments.
- Ability to handle new types of work without exceptions.
- Number of exceptions.
- Percentage of work in exceptions after change.
- Percentage of work in exceptions before change.
- Number of shadow systems before the change.
- Number of shadow systems after the change.
- Employee turnover before the change.
- Employee turnover after the change.
- Volume of work performed.
- Range of transactions.
- Extent and depth of analysis performed by users.
- Average time to do specific transactions before the change.
- Average time to do specific transactions after the change.
- Were the same financial measurements used that were employed to define and approve the project?
- Was ROI measured?

Figure 15.14   The benefits scorecard

Customer/user satisfaction scorecard

The customer/user satisfaction scorecard is given in Figure 15.15. This applies to most of the chapters since user involvement is a critical success factor for projects.

- Number of user complaints.
- Number of user requests.
- Average time to investigate a user complaint.
- Percentage of complaints handled.
- Percentage of complaints outstanding.
- Average time to handle a user complaint.
- Do users try to employ other people to handle problems instead of IT?
- Percentage of complaints that are valid.
- Measurement of benefits of IT and projects.
- Distribution of user complaints across departments.

Figure 15.15   The customer/user satisfaction scorecard

Vendor and consultant scorecard

The vendor and consultant scorecard is given in Figure 15.16.

- Number of vendors involved in the project. The more vendors involved, the greater the complexity and number of issues.
- Number of vendor staff assigned to the project.
- Turnover of vendor staff.
- Percentage of team members that are vendors. This can be an indicator of dependence on external help.
- Number of vendor-related issues.
- Number of vendor-related open issues.
- Percentage of open issues that are vendor related.
- Percentage of issues that are vendor related.
- Average time for vendor to resolve an issue.
- Age of the oldest outstanding vendor issue.
- Number of future tasks assigned to vendor.
- Percentage of future tasks assigned to vendor.
- Percentage of future effort assigned to vendor.
- Vendor task schedule performance.
- Vendor cost performance.
- Number of requirement changes from vendor.
- Quality of vendor work.
- Relationship of vendor staff in team to other vendors.

Figure 15.16   The vendor and consultant scorecard

- Percentage of vendor tasks that are joint with IT.
- Percentage of vendor tasks that are joint with users.
- Percentage of vendor tasks involving more than one person.
- Knowledge level of vendor staff in project.
- Number of surprises from data supplied by vendors.
- Extent of knowledge transfer from vendors. This could be measured by the number of times you have to get answers from vendors.

Figure 15.16   (Continued)

scorecard for rejected project ideas

The scorecard for rejected project ideas is given in Figure 15.17. This list relates to Chapters 3 and 5.

- Is there a formal process for defining new project ideas? This is better than *ad hoc* approaches since it will tend to ferret out more ideas.
- What was the percentage of ideas rejected? It is not evil or bad if this percentage is high. It does not mean that they were poor ideas. It could mean that IT group and the business units have limited resources.
- What were the reasons for rejection of project ideas? If there is no reason given, it may discourage future ideas. A systematic approach is to have standard checklist for rejection.
- Distribution of reasons for rejection. How is the bad news disseminated? This applies in particular to business units which proposed project ideas that were turned down. They could turn hostile. IT should make an effort to determine some Quick Hits to fix problems, if possible.
- Are rejected ideas revisited? They should be since you can often salvage or turn a rejected idea into a valuable one.
- Is there a formal process for reviewing rejected ideas?
- If you could replace a current project with one of the rejected ones, what would it be? Why?

Figure 15.17   The scorecard for rejected project ideas

Project termination scorecard

The project termination scorecard is given in Figure 15.18.

- Percentage of projects that were terminated. This should not be zero. New requirements and demands can cause a redirection of resources necessitating that the project be stopped.

Figure 15.18   The project termination scorecard

> - Percentage of projects that should have been terminated. Why does this occur? One reason is politics. Some managers may have too much at stake for the project to be killed.
> - Were lessons learned gathered after termination? Often, this is not the case. People just want to forget it. However, there can be valuable lessons learned that can be later applied to project evaluation and selection.
> - Is there a formal method for salvage of projects that are ended? You really want to salvage from any project that is stopped. One reason is to better start it later. Another reason is for lessons learned. A third is to identify some Quick Hits that can mitigate the impact of project stoppage.
> - How are resources reallocated from terminated projects?
> - Is there a formal method to evaluate projects for potential termination?
> - How are lessons learned from terminated projects applied to existing projects?
> - Is there an effort to implement methods to predict failure?
> - What is the percentage of projects that are terminated too late?
> - What was the number of hours consumed in terminated projects? This can be employed to improve the project selection process.

Figure 15.18   (Continued)

Resistance to measurements

Resistance to measurements as well as planning and undertaking the measurements is not uncommon. You should anticipate some resistance thereby avoiding an unpleasant surprise. Here are some points of resistance that we have commonly encountered.

- Some managers want simplified measures. They want some "quick and dirty" measure. An example is, "Are we on schedule?" If they ask for no other measurement, then this is oversimplified. To head this off, you should proactively identify multiple measurements at the start of the project.
- Some managers are short-term focused and not long-term. They avoid looking, for example, at whether there will be change after the project.
- Business units may not want their non-performance measured. This implies that you should employ multiple measurements of their involvement and participation.
- Some may think that implementing the measures is too much effort. You want to prevent this by showing that the early measurement effort is reasonable.
- People may be afraid of the changes and impacts that may result from the measurements. You want to demonstrate that many measurements are for understanding.
- People may fear the amount of effort in measurement. To counter this you want to limit the measurements used.

Mapping to the PMBOK and PRINCE2

In both methodologies measurements are stressed as critical in planning, execution, and closure of a project. Measurement is included in each of the strategic plans in

PRINCE2. It is also included in the knowledge areas of PMBOK as well as the setup, implementation, and management of projects. The contents of this chapter fit into both methodologies.

Lessons learned

One basic lesson learned is to plan the measurements for a project in advance. If you start implementing measurements on an *ad hoc* basis, it can be disruptive to the project team and management. Moreover, *ad hoc* measurements can impact productivity negatively.

Another lesson learned is to scale the measurements. In multiple projects, the ones that appear to have few issues can have fewer measurements. The ones with more issues get not only more attention, but also more measurements. There is not enough time to give all projects equal treatment.

Scaling the measurements also applies to a single project. If there are suddenly more active issues, then you will probably measure the work and milestones in greater depth and detail.

Treat measurements as positive. You can tell people if there is a lack of measurements, then they are not as likely to receive recognition for their work since there were few measurements.

It is often the case in projects that measurements related to cost and schedule get priority over those related to quality. The project leader supported by management should employ a balanced set of measurements that include quality.

Guidelines

Here are some guidelines for measurements.

- Financial project management measures are trailing indicators.
- Issue management and handling are leading indicators for projects.

What is success in measurements? Measurements should direct the project leader and management to address problems and issues earlier. Also, with measurements there should be fewer unpleasant surprises later. This can result in less rework and extra work. Often, a standard approach to measurements that is scalable as addressed above should lead to a higher success rate for projects.

It is sometimes the case that measurements lead to the project being cancelled. This is natural and should be expected. It is positive in that resources can be deployed into other work. Also, if some projects are cancelled, it can reduce any complacency among the project teams.

Some measurements likely result in actions. Other measurements are more passive. The measurements related to issues, risks, and quality tend to result in actions.

The traditional balanced scorecard includes financial, learning, process, customer factors. In project management you need more, including the following:

- Process
- Methods and tools
- Team and organizations
- Vendors
- IT and systems
- Financial

You can identify the following stages of using measurements:

Stage 1—Assess where you are now.
Stage 2—Implement measurements for selected projects.
Stage 3—Raise the level of awareness and support for measurements.
Stage 4—Analyze the mission, vision, and processes in terms of measurements.
Stage 5—Use measurements to rate projects.

Here are some additional guidelines:

- There is a need to implement using a low key approach.
- Beware of information hiding and unwillingness to share information.
- Measurement is a good place to start in terms of getting multiple project analysis started.
- Develop specific goals for the initial measurement effort.
- Collect data on current and recent projects.
- Establish a measurement database.
- Consider developing and implementing performance measures bottom up as well as top down.
- Use existing data sources as much as possible—avoid additional, overlapping work.
- Incorporate data collection into project reporting.

Questions

1. Research the Web for a failed project. Examine what measurements were used to determine failure. Propose some additional measurements that could have been employed.
2. A project seems to be on course because there appear to be a limited number of active issues. Later, the project suddenly runs into trouble. A nasty surprise. What additional measurements related to issues could have been used?
3. Organizations have for many years employed actual cost versus planned cost and actual schedule versus planned schedule as key project measurements. Why are these poor indicators and late indicators of problems with projects?
4. A project is completed successfully. The team is dissolved. Yet, problems start to surface with the systems implemented as well as with the business process. What measurements could have foretold this?
5. IT often employs measurements. In many organizations they do so far more than business units. What is the value of measuring business processes? How could you market measurements of business processes to management?

What to do next

1. Take a recently failed project and review the measurements that were used. Could earlier, more extensive measurements have predicted the problems earlier?
2. Review a current project. Have there been any unpleasant surprises? What measurements could have detected the problems earlier?
3. Identify what measurements are in place with respect to issues?

Summary

In many organizations there is the same standard set of measurements for all projects based on schedule and cost. This presents a problem since not all projects are created or implemented equally. There is a need to have a large set of potential measurements that can be triggered based on some of the following factors:

- Number and type of project issues.
- Importance of the project to business vision and mission.
- Impact on the business unit if the project is not successful.
- Extent of resources consumed in either or both of IT and user departments.
- Scope of the project.

Note that size is not on the list. That is because the size of the project alone does not indicate either importance or risk. A routine, large project may require few measurements.

Part four
IT activities

16
Software development

Introduction

The system development life cycle

We define the System Development Life Cycle as a structured approach for work that begins with project definition and ends with system implementation and operation. Everyone agrees that you need some organized approach for defining, designing, building, and implementing software systems. In construction you define the project. With the idea in hand, you can then determine if it is feasible. Now you can gather requirements. After these have been reviewed, you begin the design of the building. This is followed by construction. In constructing a building you have to integrate the various pieces—electrical, air conditioning, and so on. Building is accompanied by integration and testing. Finally, you can move into the building after inspections.

So it is natural that early software development and the SDLC was done with a similar sequential and structure approach consisting of the following stages:

- Define the project;
- Determine the feasibility of doing the project;
- Gather requirements for the system;
- Design the new system;
- Program and unit test the software;
- Integrate and test the software;
- Implement the software.

Included in the later stages were data conversion, user training, and operations procedures. Documentation was produced in each stage to be reviewed. Managers reviewed the documentation for the end products rather than the end products themselves. A baseline is established that freezes the products of the development after each stage.

In the early days of programming and development, there were few software tools and programming was extremely tedious and labor intensive. You really wanted to get each stage right before moving on to the next, because of the effort in making changes and rework. Thus, from the start, the SDLC was viewed as sequential stages.

Probably, the oldest sequential version of the SDLC was the Waterfall Model. This is a truly sequential model spanning definition through maintenance. Due to the sequential nature of work, after the requirements have been signed, there is no formal process to make changes due to new or modified requirements. As a result some systems that were implemented became obsolete on day 1 of operations. This is especially the case if requirements are not well-known and are fuzzy. This is especially true for projects that are complex or are long in duration.

Some version of the SDLC is employed by almost every methodology. This is obvious since you have to know what you are going to do (requirements) and how to do it (design) before you can do it. However, change was in the wind due to:

- Maturity of knowledge due to gathering experiences from development;
- High failure rate of projects;
- Real business need and benefit to be more adaptive to legitimate requirement changes;
- New methods and tools including programming, designing, testing, and integration methods and tools;
- Frustration with the sequential nature of the traditional life cycle.

Evolution of development methods and tools

Over the years many methods and tools for development have emerged. Tools are software packages that aid in the performance of specific tasks. Methods are approaches to undertaking design, development, and other work. Tools support methods. Failure can occur because of some of the following factors:

- The method is unsupported by a tool so that the staff must resort to manual methods.
- The tools are not compatible with each other, resulting in substantial duplication and even contradictory work.
- The method or tool is inflexible, making it inappropriate for some projects (e.g., large or small projects).
- There is no or inadequate vendor support for the tool.
- The learning curve and time consumed using the tool outweigh the benefits.
- There are no management expectations to give the staff a clue as to what is expected of them and their work if they use the method or tool.

The more successful tools have tended to aid programming (editors, compilers, interpreters, debuggers, testers, documentation, and so on), system management (such as network management and configuration management), and reduced programming (such as object-oriented tools and fourth-generation languages (4GLs), and database management systems). Tools to aid system analysis and design (e.g., CASE—Computer Aided Software Engineering) methods, diagramming, and documenting have been less successful. Tools that generate code from design input have been developed, but these have met with limited success. This is because the resulting code must be customized and completed.

Even with various methods and tools, system development efforts and projects have suffered from the following complaints and concerns:

- Business requirements and, hence, system requirements change.
- There are sometimes missing methods, tools, or gaps between them that necessitate manual, *ad hoc* work.
- Benefits from the system resulting from the project are less than estimated.
- Schedules stretch out.
- The project scope expands and changes.
- The role of the business unit and its staff is vague and ill-defined.

There is no magic solution to addressing these issues in the form of off-the-shelf tools. Therefore, you must address these factors through project management of the overall development process.

Alternative development methodologies

Several variants of the waterfall model are: the incremental model, the spiral model, and prototyping. Let's examine each of these briefly before we consider others. Note that since the book is about project management, not all methodologies are covered. Nor is there adequate space to cover each in detail.

Incremental model

The incremental model overlaps the stages of the life cycle to make up for the long development time of the waterfall model. A system can be broken down into parts during requirements and the each part can be designed and developed separately with coordination between the parts. The breakup of the project could even occur during definition of feasibility. An example might be to build a Web-based front end to an old system before core of the existing system is replaced. Unless attention is paid to the interfaces and integration of the various parts, there could be problems later—resulting in sometimes substantial rework. Psychologically, this is appealing since the project team can show users and management earlier results.

Spiral model

The spiral model is based on starting with a limited set of requirements and marching through the development cycle to completion, but not installation. This is the initial iteration or the inner part of the spiral. Each successive iteration adds more capabilities and features resulting in a spiral. Once development is completed, installation and implementation of the system follow.

The benefit of this method is that development can start before all of the requirements have been collected. Moreover, if management changes their minds and stops work, the resources consumed were less than that of the sequential approach. Another benefit is that the team builds more expertise through experience in each iteration.

Prototype model

In prototyping, after requirements you would select some part of the system to model or prototype. The most common part is often the Graphic User Interface (GUI) since that will be how the user interfaces to the system. This prototyping is commonly referred to as Rapid Application Development (RAD) or Rapid Prototyping. Feedback from the prototype is then used for refinement. The method was most useful when users had less experience with online systems. With the growth of Web-based development, its popularity has diminished.

There are several benefits and drawbacks to this approach. One benefit is that the development time may be faster. Another is the users become more involved, as opposed to waiting until the end of the stage. Experience shows that the more involved the business users are, the fewer the requirement changes and the more likely that the benefits will come true. The application software developed during the prototype is often discarded later. The prototype also provides for verification of requirements.

There are several drawbacks. One is that users' expectations are raised due to the short time of the prototyping. Another is that once they see a partially functioning prototype, they think it can be used in production. False. In prototyping difficult problems may be deferred until later. Prototyping also does not include integration or the incorporation of most of the business rules of the business processes.

SCRUM

SCRUM is a term from the sport of rugby. It is a team pack in which everyone works together to move or advance the ball. Developed from frustration with the standard waterfall method, the stages were reduced to four: requirements, design, prototype, and acceptance. This results in overlap and reduced time. This method emphasizes teamwork. Management's role changes from reviewing milestones at the end of phase to acting to deal with problems during the work. The completion date as well project cost are determined during development. If requirements are not defined well early in the project, this method helps to refine these.

Agile development model

Again, from frustration, a number of developers met and created in 2001 a statement or manifesto for Agile software development. This led to the Agile Alliance, a non-profit group, to promote the method.

The method emphasizes the following four principles:

- Individuals and their interaction are favored over processes and tools (corresponds in Agile project management to people over the work).

- Developing working software is given priority over complete documentation.
- Collaboration with the users and/or customers as opposed to formal contracting and negotiation.
- The priority of responding to needs and change is favored over sticking to the plan.

From these principles flow the following:

- Working software is delivered through successive releases.
- Projects center on individuals not work.
- Changes, even late in the project, are tolerated.
- Close coordination on a daily basis is required between users and developers.
- Progress is measured based upon the working software.

Benefits include improved user involvement and satisfaction. Another is simplicity. A third is the ability to respond to change more rapidly.

SCRUM is one variation of the Agile method. It appears at the first glance that Agile is almost the direct opposite of the traditional SDLC. Agile methods incorporate incremental development. Agile differs from prototyping in that under Agile the software delivered in each iteration is functional. Agile is also similar to the spiral method in that iterations are used.

Here are some comments on the measurement of Agile work.

- The team is involved in the specification and design of the measurements. They know then how to focus their work better since they know how it will be measured.
- One of corollaries of Agile is to maximize the work not done.
- Instead of measuring output, you measure value to the user.
- Select only a few metrics or measurements and avoid measuring too much detailed work.
- Try to collect measurements through software tools, rather than manually.
- Measurements are taken at each iteration.

It is possible in some projects to combine methodologies. For example, the user interface part of an online system could be developed using Agile or SCRUM, while the batch part following a waterfall type of method.

Requirements for a development approach

Let's begin by considering what development will be based on. Traditionally, you go out and collect requirements. You obtain many of these from the business unit staff assigned to the project. However, requirements, if just stated by business staff and not verified, are subject to being inaccurate and incomplete. Remember that there is no penalty for giving partial or incomplete information. Moreover, requirements are often not verified until the entire set of requirements is presented to the business unit for approval and sign-off. Experience shows that sign-offs have some, but limited, value. Why? Because they are not a legal, enforceable contract. Because business units may later learn more about the new system features and capabilities and so require changes.

Where will you determine and evaluate requirements? Requirements reflect the activities of the business. As such, it makes sense to observe and analyze the current business process. Requirements for both an improved process and system can be generated. It is also evident that when you observe a business process, you are seeing discrete work—in systems terms transactions. Include management information, reporting, and other work using the systems as transactions. Batch processing is embedded as steps in update transactions (labeled as batch). If there were no current business process, then you would invent the process first to define requirements for a supporting system.

Experience reveals often that interviewing, a traditional method of gathering requirements, has limited value. This is sometimes based on political considerations. The interviewee may not want to reveal their ignorance so they state requirements. The system analyst does not know the business process in detail. So these erroneous statements are incorporated into the requirements. Moreover, if the interviewee is a supervisor, then that person may not be aware of how the current work is performed at the detailed level.

Many types of transactions are available for incorporation into requirements, including both regular and exception transactions. In order to gather them all, you have to spend effort over an extensive elapsed time. Thus, if you take a totally sequential approach, your project will likely fail because the time will run out before all of the requirements are known. As was stated earlier, you want to focus on common transactions. That is where the volume is. You could include critical exception work. What is "critical"? Critical can be defined as work necessary to be included in requirements that is required to achieve the benefits and process change.

Now move ahead to design, development, integration, and testing. If these are treated sequentially, the project elapsed time extends even further. Your approach must be modular to take advantage of the transaction information as it is developed. Information on separate, unrelated transactions gathered later should not disrupt what you have already done. The approach must also be parallel so that additional analysis, design, development, and integration can proceed to the extent possible at the same time. You also have to be open to new methods and tools that are becoming available for intranets, client-server, and object-oriented development.

Let's summarize factors that impact development:

- Base requirements on information about the business process gathered directly or verified with the process.
- Support concurrent design and development for transactions that have already been defined along with continued data collection for other transactions.
- Accommodate linkage between the new and current (including legacy) systems in design efforts early.
- Relate benefits of the system investment to the combined improved business process and the new system.
- Provide an effective management and control approach for development.

- Given that the transactions in the new process will closely integrate manual and automated steps, it is logical that the user procedures be included in the operations manual with the process.

Steps in a development approach

The method described in the following steps is targeted at the preceding factors. These steps are not carried out in sequential order. Experience has shown that work can be going on concurrently in several different steps at the same time.

- *Step 1*: Understand the current business process and transactions as well as current systems in terms of potential interfaces.
- *Step 2*: Define a new or modified transaction and then business process.
- *Step 3*: Determine the benefits, user requirements, and system requirements from Steps 1 and 2 for both new development and modifications and interfaces to current systems.
- *Step 4*: Design the new transactions and system as well as the interfaces with the current systems.
- *Step 5*: Undertake development, testing, and integration.
- *Step 6*: Prepare business operations manuals (which include user procedures), training materials, and operating procedures.
- *Step 7*: Carry out conversion and data setup for the new system and process.
- *Step 8*: Establish business policies, carry out training, and convert to the new process and system.

For each step it is necessary to answer some or all of the following questions:

- What are the end products or deliverable items?
- What are the roles, responsibilities, and tasks involved?
- What are criteria for success?
- How should work be performed?
- How should the work be managed?

What are appropriate methods and tools to support the step? Some of these are established in your organization so that they will not be covered. Guidelines will be covered separately at the end of the chapter.

What are some of the implications of using these steps?

- The burden of managing the project is more intense than traditional development because the approach is conducted in parallel with multiple steps being active.
- The steps support the modular approach mentioned earlier.
- Requirements changes are less because of the way the work is performed with the business unit staff more involved in the project.
- Modern new methods and tools can be applied in any given step.

Step 1: understand the current business process and systems

End products

- Operations procedures or manual of the current process including exceptions as well as issues in the current process. This documents the current business process in terms of transactions and so provides an up-to-date user manual. It explains how the current system is used. This can be a useful side benefit to the business unit from the project, which may never have had such documentation before.
- Interfaces involving and using the current systems. This includes documenting the interfaces in place along with identifying issues, problems, and opportunities for improvement.

Roles and responsibilities

Although a systems analyst or project leader can begin the work and provide guidance, it is essential that the employees of the business unit perform much of the effort. This had several benefits. First, they develop a more formal understanding of the work. Second, they understand the problems with the current situation and can relate these problems to the process and system. They are more eager for change. Third, they become more committed and involved in the project. Given the extensive effort required, consider employing junior staff in the business unit who have more available time. Systems staff will have to support the definition of the interfaces.

Criteria for success

One criterion is the rapid collection and documentation of the work. A second is increasing enthusiasm among business unit employees regarding the project. In addition, you flesh out more exception transactions that lead to having more complete requirements.

Work methods

Consider building the table shown in Figure 16.1 for each transaction. In this table a transaction is divided into discrete steps that can be manual or automated. For each step, identify who (person, computer, customer, and so on) performs it and what actions are performed. These two columns are based on the documentation method known as Playscript. The current automation for the step is described in a column. Business rules is the column where you can supply calculation and logic rules. The column of issues identifies both problems and opportunities. The last column is for impacts due to the issues. You might want to include an additional column on the degree of risk or uncertainty in the definition of the transaction. You must admit if you are not certain about specific issues so that you can concentrate on these areas in this and the next step.

Step	Who	What	Business Rules	Current Automation	Issues	Impacts

Figure 16.1   Existing transactions

Completing this table requires that you carefully cover each significant action. Include such actions as opening mail and contacting customers, but do not get down to hand movements (as in the old days of industrial engineering). From lessons learned it is suggested that you define an initial list of transaction types. Then build the table for several transactions with business staff and conduct a review. These transactions can serve as a model for other transactions—reducing the review effort and improving quality.

Note that you can generate the basis for operating procedures and the operating manual using columns 1, 2, 3, 5, and 6. This is in line with the goal of trying to derive as many benefits from the work as possible.

Management of work

The analyst or project leader establishes the first transaction of each type as well as the overall list of transactions working together with the business unit staff. Coordinating the work of the business unit staff in building additional transactions is accompanied by directing reviews of the work. Reviews may typically add or combine steps as well as leading to the identification of more transactions. Each major exception has its own table. Small variations can be covered within the business rules column.

Methods and tools

The most useful method is to develop an initial set of transaction tables with reviews. This will help in establishing work patterns. A spreadsheet file or database management system application on a network server will suffice for a tool. Team members enter their own information. Network access supports reviews.

Step 2: define the new or modified business process

End products

- New transactions based on the new system and improved business process. These transactions are developed by considering several different alternatives and then documenting the one that is selected. This end product is critical to determining benefits, the difference between the current and new transactions, specifying the automation required in each step, and preparing the new operations manual.

- Information requirements for interfaces between the new and existing systems. These include data elements, edits, timing, backup, frequency, and volume for each transaction type.

Roles and responsibilities

Early in Step 1, the project leader or analyst can define several alternative approaches for defining transactions. Once an approach is defined and is acceptable, then the business unit staff can participate in defining the new transactions. The project leader can track down the details of interfaces with programmers.

Criteria for success

All new transactions must be defined on a timely basis as well as being complete and correct. Success, though, means that the new process is significantly better than the current process so as to justify the cost of the system and change. If the benefits do not appear to be sufficient now when you have creatively defined the new process, then you may see even fewer benefits later when the constraints of the technology come down on the process.

Work methods

Construct a table similar to that used in Step 1, as in Figure 16.2. The first four columns will feed the new operations manual and user procedures. This allows business rules to be modified. The table supports a linking between the old and new process steps. This column entry can be blank for a new step, or have one or more entries. The system requirements pertain in most cases to software. The benefits column relates to business benefits. In the comments (last column), address how the issues in Step 1 are handled in the new work flow.

Step	Who	What	Bus. Rules	Old Process	System Rqmts.	Benefits	Comments

Figure 16.2   New transactions

Use several different ways to address each transaction, including the following:

- *Improvement with no additional automation.* This shows you how far you can push the envelope without the new system.
- *Improvement maximizing automation.* This pushes the boundary of the technology.
- *Improvement based on simplifying the degree of user expertise needed.* This tests how the process can be stripped down to essentials.

Once you have carried this out for a number of transactions, you can select the approach with the greatest overall benefits. Keep the others in reserve if needed later.

The system requirements can be aggregated at the transaction level first. Then you can work with the volume and performance information specified in the first step to determine the requirements for the system and for interfaces.

Management of work

Whereas the first step required detailed analytical work, this step benefits from creativity in determining how to simplify and/or automate the transactions. The project leader can lead and conduct simulation of the alternatives of the new transaction.

After this creative part, you now must push ahead to define as many other transactions as possible. Concentrate on having a range of transactions as well as including those that have the greatest uncertainty or risk, due to a lack of knowledge, for example.

Methods and tools

The same methods and tools followed in Step 1 can be employed here. Again, make sure that all the data is based on the network so that people can share information. If you employ a database management system for the table, then you can combine and analyze the two tables more easily. Dialogue among team members can be recorded for later use because it will contain lessons learned.

Step 3: determine the benefits, user requirements, and system requirements

End products

- Comparison of current and new processes and requirements.
- Estimation of benefits to the business based on the comparison.
- User requirements that include process, organization, and personnel as well as those pertaining to automation.
- System requirements for new system as well as interfaces.
- Update the estimate of costs of the project and system based on the requirements.

Roles and responsibilities

Business unit staff must be very heavily involved in this step. It is here, after all, that the benefits are pinned down along with the new process. Gathering any additional information related to volumes of work, estimated savings, and so on is the responsibility of the business unit. The analyst can prepare an initial version of user and system requirements for review. Note that in the traditional life cycle this step is either not done or is undertaken by information technology.

Criteria for success

One measure of success is that there are substantial benefits that will outweigh the costs that will be estimated based on the requirements. If the benefits do not appear to be sufficient, what do you do? First, determine where the greatest areas of costs lie. Can these be reduced? Second, determine if the new process be scaled back to require a less costly solution.

Work methods

Benefits have been identified for each transaction so that it is possible to generate benefits at the transaction level. What must be added are volumes, personnel time, the value of the benefits, and costs. The table in Figure 16.3 can serve as a starting point. This table builds the benefits at the transaction level. The second column summarizes the benefits from Step 2. Monetary benefit along with the justification and reasoning are the other two columns. Note that justification and reasoning will be extremely important later when you present the results of the work to management for approval and credibility.

Transaction: _____

Step	Benefit	$ Benefit	Justification/Reason

Figure 16.3   Individual transaction benefits

The transactions can now be rolled up in the table in Figure 16.4. However, you must grasp the overall benefit at the function level to determine actual savings. Use Figure 16.5 to make this determination. Function can refer to a position or group within the business unit.

Transaction	Benefit	$ Benefit	Justification/Reason

Figure 16.4   Benefits by transaction

To obtain user and system requirements, proceed in the same way as you did for evaluating the benefits. Consider constructing the table in Figure 16.6 first. Then move up to the function level to generate Figure 16.7. You can then invert the table to obtain the tables in Figures 16.8 and 16.9 for user and system requirements, respectively.

Function: _____

Transaction	Volume	$ Benefit	Comments

Figure 16.5   Analysis by function

Transaction	User Requirements	System Requirements	Comments

Figure 16.6   Requirements by transaction

Function	User Requirements	System Requirements	Comments

Figure 16.7   Requirements by function

User Requirements	Function	Comments

Figure 16.8   User requirements

System Requirements	Function	Comments

Figure 16.9   System requirements

Management of work

From experience it is recommended that the project leader or analyst work with the business unit staff and managers to develop the tables. IT can function in a coordination and support role, while business unit staff define benefits.

A lesson learned here is that after the first time this is done, the benefits will probably not match up to the costs. This has the positive effect of encouraging the business unit to consider changes in organization, policy, and so on to achieve greater benefits. IT should be politically neutral here by pointing out that the benefits do not justify the cost.

Methods and tools

The tables can be based on the network server. Work from earlier steps should be available. As group members create new tables, they should have space to indicate their reasoning and logic in construction. In a conference room establish a PC connected to the network with a projector so that the group can review the tables together.

Step 4: design the new transactions, system, and interfaces

The following activities can be performed in parallel assuming that the staff are available.

- Design of interfaces to current systems.
- Design of the graphic user interface (GUI).
- Design of a representative transaction within classes of transactions.
- Design of the database.
- Design of batch programs.
- Design of a prototype of the system.
- Pilot of the process and system.

The second task provides the standard to simplify and make uniform the user interface. The third task provides the start of an object-oriented approach. Add more activities for client-server and intranet applications. For both, tools will have to be acquired and installed. Staff have to be trained. In client-server applications the middleware will be designed. The prototype tests the design of the system. The pilot tests the combination of the system and the new process.

End products

The end products of this step include the following:

- Database design
- Interface design for links to current systems
- Design of representative transactions (objects)
- Design of batch programs
- Design of new interfaces
- Prototype results
- Pilot results
- Mapping of the design against the requirements and process
- Update of benefits and costs

Roles and responsibilities

On the surface, much of the review except for technical review is in the hands of the systems organization. What can the business unit do? Well, remember that Steps 1, 2, and 3 are not dead. Work must continue on the transactions not defined at the start of this step. In the prototype and pilot areas, there is much for the business unit staff to do. First, they can test the prototype system as part of the team. Remember that this is restricted to only the system. Then they can fully participate in the pilot because it tests the prototype system in the context of the new process. The pilot helps to validate the system and process together.

Criteria for success

Success in design can be reflected in quality end products and in integration. You can really add that success is when the benefits and costs fall in line or are better than original estimates. Success is also the acceptance of the prototype and pilot.

Work methods and methods and tools

Follow the accepted methods of design in your organization. In terms of the prototype and pilot here are some guidelines.

- The prototype includes complete transactions except for the interface to the existing systems. In that way, you can simulate the entire transaction.
- The pilot includes all manual and automated steps for the transactions covered in the prototype.
- The pilot is tested with many employees in the business unit. This not only validates the system and process, but also acts to build grassroots support for the new process and for change.

Management of work

The key role is that of the project leader. The project leader must not only coordinate work in this step, but also the ongoing work in the previous three steps. Business unit managers are to be involved in conducting and supporting the pilot effort.

Step 5: develop, integrate, and test the system

Here are the end products:

- Completed application system
- Completed system interfaces.

The techniques used depend on your environment. In an object-oriented approach, keys to successful development are configuration management and control. The initial transaction in each class can be tested and evaluated. As information becomes available on other transactions, then these transactions can be programmed as objects within their respective groups.

Successful project management means that you will have to oversee the testing and configuration controls. More standard supervision applies to the interfaces and to batch programs. Base your transaction testing on test scripts generated by the business unit. These rely on work in Step 2 and help to validate the results in the earlier steps.

Step 6: prepare operations manuals, training materials, and operations procedures

The operations manual and training materials can be based on the work in Step 2 as well as the prototype and pilot of the design step. As the user interface and the exact handling of transactions are known, then this detail can be added. Operations procedures for the system follow internal practices and policies.

It is important in managing this step that you have business unit staff available to generate transaction procedures early before programming is completed. It is recommended that test scripts, training materials, and operations procedures all be undertaken together as design and development progress. The additional details of how the GUI (graphical user interface) works can be added when available later. In addition to procedures, an effort will be required to define new policies and even job descriptions.

Step 7: convert and set up the system and process for operation

Much of the information in the system that is being replaced may be unusable for several reasons:

- Data fields in the new system are incompatible with the current system. Making these compatible can be a major issue.
- Data in the current system may be incomplete or inaccurate. Making manual corrections after conversion is a problem.
- The new system typically has new and different fields than the current system. The content of these fields has to be added.
- The structure of the information may be different in the new than the old.

What do you, as a project leader, do during the conversion step? Early in the project, in the first three steps, evaluate the quality of the data and its completeness in the current system. If it appears that conversion of the data directly is not useful or will only be partial, then consider establishing an initial database for the new system. Include the following tasks:

- Developing software to aid in data cleanup, data field addition, and data entry.
- Working with the business unit to schedule when and what information will be compiled for data entry.
- Obtaining business unit resources for data collection, data entry, and validation.

Step 8: convert to the new process and system

Here the new process and system are turned on. Business unit staff must be trained. All work in previous steps must be completed. The system must pass operational tests. Training must include both the process and the system. The business unit is responsible for training in the business process. Because new employees will be hired after the system is operational, the business unit can also carry out training procedures on the system for their staff. Establishing a method for training the trainer might be useful here.

Cases and examples

Arcadia Health Services

Arcadia Health Services was a medium-sized health maintenance organization that survived with legacy systems for patient records, accounting, inventory, and other functions running on a proprietary operating system. For convenience let time begin at year zero (0). In year 0 Arcadia saw the need to modernize its systems and establish more flexible software.

The legacy systems suffered from the following problems:

• The systems lacked some of the source code.
• It took an average of more than 4 months to handle a maintenance request because the systems were so old, the staff was new to the systems, and documentation was almost totally lacking.

The systems group reviewed several software packages and made purchasing recommendations to management. Management rejected these recommendations because most funds were committed to expansion. The systems group was not informed of this reason, but instead was told that funds were not available—period. The systems group was told to come back with a proposal for internal development that would cost less money. This revision was approved.

In year 1, analysts collected requirements based on current problems, the current system, and assuming a moderate growth rate. No work flow was analyzed. No assessment was made of the business direction. The requirements and the underlying assumptions never made it to upper management. They were derailed by a middle-level manager who feared that if the requirements were adjusted to fit reality, the project would be dropped.

Senior management meanwhile had decided that Arcadia was at a crossroads—either grow quickly or be acquired. The health maintenance industry was undergoing a shakeout. Management chose growth. In year 0 Arcadia had 250,000 customers. This was the volume used by the systems group in estimating volume for the new system. By year 4 Arcadia had 1.5 million customers—an increase of over 400 percent in fewer than 4 years. As each new acquisition was made, its customers had to be added to the existing system. This robbed programming resources from development.

In desperation the systems manager chose to isolate the development team so as to keep it off limits from the conversion work. When the developers asked how many acquisitions there might be, the systems manager replied that he did not know, but the team had to continue development to meet the schedule.

At the end of year 1 the design was finalized to match the requirements in size with some growth. The new system was based on a 4GL (fourth-generation language) and was to offer many new features and data elements that were not available in the current system. However, the internal staff had to be trained from scratch to learn it resulting in more delays. Requests for consultants to help in the programming or even to do reviews were turned down.

The new system went online in year 4 (over 2 years late). It was an immediate disaster. Here are some of the critical technical and management problems that surfaced:

- Management decided to convert all customers in one shot. This was a big mistake because of data problems in the old system. At the time of conversion there were 1.9 million customers spread across more than 45,000 accounts. When the conversion program ran, it halted when it encountered one error in a record. This halted the entire account. After this was fixed, it was rerun and the next error was hit. Conversion fell behind. It was a nightmare. If an account had 100 errors, the system would halt each time it found one and then processing would have to be repeated after the fix to one record was made.
- There was no cleanup of existing data. The old system tolerated many errors and the new system was unforgiving. For example, in the middle of the conversion it was discovered that the key customer identifier had erroneously been placed into the date of treatment for over 100,000 customers. It took 15 minutes to enter a new customer versus a target of 6 seconds.

What was the business fallout?

- Uncollected bills soared to over $400 million.
- Monies due to care providers (doctors, clinics, etc.) totaled over $650 million.
- The price of Arcadia stock plummeted by over 50 percent.

The development project was a disaster. What are some lessons learned here?

- Don't freeze requirements—ever.
- Keep communications open between upper management and the development team.
- Make the design flexible for growth.
- If you are going to use new technology, hire someone who knows it.
- Don't isolate the development team.
- Carefully analyze the business process, business rules, and data.
- Plan the conversion. Start with small accounts and build up to larger ones.

Questions

1. Let's suppose that you are not going to freeze requirements. The problem then is that you might get inundated with change requests. Develop questions that you would want the requester to answer that would not only justify the request, but also ensure that only the most important changes resulted.
2. What steps could you take to give visibility of project team members to management?
3. Discuss how you could make IT staff more aware and informed about the business. What are the costs and benefits of doing this?

Lessons learned

In some areas such as E-business, implementation tends to involve buying software tools, using existing systems and interfacing to these, and doing some development. Some of the risk management concerns in development are as follows:

- The development effort must be kept limited since there is tremendous time pressure to implement.
- Any development effort must be traded off against integration, testing, and quality assurance work. The more that you develop, the more generally is the time for quality assurance.
- The competitive edge in technology for a firm will be in quality assurance and integration not in the developed software. This is because transactions must be completed in near real time across multiple systems.

It is often the case that successive methodologies and versions of the methodologies try to fix problems with the current methods used. In addition, the new methods reflect greater experience with modern technology. Thus, we recommend that you carefully review any new methodology that surfaces. We don't advocate replacing your current methods with the new, but you may be able to take parts of the new and incorporate them into your existing methods to improve them and your work.

Guidelines

- Business unit staff may be reluctant to assume some responsibilities, especially those in Steps 1, 2, 7, and 8. There is really no alternative since their participation is essential to gain their commitment. Their commitment is key to the success of the project. Not insisting on full-time participation by the business unit senior staff combined with flexibility in work will help.
- An effective method for carrying out Steps 1 and 2 is to divide the team into sub-teams that review the work of the other groups. From experience this had been found to be more effective than a separate review. It also corrects early any trend toward incompleteness or errors.

- In the initial period there is always a tendency to zero in on the first good alternative to the current process. Avoid this. You may need to change the workflow during later steps and have some flexibility by having alternatives available.
- Evaluate the new transactions by considering the following:
- How stable is the new process? How can it evolve without controls if people take short cuts?
- How will you conduct an audit of the new process?
- If someone were to create a new exception manually, how could you detect this?
- At the most detailed level in your project plan, put each transaction in the plan as a task. This is important for several reasons. First, it helps you track the work. Second, it shows how important the tasks and transactions are. This is the same approach recommended for programs. Each program, no matter how small, can be a task in the plan.
- Consider establishing a lessons learned database with input from the team members as they work on the steps. This will be a valuable addition later.
- When presenting the new process to management, have the business unit staff take the lead. After all, they did a lot of the work and they will be very credible. Give specific transactions as examples. Get down to details before you start summarizing the benefits and costs.

Questions

1. Research the Web for the method termed "Lean Development". Compare and contrast this with Agile and the waterfall methods.
2. Try to find examples of success and failure using the Agile method. What benefits and limitations result from the Agile approach.
3. Let's assume that you are going to lead a team of five on a project that will last 1 year. The requirements seem to be fuzzy. What is the most appropriate methodology to use?
4. A project has been using the traditional waterfall approach, but it is falling behind schedule and going over budget. Discuss the pros and cons of moving to a new methodology in the middle of the project.
5. You are put in charge of a large global project involving five countries that will take 2 years. How could you take an approach that combines the waterfall approach with that of Agile?

What to do next

1. Prepare a project plan template for development following the steps in the chapter.
2. Identify potential issues and resistance to business unit staff in the expanded business unit role. Discuss how these can be addressed by stressing the positive aspects of involvement.

Summary

To stabilize requirements and ensure benefits development you must involve the business unit staff at all steps. Any sustained absence will create problems later in the project. Changes in the business process are made possible by the new system and modified policies and procedures. Reengineering changes are much more sweeping than this; however, the approach employed in this chapter can be employed within process improvement projects.

17
Operations, maintenance, and enhancement

Introduction

Let's begin with some definitions. *Operations* here includes all production support activities. Examples are network support, setting up parameters for a production run, doing recovery and restart, fixing problems encountered during a production run of a system (emergency fixes), doing online diagnostics, performance analysis and tuning, and similar work. *Maintenance* is the repair of problems and doing work so that the agreed upon requirements for performance, function, and features are met. Examples of maintenance are repairing errors or bugs in the code, increasing performance of the system to the set performance levels, and even improving user procedures for greater ease of use. *Enhancements* are changes to the system to address new requirements. Handling new features, interfaces, integration, and supporting additional users are examples of enhancements.

Much of systems work is devoted to these activities. In many organizations these activities consume over half of the programming staff time and most of the network and operations support as well. As a system ages, its complexity increases. There is staff turnover, so that over a period of years many different programmers may work on a system. The size of the programs typically grows along with the size of the databases and files. The quality of documentation sinks because little priority is given to its maintenance. It is not surprising that it takes longer and longer to make changes to a system under these conditions. This is not surprising when you consider the specific tasks that are performed. In an emergency fix for operations support, a programmer must work under intense pressure to find the source of the error and fix the code. Often, there is not time to examine the large programs so that the programmer fixes the symptom of the problem. The problem may still remain. In maintenance and enhancement, the programmer must first review the code to find the areas to be addressed. Then after repair, the code is unit tested. Many times there is insufficient time and resources to fully test the program and system, much less to document the changes.

A recent trend has been the emergence of *cloud computing*. Firms such as IBM, Microsoft, and others provide computer applications through the Internet. Business users access these with their Web browsers. The use of cloud computing by a company is governed by both contracts and SLAs. The benefit to company customers is that they don't have to have an internal IT operations and development staff. These are provided by the vendor. The downside is that the company is limited to the applications available from the vendor. This can limit business flexibility as well as not having unique systems as part of the company's competitive position.

Does it matter how a particular activity is categorized in terms of operations, maintenance, and enhancement? Yes, it does. Operations support comes first. The system must perform or be available. Many organizations then rate maintenance second with enhancements coming up last. This is because you can live without the additional features. Given the resources consumed and importance, you might think that this area would receive a great deal of management attention. Such is not the case. People accept the amount of effort as part of doing business—just like business units suffer from their business processes that cry out to be fixed. Here are some of the problems encountered in these areas:

- There is a myth that this area is basically incapable of being planned and controlled. Management just assigns a specific level of effort to the work and leaves it alone. The worst case is when management designates specific programmers to work full time on one system in maintenance.
- The resources consumed in these activities deny resources to new projects or major work on current systems.
- Left on their own lower level systems, supervisors sometimes cut deals with their counterparts in the business units. The department gets to keep the *status quo* along with a few "goodies" while the programmers work on relatively easy work. Upper management in both information systems and the business unit has little awareness of what has been negotiated. This has been observed in several organizations.
- There is little or no cost justification for the work. Every project must define benefits and costs. Yet, somehow maintenance and enhancement are often exempt.
- There is a lack of strategy as to what to do with these systems. It is easier to just patch them up each year.

Management gets frustrated when the current systems cannot handle new requirements. This gives encouragement to those who advocate acquiring software packages. However, even when a package is acquired, the same lack of management control persists and impacts the package through interfaces with current systems.

What are your goals for operations, maintenance, and enhancement work? Here is a reasonable list of concerns, which will be addressed in this chapter:

- Define a strategy for each system covering what work will be done in the future, where the system will end up after a certain time, and what resources will be required.
- Implement project management across all of these activities.
- Aim to maximize tangible benefits from work in operations, maintenance, and enhancement.
- Implement more disciplined management of the support-related work.

A proactive management approach

If you start with imposing plans and controls on the work in these areas, you will achieve some tactical results, but you may miss the major benefits. You must take a wider view that answers the following questions:

- What are the business processes and their related systems that can benefit from effort?
- What are the overall plan and concrete goals for operations and maintenance? Should not one objective be to reduce the effort except for emergency fixes?
- How can you move away from the policy of dedicating human resources to specific systems?

Whether generated within information systems or by business units, maintenance and enhancement requests must identify benefits and be structured to lead to projects. An example of the list of things to include is shown in Figure 17.1. This list identifies the project and provides for its description, justification/benefits, and costs, if approved for action. It also discusses the fit of the request with elements of plans that will be discussed. The item on resource conflicts indicates whether there are competing demands for the same systems resources.

- ID—identification number of the request
- System
- Date
- Business process
- Submitted by
- Benefit of change to business process
- Impact on the business process, if not done
- How benefits will be measured
- Date required
- Reason for date
- Fit with the process plan
- Fit with the department automation plan
- Fit with the strategic IT plan
- Cost of work
- Cost-benefit analysis
- Resources needed
- Resource conflicts
- Action taken
- Date of decision
- Reason

Figure 17.1   Items to include for maintenance and enhancement requests

A series of steps can be defined to support a more proactive approach:

- *Step 1*: Measure the allocation of information systems and related resources to determine where they are being allocated (*information systems measurement*).

- *Step 2*: Develop a *process plan* for each critical or key business process. The scope of this plan includes the supporting systems.
- *Step 3*: Define an overall *strategic systems plan.* This combines the results of the process plans with other architecture, development, and software acquisition projects to yield an overall plan.
- *Step 4*: Based on the process and strategic systems plan, determine an automation plan for each major department (*departmental systems plan*). This makes the strategic systems plan more concrete and reveals how the process will be improved through systems.
- *Step 5*: Set priorities for all systems work including planning items from Steps 1 through 3, maintenance, enhancements, and operations support. This will be called the *slate of work.*
- *Step 6*: Follow through on the slate of work and measure the results.

These six steps provide for a proactive approach to gaining control and setting priorities. Each step will be discussed with an emphasis on operations, maintenance, and enhancement. Step 1 reveals the current situation and dilution of resources. Step 2 defines an overall plan for critical processes. It helps set priorities for systems work. Step 3 is the construction of the enterprise systems strategic plan. This is applied to specific departments in Step 4. Steps 1, 2, and 4 have direct relevance to departments and help gain support for more proactive work and reduced maintenance. Step 5 is crucial because it is here that the reallocation occurs. Rather than spread out resources across all systems, this step typically focuses resources to gain results for systems that support critical processes. In Step 6 you follow through on the allocation and prevent resources from being robbed by *ad hoc* requests. What will happen if you shortcut this step? Without measurement, you will have no idea of the current situation and the results of doing work. Without the plans for the business process, enterprise, and departments, how can you proactively get ahead of the work and gain business unit support for changes in priorities? If you do not set priorities (Step 4), then each request will be considered on its own as it arises—frittering away resources.

Step 1: measure information systems allocation

Let's consider measurement as it relates to operations, maintenance, and enhancement. You can develop several tables here. The first is the allocation of staff to specific systems support.

	Systems			
Staff	**System 1**	**System 2**		

Enter the number of hours that each person spends on a given system. Doing this requires either an estimate by supervisors or tracking of personnel time. Next you might want to determine the number of hours spent in operations support, maintenance, and enhancement. This can be too time consuming to gather and track. Instead, you might consider building the following lists. The first is intended to pin down known operational problems. The second provides for tracking of maintenance and enhancement requests. Status can be open, closed, being worked, shelved, and combined with another request.

System: _____

Known Problems	Severity/Impact	Resources Required to Fix

System: _____

Mainten/ Enhancement Reqmts	Description	Status	Benefits	Costs	Schedule	Resources Assigned

You can now roll up the numbers to obtain a summary. This gives the total effort spread across systems.

Systems	Operations	Maintenance	Enhancement	New Developmt/Packages

Aggregate the information by business process and by department. In many cases, only one system supports a business process, but there are cases where the process may use network tools such as groupware as well as an application system.

Business Processes	Operations	Maintenance	Enhancement	New Develop/Packages

Departments	Operations	Maintenance	Enhancement	New Develop/Packages

You can use these tables to answer the following questions.

- Is the systems staff working on the processes and systems that are the most important to the organization?
- Are staff being dedicated to lower priority work because of their in-depth knowledge of the application system?
- Is the split of resources across departments logical, given the differing levels of importance each has to the organization?

Step 2: develop process plans for key processes

From the standpoint of the business, there must be an overall plan for the top critical business processes. Called the process plan, it defines the future direction for the process (both manual and systems parts) toward which resources can be applied in the future. A process plan contains the following elements:

- Assessment of the current process in terms of issues, problems, and areas of improvement;
- Costs of the process as well as systems support;
- The long-term new business process that serves as a goal for both the business unit and information systems;
- Benefits accruing if the long-term process is achieved;
- Systems and technology required to deliver and support the long-term process.

The process plan requires work because you must understand the current process and systems, business trends, and new technology and its potential, and you must be able to define a new process. Therefore, with limited resources it is recommended that you spread out the development of the process plans over several years.

What if there is no process plan? The business unit has no direction for the process. Instead, members of the business unit will react to new technology that they see and put in *ad hoc*, unstructured requests. These will more easily pass through the business unit into information systems. With a process plan in place, there is something to measure a new technology or request against. Will the new technology or request take the process in the right direction?

How do you develop a process plan? Start by identifying 5–10 critical processes. Develop one plan and use it as a model for the others. Pick as the first process the one that crosses multiple departments and has systems that have substantial interfaces. This will be the most complex situation. For the process, develop the table in Figure 17.2. This gives the steps in the process, their descriptions, current automation, and issues. Each step is described along with the major business rules in the second column. How the current system supports the process is given in the third column. Exceptions and volume information are listed in the fourth column. The last column provides for issues and comments.

Process: _____

Step	Description/ Business Rules	Current System	Exceptions/ Volume	Issues/ Comments

Figure 17.2   Analysis of the current business process

This action helps you understand what is going on at the step level in the process. Next, move up to the process level and identify issues and opportunities associated with the process. Figure 17.3 provides an example. Issues and opportunities can include system replacement, enhancements, maintenance, and operations problems. The impact of the problem on the organization overall, the business unit, and systems are addressed along with benefits. In the comments column you might refer to the specific steps where the impact or benefit can be felt.

Process: _____

Impact if not addressed   Benefits

Issue/ Opp	Priority	Organ.	Business Unit	Info Systems	Organiz	Bus Unit	Info Systems	Comments

Figure 17.3   Issues and opportunities at the process level

The new process can be defined by the following elements:

- Objectives in the design of the new process
- Business assumptions
- Technology assumptions
- Steps in the new process
- Table of analysis (see Figure 17.4)
- Benefits of the new process for the organization, the business unit, and information systems

Process: _____

Step	Automation Needs	Business Needs	Current Process	Issues/Opportunities Addressed

Figure 17.4   Analysis table of new process

A potential outline of the process plan document is as follows. The tables presented above are included in the plan.

- Introduction

    Purpose and scope
    How the plan was developed
    How the plan is maintained

- Assessment of the current process

    Summary of the current process
    Issues and opportunities
    Impacts, if not addresses

- Long-term business process

    Summary of new process
    Assumptions—business, technology
    New versus current process

- Benefits of new process

    Organization
    Business unit
    Information systems

- Systems and technology requirements for the new process.

Note that there is no detailed project plan because this is a strategy document.

Step 3: create a strategic IT plan

Time and space do not allow a step-by-step approach in developing the strategic IT plan. It is assumed that the plan sets forth:

- Issues and opportunities facing information systems
- Objectives of information systems
- Constraints (factors that must be accepted because they cannot be changed)
- Strategies (approaches for getting around the constraints and working toward the objectives)
- Action items and project ideas (specific actions and projects that support the strategies)

The plan can draw on the process plans developed in Step 2. Using the plan you can develop a table that assists you in evaluating your current and future work. These are given in Figure 17.5. Each issue or opportunity pertaining to operations, maintenance, and enhancement is given in the first column grouped by business process and system. The second and third columns give the issues/opportunities and objectives that the item supports. The fourth column gives the strategies, and the fifth lists the action items and project ideas that pertain to this issue or opportunity. If an enhancement has

Process: _____

Operations, Maintenance, Enhancement	Issues/ Opportunities	Objectives	Strategies	Action Items/ Projects

Figure 17.5   Operations, maintenance, and enhancement versus elements of the strategic IT plan

a blank entry, this means that doing the enhancement does not support the strategic systems plan. You have to question whether it should be done.

Step 4: construct departmental systems plans

Department or division automation plans can be initially generated by projecting down the elements of the strategic systems plan and process plans. Using this as a start, you can now identify specific items of relevance to the department. The same tables can be employed as for the strategic systems plan. In both cases, you are attempting to determine the fit of operations, maintenance, and enhancements to the strategic plans. Note that this fit is part of the request form in Figure 17.1.

Step 5: set the slate of work

Setting the slate was discussed earlier at a general level. On a quarterly basis, management can review the existing work and requests for changes and set priorities again. The slate of work consists of all approved projects, requests, and other tasks. If there is no organized approach for setting the slate, requests will be handled one at a time. People who scream the loudest or who have the greatest political clout often get their requests approved first. This leaves few resources for the remaining work. It is no wonder that when information systems reported to finance, finance systems received the highest priority. In many cases, the systems of the people with the greatest political muscle are not the ones that should be given attention. Other systems that cross multiple organizations might benefit the organization more from work.

Over the years, organizations have grappled with the problem of setting priorities. In addition to the reactive mode already mentioned, one approach has been that of fairness. That is, resources are spread across all systems and business units. Each system receives some attention. However, this yields only minor improvements because there is no concentration of resources.

A better approach is to impose a formal review and approval process that cannot easily be overridden unless there is a true emergency. Under this approach, projects and work are only approved if there is a plan of action accompanied by tangible benefits. It is not enough for business unit and systems staff to estimate intangible benefits. These may not come true. The criteria must be tangible benefits and support for the long-term architecture of the organization. The setting of the slate of work must also be accompanied by active measurement to ensure that the benefits were realized. Where do you achieve tangible benefits? A popular myth has been that the benefits are in systems. This is generally not true. The benefits really lie in the business units. They reside in the improvements to business processes. That is where the benefits can be shown and measured.

Let's now examine the process of setting the slate of work. Identify a person who will gather requests and help employees formulate requests. This person who fulfills this centerpost role will provide the following services:

- Offer support for preparing requests.
- Review requests for completeness and accuracy.
- Track requests.
- Develop several "straw man" allocations of resources for management to review.
- Measure the benefits of the changes after they have been made.

Unless someone is formally named to this role, it will be difficult to support an allocation process. The fallback will put the systems manager in the middle of one-on-one negotiations with business units.

Requests can be categorized as follows:

- Streamlining and cleanup of production systems to reduce operations support;
- Maintenance requests;
- Enhancement requests to meet government reporting requirements, user requests for changes, and so on;
- Backlog of previous requests that were not approved;
- Ongoing development projects and installation of software packages;
- New development and software acquisition requests;
- Policy and procedure changes;
- Time set aside for operations support;
- Ongoing maintenance and enhancement work;
- Implementation of new technology to improve the systems architecture (such as hardware and network upgrades).

With these categories defined you can proceed with actions to evaluate the requests.

- **Action 1: Review and place requests in categories.**
  Each request is reviewed and placed in the appropriate category. Some requests will be eliminated because they have little benefit. The need for some of the backlog items may have disappeared. Other requests may be combined due to their similarity.
- **Action 2: Evaluate requests in each category.**
  You have a stack of requests in these categories. What do you do next? How do you evaluate them? Each category is unique. For example, policy and procedure changes

do not require money or staff but may require training and other investments. The time set aside for operations support will depend on the system and even the time of year (e.g., year-end closing). As each category is discussed, keep in mind that your objective is to weed out as many requests as possible. There are very few resources and many requests. When you consider only critical programmer resources, you are likely to find even more potential conflicts.

- *Streamline production systems.* Programmers here will go into the code and begin to clean up past production problems that were temporarily fixed. The payoff is fewer hours in the future for support and reduced downtime for the application system. This sounds like a good opportunity. However, no new features are added for the business unit. Also, an old system may be in such bad shape that it cannot reasonably be fixed. You will probably only give one to three requests in this category any priority. The others will be eliminated due to resource conflicts, limited benefits, and the condition of the system.

- *Maintenance requests.* These are requests by the business staff to making relatively minor changes in the system. It is very attractive to spend time here because it appears as low risk with some benefit. However, there is often little real benefit. The system is not really improved. Nor are there substantial benefits in the long term. Based on these factors you can probably eliminate half or more of the requests.

- *Enhancement requests.* Some of these requests may be mandated and so cannot be avoided. Other requests can be prioritized based on benefits and extent of effort. You want to avoid giving high priority to requests that involve large-scale effort over an extended time (such as more than one person for over 3 months).

- *Backlog of requests.* A request is in the backlog because it did not receive a high priority. Your goal here is to eliminate such requests. After all, the business unit was able to get by without the change until now. Some of the requests can probably be combined with requests in other categories.

- *Ongoing development and software package implementation.* The tendency here is to automatically approve these projects because they were approved earlier and they are in process. However, this is a good opportunity to revisit the purpose, scope, budget, and progress of the projects. You will find that it is desirable to restrict some of the projects that appear to be dragging out.

- *New development and software acquisition requests.* This is one of the categories that you want to make a priority. Rank these requests here by impact on the business and fit with the long-term architecture that you are trying to build.

- *Policy and procedure changes.* Many people don't include these as project ideas. Yet they are, because it may take a project to implement them. By giving the policy and procedure changes visibility, you will accentuate their importance and benefits. You are likely to retain all of these for the final selection.

- *Time for operations support.* This includes normal support as well as emergency fixes. There is a tendency to use last year's experience to estimate requirements for the next period. This is not a good idea because it perpetuates setting aside a "systems slush fund". It is better to cut this back each year.

- *Ongoing maintenance and enhancement work.* Normally, this category is untouchable. However, you do want to evaluate progress, purpose, scope, and benefits.

You may find that some work can stop because it yields fewer benefits than originally estimated.

- *Implementation of new technology.* This category often gets little attention. People don't see the benefits of the technology. The technology projects that can be selected are those that are needed to meet performance goals due to workload growth and those that support new systems. You may end up combining some of these items with projects in new development and software acquisition.

- **Action 3: Develop alternative work slates.**

  To help you in developing alternative work slates, you might want to prepare some tables. Figure 17.6 is a basic table. Here you will list the project ideas from each category as rows. The columns are the individual systems staff. In the table entry you will provide the number of hours required by the request.

Project Ideas	Person A	Person B	Person C	Person D

Figure 17.6   Project ideas versus resources

Next, you can use this table and separate out the work for which there is little or not conflict. This is because staff are not interchangeable and are specialized. You will find that because of this, some programmers will be working on lower-priority work. Reconstruct Figure 17.6 so that the requests that are handled by this sorting are at the top of the table. Draw a heavy line below these and the remaining requests. There must be an underlying purpose for each alternative. Here are some that have been used in the past.

- Focus on maintenance and enhancement. Under this alternative, you find that there are substantial business pressures to curb costs. The business units are also under pressure to control costs. You are just trying to maintain. There will be no long-term improvement here, but this alternative is useful because it shows what will happen if you stand still.
- Focus on long-term improvement. Here you will minimize effort in maintenance and enhancement as well as in production support. Backlog will get a low priority. The resources will go toward new development, software acquisition, and architecture improvement. This is the most aggressive alternative and shows you what can be done if you maximize effort in these categories.
- Give emphasis to tangible benefits. Under this alternative you will give highest priority to the requests that yield the greatest tangible benefit.
- Focus on a specific business area. Here you will give priority to requests from a specific business unit to which management gives high importance. Minimize work for other areas.
- Fit the priority with management goals. Requests that are favored here will fit with management's goals. This can be revenue production, cost control, or improvement in business practices.

- **Action 4: Determine the slate of work.**
  Make sure that you define all of the preceding alternatives. Now consider which work slates are similar. You are going to be lucky if the alternatives of long-term improvement, tangible benefits, and management goals are very similar. This is how you will want to present these to management. Experience shows that you will be more successful in marketing if you can show that a particular slate fits several objectives.

Step 6: follow through on the work

Each approved request should now have a project plan. The project plans should fit into the templates that have already been discussed. Each request should have a designated project leader. You will also want to apply measurements to the work. There is the obvious measurement of tracking the budget versus actual results and the schedule versus the plan. Beyond this is the achievement of the true benefits that were projected when the request was prepared. Remember that the business unit is responsible for achieving the benefits. Information systems can only provide the systems and support. Whether there are increased sales, improved efficiency, or reduced costs will depend on what the business does after the project work is completed. That is why it is recommended that the changes in the business processes, procedures, and policies be made a part of the project. It is recommended that you employ a standard, formal process for assessing the benefits of the work. Figure 17.7 gives the elements that can be used for this purpose.

- Request
- Date
- System
- Business Unit
- Business Process
- Estimated Schedule
- Actual Schedule
- Estimated Cost
- Actual Cost
- Estimated Benefits
- Actual Benefits
- Reasons for Variance of Actual with Planned
- How Benefits were Realized
- Lessons Learned

Figure 17.7   Measurement of benefits for a completed request

- Justification or explanation is required for variance in schedule and budget.
- In addition to the benefits achieved, the form requires a discussion of how these benefits were achieved.
- There is also space to capture lessons learned from the work.

If there is no measurement, then people just move on to the next project. The knowledge and experience of the previous work are not captured. You then lose a valuable chance to improve the process of maintenance and enhancement as well as other work.

What are some of the reasonable tasks for tracking maintenance and enhancement work? You can generally divide up the work into the following categories: initial investigation and review of the code, design and programming changes, testing and rework of the code, documentation, and further testing. In addition, there may be need to training, data conversion, and other tasks as well. Employ a standard template of these tasks. You have several alternatives for having programmers report their time. They can report on time cards the precise tasks that they worked on along with the hours worked. This is often corrupted by people who create a political picture where investigation is reduced and coding is increased. Another approach is to have the programmers put down the total time per project. Then separately, in a project management system, they can input the status of the work.

Managers often treat maintenance and enhancement as stand-alone activities among their programmers. They don't consider collaboration important because the programmers are working on different systems. This is another lost opportunity. Here is an area where you can make a difference. Encourage the programmers to share experiences in making changes. Have them walk through the changes that they made and share lessons learned. This has a number of benefits to this, including the following:

- Lessons learned to improve the work of younger, less senior programmers;
- More cross training of programmers so that there is less specialization over time.

Maintenance and enhancement are not exempt from issues and lessons learned. There should be a lessons learned database that includes information about each system as well as programming practices. In terms of issues, the programmers can surface a number of problems and potential improvements that can be worked on later if time were available. This is another opportunity to gain information from their work. It also shows programmers that management values their work.

Cases and examples

Rapid Energy Company

Rapid Energy Company is a large multinational energy company. Some years ago the company experienced substantial growth. Information systems had expanded, implemented software packages, and still maintained many old systems. When times were good, no one really paid attention to allocation. Then the price of oil dropped and times got rough. The information systems group was forced to economize. The choice was either to lay people off or to restructure the work or the organization. There had been no measurement and little planning in place. The first step was to measure what was going on. It was found that almost half of the maintenance and enhancement requests could be halted as they yielded little benefit. In addition, when the business units were surveyed and key business processes studied, a number of major needs surfaced that had very tangible labor-savings benefits. Using the priority approach described in this chapter, work was redirected toward these major enhancements. The resulting savings prevented any major layoffs except by attrition. Management support for information systems was greater than it was in the good old days.

Questions

1. Given that you are the new IT manager, how would you evaluate the effort going on in operations, maintenance, and enhancement?
2. At Rapid Energy it was found that business users approached programmers directly for some changes. These were then made. What is the impact of this on overall IT productivity? As the IT manager how would you go about restructuring communications with the business units?
3. In most IT groups the project leaders and supervisors have a great deal of informal contacts with business unit supervisors. How could you exploit this to increase IT effectiveness?

Lessons learned

You should assume that there will be substantial ongoing change and enhancement—more than that for systems in the past. Why is this? Here are some reasons.

- Marketing will require more creative promotions and discounts to be supported.
- Changes in all versions processes have to be coordinated and synchronized. This requires more systems work.
- The business is evolving so that competition and marketplace pressures will mean more enhancements.
- If there is substantial traffic growth, there will have to be major hardware and network upgrades.
- Technology is changing—meaning more work.

Guidelines

- Each year develop a combined list of benefits for the work performed by information systems. You can create a table where the rows are the various projects and work and the columns are areas of benefit (cost savings, performance improvement, revenue increase, and so on). Then sort this table by business unit, business process, and technology area. This will give you a better understanding of what the information systems group is accomplishing.
- Visit each programmer individually and discuss that person's technical work. Have each programmer identify issues and lessons learned, and put these into databases. Next, gather the programmers together in a meeting and show them how they share

the same issues and lessons learned. Build informal collaboration and information sharing.

- To support a project management atmosphere you should have each programmer participate in the development of project templates for maintenance and enhancement. You may have a number of different templates that depend on specific types of enhancements.
- Market the changes in the current method of operation through self-interest. The programmers gain by showing that their work is important and valued. The business unit gains by having its high-benefit requests undertaken. Management gains through visibility of the information and achievement of benefits. The information systems unit gains by implementing project management across almost all work.

Questions

1. Discuss the possible definitions and distinctions between maintenance and enhancement?
2. Some systems seem to undergo substantial work in terms of maintenance and enhancement while others have little activity and work. What are some of the possible implications and causes for this to happen?
3. In cloud computing operations are supported by a remote vendor in a similar way to e-mail with Yahoo or Google. Discuss the advantages and disadvantages of a medium-sized firm using cloud computing.
4. Research the Web to identify security issues related to cloud computing.
5. There are arguments for either or both centralized versus distributed computing. Discuss the advantages and disadvantages of each.

What to do next

1. Measure what you currently have and what is going on. Identify the projects and work, and place them into categories as was discussed earlier. Then examine the allocation of effort. If this same allocation continued for several years, would there be any major benefit or change?
2. Using the results of the first item, evaluate the benefits of the work. Evaluate the benefits that were achieved from the previous maintenance and enhancement work.
3. Identify potential projects that can be performed if resources were available. Develop an alternative using data from the past to indicate what may have been possible if resources had been redirected toward this more productive work.
4. Examine how people report their time on production, maintenance, and enhancement. Is there sufficient detail to determine what is going on? Are the programmers sharing any lessons learned? Is there an awareness of outstanding issues with each system?
5. Is there a real effort to identify benefits for each request for maintenance and enhancement? Is there any follow-up to determine if the benefits were achieved?

Summary

Many people believe that maintenance and enhancement fall outside of project management. They feel that imposing project management on such small work and limited tasks is too great a burden. However, maintenance and enhancement tasks can stretch out for months. Without any controls or formal approach, a substantial percentage of available resources can be drained off into work of lower priority. In this mode maintenance and enhancement work is reactive. To make it proactive you must actively seek out opportunities for systems work and put them into the planning process. Doing this will give greater visibility to the work as well as increase awareness that tangible benefits count.

18
Software packages

Introduction

Many firms have acquired or are in the process of acquiring software packages to replace some or all of their legacy systems with standardized, integrated software. Examples include SAP, Oracle, Salesforce, and others. This trend will continue for years as companies move to employ software packages rather than customized software solutions. The benefits of software packages include the following:

- Reduced or eliminated development effort.
- Ability to control staffing levels in information technology related to programming.
- Faster availability of software and features.
- Reduced risk because of less development.
- With new systems in place, there is less maintenance and perhaps greater flexibility to support enhancements.

The packages can either be run on a company's computer or from a vendor (e.g., cloud computing). The risks and costs of using packages are still substantial: If the wrong package is selected, the entire project can fail.

- The company must still struggle to be competitive with other firms in the same industry using the same or similar software packages.
- If the business processes and packages don't fit together, then something has to give and the business suffers.
- Changes to the software will have to be made by the vendor or someone approved by the vendor.

The process of selecting and implementing such packages is quite different and more complex than was the case in earlier times. Some of the critical factors are as follows:

- In the past, a package augmented existing business processes. Today, the business processes must fit closely with the package to achieve substantial benefit. As an example, suppose that your firm would like to ship equipment to good customers without the paperwork. However, if the package requires the paperwork first, you cannot really ship the equipment right away.

- The packages are integrated today, which means that their use involves multiple departments and divisions. Departments that never really had to work together now find that, because of software, their patterns of behavior must change. Project management of the implementation process is much more complex.
- Due to the complexity of the software and the long learning curve, most firms find that they have to hire consultants to support the installation process. The cost of the consultants often far exceeds the cost of the software package.
- Implementation can take months or years as company management defines new or modified business processes. Who will perform the normal work during this period?
- The benefits of the software accrue to the company's general management and to the company as a whole more than to individual department staff. Their workload and complexity may actually grow. It is very difficult to motivate the lower levels of business unit that the package is in their best interests. The effect of a mandate from management can be dissipated over the years of installation.
- The company must endure risk as resources are applied to the implementation. Flexibility and staff resources that are normally available are now consumed in the implementation of the package. Changes to existing software that will be replaced will likely be turned down. Programmers who supported the current legacy systems to be replaced are devoted 100 percent to the new software package. Do you think that these people are going to eagerly support the package? Their resistance could create another project management problem.
- Interfaces must be built that link legacy systems—which will not be replaced by the software package—and the software package. This can be complex because the content, meaning, and other characteristics of the information may differ between the package and legacy systems.

Why do failure and problems occur? Here are some reasons:

- The culture of the country and that of the firm do not fit with the software. This is discovered too late and the project fails.
- The business units and corporate management are too inflexible to make changes in business processes that will accommodate the software package.

The company fails to take advantage of the new features of the software and instead thinks of the software as a straight replacement for the existing software.

The information technology organization is faced with many challenges in implementing a software package:

- How to maintain current systems during the transition.
- How to manage such a large project.
- How to transition current systems staff to the new technology.
- What to do with the other software not touched by the software package.

The purpose of this chapter is to determine an approach for managing the selection and implementation of large software packages.

There is some basic general rules that you should apply to both software package evaluation and implementation. Give high priority in evaluation not to the features pitched by the vendors but instead to whether your business transactions will flow through their systems. In implementation give attention to not only the software, but on how you will fill the gap between what the package delivers and what you need. In some cases, you may have to invent new shadow systems and workarounds—even for the new package.

Steps in implementation

The package project can be divided into these steps.

- *Step 1*: Assess your current systems, processes, and technology.
- *Step 2*: Evaluate the software packages and vendor support required.
- *Step 3*: Select and negotiate contracts with vendors.
- *Step 4*: Manage the initial software setup and training, and conduct a pilot project.
- *Step 5*: Undertake full-scale implementation.

Before proceeding with each step, please note that each situation is unique. The following suggestions will serve as guidelines and lessons learned—not as inflexible rules.

Step 1: assess your current systems, processes, and technology

Why go through this step? Why not just plunge in and select the software? Knowing what other problems you will face is one reason. Another reason is to prepare the organization for change in business processes. Here you must uncover and unearth your shadow systems, workarounds, and exceptions.

The end products of the first step include the following:

- Identification of upgrades or replacements for hardware, system software, and network components and systems required to support the software package.
- Determination of the business processes, business units, and managers that will be involved in the other steps.
- Assessment of the scale of effort, costs, and issues that will have to be faced in implementation.
- Estimation of benefits from implementation of the software package.
- This step can be undertaken even if there is a management directive to implement a specific software package. The preceding information can contribute later for generating a realistic perspective of the requirements for implementation.

Several activities can be performed in parallel.

- **Action 1: From basic requirements of the software packages being considered, determine the potential future hardware, software, and network environment.**

Most packages can operate on a variety of machines, operating systems, and database management systems. If you already have such an environment, then you can determine the incremental additions required. In other cases, the company is faced with acquiring a new platform to support the database management system. This is a major step because the interfaces required between the old systems and the new package will cross the network with multiple platforms.

The network and workstations are another part of the puzzle. Although you may be able to support the package in a minimal form with the current network, you are just asking for trouble. The business unit will change its pattern of work by using the network and PCs even more than it currently does. Existing PCs may have to be upgraded or replaced along with network interface cards, hubs, routers, and other network components.

How are the costs of upgrades accommodated? One view is to associate them with the software package implementation. Another view is to consider the upgrades part of the normal price of doing business using technology. If the upgrade issue is not faced early, then it will hit with full force when the new system is being implemented. The implementation schedule will suffer as resources have to be pulled off to handle the upgrade.

From lessons learned, the upgrade can commence after software selection and negotiation. This will support focus on the software later. Network implementation is considered in more detail in Chapter 19. Here it is recommended that the scope of installation, testing, training, and support be identified to assist in planning during later stages.

- **Action 2: Identify the business departments and processes to be affected by the software package.**

Let's assume that you are considering payroll and human resources software. You might think that only these departments are involved. You might be wrong. Some of the packages move data entry and capture out to line business units. They have to be included in the project as well. In some cases, you might find it easier to determine which departments are not involved. Consider creating a table of department involvement. An example is shown in Figure 18.1. In the second through fourth columns, the roles of the departments can be listed in terms of evaluation and implementation. The last column indicates the department's role with respect to the business process.

Dept.	Evaluation Involvement	Implementation— Pilot	Implementation— Full Scale	Business Process Role

Figure 18.1   Table of department involvement

In contacting departments to collect this information, identify people who will be involved in evaluation and implementation. You might wish to use the table in Figure 18.2 for this. It identifies their roles as well as expertise. With respect to business processes identify both formal and informal processes.

Dept.	Person	E-mail/Telephone	Role/Expertise	Comments

Figure 18.2   Roles of staff

- **Action 3: Analyze business processes and transactions in terms of standardization and potential limitations.**

This can be the most time-consuming action, but it is limited here to getting an initial assessment of uniqueness and culture. Detailed analysis will come later. Here you have to determine the degree of flexibility of the processes and organizations to accommodate to the packages.

Concentrate on defining detailed transactions in the current business processes that can be employed in the evaluation of the software packages. Gather both typical and exceptional transactions. Collect some sample data as well. For each transaction, identify the steps, business rules, and exceptions that can occur. Try to pin down the reasons for exceptions. A list of tasks for Step 1 is given in Figure 18.3.

```
1000   Project Planning
       1100   Purpose
       1200   Scope
       1300   Establish Lessons Learned Database
       1400   Establish Issues Database
       1500   Set up Project Management-Related Software
       1600   Train Project Team in Project Methods and Tools
       1700   Establish Project Reporting Process
       1800   Establish Issues and Lessons Learned Processes

2000   Initial Data Collection for Software Packages
       2100   Identify Software Packages
       2200   Survey Software Packages
       2300   Define Technology, Support, and other Requirements for each Package
       2400   Collect Information on Experience, Use, Contracts, and so on
       2500   Define Business Process Requirements for Each Package

3000   Estimate Future Network, Hardware, and Software Requirements
       3100   Review Current Workload and Systems
       3200   Estimate Future User Base and Volume for the Software
       3300   Define Network Structure and Components for the Future
       3400   Identify Hardware and System Software for the Future
       3500   Conduct Sizing Analysis to Determine Quantity by Component Type
       3600   Itemize Upgrades Required
       3700   Define Migration Path from Current Architecture
       3800   Estimate Costs and Determine a General Schedule for Migration
```

Figure 18.3   Tasks for Step 1

4000   Identify Business Units and Processes to be Affected

  4100   Identify All Departments and their Potential Involvement
  4200   Define the Roles and Responsibilities of Each Department
  4300   Identify Business Processes and Relate them to Departments
  4400   Identify Key Individuals and Roles by Phase of Implementation
  4500   Establish Project Team

5000   Analyze Current Business Processes

  5100   Analyze Central Processes to be Impacted by Software Package

    5110   Determine Business Transactions
    5120   Analyze Key Transactions
    5130   Define Issues and Opportunities for Improvement for Current Work
    5140   Identify Other Manual and Supporting Systems
    5150   Identify and Analyze Cross Process Transactions

  5200   Analyze Related Processes for Interfaces

    5210   Identify Exact Interfaces
    5220   Determine Problems and Impacts with the Current Interfaces

  5300   Analyze Existing Software that Will Interface with the Software Package

    5310   Determine Current Interfaces
    5320   Define the Problems and Impacts of these Interfaces
    5330   Assess the Ability to Make Changes to Current Systems

  5400   Define Format, Quality, Completion, and Condition of Data in the Current Systems

    5410   Identify All Relevant Data Files and Control Tables
    5420   Conduct Analysis of the Data and Tables
    5430   Review History Files
    5440   Evaluate Potential Migration Approaches

6000   Estimate Costs, Benefits, Risks, and Schedule for Package Implementation

  6100   Develop First Cut at Costs for Technology, Systems, and Implementation
  6200   Identify Business and Technical Issues related to Implementation
  6300   Define the Benefits for the Package and How these would be Realized
  6400   Develop Initial Implementation Plan and Schedule
  6500   Perform Cost-Benefit Analysis

Figure 18.3   (Continued)

Step 2: evaluate software packages and support requirements

Traditionally, you define a list of features for the software that you can then prioritize into those that are absolutely required and those that are desirable. Each package can then be evaluated and scored. You can generate a total score by weighting the various features (multiplied by the score). This is most useful if you can identify some features that are very unique. Then the scoring can eliminate some of the alternative software packages. However, it is often the case today that most of the packages are flexible enough to possess many features.

Because the software integrates with the business process, following only this approach may result in problems. You must also determine the fit between the software package and the business process. If possible, take the transactions gathered in the previous step and apply them to the software packages. This may not be possible, because a massive effort may be required to set up the tables and parameters just to get ready to run the transactions. There are several fallback positions. First, working with the vendor, you can simulate how the transactions will be handled. Ask questions about how the package is to be set up and how each step of the transaction will be addressed. A second approach is to interview current users of the software package. Some of the questions to ask are given in Figure 18.4.

Technical

- What are alternatives for hardware, system software, and networking?
- Is the application offered via cloud computing?
- What software is required beyond the software package?
- What systems management methods and tools are needed?
- What network management methods and tools are required?

Business

- What industries does the firm support?
- What business processes do the company's products support?
- In what countries and regions does the company offer support and sales?
- What productivity and activity statistics are offered through the system?
- What security measures are offered and supported?

Functional/General

- What is the financial condition of the firm?
- How many employees does it have in development and support?
- Are regular new versions and releases issued?
- Does the firm have new products coming out that would cause you to wait for them?
- What is the direction of development for the firm?

Existing Users

- What are the greatest strengths of the product?
- What are the weaknesses of the product?
- What was the quality of support during installation?
- What parts of the old system still have to be used?
- What were the benefits of the new system, as compared to what was expected?
- How well was the implementation project organized?
- What were the surprises encountered?

Figure 18.4   Questions related to software packages

Some additional suggestions are as follows:

- Ensure that you include exception transactions as well as normal ones. It is often the exceptions that contain business rules that cannot be handled by the software.
- Make sure that business unit staff are involved in the evaluation. If they don't participate, they may feel left out here and then feel that the package is being shoved down their throats later.
- Review and document results as you go. Also, record questions and issues that may impact implementation.

Figure 18.4   (Continued)

What is "success"? You might say that it is selecting the most cost-effective package that fits the requirements. That is insufficient today. The business unit must not only agree, but also commit to implementation and to change. Otherwise, the installation of the "best" software will end up on the rocks.

Let's define the role of the business unit in this step. In the preceding step the business unit participated in defining and assessing the current business process. Here the business unit must be involved in the evaluation through direct participation. During the evaluation, there will be times when the current process does not work with the system. The process will have to change. Get this out on the table. Have the business unit react. Otherwise, work-around efforts might be necessary later to circumvent the software package and preserve the current business process. IT cannot agree to the new process and change. That is the responsibility of the business unit, which will have to identify the necessary changes to its pattern of work. Act as a coordinator and scribe to record the results and changes. There may be implications for policies and organization as well as procedures.

You will likely require consulting support to implement major software packages. The identification, evaluation, and selection of the consultants can make or break the project. Many firms select the software first and then find the consultant. This is a very bad idea for several reasons. First, the consultant costs will likely exceed the cost of the package many times. Second, success will depend as much on the consultant as on the package. You can also select a package where the assistance in your area or country is limited or where assistance is very expensive. It is recommended that you consider evaluating several consulting firms when you have narrowed the software packages to two alternatives. Some criteria for evaluating consultants are listed in Figure 18.5.

- History and track record of the firm
- Length of time and number of engagements involving the software package
- Available support by region and country
- Experience with specific firms in your industry

Figure 18.5   Criteria for evaluation of consultants

- Range and scope of tasks that the firm can address

  - Planning for implementation
  - Analysis of business processes
  - Set up of software package
  - Design of new business processes using the software package
  - Installation of the software
  - Customization of software
  - Training in the software
  - Measurement of use and results

- Number of current engagements and commitments
- Ability to support multiple locations
- Status of the consultant from the perspective of the software vendor
- Previous clients and recommendations
- Cost
- Availability of staff
- Guarantee of work
- Problem and issue management

Figure 18.5 (Continued)

Narrow the candidate software packages to two. Ranking should not be on the basis of cost, but on the benefit that the company will derive (as the benefits far outweigh the cost of the software). When considering cost, focus on the total cost that will include hardware, consultants, and internal staff support. Thus, it is important for the business units to define the benefits for each package. A checklist is given in Figure 18.6.

Costs

- Software package—basic
- Software package—additional modules
- Related system software required
- Related database management software required
- Utility software required
- Network hardware upgrades and purchase
- Network software upgrades and purchases
- Server hardware upgrades and purchases
- Server software upgrades and purchases
- Client hardware upgrades and purchases
- Client software upgrades and purchases
- Labor costs to support upgrades and purchases
- Facilities upgrades
- Vendor software installation support
- Vendor software implementation support
- Consulting support—planning

Figure 18.6 Cost and benefit elements

- Consulting support—installation
- Consulting support—implementation
- Data conversion effort
- Pilot system implementation and testing
- Vendor software maintenance and service
- Hardware/network maintenance and service for additional items due to software package
- Dedicated staff support for software package implementation
- Ongoing staff support for software package

Figure 18.6 (Continued)

Packages that leave the current process intact will appeal to the business unit, but will lack sufficient benefits. Management benefits such as availability of centralized information must be quantified. What if management attempt to impose a choice? Include another package and perform the evaluation. You still must evaluate the package against management's choice. Figure 18.7 contains a sample list of tasks for this step.

1000 Determine Candidate Software Packages/Consultants and Collect Data

    1100 Collect Detailed Information on Each Package
    1200 Define Feature and Capability List
    1300 Collect Information from Existing Users
    1400 Survey the Web and Literature for Reviews and Experience
    1500 Identify Potential Consultants
    1600 Define Evaluation Criteria for Consultants
    1700 Collect Information on Consultants
    1800 Collect Data from Consultant References and the Web

2000 Preliminary Evaluation

    2100 Develop Evaluation Approach and Criteria
    2200 Perform Quantitative Analysis

        2210 Define Weighing Method for Features and Capabilities
        2220 Carry out the Scoring and Evaluation Analysis
        2230 Document Evaluation Results

    2300 Transaction Testing

        2310 Identify Transactions for Testing
        2320 Determine Testing Approach
        2330 Identify Data for Testing
        2340 Define Anticipated Testing Results
        2350 Conduct Transaction Testing
        2360 Evaluate Test Results
        2370 Document Test Results

Figure 18.7 Tasks for evaluation of software packages

```
2400   Conduct Evaluation of Consultants

    2410   Assemble Information for Evaluation
    2420   Perform Evaluation of Consultants
    2530   Identify Primary and Secondary Selected Consultants
    2540   Document Results of Analysis

2500   Prepare Initial Evaluation of Software Packages

    2510   Software Packages only
    2520   Consultants only
    2530   Combined Software Package and Consultants
    2540   Select Finalists
    2550   Document Results
```

Figure 18.7   (Continued)

Step 3: select the package and negotiate the contract

Now you have narrowed the field to two packages. You must select one along with the consulting firm and then negotiate with both the software vendor and the consulting firms. Note that the consultant choice is linked to the package choice. The consultant will eventually disappear, so why have the consulting firm involved here? Because of your dependence on the consultant for success of implementation, the package and its support are tied closely together.

Final selection

With both finalist packages suitable, how are you going to decide which to choose? Here are some guidelines:

- Any cost differential that is present now may disappear as the implementation progresses. Since much of the cost lies in labor associated with implementation and these costs are often comparable for different packages, cost may not be the deciding factor.
- A deciding factor may be your firm's willingness to change its business processes and policies. Each package will have its own requirement for business change. Business change in turn relates to the degree of benefit. Thus, if two packages have a similar cost to implement, you might decide in favor of the one that offers the most benefit because management is willing to make changes. On the other hand, you might decide in favor of the one that requires less change, if it is politically acceptable despite the fact that it offers fewer benefits.
- Another criterion for selection is that of risk. Risk in software packages will often lie in implementation. Implementation will depend on the combination of the software vendor, the consultants you select, and your staff. Here the consultant alternatives for each package may count more than the actual software itself.

Contracting

You would follow the guidelines in Chapter 14. Figure 18.8 provides a list of contract issues for both the software vendor and the consultant. Among the most critical questions in terms of contracting are the following:

- What is the role of the software vendor in providing initial installation and training support?
- What are the responsibilities of the software vendor in fixing problems with the software?
- What is going to be the responsibility of the vendor, consultant, and you in managing the implementation? What roles will each play?
- How will the consultant be measured and monitored?
- How will problems and issues be resolved between the vendor, consultant, and you?

Software package

- Functions and features included
- Hardware, network, and system software environment required
- Installation support provided
- Implementation support provided
- Warranty
- Performance standards
- Acceptance criteria and testing
- Maintenance and ongoing support
- Cost structure and discounts
- Upgrade policies

Consultant

- Available staff and their qualifications
- Types of service to be provided
- Ownership of any customized work
- Protection of company operations information
- Termination
- Level of effort
- Work quality evaluation
- Replacement/substitution of staff
- Billing and payment terms

Figure 18.8   Contract issues

Step 4: install the software and conduct a pilot project

Begin forming the project team. Consider having three project leaders: one from the vendor, one from the consulting firm, and one from your firm. These leaders are not equals because you are the customer. An alternative is to have four leaders: one from the business unit, one from IT, one from the vendor, and one from the consultant. However, this can become unwieldy and difficult to manage. Almost all successful implementations involve multiple leaders so that decisions can be made quickly and parallel subprojects can be undertaken.

The roles of each group must be defined. These are as follows:

- *Internal information systems.* General project management, design and programming interfaces, operations procedures, and data conversion.
- *Business unit.* New operations procedures, training materials, estimation and responsibility for benefits, and testing.
- *Software vendor.* Software installation, training, support for testing, troubleshooting, and testing.
- *Consultant.* Implementation support, support through lessons learned and experience, training of systems and business unit staff, and testing.

Note that there is overlap because some functions involve multiple organizations. The three project leaders develop an overall summary plan that includes the tasks in Figure 18.9.

```
1000   Project Management

       1100   Identify Roles and Responsibilities
       1200   Identify Team Leaders
       1300   Identify and Select Team Members
       1400   Develop Detailed Tasks and Milestones
       1500   Establish Detailed Project Plan
       1600   Management Review and Approval

2000   Software Installation

       2100   Review the Environment for the Software Package
       2200   Acquire Additional Hardware, Network, and Software to Support the
              Package
       2300   Install and Test Supporting Hardware, Network, and Software
       2400   Train and Prepare for Software Package Installation
       2500   Install Software Package
       2600   Test Application Software in Network

3000   Training and Setup

       3100   Training for IT and User Staff
       3200   Definition of New Business Process Transactions
       3300   Definition of Parameters and Table Values for System
       3400   Setup of Parameters and Table Values
       3500   Preliminary Testing of Parameters
       3600   Training of IT Staff for Interface Programming
```

Figure 18.9   Tasks for initial implementation of software package

```
3700   Design of Interface Programs
3800   Programming and Testing of Interface Programs
3900   Documentation of Business Process for Pilot

4000   Data Conversion

4100   Review Analysis Findings with Respect to Data
4200   Determine Data Conversion Approach
4300   Define Schedule for Data Conversion
4400   Develop and Test Software for Data Conversion
4500   Perform Initial Data Conversion

5000   Pilot Project

5100   Train Business Staff as Part of Pilot
5200   Load Data and Setup for Pilot Project
5300   Establish Network and System Environment for Pilot
5400   Define Acceptance and Measurement for Pilot
5500   Conduct Initial Pilot Test
5600   Review Results and Refine Tests
5700   Redo Pilot
5800   Measure Results and Estimate Benefits
```

Figure 18.9   (Continued)

Next, each manager works with his or her own staff members to identify their tasks in detail. Several joint working sessions can be held to refine the tasks and schedule. Attendees also should include business unit staff as well as employees from the other groups. This collaborative approach not only heads off problems later, but also supports gaining the employees' commitment and involvement. By working together the team will acquire a common vocabulary.

Software loading

Loading software used to be easier when it resided on a mainframe computer. Today, most software is client-server or intranet based. This means that there are many components and more people involved in setting up the software. You will probably want to establish the software package on a separate testing client-server network. This will not only ensure integrity of the current network, but will also support training, development of system management and operations procedures, and testing. You will also want to have key systems programmers, network support staff, and application programmers involved in these tasks to aid in their learning.

What are some of the issues that you may face here? One is that you may suddenly find that the network software or hardware must be upgraded to support the software package. A second issue is the challenge of making technical staff available to work with the software package in addition to their normal work.

The end products of the software loading are as follows:

- Functional software on a network;
- Technical staff trained at a basic level in installation and operations;
- Established framework for the systems and network management and operations procedures.

The procedures can be finished during the pilot.

Training and setup

Training requirements for integrated software packages are extensive. This is because exact parameters and table values have been loaded into the system. This requires business unit staff and managers who know the current business process in detail, understand what the new process will look like with the new package, and are empowered to make decisions. This is a tall order, given that there are very few of these people and there is a need to continue to support the current process. The role of the consultant is helpful here because he or she can explain what alternative parameters mean in terms of the business.

How can you track the training and setup? The most complete approach is to list each table that must be specified as a task. You will really know where you are and what progress is being made. However, maintaining such a detailed schedule will take time. Going to this level of detail provides some additional benefits. Building the list of tables and tasks with the consultant and business unit staff will show the business unit staff what is ahead of them. If they are encouraged to update their own schedules, then they can use the schedule as a checklist. In building the tables for the software package you will come upon unknown factors that require further analysis. Enter these factors into the issues database to ensure that they are addressed later. Then the team can go on to other tables. It is similar with lessons learned. As you learn about a specific table and what its impact is on the system, you can enter this information into the lessons learned database.

What challenges do you face in the setup? One is getting the right human resources from the business units to participate. Another is maintaining a steady effort over several months of setup. It is difficult to maintain momentum when the people still have to perform some or all of their normal tasks. A third challenge is tracking down unresolved issues and questions. Not resolving some key questions can mean that the pilot cannot test this area of the software package.

The end products of training and setup are as follows:

- Business unit managers and staff have been trained in the setup and use of the software package.
- Parameters and tables of the software package are established.
- The software package is ready for the pilot.
- A start has been made on training materials and procedures.
- Decisions have been made on the detailed changes to the business process that will be tested in the pilot project.

Pilot project

A pilot project is important for any major software package. First, you validate the parameters of the tables of the system as well as the training of the staff. Second, you can use the pilot to build procedures and training materials. Most important, you can determine what changes in the business process will be necessary to fit with the software (the parameters and tables have only limited flexibility). The pilot then develops the new business process and helps to validate the benefits that were estimated when the package was justified to management.

What are some of the risks in the pilot? One is that the pilot does not exercise enough of the features and capabilities of the software package. If this occurs, then the business process will be in a state of flux during implementation leading to more problems. This happens when management attempts to rush the pilot project so as to begin implementation earlier. Another risk is that the pilot does not exercise all of the exception transactions and conditions of the current business process. A third risk is that the business unit may attempt to run the pilot with the old business process. This may lead to rejection of the software package.

The end products of the pilot project are as follows:

- Validation of the software package tables and parameters;
- Definition and validation of the new business process along with the software package;
- Completion of operations procedures and training materials for end users;
- Completion of systems and network management procedures as well as computer operations procedures;
- Trained core of business unit staff who are confident in the software package.

It is, perhaps, the last item that is most important. It is a big leap from a pilot to full-scale implementation. If the pilot yields many unresolved issues, then consider addressing these issues, followed by carrying out a second, limited pilot. Doubts about the system will have a major dampening effect on its implementation.

Step 5: undertake full-scale implementation

A list of tasks for this step is given in Figure 18.10. What areas have risk? Here are several that seem to surface repeatedly:

Conversion

While some reference tables are easily converted, the basic files are a different matter. Will the master file be converted? If so, how will missing data be captured and entered? How will the data in the master file be cleaned up? Some companies have found that it is easier to establish a starting date and enter all transactions into the new system

1000　Business Process Change and Preparation

1100　Review Results of Pilot
1200　Prepare and Review Policies and Procedures
1300　Prepare Training Materials
1400　Determine Migration Path for Existing Data
1500　Establish Data Entry and Cleanup Squad
1600　Verify and Validate the Converted Data
1700　Dry Run and Test the New Business Process

2000　Network, Hardware, and System Software

2100　Determine Exact Requirements Using Pilot Experience
2200　Implement Hardware, Network, and Software
2300　Conduct Network, Security, and Performance Testing

3000　Interface Programs

3100　Complete all Interface Programs
3200　Conduct Tests of Online and Batch Interfaces
3300　Conduct Tests for Backup, Recovery, and Restart of all Interfaces

4000　Software Package Customization

4100　Define Customization Requirements Based on Pilot
4200　Design Software
4300　Program and Test Customized Software
4400　Conduct Interface Testing
4500　Document and Establish Software in Production

5000　Operations Procedures and Setup

5100　Define Operations Procedures for Normal Operation
5200　Develop Backup, Recovery, Security, and Restart Procedures
5300　Validate and Test Procedures

6000　Training and Cut-Over

6100　Conduct Training of End Users
6200　Establish and Test Production Environment
6300　Go Live with System
6400　Verify the Changes in the Business Processes
6500　Measure Benefits and Impacts of New System and Processes
6600　Identify Any Unresolved Issues and their Impacts

Figure 18.10　Tasks for full-scale implementation of software package

from that date forward. In this case, you might start several months prior to the planned cutover date.

Another major issue exists with history data. Given that the history data is useful to the business, it must be accessible in some form. Business units often want several years of history data. It is infeasible to convert and clean up all of this data, which might require years of research. A frequently used approach is to archive the information to microfilm or image for access manually later.

Interfaces to current systems

Several types of interfaces are required. One type is permanent. That is, the software package will interface with existing software for the foreseeable future. An example might be a case in which the software package will feed an existing general ledger system. There is no plan to replace the general ledger.

The second type of interface is a temporary interface. Here the software package is composed of many large modules or parts. It is impossible to install all of the parts at once. Therefore, the first module of the software package must interface with the existing software that will eventually be replaced by other package modules.

Interfaces sound straightforward enough. But are they to be online or batch? What happens with the conversion of data from the package into the old software and vice versa? How will data be saved from one module of the software package to be input into another module that will be implemented later?

Integration of the system into the business process

This has been mentioned repeatedly. The new business process must clearly be defined as being separate from the current process. The project leaders make an effort to begin measurements of the new process and system to validate benefits. Unfortunately, this often means creating shadow systems or making process changes to address the parts of the process that the software cannot handle.

Cases and examples

South County—A near disaster

South County is a local government agency that had a number of legacy systems. These systems operated on obsolete hardware. A logical three-part strategy was formulated to achieve modern systems. The first part was to implement new hardware, PCs, and a wide area network. This was successfully managed. The second part was to select the initial software package that would run on the new hardware, convert over the other legacy systems, and interface them to the package. This step in the strategy fell apart. It cost more than 300 percent and over a year longer than anticipated to implement the software package. Conversion and interfaces were pushed back further.

What went wrong? The decision was made to select and implement a general ledger system. General ledger has unique characteristics that make it very difficult to implement compared to other software. The software requires extensive interfaces to all systems that feed the general ledger. If the old chart of accounts is not adequate, then intensive, detailed work is required to define a new chart of accounts. This is in addition to data conversion. Data conversion often does not work because the level of detail in the old system is insufficient for the new system. The existing legacy systems were based around the old chart of accounts. To have a meaningful general ledger, the old legacy systems had to be modified in addition to interfaces.

What might have been done? Systems that fed the general ledger would have had more users and benefit. The existing general ledger was adequate, but did require improvement. Had South County picked payroll, accounts payable, or accounts receivable, there would have been more users and greater benefit. The general ledger only had 11 online users. The other systems had at least three to five times as many.

Questions

1. Most organizations now employ software packages extensively. What is the objective in implementing a package relative to building internal staff skills? How much do you think internal staff should know about a software package?
2. A vendor had proposed using cloud computing to meet the needs in accounting for South County. This was rejected at once by management. What would have been the advantages of cloud computing for South County? What would have been the drawbacks?
3. This case highlighted the importance of considering related software needs as a group. What are barriers in an organization to this approach? How could you market the idea of considering them as a group?

Vixen Manufacturing

Vixen Manufacturing decided to acquire a large-scale integrated manufacturing system. This system was table driven and required that Vixen operations managers and staff change their processes and procedures extensively to use the software. Vixen management recognized that the operations staff were critical to the success of the project. They provided for resources that could help the business units in both current work and conversion. Vixen managers also indicated to the staff that they were very flexible in terms of rules and policies. They encouraged the staff to first understand the software and then to be creative in their use of the software.

Vixen established a four-person steering committee composed of the business unit, consultant, information technology, and management. The project was divided into subprojects: initial installation and training, business process definition, initial implementation and evaluation, and full-scale implementation. The use of subprojects provided focus to each area of the project. The projects were managed in an open environment. Group sessions were held to simulate alternative new business processes, procedures, and policies.

Even with all of this, there were problems. First, Vixen moved from an initial small pilot implementation to full-scale implementation in one step. This was a problem because not enough people were trained from the pilot to support full-scale implementation. The schedule slipped, and Vixen had to fall back and establish several intermediate stages of implementation.

Questions

1. In implementing a software package, you have to take into account the morale of the staff maintaining the current systems. What concerns should you address? How could you keep the morale of the maintenance staff high?

2. Firms such as this one often plunge in and attempt to implement an entire system at one time. What are the advantages and disadvantages of this approach?
3. Suppose that management wanted to select a major new manufacturing software system to address its process problems. How would you sell the idea of in-depth analysis of the processes before plunging ahead?

Lessons learned

Software packages can include network utilities, firewall software, shopping cart software, credit card processing and authorization, and similar software. Attention here is on integrating the software and interfacing it to the legacy systems. New business software continues to emerge so that evaluation of the software is more complex. During the evaluation, you want to give emphasis on flexibility to support marketing and to interfaces.

Never assume that a software package will address all requirements in the business work. Often, the parts that the packages do not address are very important. Moreover, in real life, you cannot leave these parts unchanged. So there may need to be a separate, but related, project that deals with these parts.

Guidelines

- At times it will be possible to keep the old methods in the business process or to adopt new ones that better fit the package. Encourage people to move to the new process. Otherwise, you will see the benefits drip away.
- Identify junior business unit staff who can be key players in building the new business process and acting as champions within the business unit.
- Determine at the start of the implementation how knowledge of the software package will be spread out among different business unit staff. Assume that there will be attrition so that you must allow for backup.
- If you cannot fit a transaction into the software package, be ready to consider a workaround of the software package. If you admit that this is possible early in the implementation, you will likely face more pressure to allow for more exceptions— watering down the benefits of the system.
- During implementation establish an ongoing user group that can be responsible for maintaining the training materials and operations manual, and for training new staff in the business unit. This is also intended to head off deterioration of the new process.
- A parallel effort is required on several fronts to reduce the elapsed time of implementation. Each module of the software package must have its own project plan. In this way, there can be at least a limited parallel effort for multiple modules of the software package.

Questions

1. Select a software package and search the Web to determine both problems and benefits that users have experienced.
2. Let's assume that management has selected the wrong software package. Their decision cannot be reversed. What actions could you take to mitigate this problem?
3. Assume that your firm has selected the same software package as three of your competitors. What can you do to implement the system so that you gain a competitive advantage?
4. For a particular application such as sales, identify three software application packages. Using the materials in this chapter lay out an evaluation of the three packages.
5. Discuss under what circumstances you would not select a software package, but, instead, would develop the software internally or with consultants.

What to do next

1. Scan the literature and Internet to find experiences and lessons learned on implementing software packages. Arrange the lessons learned in terms of management, technology, the software vendor, the consultant, and the business unit. This will assist you in defining roles as well as providing guidance to the people on what can happen.
2. Evaluate your last software package acquisition. Answer the following questions:

   - To what extent was there a complete project plan for implementation?
   - Were the roles of the different players defined at the start of the project or did they evolve?
   - What major issues were encountered in the project?
   - What lessons were learned from the experience?

Summary

Software package acquisition is a growing trend in industry and government. What was once a fairly straightforward project of implementation has grown into a complex one in which you must partner with the software vendor, business unit, and consultant for implementation. This is because business process improvement is linked to the software package. The technical part of the project has also become more complex due to the size of the software package, its interrelationship with the business, customized interfaces with legacy systems, and data conversion risks.

19
Technology projects

Introduction

So far in this part of the book, development, maintenance and enhancement, and software packages have been discussed, covering software and some other systems projects. However, there are other projects involving networking, implementation of new technology, and so on that do not fit into these categories. Here are some examples of technology projects:

- Installation of a wide area network
- Upgrading or replacing central computers and servers
- Implementation of groupware, electronic mail, or other general network-based software
- Installation of new PC software on all users' machines
- Wholesale hardware replacement
- Implementation of intranets and access to the Internet
- Implementation of geographic information systems (GISs) and geographic positioning systems (GPSs).

These "technology projects" are different from software projects in a number of ways:

- The technology often touches a wider group of users and business unit staff.
- There is potentially more exposure and risk because the organization at large becomes dependent on the technology.
- The projects have substantial costs that in some cases these outweigh software project costs.
- Internal knowledge of the technology is limited because it is new to the organization.
- A wider range of skills in implementation is often necessary for successful implementation.
- Benefits are more difficult to pin down because the business processes might not be changed by the technology alone.

- There is substantial, ongoing support in upgrades, operations, and training.
- Technologies may have to be integrated, generating even more work and costs.

Based on these factors it is no wonder that organizations defer technology projects and concentrate on software projects. Upgrades and replacements to current technology are often delayed because management sees the cost, but not the benefits. Given the wide scope of the project along with the cost, the IT organization may view such projects as daunting.

These key questions must be answered:

- What technology projects should be undertaken?
- How do you evaluate and select new technology for implementation given the wide variety of choices and the obsolescence of new technology?
- How should a technology project be managed to minimize total costs over time?
- How can you minimize risk?

Your information systems and technology architecture/infrastructure

A systems and technology architecture is the structure of the hardware, software, and network components of your organization. The architecture is more than a list of products and components; it is also the glue and interfaces that tie the parts together. At Beaumont Insurance maintenance costs of the hardware alone consumed more than $15,000 per month. The mean time to repair problems was in some cases days long due to the problems of the vendor finding staff who still knew the old technology and the difficulty in getting parts.

In comparing modern and old architectures you can begin to see the benefits of a modern, up-to-date architecture, such as the following:

- **Information systems benefits.**

  - It is possible to now acquire a range of modern software packages.
  - It is easier to hire staff who are familiar with the new technology than it is to find people familiar with the obsolete technology.
  - The dependency on the few critical staff who knew the technology is reduced.
  - Maintenance costs may be substantially reduced.
  - New software development is now possible.
  - Network management and performance are improved with modern tools.
  - Operations staffs may be able to be reduced due to central network support.

- **Business unit and management benefits.**

  - The business can now offer modern and innovative insurance products.
  - There is less user training due to working with Windows-based software compared to the old terminal-based systems.

- Employees will have access to electronic mail, groupware, and other software that were not possible in the old architecture.
- Reengineering and process improvement can be more easily supported with modern technology.

Are the benefits always achieved? No. One reason is because the new technology raises expectations among business units for more services. Thus, any savings are offset by greater demands for information and processing support. Another reason is that the new technology touches many more people—leading to greater expense.

Risks in technology projects

You can just jump in and start a technology project. However, that is not a good idea due to the risks and uncertainty. Here are some things that can change or go wrong in a project:

- The number of users of the technology can be underestimated, meaning that a larger investment in hardware, software, and the network will be necessary. This occurs often with intranet and client-server systems.
- The technology does not interface or integrate with existing systems and technology well. This leads to either reduced capabilities or higher cost and more time. This has occurred with some network technologies.
- There was no strategy, so the technology acquired was not complete. This then requires more purchases of additional software and hardware to support implementation. Many technology projects are generated by business unit or management request. IT reacts to this without a strategy.
- The situation was not measured before the new technology project. Hence, at the end of the project, no one has a clear idea of the benefits. There is no before and after comparison. This is very common, in that measurement was not planned.
- If not planned, the new technology may not replace the old in all cases. This means that IT must now bear the burden of supporting both the old and new systems in parallel. This sometimes occurs when a legacy system cannot be totally replaced.
- Staffing support requirements are underestimated. With a fixed headcount in information technology, this means that management must play a zero-sum game in allocating resources. This was the case when PCs were acquired in the 1980s. End user computing support requirements mushroomed.

Costs and benefits of technology projects

Technology projects have associated costs and benefits that can be identified now for later reference. Figure 19.1 lists a number of the cost elements of a typical technology project; Figure 19.2 lists benefits. Note that you extract from these for your specific technology and organization situation. Note that these are only summary and partial lists.

Hardware and related software

- Hardware
- Peripherals
- Network servers
- Print servers
- Database servers
- PCs and workstations
- Operating systems
- Utilities
- Compilers and development tools
- Database management systems
- Fourth generation languages
- Web hosting software
- Cloud computing software
- Firewall hardware and software
- Routers, hubs, and gateways
- Patch panels
- Test equipment
- Monitoring equipment and software
- Network management software
- Security software
- Connectivity software
- Monitoring and troubleshooting software
- Testing software
- Cabling
- Cable interface units
- Telephone, leased lines, satellite links
- Internet service provider

Software

- Electronic mail
- Collaborative software
- PC software
- Intranet software
- Groupware

Personnel

- Installation support

     Cabling
     Network
     Hardware and data center

- Systems programming
- Data management
- Network management
- Security

Figure 19.1   Examples of costs associated with technology projects

- Network support
- Consultant and vendor support

Maintenance and ongoing support

- Hardware maintenance
- Software upgrades
- Hardware upgrades
- Software maintenance and support

Other

- Duplicate and overlapping support during transition
- Facilities work in the data center
- Facilities work in business units
- Uninterrupted power supplies and backup
- Physical security and access control
- Furniture and office equipment
- Telephone system

Figure 19.1   (Continued)

Information systems and technology

- Reduced maintenance costs
- Ability to hire new staff
- Reduced reliance on critical staff with the old architecture
- Flexibility in placing data and software
- Increased ability to manage and support the network and users
- Improved security
- Improved management and troubleshooting
- Ability to implement new solutions
- Ability to use new development methods and tools
- Ability to acquire new software packages
- Potentially less effort in interface support
- Improved productivity with new methods and tools

Business units

- Access to new functions and capabilities
- Access to new software packages
- Benefits from new development
- Increased sharing of information
- Improved productivity of staff
- Increased computer utilization
- Support for process improvement

Figure 19.2   Examples of benefits associated with technology projects

In terms of costs, network-related components today consume more cost and effort. This is due to the complexity of integrating a number of components as well as linking to many business units in different locations.

Note that many of the benefits occur only after application software has been developed or purchased and implemented for the business units. As stated earlier, the benefits of systems generally rest with the business units. However, some benefits, associated with increased efficiency and effectiveness, are within the information technology unit.

Steps in a technology project

Given the risks and benefits as well as limited resources, an organized approach to technology projects is needed. Here is a series of steps that can be followed:

- *Step 1*: Determine technology opportunities. This proactive step identifies as many opportunities as possible for new technology.
- *Step 2*: Define the long-term new systems and technology architecture. This is the systems and technology environment that you wish to achieve in a 3-to-5-year period.
- *Step 3*: Develop a strategy for technology projects. This involves the sequencing of projects to support the implementation of the new architecture.
- *Step 4*: Evaluate and select the vendors and products for the new technology.
- *Step 5*: Develop the project plan for implementing the technology. This includes measuring the current technology and architecture as well as estimating the benefits of the new technology.
- *Step 6*: Carry out the technology project. The scope includes not only technical implementation, but also use by business units.
- *Step 7*: Measure the results of the project.

Some comments are useful before each step is examined. In general, you perform Steps 1 through 3 one time for a series of technologies. Then you update the architecture and strategy periodically. Thus, Steps 1 through 3 spawn a group of technology projects carried out over an extended period. You will initially define the costs and benefits of the new technology in Step 1 to solicit management support. These will be refined in successive steps. In Step 5 you will determine the costs and benefits in more detail as part of the project plan.

Step 1: Determine technology opportunities

The first action in this step is to define your current architecture. This can be done by first listing the various components (hardware, software, and network). Then you can develop network diagrams and text to describe how the components interface and integrate. This is similar to the figures discussed earlier except that you must give more detail on each component.

Now have the architecture lists and diagrams reviewed for accuracy and completeness. As you are doing this, also have people indicate where they think the problems are in the architecture and with the architecture overall. Ask the following questions:

- What components are missing?
- Where are the poor quality interfaces?
- Where is integration needed, but does not exist?
- What does the architecture prevent the business units from doing?
- In what areas is the support effort the highest?
- What is the distribution of costs across the architecture?
- What prevents the architecture from being expanded?
- What is the distribution of incidents of failure in the architecture?

You have a list of issues, problems, opportunities, and gaps in the current architecture. Take a diagram of the architecture and show by arrows and labels where the problems occur.

Step 2: define the long-term architecture/infrastructure

You can now proceed with identifying potential components to the architecture defined in the first step. The first action is to determine your overall approach to the new architecture. Today, this typically means that you will identify the following:

- Operating systems for the architecture levels (host, network, and PC/workstation);
- General network approach (protocols, connectivity, topology, and hardware);
- Scope of the new architecture (which users, business units, and so on will be connected);
- Database management systems/fourth-generation languages to be used;
- Development languages, compilers, and so on to be employed.

You have now defined the framework for the architecture. The second action is to flesh out the architecture in terms of hardware, software, and network components. Here you will specify each type of component that you require. You will not, however, indicate the quantities required. The results of this action can be reviewed by internal technical staff as well as selected vendors with whom you have relationships and whose products will be part of the long-term architecture. The third action is to determine more precisely the quantities required as well as to estimate the support requirements in terms of staffing.

As the fourth action, you will now develop a list of benefits and costs as well as projects required to move from the current architecture to the new architecture. The costs and benefits can only be rough estimates. With the completion of this step you have defined the new architecture. You are not ready to present it to management, however, because you lack a strategy for implementation. All you get from non-technical management now is puzzled support because you have no plan of action.

Step 3: Develop a technology project strategy

A partial list of projects for Beaumont Insurance follows. With the list of projects defined, you must now determine the priority and sequencing of the projects. This is the technology project strategy. It is your implementation strategy.

- Selection and implementation of new host hardware;
- Implementation of the wide area network;
- Installation of database management systems;
- Upgrading and expansion of PCs for business units;
- Implementation of electronic mail;
- Internet access project;
- Implementation of improved local area networks;
- Conversion of the existing software applications to the new host hardware.

Let's use the Beaumont example to show how to develop the strategy. You first want to determine which projects depend on others. Here electronic mail and Internet access depend on the wide and local area networks. Database management software depends on the new host system as does conversion of the existing software applications.

The second action is to see what can be done in parallel to reduce the elapsed time of installation. Note that you want to reduce elapsed time because the longer the transition, the more expensive and risky will be the projects as you are maintaining the old architecture in parallel with the new. Here you can see that there are three parallel projects: the new host hardware, the wide area network, and the local area networks. You can upgrade the PCs at any time. However, because this may involve substantial training and support, it can wait. This will be our first phase of modernization. At the end of the first phase, there are few benefits and many costs because you are setting up the structure for the software.

Now assume that the first phase is complete. What is next? Obviously, the priority is to convert the existing application software so that you can eliminate the old hardware. However, access to the online applications means that the users must have PCs. The second phase then includes software conversion and PCs. At the conclusion of the second phase, you will have operational systems on the new host and network. Users will be working with PCs instead of terminals. There are some benefits here, but there are even more costs.

The third phase is to establish additional user functions as well as the development and production environment for the future. The projects are electronic mail, Internet access, and the database management software. At the end of this phase you are able to evaluate and select application packages as well as to do development.

To summarize so far, the three phases are as follows:

- *Phase 1*: Implement the basis structure of hardware, system software, and the network.
- *Phase 2*: Establish the operational systems on the new architecture.
- *Phase 3*: Implement the development and user functions that take advantage of the new environment.

You have incurred major costs and have received limited benefits. This is a general pattern with technology projects. Even with smaller projects that involve limited new technology, this is often the case.

Now suppose that you have an architecture in place. You can bypass the first two steps to some extent. You will still have to specify how the new technology fits within the architecture. You will also have to develop an implementation strategy for the technology.

At this point you are ready to prepare a presentation and deliver it to management. Many of these presentations end in disaster. Management asks about the benefits to offset the costs. It is likely that you will be unable to identify sufficient benefits to justify the costs. As a result, management turns down the technology project. How do you prevent this outcome? From experience it is recommended that you emphasize the results if the technology project is not carried out. Ask and answer the following questions.

- What will happen to the architecture if deterioration continues over several years?
- What is the impact on the business units if modernization does not occur?
- What will be the comparative position of the organization in industry?
- What are competitors doing with technology? What can the competitors do that you cannot do with your current technology?
- What is the impact on the ability of IT to respond to business unit requests?
- How will the business units benefit from the new technology in the near term?
- How will the business units benefit from the new technology in the long term?

This approach emphasizes the downside of continuing business as usual. It is the key to getting management support. At the end of the presentation you will indicate that the next steps are to identify precise quantities of each component and develop a project plan. You will then return to management with the results of these two steps. Can't you do these steps first and then present the whole thing? You can, but it is not a good idea. Use this presentation as a means of showing management a vision of the future.

Step 4: Evaluate and select products

Prior to this step you have gathered some information on products. For database management systems you may have narrowed the field to two or three products, for example. Create a project plan to perform the evaluation and selection. Because evaluation and selection were already discussed for software packages, the attention here will be on what has to be included in evaluation and selection.

Involve the business unit managers and staff in this step and those that follow. The business unit will have to support the selection as well as the plan and benefits. If the business unit is not involved here, but only later in implementation, then there is a risk that the project will be labeled as only an IT project. This can doom management support when you present the plan.

You must ensure that the lists of components and support tasks are complete. If you miss something important and have to return for approval, you risk the entire project as well as your own credibility. Make the effort to contact existing users of the technology and find out what components they acquired, their experience in implementation, and some idea of the costs incurred and benefits received.

You can contact the vendor at this stage to review the list of components and to get ideas related to the implementation plan for the technology. It is important that you get the vendor on board because the vendor will later be asked to provide support. Through the vendor's participation you protect yourself in terms of being complete.

Step 5: Develop the project plan

Although the project plan for a technology project depends on the specific technology, there are some general stages of work in the project. Divide the project plan into these stages:

- *Stage 1*: Make preparations for installing the technology. This might include initial technical training in the technology, facilities work, staff assignments, procurement, and related start-up tasks. At the end of this stage, you are prepared to install the technology. Here you will also measure the current business process and technology with the business unit.
- *Stage 2*: Install the technology. This is followed by testing to ensure that it is functional. Of course, it is not connected or integrated with anything as yet.
- *Stage 3*: Employ the technology in a prototype mode. This includes the initial loading of data, establishing some of the interfaces with the technology, and starting on any customization. During this stage both IT and business unit staff will become familiar with the technology. Benefits can be estimated again.
- *Stage 4*: Complete the implementation of the technology. The technology is used in production. The results of using the technology are measured and compared with the estimated benefits.

This stage-wise approach has several benefits. First, each stage has defined, measurable milestones. Second, mistakes or errors can be addressed prior to full-scale implementation and use. Third, employees are given time to work with the technology. Fourth, you get an opportunity to show managers what is going on and how you are protecting the business unit from any unforeseen problems.

It is important to have both the business unit and vendor involved in project planning. This joint effort will build participation, commitment, and support for the project and the technology. The business unit will have to make the technology work within its business processes.

It is now time to review the selection and plan with management. You will want to focus on the business and management aspects of the plan and the technology. Thus, you focus on how the technology can be used in the business processes and what benefits it will provide. You will not focus on how it works or the details of the technology. Have the business unit manager give the part of the presentation dealing with the use of the technology and its benefits.

Step 6: Implement the technology

The implementation will proceed following the stages of the plan. Consider having a separate project team for each stage because the major tasks in each stage are different. Business unit involvement in the first stage is limited to learning more about the technology. There is no or little involvement in the second stage of installation. Involvement grows in the third stage. Several people from the business unit will be involved. They will have to prepare operational procedures for the technology, define how it is to be managed, support the conversion, and perform testing. The business unit role expands sharply during the implementation stage.

Technical staff such as systems programmers and network staff are involved in supporting the installation in the second stage. Programmers and analysts take over for the third and fourth stages. Vendors support the first three stages.

Beyond the project organization, it is very important that you select the right first application of the technology. If you pick one that has time pressure, then you risk failure because the project team is just learning the technology. If you select an application that involves a business process that is in trouble, there is also unnecessary risk. The critical lesson learned is that you select the application that (1) allows ample time to learn the technology, (2) presents little time pressure, (3) offers clear benefits to the application, and (4) is arranged so that the business environment of the application is representative of the potential applications.

Picking the first application is part of your implementation approach. It is hoped that you will have the same project team members available for the second and third applications of the technology. Choosing the first application was based on minimizing risk and maximizing the chances of success. Selecting the second application must be based on benefits. Therefore, the second application typically involves more users and a greater number of interfaces.

After each application of the technology, measure the project as discussed next. You will also want to gather lessons learned so that your plan, issues, and how you approach situations will be more effective as you go. In one large implementation of fault-tolerant computing, there were eight different applications of the technology. The second application produced more benefits due to a wider scope. Lessons learned and new experiences were gathered during the first four implementations of the technology. It was only during the fifth implementation that little new was learned.

Step 7: Measure project results

The scope of the first stage includes measuring the current business process and system. The last stage encompasses the measurement of the business process after the technology has been implemented. In this step you will also gather lessons learned from the IT and business unit staff. Some areas of lessons learned will bring forth the following questions:

- What surprises were there at each stage?
- How did the business unit ensure that the benefits were achieved?
- What technical tips were gained as a result of the experience?

- What experience and knowledge were gained from the implementation and use of the technology?
- What new information was gained on the condition of the old business process?

When implementing a new technology, the current business process is often streamlined and reengineered to take advantage of the technology. This work, begun in Stage 3, provides you with insight as to the detailed problems with the current process. The IT staff may also have ideas about how to further improve the architecture to take advantage of the technology.

In documenting the measurement, begin with describing in detail how the current and new business process work. Then you can show the differences before and after. Follow up by identifying the areas of benefits and costs associated with the project. You will change the order when you present the results to management. In the presentation the business unit manager will show the current process and highlight the benefits of the technology. If necessary, you and the business unit manager can show the difference between the old and new by showing a sample business transaction that takes advantage of the technology.

During this step, also try to identify the most efficient and effective means of achieving ongoing support for the technology. When people installed PCs for the first time on a wide scale, they were caught by surprise by the quantity and persistence of the end user computing support required. New users needed not only initial training, but continuing hand holding as well.

Things that go wrong and what to do about them

Many things can go wrong in technology projects. Here is a sample of some of the potential pitfalls, gathered from experience, observation, and war stories.

- *Mid-implementation paralysis.* In this case the technology was successfully installed the first time. However, due to the problems encountered it was decided to eliminate or delay any further implementations. This means that the economies of scale of support for the technology on an ongoing basis are spread across a smaller number of users. This occurred with some applications of database management systems.
- *Niche technology.* The systems group or business unit identifies a technology that has very limited application. It is successful, but it consumes too many resources to do the implementation. This occurred with early implementations of image technology.
- *Failure without backup.* One company tried to use digital cameras to capture photos and then transfer them over the Internet. The quality of the pictures was not acceptable and the camera did not hold enough pictures. The company dropped the project, wasting both money and a good idea. The company might have gone back to using standard 35 mm cameras with scanning but did not consider it.
- *Business unit is difficult to work with.* IT finds that the business unit staff lack interest in the technology and, therefore, fade from the project. Instead of facing this problem head on, IT pushes ahead to implement the technology, based on the belief that when the users see the technology installed, they will like it. This is unlikely, however, given the users were not involved.

- *Too many technologies in one project.* Many early client-server projects failed because their scope included middleware, client, server, and host interface development. The project was too ambitious.
- *The technology has just appeared.* The early personal digital assistants (PDAs) were often failures due to their limited recognition ability and processing power. Applications based on these failed. You want to select technologies that are sufficiently mature for industrial strength use. How do you know when this is the case? When other companies have applied them. Don't be a pioneer. You can end up with arrows in your back.
- *First application requires extensive integration with legacy systems and data.* This project will turn into 90 percent legacy system programming and 10 percent new technology. Many early efforts at work-flow software and client-server systems suffered this fate.
- *Implementation gets out of control.* The initial application of the technology was extremely successful. Rather than measure the results and regroup the resources, the team is forced into a large project. They encounter too many problems. The project is stopped and termed a failure. This occurs when a limited pilot project is followed by a desperate desire to implement fully.
- *Selected technology is undergoing rapid change.* In the early 1990s network technology and operating systems were undergoing change. This accelerated in the mid-1990s. As a result, some companies that plunged in to get a network operational ended up having to redo the project based on the latest technology. Select technology that will be stable over some payback period.

Cases and examples

Sycamore University

Sycamore University is a large university with over 20,000 students. Many departments and schools have their own internal IT groups. These IT groups would often go out and acquire new technology. In most cases, this was not thought through. There was no cost-benefit analysis. There was no thought of maintenance of all of the technology and systems acquired. The central IT group was faced with a nightmare—how to provide support, provide for limited autonomy, and increase cost-effectiveness of IT across the campus.

The first attempt was initiated by upper management who decreed that departments would have to identify all current technology and get approval for new technology. IT centrally was not equipped or manned to support this. The decree was even issued without IT involvement. As a result, what happened? Nothing. No change.

The second attempt was to make contacts with the larger schools such as medicine, engineering, and arts and sciences. A marketing approach was employed using fear. The question was raised, "What would happen if their internal systems failed?" This produced results. Some systems were eliminated. Others received central support. Separately, IT initiated investigations into new technology. They took steps to involve departments. This was done to ensure a more structured approach to evaluating, selecting, and using new technology.

Questions

1. Why would a department or school establish their own IT group and their own internal systems? Why would their management overlook the potential problems and pitfalls?
2. This chapter has focused on new technology and systems. Discuss how you could eliminate old, obsolete technology that continued to be in use?
3. Discuss the conditions under which you would continue to use obsolete technology.

Lessons learned

Technology implementation is a key component to IT implementation and support. You have to upgrade the network, provide additional computing capacity and servers, provide for backup and recovery, support testing and quality assurance, and move to a 24 hour a day/7 days a week support environment. Keep in mind that the technology must be scalable. The spread between high and low levels can be hundreds of percentage points over the low level.

Guidelines

- As technology changes, you might be tempted to undertake many technology projects to keep constantly up to date. This is the other extreme to doing nothing. Too much technological change is disruptive and counterproductive. Moreover, it drains resources away from other projects and halts projects while the technology is being put into place.
- Consider the long-term use and potential application of any new technology. This will aid in determining your strategy for the technology.
- Many organizations underestimate the cost and effort of getting rid of an existing technology when implementing the new one. It is not just conversion, but also training, interfaces, and an extensive testing and shakedown effort that are required.
- If you have a legacy system that depends on obsolete hardware or software, then you must consider replacing the legacy system as you replace the hardware and software.
- Major costs of obsolescence lie in ongoing maintenance as well as in declining staff morale for people surrounded by dinosaur products.

Questions

1. Using the Web try to find an example where a company attempted to install a new technology and failed. Examples in the past few years have been some involved RFID (Radio Frequency Identification).

2. Cloud computing in which companies depend on Web-based software for their needs is growing more popular due to lower costs. What are some advantages and disadvantages of cloud computing?
3. A common argument is technical staff should keep up their skills and learn new methods and tools. Yet, in all cases there are legacy systems to support that are not suited to the new methods and tools. What are some arguments for and against a senior technical employee making the effort to keep up with new tools?
4. Many firms wait too long to replace old systems. They believe in the adage "If it is not broken, why fix it?" If you were the IT manager in such a firm and wanted to change and modernize the technology, what approach would you use?
5. Research the Web to identify issues and problems in interfacing new and old technologies.

What to do next

1. Answer the following questions about your current systems and technology architecture.

   - Do you have a defined architecture that employees are aware of?
   - Is there a formal approach for evaluating and selecting new technology?
   - What cost-benefit analysis is performed for a new technology?
   - Are technology projects treated and managed differently than software projects?

2. Based on your knowledge of your organization and its technology, identify areas where the architecture must be modernized. What are the tangible benefits of modernization? In implementing the technology, what interfaces are necessary?
3. Find some technology that has been in limited use but that had been projected to be used on a wider scale. Why wasn't its use expanded? What are the ongoing support costs and issues associated with the technology being limited to a few users? How does this technology lock its particular users into limited future change? Is it better to continue using the technology, or should it be pulled out and replaced?

Summary

Your systems and technology architecture is a dynamic structure that requires you to spend time periodically to consider improvements and upgrades. If your technology becomes obsolescent, then you would have likely been blocked from acquiring new software packages and carrying out much new software development. In other words, a poor architecture acts as dampening force on your ability to improve your business processes. Moreover, the more you fall behind, the more expensive and time consuming it will be to catch up. Technology projects have long-term structural goals for the architecture as well as near-term goals to support the organization.

Part five
How to successfully address project issues

20
Business issues

Introduction

This chapter, and the others in this part of the book, begins by introducing each issue. This introduction is followed by a discussion of factors that give rise to the issue, the impact of the issue if not treated, how to prevent the issue from occurring, and what to do if the issue arises. The chapters are arranged slightly differently from other chapters in that the examples and guidelines are included within the discussion of individual issues. How can you use this material? The first answer is obvious—employ it when the issue arises. A second answer is to create a checklist.

As systems organizations direct their resources toward client-server, intranet, extranet, data warehousing, and other applications that closely touch the business, the number and extent of business issues will continue to rise. Unlike personnel or technical issues, business issues force the project leader to move outside of the project team and deal with managers and employees in various departments. To head off problems here, it is likely that the project leader will spend even more time with the business issues as opposed to the technical areas of the project.

Issue: the business unit changes requirements frequently

This is one of the most common complaints voiced by systems managers and staff. It has been so for the past 30 years and is not likely to disappear soon.

How this occurs

Are the requirements really changing? If the requirements are based on transactions in a business process, in management, or with external forces, then requirements have changed. If the source of the change is what a middle manager might like, then it may relate to style or politics rather than substance. A manager can even seek change for political gain or to delay the project—these are sinister, but possible sources of the change. There can also be a lack of understanding of systems and technology.

Potential impact

A change to the requirements is often viewed with alarm by the project team. Team members see their work being undone and, in the worse case, fear having to start over. This can be frustrating and demoralizing. This situation is made more severe if people have experienced requirements changes repeatedly on multiple projects. They may just become resigned to having it happen again.

How to prevent the problem

To prevent this from happening, the systems group must become more proactive at the start of the project. The scope of the project must be negotiated. This is important because it is one of the leading areas where requirement changes occur. The second step is to base requirements on the definition of a new business process. Requirements based on detailed business transactions and rules are less likely to change. Any change in requirements can affect the business process. The business unit staff must be heavily involved in defining, understanding, agreeing, and carrying out requirements.

How to address the problem

If a requirements change occurs, answer the following questions:

- Why did the change appear now?
- What is the impact if the change is not addressed?
- What is the impact of the change on the underlying process?
- Can the requirement be met through procedure or policy change rather than a systems change?

Consider reopening all requirements and specifications with the business unit. Additional requirements can be identified now to minimize impact on development.

Issue: the business unit does not provide good people for the project

Business units today do not have a surplus of people. Many departments have downsized. As a consequence, only a few people have in-depth knowledge of the business rules and transactions. Others may know what to do, but they do not understand why they are handling the transactions in that way.

How this occurs

When asked to provide someone for a project, a business manager cannot afford to release the most experienced person. The department might really suffer. In addition, the manager may lack confidence in the project and might not want to risk good people in the project. Managers are often likely to provide individuals whose loss might have the least impact. They may have had poor project experiences in the past. Timing may be bad—the change might be conflicting with the year-end closing, other projects, or a peak work time of the year.

Potential impact

If you assume that the business people provided to the project can speak for the department, you are likely to be sorely disappointed. Getting information from them without validation and checking on completeness can be a problem. The team might carry out work that will later have to be redone.

How to prevent the problem

Ask for someone to be on your team who is junior in the business department and request only their part-time involvement. Assume that they have a limited knowledge of what goes on in the department. Request that a group be appointed to review the work for validity. If this is not done, then find other people to review the work. You are picking a junior person because their absence will least impact the business and because you really do not know what you need yet. This has a side benefit of gaining broader participation in the project from the business unit. You know that you understand the unit's limitations.

How to address the problem

If the business unit provides no one, then question the project. If the business unit is uncooperative at the start of the project, then things will likely go downhill from there. Meet with the business manager to indicate your minimal known requirements and your sensitivity to his or her staffing problems. Also, point out that because the project is just starting, you really do not know who and how much of the person's time will be required.

Issue: the business unit is unwilling to change the business process

How this occurs

Members of the business unit can become convinced that the way that they are handling their work is the best and only way. After all, it has been proved through years of use. They may also fear change and the impact and disruption likely to follow. They may feel that any change will make matters worse. They were promised much by

IT and may feel that they received little. Middle managers may resist due to fear of loss of jobs and power.

Potential impact

Resistance can be open or subtle. Delays in making decisions are one sign of problems. Change of mind and indecision are the other signs. The project now suffers due to a lack of defined specifications. The business unit employees may keep trying to bring the project back to the current system.

How to prevent the problem

What was said in earlier chapters applies here. The scope of involvement and role of the business unit have to be nailed down in the definition of the project concept. This has to be reinforced as the project proceeds. Not only must the benefits be stressed, but the problems must be stressed also if the current process continues.

How to address the problem

If the business unit wants a new system and also wishes to maintain the current process, then you must answer some fundamental questions:

- What is the benefit of the system if the process is unchanged?
- How will exceptions not handled by the current system be addressed by the new system operating with the old process?
- If the business unit won't change the process, what sign is there that it is even willing to accept a new system? Won't the business unit want the new system to be just like the old one because it fits well with the current process?

Show how the new system fails to mesh with the current process—creating more problems.

Issue: several business units cannot agree among themselves

Major systems projects with substantial benefits often cross multiple departments or divisions, making this issue more common.

How this occurs

Many departments have never really worked together on a systems project. Each brings its own history, opinions, and preferences into the project. Each department's relative power structure also comes along. This makes for an impossible situation if the project manager is naïve. The same can be said of projects that involve multiple offices spread across different parts of the country or the globe.

Potential impact

The project can become paralyzed because no decisions can be reached. Any decisions that are achieved may be undermined by departments who feel that they lose power if the decision appears to go against them. If hostility continues to rise, it may be impossible to continue the project without major and ongoing involvement of upper management.

How to prevent the problem

Try to understand the politics of each department at the start of the project. Meet with business managers and identify the potential problem of generating consensus. Seek agreement on a method to resolve problems in advance. Identify potential conflicts with the project team at the start. Show how the approach and solution fit within each department's self-interest.

How to address the problem

If a problem arises that is due to disagreement, then work with each department individually to get opinions and concerns. Don't address this in the group at first—it will likely solidify positions. Develop a solution and interpret it from the perspective of each department's self-interest. Follow this up with additional sales efforts. Take this problem seriously. Such issues can appear trivial to an outsider, but they are not to the people in the trenches.

Issue: the business unit cannot consistently resolve issues

You thought you had resolved an issue, but each time you turn around, the situation is changed. The issue is still unresolved.

How this occurs

Indecision may be due to lack of understanding of the issue and its consequences. People in the unit may not be prepared to make decisions. Alternatively, there may be a power struggle with different factions within the department. A fourth possibility is that people in the unit do not know their own business process in sufficient detail. The situation can be made more complex if there is lack of communications between levels of the organization.

Potential impact

The project may become frozen. The systems people may throw up their hands and state that they will await the final decision. Morale in the team may drop. If the decision is forced, the possibility of it resurfacing remains.

How to prevent the problem

Issues must be analyzed in terms of the basic business process, which is more likely to yield truth than opinion. Any resolution based on the process is more apt to stick. However, you will then have to provide a political slant on the decision for each department. Don't wait for the department to point out the problems. Be proactive. Each new issue is to be reviewed in terms of what has already been resolved to see if it is a variation.

How to address the problem

Let's assume that you get conflicting signals. What do you do? Consider the issue again along with all outstanding issues. Use this as an opportunity to review the roles and responsibilities of the department as well.

Issue: the business unit staff members do not know the business process

How this occurs

On the surface, this sounds absurd. However, today, with downsizing and change, it is true more often. The people who possessed the deep business knowledge might have retired or disappeared. Although individuals know pieces of a business process, no one knows the whole. In addition, people do not know why they perform the work the way they do. There may be a difference between the way people think that the process is being done and the how it is actually being performed. Knowledge may be fragmented through the group. There was once a soldier who appeared next to a bench and guarded the bench from 11:00 A.M. until 2 P.M. When asked why this was done, the soldier replied that he didn't know, but that it had been going on for years. When a probe was initiated, it was found that 4 years ago, the bench was painted. An officer who failed to notice got wet paint on his uniform and then ordered someone to guard the bench while it was wet. The order was never rescinded.

Potential impact

You cannot assume that business knowledge or information is complete or accurate. This can also lead to problems in specifications and design. When there is a lack of information, there is the danger of a process being invented from a technology view without business involvement.

How to prevent the problem

It is best to observe the business directly and see the situation first hand. Ask to be trained as if you were a new employee. How many people does this process take? Are the instructions incomplete or contradictory? How often do you have to ask for assistance? Doing this will provide you with contacts as well as information on the state of documentation, the extent of staff knowledge, and the existence of formal procedures.

How to address the problem

Requirements may be provided by managers and staff. However, they may be incomplete and fail to address exceptions. As you are provided with these requirements, verify them with the business process directly.

Issue: the existing business process is in poor condition

A business process can deteriorate like a system over time. More work may be handled informally outside of the process. The error rate may be high. Transactions may have to wait for a specific person to handle them due to overspecialization. The supervisors may be handling a substantial percentage of the work themselves. The department may be using homegrown PC-based solutions that are incompatible with the major systems.

How this occurs

Deterioration in a process often sets in because people take the process for granted and fail to give it any attention. No one thinks to put money in the budget to fix the process. After all, processes fix themselves right? Once the situation worsens, managers may be reluctant to address the problem especially if the process works at some minimal level. They fear upsetting the department and making the situation worse.

Potential impact

Any system linked to a deteriorated process may suffer from faulty data, disuse, or abuse. The system may not be employed as intended. A new system has a small chance of success if the process problems are not addressed. You cannot assume that the new system will fix the problems of the business process.

How to prevent the problem

Investigate the state of the business process as part of the initial work toward a new system. Include the process within the scope of the project. Measure and document the condition of the process at the start. Separate out what can be handled in a system rather than the process.

How to address the problem

If work has begun on a new system without an in-depth review of the process, your project is in trouble. Validate the design against the process. This will draw attention to the condition of the process.

Issue: middle-level business unit management resists change and the system

How this occurs

Who is threatened by the new system? People who work with the current process and system may be terrified, but they have little to fear. Transactions will still be processed—only with a new system. More directly threatened are managers above the immediate supervisors of employees who perform work in the process. If not brought into the project and without a future role being defined, they can be resentful and disruptive.

Potential impact

Lack of cooperation by mid-level managers can create problems at lower levels. It will take longer to gain support and reach decisions. Project progress will slow down.

How to prevent the problem

Planning ahead, you will want to work with upper management in the business unit to gain support and to ease any fears of change. If some managers are to be released later, then the project team can be guided around these people. When asked, the team can indicate that the scope of the project includes the process and system, but not the organization. It is best if high-level managers identify their future roles to gain their participation.

How to address the problem

If you encounter resistance from mid-level managers, then you can take several courses of action. One is to sympathize and indicate the project scope. Another is to minimize contact so as to prevent confrontation. In the most serious cases, you can contact upper management in the business unit. Push for role definition. Do this rarely as you don't want to be labeled as someone who "cries wolf".

Issue: the business unit attempts to dominate the project

How this occurs

Business managers who realize the importance of systems in relation to the business process may seek to dominate the project. This is due to a desire to craft the new process and to fix errors. It may also be a defensive move to retain control. They may also fear the project results if they release control.

Potential impact

Although the initial impact may be positive to give more support to the project, the longer-term effect may be more changes in the project due to meddling. There can be an attempt to retain the current process.

How to prevent the problem

The situation may be prevented by defining the business role at the start. This can be followed up by having the business unit involved in resolving issues related to the project. Once implementation has begun, the business unit will, after all, play the major role. This might make the business manager hold off from over-involvement.

How to address the problem

If domination occurs, don't discourage it. Try to channel it toward issue resolution. Define roles through assigning areas of tasks to the business unit.

Issue: the business unit view does not fit with that of upper management or the industry

How this occurs

You have approval for the project. Management sees the project as critical for success in competition. Yet the business unit takes a local view for its own interests. The two views are dramatically different and opposed. This is not unexpected given the mission and charter of the business unit. The business unit may also be out of touch with trends and practices in the industry today.

Potential impact

Left unaddressed, the clash in purpose and scope can harm the project. Relations between the business unit and management may deteriorate. Upper management may not want to take on the department so that the project is either warped or flounders. Alternatively, there may be no surface conflict, yet conflict does exist.

How to prevent the problem

The issues of purpose and scope must be handled in the project concept. This will give management a forum to direct the business toward a wider goal. An effort must be made to relate the wider goal to the operation of the business unit.

How to address the problem

Resistance to a larger project can still emanate from lower levels of the business unit. The project team acts as a marketing arm of management to reinforce the wider project view and to show how new work processes and systems support both the department and management views.

Issue: business unit managers and staff lack technical knowledge

No one expects business managers and staff to be programmers or analysts. However, lack of knowledge of basic technology concepts can impact a project because it makes the fit between the system and process more difficult.

How this occurs

Individuals can go to school and then work in a department for many years using technology. However, they may lack awareness of its potential and may not be up to date with the technology. This is not a surprise because the technical staff lack knowledge of the business department. In such situations many departments just accept the technology with which they are provided. The business unit staff may not see the benefits in their jobs from training in the technology.

Potential impact

Though there is acceptance, employees may be reluctant or lack creativity to develop new ideas for systems improvements. When systems staff ask about new requirements, they may be met with blank stares. They do not comprehend how the system will provide benefit.

How to prevent the problem

You are not expected to train everyone in technology. What you can do is explain new technology in terms of the information on the business process that you have collected. Staff members are more likely to be interested because it is relevant to them. This can stimulate their creative thinking as they respond. You can treat the technology as a "black box".

How to address the problem

When you encounter resistance to technology, it may be due to ignorance and fear. Do not assume hostility. Take time to explain the technology in terms of how staff members can use it and what its benefits might be. Don't explain the details. Show that it performs similar functions only better.

Issue: business unit management is replaced

How this occurs

In any project with an extended life span, it is possible that key business unit managers who provided support to the project may be promoted or leave. Change can occur through reorganization, mergers, and so on as well.

Potential impact

The impact of management change is often viewed negatively. People want to put the brakes on the project until things settle down. This can cause the project to stall. By putting a positive spin on the impact, you create an opportunity for new support and fresh ideas.

How to prevent the problem

If your project lasts a year or more, then anticipate management change. Market the project concept to as wide a group of managers as possible. Keep them informed and involved. The negative impact caused by the departure of one manager is minimized. Within the business unit build project support at the grass roots. This will come in handy in dealing with new managers. Make sure that you work quickly to bring new managers on board. Get them involved in issues that are not time sensitive so that they can adapt to the project and adopt it as their own.

How to address the problem

If you encounter sudden management change, establish communications with the new manager. Don't wait for the manager to come to you. Point to the progress and benefits as well as the manager's role in the remainder of the project. Involve managers in issues.

Issue: the business unit has no interest in the project

How this occurs

Even if something is in your best interest, you may not have the time or energy to devote to it. It is that way for financial groups during the annual year-end closing of the accounting books. It is the same with shipping and distribution firms during peak periods. Alternatively, people in the business unit may be keeping their eyes on their immediate issues. They fail to see the benefit of the project even though company management wants to see the project completed for overall benefit.

Potential impact

Lack of interest can spell doom or delay for a project. If you attempt to reverse and fail, the project can be cancelled. Upper management support for the project can be countered by tactical arguments that there is too much work that is more important than the project. This leaves upper managers with few options—they will delay the project. To understand the impact, you must understand the cause.

How to prevent the problem

During the initial definition of the project, point out the project benefits to appeal to the self-interest of the business unit. If the senior management of the business unit does not show interest, move down in the organization to obtain support. If there is little benefit to the business unit directly, then discuss the potential problem with upper management to get ideas of how to address the issue before it arises. You seek to establish support for the project at the top and the bottom.

How to address the problem

Suppose that there is not interest in the department, but there are project benefits. Consider involving other departments who will benefit and get them to help you bring the reluctant department along.

Management interest in the project may also wane over time. This might be due to problems in the project or in the perception that the benefits will be less than anticipated. Revisit the project concept and determine if you really want to go ahead or change the project.

Issue: other work or projects have higher priority for the business unit than your project does

How this occurs

Your project is underway. People assigned by the business unit are reassigned to other work. They disappear. Priorities can change. Problems can arise in the department that require the specialized skills of the team members. Remember that in many cases in business units, the expertise of all of the trained staff is required to address all of the exceptions.

Potential impact

Without any notice, the project can be stranded in a vacuum. Questions will soon arise that require answers from the business unit. If you hassle the people who returned to the department, they may resent the additional work and may not want to return to the project. Although parts of the project can proceed at a slower pace, there will be a noticeable effect as work is deferred waiting for answers.

How to prevent the problem

At the start of the project, never ask for people from the business to be assigned to the project on a full-time basis. Try to involve a number of people so that you are not overly dependent on one or two. Keep contact with the business unit manager so that you know what pressures the unit is working under. If you sense that the team members are required back in the department, work with the business unit directly to plan on how to cover the gap. In a project that will last from six to nine months, plan on work of higher priority arising and attempt to schedule it in the project.

How to address the problem

If there is a sudden crisis and departure, expand your network of contacts in the business unit. Develop a contingency plan to keep the project going prior to contacting the business manager about the problem. While indicating the impact, sympathize with the manager.

Issue: the business unit has existing technology that conflicts with that of the project

How this occurs

There is probably technology in your home with which you feel very comfortable and that you don't want to replace. It is the same in business. A department may like its procedures, policies, and systems. People in the department don't see a need for change. They may have created PC solutions that they don't want to lose.

Potential impact

Not only can the project be derailed, but you can encounter long-term, deep-seated resistance. You may fight a constant uphill battle as the business staff find numerous holes and gaps created by the new system replacing the old.

How to prevent the problem

When you begin the project, be sensitive to people's feelings. Indicate that any new system or technology can build on the experience and knowledge associated with the existing system. Also, show them that many procedures and policies can be reused. The new system is then an evolution from the current. Reinforce this benefit by focusing on the additional features and capabilities of the new technology and system that are lacking in the current. Show how the functions performed by PC and other systems are addressed in the new system.

How to address the problem

If you sense resistance, then expand your contacts in the business department. Take more time to understand how the current system and process work. Ferret out the PC systems. Lower the profile of the project to avoid being a target. Disseminate information about the new system to show how the new is better than the current.

Questions

In each of the chapters on issues there are five to six questions. The first question identifies areas under the subject of the chapter and asks you to search the literature and Web for examples. The second question requires to do a search for guidelines for the areas covered by the chapter.

1. Search the literature and Web to find examples in the following areas:

   - Role and activities of the business unit manager;
   - Business unit staff;
   - Processes employed in business units and departments;
   - The actual work in business departments;
   - Work in related departments.

2. Search the Web and literature for guidelines in the above areas.
3. What is the difference between limited user participation, involvement, and commitment by users?
4. Research the Web on the issue: the business unit manager used to be in IT.
5. Research the Web on the issue: the business staff want to get too involved in the IT work.
6. Research the Web on the issue: there are new exceptions surfacing while the project is going on.

What to do next

1. With your list of issues in hand, separate out the business-related issues. Look for patterns in the issues. Review your relationship with all levels of the business unit to identify potential actions you can take.
2. Taking a wider perspective, review the history of the project to assess how business-related issues were handled. Add this analysis to the results of item 1.

Summary

Constantly monitor the relationship between the project and the business units involved in project. This is not only to detect potential problems, but also to identify opportunities for increasing the involvement by the business unit as well as its participation in addressing issues. The importance of the business unit contribution to the project can be highlighted by indicating results from the involvement.

21
Human resource issues

Introduction

Personnel issues in projects were of concern in ancient history, prior to the formal definition of projects and project management. Attention and concerns have grown due to a number of factors:

- Downsizing has forced companies to do projects with fewer people so that the performance of the staff on the project becomes critical.
- Deadlines for systems and technology projects are tighter along with budgets as management realizes the role of systems in competition and business operations.
- Business processes depend on systems more than ever—raising the level of importance of projects.
- People are shared among projects, creating more issues and tension in managing human resources.
- It is more difficult to attract and retain good people.

Human resource issues focus on the project team. The project team may include staff from business units as well as internal systems staff.

Issue: turnover of project team members

Let's begin by acknowledging that some staff turnover is expected in a systems project that spans a year or more. In addition, it is sometimes favorable that certain individuals leave the project team. Thus, turnover is not bad in general. When a person leaves the project on schedule and as planned, then it is not counted as turnover. However, if the extent of turnover is great, or if critical people leave, then there is a problem. Note that the approach of having a small core team with many part-time people or players helps mitigate the turnover problem, except within the core team.

How this occurs

Individuals can get tired of the project or begin to feel that their work is not appreciated. There may be many issues in the project. People may feel that because the project is in jeopardy, their jobs are at risk. Team conflicts and personality clashes can be another cause. Because many systems people are often quiet and not outspoken, it is sometimes difficult to detect problems among them until it is too late. The team member then seeks to return to the line organization and be assigned other work.

An alternative reason for turnover is that a person (including even the project leader) gets an attractive offer either internally from another department or externally from another firm. The individual may discuss it with his or her line manager. It may not even be brought up to the project leader if the leader and the employee lack a close relationship. If the project leader is not in regular and constant contact with the project team members, then many times the situation cannot be turned around. The person leaves.

Potential impact

Damage occurs if the project manager is caught off guard. Then the leader does not look like a leader. Faced with such a problem, you must scramble around to find someone else and to carry out damage control within the team and with management. The problem is compounded if the team member involves the line manager. The line manager may question the project leader and the leadership itself. It will obviously be more difficult to attract a replacement into the project.

If the person is hired from outside, then another set of problems emerges. The remaining team members may feel that they can do better outside. The departure of one person may lead to a rout. This is often precipitated by headhunters and search firms who attempt to systematically raid an organization of its technical talent. This results in more pressure on the team.

How to prevent the problem

The project manager must perform several important activities. One is to stay in close contact with team members. The project leader must establish sufficient rapport so that the team member will alert the manager to problems and to headhunter activities. As a project leader, you must keep such information to yourself. You cannot attribute it to the particular individual; otherwise, you impact the communications. The person may not take you into his or her confidence again.

Ask if the team member has any concerns or problems with the project or the team on a regular basis. You can do this in a positive way by inquiring as to any of the person's ideas that might improve the project. The ideas you solicit may lead you to the problem (reverse engineering).

On the recruitment and headhunter front, bring this up in a project meeting at the start of the project. Point it out as a possibility, as the team members are in demand. Indicate that you expect them to contact you before they take any action. Remain vague as to what action you will take.

How to address the problem

What do you do when the problem occurs? First, determine what is going on. Why is the person thinking of leaving? Do not plunge in, in an attempt to save them for the project. This shows desperation and may raise more panic among the team members. Embark on several parallel tasks:

- Find out what the team member's reasons are.
- Work with the team member to define what must be done before the person leaves.
- Analyze the project plan to see how the project can be restructured to keep momentum.

This information can help you determine whether you must make the effort to retain the person on the team. You may need to meet with the person's line manager to discuss the issue and to plan for a transition. Concentrate your attention on the project and not on the person. Some project managers neglect the project and focus on keeping the person on board. For you as a project leader, the project comes first. In project planning, see if you can reassign tasks and restructure work so that the impact of the loss of the person is minimal. Turnover is an opportunity to shake up the project and team, if that is required.

What do you do with the project team? Contact each person and answer any individual questions. Be honest and tell them why the person is leaving. Indicate what you are going to do as the project leader. Be positive. The person leaving is going for a new opportunity. This would not have been possible without the project. The situation allows the remaining team to be involved in restructuring the work and having a say in determining the type and characteristics of the replacement person. If you sense other people are thinking of leaving, then hold off on a project meeting. Instead, follow up as was discussed earlier. Prior to the project meeting, make an effort at restructuring the project based on input. Also, start the process of finding a replacement. At the project meeting, review the situation and discuss what is going to happen next.

Issue: lack of commitment

Commitment to a project involves attitude and feelings. The benefit of commitment is difficult to quantify. You have seen projects where the lack of commitment among the project team can mean failure of the project. The team members just cannot resolve some problem or issue. There is evidence that commitment can spur greater effort in a project at a critical time. Commitment is also a matter of time. At the start of the project, people often feel tentatively committed to the project. During the project their level of commitment or dedication can rise or fall. At the end of the project everyone feels committed because it is near the end and they want to see the project completed.

How this occurs

Lack of commitment can be due to lack of interest. This is most often the case among part-time team members who are involved in many other projects. They do not have the time or dedication to be committed to one project. Fortunately, less commitment is often required among these team members. Where commitment matters most is in the core team. These people have to often spend extra hours and reschedule their lives to accommodate the project.

Individuals can lose their sense of commitment for a variety of reasons. Their commitment may have been very high at the start. They got burned out in the project. The project leader may not have recognized their efforts. Management begins to assume that they can devote 100 percent of their lives to the project. People then get burned out and seek to leave the project. This is referred to in some companies as the "death march project". Events in the project can also lead team members to become discouraged.

Potential impact

Lack of commitment is not felt in the everyday and routine tasks in a systems project. The crisis occurs during integration, final testing, and debugging, where extra effort is required. If one person lacks commitment, the attitude can rub off on others, affecting the entire project. Lack of commitment then translates into lack of effort. The schedule begins to slip.

How to prevent the problem

You, as the project leader, must seek to involve the team members in all aspects of the project and project management. By handling issues, actively updating individuals about the project, and reviewing each other's work, involvement increases. Positive involvement and progress naturally lead to commitment.

How to address the problem

You may be able to sense a lack of commitment among some team members by their jokes and comments about the project and their work. When you notice this, you first want to determine what underlying problems have led to this situation. What you do depends on the project state and status. If there is no crisis or schedule push, then you have time to get to the root causes. If there is a crisis, then work with each team member to define a work schedule that will accomplish the project goals while at the same time not exhausting the team member.

Issue: lack of knowledge

Project leaders often make the mistake of assuming that certain team members have specific levels of technical knowledge or that they have extensive knowledge of the business process. Then the leader is surprised to find out that the knowledge is lacking. This has become more commonplace due to the wide range of technical and business knowledge that a project requires today. A project manager may expect that there will be gaps and holes in the knowledge of the team.

How this occurs

The demands of the project for detailed knowledge have been cited as one reason. Another factor is that people naturally do not like to reveal what they do not know. This is especially true for individuals who are hired into a company to work on a specific project. They may overstate the extent of their experience. If the project leader fails to assess the actual skills and knowledge of the team members in advance, there are likely to be many unpleasant surprises in terms of knowledge gaps.

Potential impact

Lack of knowledge often does not surface until the project and tasks have been active for some time. Individuals, on their own, may try to hide the gap or work around it. The first impact is the slippage of the task involved. If the knowledge is critical, the project leader may have to find new resources to fill in—adding to both expense and duration. There are also social impacts. The other members of the team may no longer trust the team member. Conflict among the project team can be created. The person may feel depressed from finally having to admit that he or she lacked the necessary skills.

How to prevent the problem

The first step is to carefully define what skills are needed. Most project leaders provide only vague descriptions instead of detailed skill requirements. The next problem occurs when the candidates for the project team are interviewed. The project leader may fail to identify questions that test their knowledge and skills. This can cause the wrong people to be hired.

Another situation is that the manager is so desperate that he or she conducts only a cursory evaluation of skills. The manager just wants to fill up the project team. This occurs often when companies want to hire people with scarce skills that are in demand (e.g., client-server, extranet, or an ERP system).

Identify team members and others who have the proper technical background to evaluate individuals for the team. Have them develop specific questions and review them with you. These questions are often best if they present a situation to which the person can respond.

An individual who lacks certain knowledge or skills may still be suitable for the project. This is especially true for business unit staff who may not know all of the detailed steps in processing exception transactions. The project leader encourages people to identify gaps or lack of knowledge. Then the two of them can work on identifying alternative solutions to address the issue. This is a more proactive and positive approach.

How to address the problem

If a team member lacks the knowledge to do the work, then you first must consider the schedule. Is there time to allow the person to accumulate this knowledge? If there is, then you can send the person to training. If there is not, then you must help identify additional resources that can fill the gap. Your goal is to find someone who can work with the team member and transfer knowledge as the tasks are performed. This will provide guidance to the team member and make the person more self-confident.

Issue: team members are inflexible

How this occurs

"Flexibility" is a vague word. You can be flexible in the use of a method or tool, but locked into only those methods and tools. Inflexibility is not uncommon in systems. Because people put a great deal of time and effort into learning the technology, they are reluctant to discard it. There is psychological commitment to the method as well. Legacy systems are often sustained by individuals who employ the same tools and methods for years. As a side note, you can easily see that a major barrier to new technology is the speed with which people are willing to adopt and support it. When a technology is new, there is even more reluctance because they don't know if the technology will last.

Potential impact

Inflexibility may impact the quality of work through the continued use of old methods. It also may mean resistance and disagreements within the project team between groups who favor the old and new. Having multiple approaches can disrupt the project.

Inflexibility may not be obvious; impacts may only appear later. A COBOL programmer, for example, can be trained in C++ and object-oriented methods. Then when he or she starts programming, the code may resemble COBOL and is not object oriented. The impact of inflexibility can be poor quality work in the project. Different individuals may adopt different styles and methods for using the same tools. Thus, the project may finish, but maintenance may be a nightmare. A more severe impact may be that your seasoned legacy system programmers resist learning client-server systems—resulting in staffing problems.

How to prevent the problem

Anticipate that many people will have limited flexibility. With technology change flexibility is difficult to achieve over time. Appeal to an individual's self-interest in learning the technology. Carry out the following steps:

- Bring the people up to date on the technology and explain why it is important for them.
- Review with them why specific products, methods, and tools were selected.
- Indicate how you will support them in learning and using the technology.
- Identify sources for support and additional information that will be available.

- Clearly indicate the goals and expectations that you have for them with respect to the technology and why these are reasonable.
- Specify the benefits that will accrue to them in terms of their own careers.

How to address the problem

If you encounter people who are inflexible and who resist the technology, do not attack them head on. Instead, visit them and elicit their concerns. Do not address these fears at this time. Go back to your office and identify steps that you can take to allay their fears and concerns. Now revisit each concern with them along with what can and will be done. A further step is to meet with the team and indicate what is available. This reinforces your support of the technology in the presence of the team.

Issue: team members resist project management

How this occurs

Many creative people have been abused by project leaders and project management. They may have been hounded to death about status every day by a project leader who lacked both managerial skills and technical knowledge. It is not a surprise that they are turned off to you.

Potential impact

Team members who resist project management may rub it off on other team members. It will likely become more difficult to run the project. Dealing with project issues will become more complex.

How to prevent the problem

At the start of the project, discuss how the project will be managed. Follow the earlier suggestions and lay out a role for the team members by identifying their own tasks, updating their tasks, and identifying and helping to resolve issues. Follow this up with actions that reinforce this. Establish patterns of behavior early in the project before these are major problems.

How to address the problem

If you sense resistance, ask the person privately about their past projects. Sympathize with the person and show how your approach is different. Reinforce the methods described earlier. It is possible that the resistance to project management masks other underlying concerns about the person's work.

Issue: conflicts within the team

A team is composed of individuals working together. Many systems managers attempt to manage by emphasizing individual work over teamwork to minimize conflict. This often leads to other coordination problems related to integration issues.

How this occurs

How can conflict arise in a team? People can clash regarding which methods or tools to use, how best to employ the technology, personality conflict, and what constitutes acceptable quality—just to mention a few. The conflict may not be noticeable at first. It may surface over an issue at a critical point in the project. Conflicts can arise between junior and senior staff or between technical and non-technical people.

Potential impact

Some team conflict is natural, unavoidable, and positive due to various possible technical solutions as well as different experience. If not directed toward resolution, then the problems can affect the schedule and productivity can suffer. Hostility can later resurface and affect decisions in the project.

How to prevent the problem

Indicate at the start of the project that conflict is almost inevitable. Resolving the conflicts will be done for the good of the project. There are no winners or losers. When you sense a conflict, make it impartial and deal with the underlying issue.

How to address the problem

Try to separate out the symptoms of the conflict, the issue itself, and potential solutions. Depersonalize the conflict as soon as possible. Attempt to address several issues at one time.

Issue: team members spend too much time on the wrong tasks

Any individual has work preferences. On the weekend, you probably like to work on some things more than others. It is not surprising that this occurs in systems projects in which people have to work on a variety of widely different tasks.

How this occurs

Given people's preferences and a lack of leadership, it can be understood why people gravitate to the tasks that they prefer. They feel that they can accomplish something even though it is for tasks of lesser importance. Certain tasks are more interesting than others to them. The project leader may treat all of their tasks as equal, sending out the wrong message.

Potential impact

If the project leader does not address this issue, the progress on the project can continue, but the actual work on the critical tasks will suffer. The overall project schedule may later slip.

How to prevent the problem

To head this off, as the project leader, clearly identify what tasks are most important and why they are important. Cut the team member some slack and indicate that it is okay to work on other tasks as long as critical tasks are addressed. Encourage a multitasking work environment, in which people work on several things at one time. This gives variety and can be narrowed to one critical task and then reopened to several.

How to address the problem

Assuming that you are aware that an individual is not working on critical tasks, what do you do? Experience shows that an initial carrot and stick approach can be successful. Indicate how important the critical tasks are, but also allow team members time for other work. Follow this up by visiting team members to monitor what they are doing.

Issue: team members are overcommitted to projects

There are many projects as well as regular work such as operations support, maintenance, and so on. People today are spread thin. Individuals with critical skills and knowledge are spread even thinner.

How this occurs

In traditional project management overcommitment is more likely and the impacts are more severe. Many project leaders are trained to treat all team members as fully committed to their projects. They may then sometimes harass team members to work on their project.

Potential impact

With multiple commitments a person may feel too much pressure. Then work might suffer. In extreme cases, the person might leave the project.

How to prevent the problem

To avert problems associated with overcommitment, become informed of all of the person's commitments. Then you can identify realistic minimal expectations for the time that you require. Monitor the person's time and, when possible, encourage team members to do their other work. If there is a conflict, be reasonable and consider what additional time you can allow.

How to address the problem

When there is a problem in the project work, approach the individual and review all of his or her commitments. If necessary, approach other managers that are involved and work out a compromise schedule.

Issue: there is a personnel gap—missing skills

How this occurs

You thought that you had everything covered, but you find that some people lack certain skills. Or as the project progresses you determine that new skills are required.

Potential impact

Tasks involving the missing skills slip. Even if you attempt to work around the problem, the impact remains. If it continues unaddressed, the work of other team members will suffer.

How to prevent the problem

You can mitigate the problem by assessing the skill levels of the team. Have other team members or outsiders to the project conduct skill interviews. You can also establish and maintain a list of consultants or contractors.

How to address the problem

In the event of a gap or hole, consider help from inside and outside the firm. Go over the options with the team members so that they are involved. Have them participate in the evaluation. Plan ahead as to how you are going to bring the new people onto the project with minimal disruption.

Issue: a team member is reluctant to leave the project

How this occurs

Individuals may establish friendships with other team members. They may feel secure in being on the team. This is a known factor for them as opposed to an unknown. They may be reluctant to move to a new, unknown situation where they have to form new relationships.

Potential impact

The productivity of the team may suffer as these people hang on. Your credibility as a project manager may suffer along with your budget. The team wonders, "Why isn't something being done?"

How to prevent the problem

Clearly identify the end point of each team member's services to the project. In addition, as the work of individual team members winds up, help them reestablish their ties to their home line organization. This will make the transition easier.

How to address the problem

If you sense that someone is attempting to hang on, schedule a meeting with the person's manager. Don't hint at problems. Indicate that it is in everyone's interest to establish and carry out a transition.

Issue: team members spend too much time in communications

How this occurs

There are projects on which a subgroup of the team enjoys socializing too much. These team members take up project meeting time with their personal lives, stories, and so on. In addition, they spend considerable time meeting among themselves. It is natural that this will occur in long projects where people may bond together through a common experience.

Potential impact

Although some communications is fine, excessive time may be consumed. In addition, other team members may feel shut out from the project—they sense a clique. Internal team conflicts may expand.

How to prevent the problem

Indicate after the start of the project that some communications is essential, but that friendships and other relationships should be carried on outside of the project. Make sure that all team meetings address issues.

How to address the problem

It is better to redirect the communications to the project each time personal items are brought up. Reinforce this behavior constantly. You may have to reorganize tasks to head off having any subgroup of team members become a clique.

Issue: a team member resists learning new skills

New technology emerges at a continuing pace. Since ancient times people have resisted change. They feel that the skills that they use today are still valid and will continue to be in demand in the future. Changing this attitude is very difficult and becomes more so as people gain more experience and seniority in their positions. The point can be made that this issue must be treated by the line organization in which the person is based. However, it is typically the project that uses the new technology. The line organization only requires the older skills and technology. This can create even more pressure for the person to leave the project or to turn down the opportunity to join the project.

How this occurs

When the project leader indicates that the team members will be able to learn new techniques or technologies, he or she thinks that this is a major benefit from serving on the project. After all, the team is getting paid to be trained, to gain expertise, and to use the technology. This raises their skill levels and makes them more saleable in the market. Sounds good, eh? The argument will work with many on the project team. However, there will be some holdouts. To some, a new technology represents a series of threats.

- Some people may feel that their current knowledge and experience will be worthless. They can begin to feel obsolete.

- They may feel overwhelmed. Perhaps, they have not learned new technology for a number of years.
- They may believe that the existing technology is better than the new technology.
- Business unit staff may feel that their current process is just fine and has served them for decades without new technology.
- Some people prefer stability to change. They resist new technologies in general.

When personal computers first emerged, mainframe programmers were some of the last to adopt this technology. In ancient Rome adoption of new technology virtually halted in the second century A.D. An example was the failure of the Roman Empire to adopt stirrups for horses. Stirrups allow the rider to fire arrows more accurately because they provide stability. The enemies of Rome used stirrups; Roman armies paid the price. The problem in systems is typically most acute among programmers. Some COBOL programmers who learn a new language such as C++ continue to design and code programs with a COBOL mentality.

Potential impact

It sounds simple. If a person resists, you can replace that person and find someone else. Or you can place pressure on the person. It is much more complex. Resistance may not be open. It may not even be evident until after the person has been trained in the new technology. Unfortunately, the person who is reluctant may often possess critical knowledge about the legacy systems and their business rules. The person cannot be replaced and will be needed. You may now have to hire additional staff.

If a business unit employee resists the new technology, there can be additional problems. The employee may return to the business unit and criticize the new technology. This may create, in turn, problems at the management level. People not familiar with working with technology may feel intimidated. They may feel that they are under too much pressure.

How to prevent the problem

As a project manager, anticipate that this will occur. You can take the following steps to pave the way for the new technology:

- Discuss the potential benefit of the technology and what other organizations and companies are doing with it.
- Point out the demands that exist for knowledge of the technology.
- Carefully indicate what improved skills each person will gain.

Next, turn to the learning process.

- Indicate the steps in learning and training and explain that help will be provided.
- Define your expectations for what the people will be able to do in the early stages of the use of the technology.
- Encourage them to voice their questions and concerns.

The item that project managers seem to miss or pass over lightly is that of the expectations. Somehow some project managers think that individual team members can ascertain expectations through osmosis.

How to address the problem

When this issue is detected, go directly to the person and solicit his or her concerns. Do not respond defensively about the technology. Show that you are open minded so that the team member will voice all concerns. Also, do not attempt to answer these now. Visit other team members and see if they share some of the same concerns. Do not openly ask; instead, get their reaction to how the project is doing in general. See if they then volunteer information.

Issue: a team member leaves, producing a gap

How this occurs

Team members can leave a project team regardless of project duration. There can be many causes. They may find work that is more interesting elsewhere. They may not get along with the people on the team. They may not be performing well. Be on top of the situation to sense problems before they are announced.

Potential impact

Much has been written about the crises that arise when people leave a project. In systems, there may be a gap, but not necessarily a crisis. The damage depends on the expertise and knowledge of the person leaving.

How to prevent the problem

If you stick to the approach of just-in-time arrival of team members and their release as soon as possible, the problem can be minimized. For critical team members you must consider backup and cross-training from the start. If you implement this later when there is a problem, you can provoke a crisis.

How to address the problem

When someone leaves, view it as an opportunity. Meet with other team members to determine a way to reformulate and reassign work. Then you can identify the remaining gap and fill it in.

Issue: the quality of a team member's work is inadequate

What is "quality"? Who defines what is acceptable quality? Are team members supposed to assume some standard that is not stated? Quality can mean different things to different people. Let's assume that the work of a team member is not acceptable. It may be that it has to be redone. It may mean that the end product failed. Important here is not only the work, but the impact on the project. If there is a major impact in terms of cost, resources, or schedule, then the project manager will have a different course of action than if there is no effect.

How this occurs

Poor work quality can result from a misunderstanding of the requirements. The work is measured against a standard different from what the person knew about. Many quality problems result from such miscommunications. They can result from communications problems between team members or from poor individual work.

Potential impact

At a minimum, poor quality can mean time spent in reworking and correcting problems. From an interpersonal view in the project, it can mean that the team members begin to lose confidence in the person's work.

How to prevent the problem

At the start of the project, indicate what is expected in terms of quality and how work products will be reviewed. Also, point out what actions are possible in terms of working with the person to improve quality.

The second step is to monitor the work early in the project to establish a pattern. Peer review is a useful way of handling evaluations. During the project watch for signs of potential problems. One common sign is that the work is lagging behind schedule. To make up the time, people sometimes sacrifice completeness and quality. Another possibility is that team members are having a major technical problem and have not made this known to others.

How to address the problem

Let's assume that you encounter a quality issue. First, determine the team member's own assessment of his or her work. If the person thinks that he or she is doing a good job, then there may be a training problem. If the person admits concerns, then you both can work to identify what can be done. Volunteer to get assistance for these team members, even if they do not admit problems. If you confront them, you risk making the situation worse.

Issue: there is conflict between junior and senior staff

How this occurs

Senior IT staff often have the knowledge and wisdom based on working with the same software, languages, and tools over many years. Maintenance and support are so important that management does not encourage them to actively learn new methods. Thus, part of the conflict stems from different methods and tools. Junior staff see benefit in the new technology; senior staff may see comfort in the existing.

Potential impact

The potential impact is serious. It can lead to open conflict and an unwillingness to work together to resolve issues or perform tasks. In some instances we observed, the work was delayed by over a month due to this conflict.

How to prevent the problem

You must assume that there will be conflict. This especially occurs with newer staff in E-Business who may view older programmers as cave men. To the older programmers the younger ones appear like pseudo programmers. To prevent the problem acknowledge that it might happen. Encourage joint tasks from the start to reduce the problems later.

How to address the problem

When the problem arises, our approach is to tackle it head on. That is, we would focus on interfaces and integration to get the people to work together. Point out that these joint tasks, while unpleasant, are essential to the project. Indicate that they can return to their separate tasks later. Actively monitor these joint tasks.

Issue: the new team member does not fit

How this occurs

In any team, a new member might not fit in. This occurs in both business units and IT. In business units, the lack of fit may be personality or procedures and policies. In IT it can involve methods and tools as well as personality. In IT the problems tend to be more striking since the individuals have a closer relationship to methods and tools. A number of IT staff also may have strong technical skills, but lack personal and behavioral skills.

Potential impact

One impact is that there is a lack of communications. This can cause problems in work quality as well as schedule. Another problem that may arise is that work slows down for many people because they are disturbed by the unpleasant work environment.

How to prevent the problem

The key here is how you recruit and bring on new team members. Beyond the normal interviewing and evaluation of skills, you should assess how they work on solving problems and issues, and how they work together in joint tasks. After the person is on board schedule a project meeting where they meet other members of the team and where they can talk about lessons learned from previous projects. These steps can help to prevent the problems as well as providing an early warning system that such problems exist.

How to address the problem

If you find that the new team member is not fitting in, then you should not ignore it. Instead, you must face it. After talking with individual team members to discover the source of the issue, you can both work on the issue and take some actions. Potential useful actions are to encourage and layout joint tasks. This will support a behavioral change early in the project.

Questions

1. Search the literature and Web to find examples in the following areas:

   - Acquisition and selection of new team members.
   - Use of methods and tools by team members.
   - Other commitments of team members beyond the project.
   - Management of team members during the work.
   - Replacement of team members.

2. Search the Web and literature for guidelines in the above areas.
3. Research the Web on the issue: how to verify if the training provided for the project work was useful.
4. Research the Web on the issue: team members fail to participate in meetings.
5. Research the Web on the issue: a team member tries to take over the project from the project leader.

What to do next

1. The following table can serve as a checklist for you to use in the project for detecting the symptoms of problems.

Symptom	Date	Incident	Description	Impact

2. The following summary table can be created from the issues database or manually.

Human Resource Issues

Issue	Priority	Date, age	Assigned to	Decision

22
Management issues

Introduction

In the past management gave less attention to IT projects. They were treated as peripheral to the business. In the last decade the situation changed as management realized that systems and technology could not only reduce costs, but also provide competitive advantage and increase revenue. Process improvement and E-Business have been two factors that have further increased management interest and involvement in IT. While this was greeted by some as very favorable, it has been a mixed blessing. Many managers lack knowledge of IT and the time and complexity to implement new systems and technology. Vendor promises, advertisements by manufacturers, and success stories have fueled both involvement and problems. A basic point here is that experience shows that trying to teach IT to many traditional managers is not always productive. A better approach is to work with managers on IT-related issues. Managers are used to solving problems so that addressing issues in a business way is useful.

Issue: management changes direction of the project

How this occurs

Due to internal business needs, changes in departments, shifting priorities, and other reasons, management can change the direction of the project. One source is that management did not understand the project at the start. This is especially true if there was no project concept defined so that later they had additional or other ideas.

Potential impact

The impact on the project team is to slow down or halt work while people attempt to determine what to do in response. While a project can withstand one or two of these impacts, any more than that and people on the team begin not to take the project seriously.

How to prevent the problem

The best prevention is back at the start when the project concept was defined and discussed. An issue that can be pointed out is change of direction. In fact, most of the issues in this chapter can be added to your initial list of issues.

How to address the problem

When changes occur, go to the business unit managers who are involved in the project and attempt to assess what the change means. Do not make changes until both you and the business manager discuss them with upper management. Otherwise, there could be misinterpretation.

Issue: management loses interest

How this occurs

Some managers show interest in a project at the start. Then as time passes, they lose interest. This can happen for a variety of reasons. First, the project may have been a diversion and they return to their other work. They really don't have time to deal with it anymore. A second reason is that you have not kept them informed so they just assumed that things were OK. A third reason is that they sense that the project is in trouble and they don't want to get involved.

Potential impact

The impact may at first seem to you to be negative. Loss of interest will let you and the team get down to work without as much interference. The real loss comes if you need to have an issue addressed that requires their support and you are unable to get to see them. Issues then take longer to resolve and the solution may not be to your liking.

How to prevent the problem

Keep management informed from the beginning. However, you do not want to run to management with many issues. If you do, then they may perceive that the project is in trouble. Focus on informal communications.

How to address the problem

You will see that management loses interest if you find that they do not have time for you or if they do not express any interest. Keep them updated and surface an issue every now and then to keep their interest.

Issue: key manager who supported the project leaves

How this occurs

There are several versions of this issue. One is that the manager leaves the company. Another is that he or she is transferred. A third is that the manager loses power and so can no longer support the project.

Potential impact

Without a champion of the project, it will be difficult to find people to take issues. Other managers may associate the project with that person and may not see any self-interest or organization interest in the project.

How to prevent the problem

The solution to this is to have more than one champion of the project. At the start indicate that it is in their own best interests to have several managers supporting the project. You are in essence building an informal steering committee.

How to address the problem

Contact the manager and get ideas for who could be a replacement. Also, contact the business unit manager. After all, they are the ones who are most involved in the project since they will receive the benefits of it. They should be the ones who should find support for the project.

Issue: management expands scope

How this occurs

Like other issues in this chapter, this can be due to external or internal factors. If the project was not defined in the project concept, then the scope of the project is not clear to all of the managers. Each person may have a different idea of what the project is to accomplish. This is a common cause for scope creep.

Potential impact

Expanding the scope is often not accompanied by either more money, people, or time. Whatever you deliver will possibly be unacceptable. The project may turn out to be viewed as a failure even if it did achieve the initial goals within the original scope.

How to prevent the problem

During the project concept, hammer away at getting a common view of the scope of the project. Make scope creep an issue. Indicate what things are outside of the scope of the project. Also, show what happens if there is scope creep.

How to address the problem

There are several alternatives. One is to review the entire project concept again. Meet with managers and business units to redefine and review the scope. Another alternative is to see if you can divide up the project into phases where the added scope items are included in a later phase.

Issue: there is no will to allocate resources

How this occurs

You received approval for the project. You think that this is great. Later, you find that management is unwilling to go to the IT manager or the business unit manager and redirect resources to the project. There are other priorities. Moreover, if the manager orders the redirection, there may be resistance and complaint about operational needs not being met.

Potential impact

The impact is that people are assuming that the project is going ahead since it was approved. The project is delayed since you cannot obtain the resources. The schedule slips.

How to prevent the problem

To prevent this from happening, raise the resource issue at the start of the project. Work with line managers and IT managers to line up resources. Make an effort to show how the project is in their own best interests. This should all be done before you get formal approval.

How to address the problem

If the problem occurs, then you can return to the manager to seek support. This, however, is an extreme step and puts the manager in an awkward position. It is better to work with the line and IT managers to get some resources to get the project going. Once you show some initial results, then you can return to these people to request additional resources.

Issue: management rules by consensus

How this occurs

Here management cannot seem to make decisions at the individual manager level. There is a fear of making decisions without involving other managers. Therefore, no decision is made.

Potential impact

The direct impact is that decisions on issues or priorities are delayed. The burden falls on the project leader to line up support with different managers. This delays the project and diverts the project leader from dealing with the other project issues and tasks.

How to prevent the problem

Prevention of this problem begins with an assessment of management and their style in decision-making. If you detect this as a problem, then you should bring this up with the business unit managers. Enlist their support in working with senior management.

How to address the problem

If the problem occurs, then you should go to the business unit manager and work out a joint approach. You should also make contingency plans for dealing with the situation in the future.

Issue: management locks onto hot topics

How this occurs

Whatever is the topic, management can seem to lock onto a specific project because it involves something that they are interested in. It may not even be critical to the business—just something that caught their fancy.

Potential impact

The result may be that managers are now showing interest in the details of the project. They want to attend meetings and be involved. While attention is nice, it is likely to be counterproductive and get in the way of work. People in the meetings will not talk openly in front of the manager. You then have to hold additional meetings without the manager present.

How to prevent the problem

Try to make the project seem mundane while it is important. Play down the new technology and other factors that are attractive to the manager. Instead, you should involve the manager in some issues so that they understand more about the project.

How to address the problem

If the problem arises, then you might want to discuss the issue generally with the manager. Your approach is to suggest that they might want to be involved in issues rather than the details of the project.

Issue: management adopts a specific package and jams it down everyone's throat

How this occurs

This happened frequently with ERP systems. Corporate decided on the package and everyone had to get in line to install it. This sometimes also happens because of the industry. If everyone is buying a particular package, then there is substantial pressure to buy and install the same package. Vendors apply pressure as well. Managers are then attracted by the lure of the benefits of the software.

Potential impact

The impact can be devastating—not just to IT, but to the business units. Implementing a complex package requires the precious few experienced and knowledgeable users. Taking these people out of the everyday work can wreak havoc on the departments. In IT the impact may cause resources to be diverted from important maintenance and enhancements. Systems staff members are forced to juggle between the demands of the package and their normal work—hurting both.

How to prevent the problem

The important thing here is not to head off the acquisition of the software. It may be the best decision. Rather, the emphasis should be on ensuring that everyone understands the effort that will be required to implement the software from both the business unit and IT perspectives.

How to address the problem

When you receive the mandate for a software package, quickly identify implementation issues related to interfaces, changes to the business processes, and the time and effort required to set up the software to meet the needs of the business. Prepare a list of issues as well as a plan. Identify situations where staff will have to split in their time to support the package. You never want to say no, but you do want people to realize the schedule impacts.

Issue: management listens too much to consultants

How this occurs

Consultants are a regular feature of the corporate landscape. Assume that it is natural that these people will want to establish and build ties with management. After all, they are seeking more work later. They hope to get it by aligning themselves with senior managers. They also are trying to protect their positions. Managers as a result sometimes overrely on these consultants.

Potential impact

It is not that the consultants are malicious or trying to cause problems. Often their advice and counsel are misinterpreted. The impact may be the appearance of a change in direction or focus. It can also mean that the project is given much more scrutiny. Either way, it is going to take more effort now to deal with this—time that could be spent on the project.

How to prevent the problem

One approach is to maintain contact with both management and the consultants. Encourage the consultants to express any of the concerns to you first. Don't try to stop them from contacting managers. This won't work and places you in a defensive position. Instead, try to make them feel as part of the team.

How to address the problem

When a problem arises, you will probably hear about it from the manager. The manager will often not credit the source, but will just identify the issue or situation. You should be ready for this. However, if it occurs, then you will obviously work to provide answers to the manager. You should also keep the consultant informed. Perhaps, the consultant will begin to realize the situation that was created. You should also assume that you will be given partial information and that you will have to investigate further.

Issue: management wants to change E-Business priorities

How this occurs

Managers are besieged with information related to E-Business. They hear about new industry trends, new products, what the competition is doing, and so on. This in turn generates requests for changes and for additional work. Examples might be targeting new audiences or stressing new or different products and services.

Potential impact

Changing minor requirements is one thing. Changing direction, schedules, and other factors in the middle of E-Business implementation creates many problems and opportunities. The impact in some companies has been that E-Business implementation was delayed for months as direction shifted.

How to prevent the problem

While the problem cannot be prevented since you do not control management, there are some things that you can do. First, base your work in implementation on business processes rather than analysis of customer behavior on the Web, and so on. This is more stable. Second, keep in frequent contact with managers. Get them involved in issues. If you do this, then you will likely find that they gain a better understanding of what it takes to get E-Business up and running.

How to address the problem

When changes of direction occur, don't immediately rush out and change direction. Instead, try to understand the source of the change and the reasoning and logic behind it. There are many different ways to accommodate changes in direction. Don't pick the most difficult. Another comment is to use this change as an opportunity to determine what other changes there might be later. This change in direction might be the tip of the iceberg.

Issue: marketing defines new E-Business initiatives with management support

How this occurs

In E-Business and even standard business, marketing strategy plays a critical role in determining the direction of the company. Marketing attempts to be creative to beat the competition. In E-Business there are many opportunities for creativity in promotions and discounts.

Potential impact

Handling traditional requests usually has meant tight, but reasonable deadlines. In E-Business this is not the case. There is pressure to get the changes made to both the systems and processes so that the new marketing campaign can get going. In the print media there is a substantial lead time for publication. For the Web it is much faster and more immediate.

How to prevent the problem

Actually, the problem cannot be entirely prevented. The best approach is to determine the range of potential marketing programs so that you can anticipate potential requests before they occur. This will help in shortening the work later after the request is made. Doing this also helps to structure the marketing organization. However, it is not guaranteed since there are still creative promotions arising everyday.

How to address the problem

When a request comes up, you are put into a reactive mode of operation. IT and the business units are placed on the defensive. To head this off, you should make a major effort to keep in regular contact with marketing staff and managers to see what ideas they are working on. This is an ongoing effort to prevent surprises. When you do receive a request, consider meeting with them and the business units affected to determine the best approach. Always consider non-systems solutions and approaches.

Questions

1. Search the literature and Web to find examples in the following areas:
   - Management communications.
   - Management involvement.
   - Management decision-making.
   - Management taking actions.
   - Resource allocation and management.
   - Management involvement and support of change.

2. Search the Web and literature for guidelines in the above areas.
3. Research the Web on the issue: management vacillates on issues and decisions.
4. Research the Web on the issue: it is difficult to communicate with some managers.
5. Research the Web on the issue: There is significant management turnover.

What to do next

1. Identify management issues associated with your current and past projects. Then address the following questions.

   - What was the state and condition of communications with management, both formal and informal?

- What was the elapsed time to resolve issues?
- Did management bring issues to you or did you present and update management on issues?
- After issues were resolved, what was the relationship between management and the project?

2. Prepare a table of the issues presented here as rows and the projects as columns. In the entry of the table indicate to what extent the issue appeared in the project.
3. Looking back on management issues that you encountered, identify what could have been different.

Summary

Management issues will not go away. History shows that many of the same issues recur repeatedly. Knowing this a suggested approach is to anticipate that these and other issues will arise with the same and new or different managers. Lessons learned from solving management issues and communicating more effectively with management are the keys here.

23
Technical issues

Introduction

When you think of technical issues, you often think of programming, hardware, or network issues. Technology and systems are much more complex today. There are more interfaces and integration between systems. Staffing resources are limited, creating more competition for scarce technical resources. Technical issues thus become more intricate and complex.

Issue: legacy system support is too resource intensive

Legacy systems will not disappear soon. They have, in many cases, been customized to the specific business environment and business rules. They have adapted to the business. They can only be replaced through custom development or by adapting the business to the software packages. Yet when new client-server, data warehousing, or intranet systems are developed, they often must interface with the legacy systems.

How this occurs

Legacy systems typically depend on a few key programmers who have lived with them for many years. They provide maintenance, enhancement, and production support. Each person often has unique knowledge and experience with the systems. These people face a backlog of work as well as demands of continuing, day-to-day support. On top of this, there are demands for interfaces. Efforts to use productivity aids and new tools achieve limited success due to the old technology embedded in the legacy systems. Training new staff in the legacy systems is often not possible due to limited resources and the difficulty in finding and training new staff in a system that lacks documentation.

Potential impact

Users are often frustrated at their inability to advance their capabilities due to these limitations. It is a Catch-22 situation—there are not enough resources, yet additional resources cannot be added. The situation becomes more difficult to improve. Eventually, of course, all legacy systems will be replaced. However, the major question is when resources will be made available to do this.

How to prevent the problem

Develop a strategy for front- and back-end systems to connect to the legacy system with modern intranet or client-server systems. This will allow business rules and additional functions to be supplied without modifying (only interfacing) the legacy system. This extends the life of the legacy system. You can add a strategy for replacement of the legacy system, if that is possible. You can also define small changes to reduce support as well as take a harder line on enhancements.

How to address the problem

Review the backlog of requests for the legacy system and cut it, if possible. Go through the maintenance and enhancement requests to see if they can be addressed in some other system or eliminated. Give the support requirements and limitations of the legacy systems more visibility in terms of their impact and resource consumption so that management is aware of their cost, restrictiveness, and impact.

Issue: there is a lack of available training for staff

How this occurs

New technology creates training requirements for the technology itself as well as interfaces. When a new technology first becomes available, training is limited and there is a lack of expertise. Employees must learn the technology through some form of training. However, their schedules, the training schedule, and the timing of projects using the technology all restrict availability.

Potential impact

If training is conducted too early, knowledge can be lost before the technology is used. If it is too late, then training is rushed and staff must learn it on their own in the midst of the project. Lack of training will slow down the project and likely create rework later.

How to prevent the problem

When evaluating any new technology, determine your training requirements and schedule as well as the availability and quality of training. Schedule training as part of the project plan. Try to find classes that offer tips and lessons learned as well as instructions.

How to address the problem

If training is not sufficient, then consider having a consultant do in-house training and provide experience and knowledge in the project to shorten the learning curve. However, ensure that you establish a cutoff time to make the staff self-sufficient.

Issue: the technology requires a learning curve that is too long

How this occurs

To employ new technology, such as that related to software or networks, you must gain understanding and then advance to some level of proficiency. One of the reasons for the failure of early client-server projects was that there was an unexpectedly long learning curve for dealing with the client, server, and middleware. Learning a technology also may require that you unlearn old habits that proved useful in the past. This is particularly true in object-oriented programming versus traditional programming. Management may also divert people from learning the new technology into maintaining the old technology. This shows the staff that management places a greater value on the existing than on the new technology.

Potential impact

If you underestimate the learning curve and do not allow time for people to gain proficiency, the project will likely slip. The new technology typically must be supported by training and education, consulting, and support. Additional software tools may be required as well. If these are not provided on a timely basis, the project schedule suffers. Not only can the schedule suffer, but the quality of work can as well. This can occur if people try to gain their knowledge through work on the project—often resulting in substantial rework.

How to prevent the problem

Consult with the vendors and existing users of the technology to gain insight into what ingredients are needed for successful implementation and use of the technology along with the estimated time for the learning curve. Develop an approach for measuring how people are doing in gaining expertise.

How to address the problem

If this problem arises, divide the tasks in the schedule and attempt to spread the learning curve among multiple staff members. In addition, work with employees to determine if any other assistance might be beneficial. Hold meetings to share lessons learned related to the technology.

Issue: there is a lack of experience and knowledge of the technology

How this occurs

If the technology is very new, available experience will be lacking. There are likely to be bugs, missing features, and other problems. Alternatively, the technology might have been out in the market for some time, but has attracted few users. Why does anyone want this technology? One reason is that people are desperate to fix problems so they want to use it right away. Another reason is that the technology fills an existing gap in the architecture. Perhaps no competing product is on the market.

Potential impact

One obvious risk is that you are going to be a pioneer in the technology. That is, the project that depends on this technology will move from one problem or issue to another. It will be more time consuming to get around problems because the vendor will have to be contacted more frequently. The situation can also occur when you are the first to integrate a particular combination of technologies.

How to prevent the problem

Make sure that learning the technology is planned within the project. Gather lessons learned from the vendor and any other users. Involve the vendor staff in the project if possible. You also must identify and pay much more attention to areas of uncertainty involving the technology.

How to address the problem

If you begin to run into a succession of problems, consider stopping to gain more knowledge of the technology. Apply pressure on the vendor for additional assistance. Slow the project down and give higher priority to training and learning.

Issue: the technology does not work

How this occurs

Not working can mean many things. The technology may not work at all, it may not work the way you require, or it may fail due to the specific configuration—it was undersized. Whatever the cause, the technology is not performing as desired. This may occur due to underestimating the requirements, misunderstanding of the technology, and vendor error.

Potential impact

You are fortunate if this issue can be resolved by throwing money at the problem and increasing capacity or capabilities. Examples are adding memory, disk, or upgrading the CPU to increase performance. However, if you are dealing with critical software, then you probably have a real problem. In the worst case, the software may actually have to be dropped and a substitute found. If you retain, you may have to work around the technology.

How to prevent the problem

Identify the minimal acceptable working level for the technology. Get the vendor to commit to this level. In some cases, you can prevent the problem by putting in additional capacity at the start. You can also attempt to test the technology prior to acquisition or right after installation. However, the problem may surface in interfaces. Thus, you must test interfaces as soon as possible. Concentrate resources there.

How to address the problem

If you encounter an interface problem when the technology is failing, consider creating a new project plan that includes only the interfaces. Manage it with much more attention. Involve vendors whose products are used in the interfaces.

Issue: ordering and delivery of the technology are delayed

How this occurs

Delays can be due to your internal purchasing process, the vendor not having the product ready, or politics or geography, such as when the technology is shipped internationally and is beset by government red tape. Many project managers do not consider the purchasing and acquisition process. They discover too late that they should have begun on this at start of the project. Delays due to problems in negotiations can also occur. People can take the mundane process of ordering and delivery for granted. Some technology projects may require specific manufacturing or customization with substantial lead times.

Potential impact

The technology is not available. The schedule is at first not impacted. People work on other tasks. Time passes. Then the problem becomes more acute. The direct impact of slippage occurs. Morale might be impacted if people begin to feel that if the project were important, the components or technology would be on hand. In one manufacturing situation test equipment was delayed, seriously impacting production.

How to prevent the problem

As a project leader, set aside time at the start of the project to concentrate on the procurement process. Understand how this process works. Volunteer to work with people in purchasing to expedite the tasks. Remember that if you show how urgent it is to acquire equipment on time, your effort will likely be met by a similar effort. Follow up in negotiation, shipment, delivery, and verification. Work with the vendors to expedite their efforts.

How to address the problem

If you are faced with delays, do two things. First, devote the time to follow up on problems. Second, contact the vendor and see if a duplicate component can be shipped immediately. You can later return the faulty component you first received. If there are purchasing delays (approval cycles, freezes, and so on), then show the impact of the delay to management in tangible terms within the schedule.

Issue: a new version of the technology will be available soon

How this occurs

Technology changes quickly. New releases of some products occur at three-month intervals. For some software, these include fixes of known problems as well as new features, functions, and performance improvements. The situation is compounded because the typical systems organization faces the issue of upgrading across multiple products from a range of different sources. The basic question is, "When should you move to the new version?" The more general question is, "What is your general strategy for upgrading many different products?"

Potential impact

New versions can create problems with interfaces and integration. Additional errors may surface. New versions can have latent errors that were not detected during testing. If you jump too soon, you risk becoming a pioneer. If you wait, you might miss important benefits. If you wait too long, you can risk obsolescence. You may face additional complexity if you made changes when you installed the last version and did not keep a record of what changes were made.

How to prevent the problem

Begin with an overall strategy for upgrading the technology. Which components link together and so must be upgraded together? Where do the most problems lie? What are your problems and how do these impact priorities? Consider creating a formal upgrading project plan.

How to address the problem

If you adopt new versions on an *ad hoc*, unplanned basis, then you can face almost non-stop disruption—like having the street in front of your house torn up all of the time. If you encounter several potential upgrades at one time, create a small group of systems staff to consider what to do in terms of a strategy.

Issue: there is a lack of support for interfaces to existing technology

How this occurs

With increased networking and integration among products from a variety of vendors, it is not a surprise that many problems exist in the areas of interfaces. This is complex because you and your staff must learn the technology on both sides of the interface as well as how to glue it together effectively. The vendors will likely only have limited knowledge of each other's technology products.

Potential impact

If you fail to give interfaces a high priority, you risk the schedule and plan. Everything can be complete except for one critical interface. Without it the project can fail or at least be put on hold.

How to prevent the problem

Interfaces are so important that you must plan the project around the interfaces and integration effort. Establish tasks that address interface testing. Ensure that test data and suites are prepared that thoroughly test the interfaces.

How to address the problem

If you encounter an interface problem that is likely to affect the project, consider setting up a subplan for the interface. Make yourself the project leader and devote your time to coordinating the tasks. Coordination of the interfaces is both complex and time consuming.

Issue: there is a gap in the technology

How this occurs

Each time a new technology is implemented, gaps are created between it and the existing technologies. This even occurs with standard interfaces because the new technology adds content or performance to interfaces. For example, a new network operating system creates gaps in network management. Features found in network management software may be included in the operating system. Information formats may be different. Many products are affected by a steady evolution of the overall architecture as new versions of current technology as well as new technology are added.

Potential impact

What happens if a gap is not addressed? You may not be able to use the technology at all. It is more often the case that you will not be able to use new capabilities until the gaps are addressed. The staff must also learn the technical details of the new technology in order to deal with the gaps. This takes valuable resources away from other work.

How to prevent the problem

Identify existing gaps in your current technology architecture. Develop a strategy for dealing with these first. Next, include the gap issue in the evaluation and selection of new technology. When people suggest new technology, make sure they are aware of the potential problems.

How to address the problem

When you encounter a gap, have staff understand the details of what has to be done. Then contact the vendors to see what help you can get. Make gap analysis and contingency planning part of the projects involving new technology. In addressing the gap, make sure that you establish many small milestones so that you can track progress.

Issue: the pilot results from the technology were not successful

How this occurs

Everyone expects success in pilot projects using new technology. After all, newer is better, right? Why do pilot projects fail? There are many possible factors:

- The objectives and scope of the pilot project were not clearly identified.
- The pilot did not address specific technical issues.
- Resources to perform and evaluate the pilot test were lacking.
- Time to do the pilot was insufficient, so the pilot was rushed.

Thus, success hinges on much more than the technology itself. A major airline conducted a pilot project for a new airplane restroom. It was placed in the middle of an open floor of offices. No one used the pilot. However, because there was no measurement or complaints, the airline assumed that the pilot was successful. When the unit was installed in planes, people got stuck in the toilet and the unit had to be removed—a pilot project with a flush?

Potential impact

What do you do after the pilot? How do you interpret the results? Can you proceed with the project, should you run another pilot, or should you stop the project? This dilemma can hang up a project for some time. If you attempt to fix the problems in the pilot during finishing of the system, then you risk having additional problems surface.

How to prevent the problem

A pilot project has specific goals and scope. The process or system must be measured prior to the pilot as well as after the pilot. Criteria for success of the pilot are established at the start of the pilot. These criteria cannot be weakened after the pilot to force acceptance unless all are in agreement.

How to address the problem

If you are faced with problems from the pilot, consider the following alternative courses of action:

- Continue with the project and make adjustments later.
- Change the purpose and scope of the project to fit the results of the pilot project.
- Rerun the pilot based on revised assumptions and setting.
- Stop the project and return to the previous stage in the project.
- Substitute other technology and either continue or run a new pilot.

To evaluate these alternatives, you must review the costs and benefits of the new project.

Issue: the performance of the technology is not satisfactory

How this occurs

In a broad sense, technology performance can involve workload, response time, security, reliability, throughput, utilization, productivity, cost, benefits, and other measures. The values of these measures depend on the work submitted to and performed by the systems and technology. If the actual workload is substantially higher than what was estimated, then performance problems are likely to arise. Performance may also not be acceptable because business units or information systems raised the standards of performance. Even with the increased performance of new technology, there are still performance issues because people expect more out of the technology than ever before.

Potential impact

Performance may not be satisfactory, but it might be minimally acceptable. In some cases, you can continue using the technology while the problem is being fixed. If performance is totally unacceptable, then it may be necessary to halt use of the technology and have the business unit fall back to another system. This happened in the early days of point-of-sale systems.

How to prevent the problem

Ideally, you should test the technology to find the limits of performance and determine at what point problems occur. Also, perform analysis to determine what upgrades are possible when performance suffers. In fact, for every new critical technology that involves potential performance problems, it is a good idea to define a migration path for improvement.

How to address the problem

What is the source of the performance problem? Can it be addressed through upgrades? If so, who is liable for the cost? Will the vendor contribute to the cost? If the problem is fixed, will other performance problems surface? You may face a series of problems. Develop a plan for addressing the problem. Make sure that it includes measurement and that adequate resources are applied.

Issue: features are missing

How this occurs

Consider software. You carefully evaluated the software package or tool. You verified features by interviewing the vendor. You received demonstrations. However, upon delivery you find that some of the features are missing or are only partially implemented. The source of this problem can be either the vendor or the customer who misinterpreted what was said. You also might have assumed that a feature was present (to support an interface, e.g.) even though it was not.

Potential impact

The project can be delayed or at least may have to be changed to adapt to the situation. The question of impact revolves around which features are missing and how dependent the project is on these features. In some cases for software packages, the system may not be able to handle your unique financial, accounting, or manufacturing situation.

How to prevent the problem

How do you verify that the technology will do what you desire? The answer is obviously by testing the work through the system. However, setting up for such testing can be very expensive. For software it may involve establishing many different tables. This requires extensive analysis, training, and even more testing. You can talk to references provided by the vendor.

How to address the problem

If the missing features are important, you may wish to consider changing the business process to fit the technology as it stands. You can wait until the features are added, but that might take years. You can also implement a procedure for working around the problems.

Issue: the technology in use is obsolete

How this occurs

Every business and household contains technology that is obsolete. New technology came along that replaced what you have. Why didn't you replace the technology? Because it still works the way you want. You don't see any reason to replace it. Another reason is that it is not very important to you and is not used much. You may also determine that the new technology involves more problems and hassle than replacement is worth.

Potential impact

For stand-alone technology, this is less of an issue. You are probably more likely to continue to use it and avoid replacement. The problems crop up in technology that requires support or is integrated with other technology. For example, let's suppose that you are using an older network operating system that has served you well. Now you want to purchase a software package. However, the package does not run on the current network operating system. To use the new software package, you may be forced to upgrade hardware, replace the network operating system, and train or hire staff.

How to prevent the problem

Dealing with obsolescence is one of the reasons to define a systems and technology architecture. The architecture can provide you with the information about integration and aging of the technology. The second step is to devise a replacement strategy. Such a strategy identifies the following:

- Which components are to be replaced?
- How they might be replaced?
- What trigger events are required to initiate the replacement?

How to address the problem

You face the need to replace the obsolescent technology. This is a good time to review all of the technology and plan an overall replacement strategy. Management will be more supportive of an overall plan that addresses obsolescence as a whole. When marketing and selling the changes to obtain funding, focus on the downside. That is, address what will happen if there is no replacement. Here are some potential impacts:

- The support effort will be increased.
- The firm will be prohibited from implementing new systems.
- The business units will be denied systems that might have major potential benefits.
- The likelihood of failure will be higher.
- It will be more difficult to obtain support.

Issue: the technology is not scalable to handle the workload

How this occurs

Undersizing of hardware and network components for E-Business is fairly common. Neither management nor IT anticipated the workload imposed by Web traffic. Moreover, they did not anticipate the high peak load and the fluctuation in the workload. Another reason is that inappropriate components were selected to save money or time.

Potential impact

The impact can be slow response time or even a breakdown. This situation then leaves to customer or supplier complaints for E-Business traffic.

How to prevent the problem

Prevention of the problem come from front-end analysis and gathering lessons learned from similar organizations to determine what their range of workload was.

How to address the problem

If this problem occurs, attention must be given not only to fixing it now, but also developing a long-term approach that involves measurement, capacity planning, and acquiring and using systems software tools.

Issue: the wrong direction in technology was taken

How this occurs

Often the wrong direction is taken because of the past. The most comfortable approach is to just use upgraded products from your current vendors. These tend to be backward compatible so that they are easier to install and use. There is much less training. If you take this approach one time, it is easier each time there is a decision. The end result can be that you have taken a tangent off of the main technology track.

Potential impact

The potential effect is that you may be stuck with obsolete or inadequate technology. This will mean that you will likely have more turnover of staff as people leave to work on mainstream, up-to-date technology. It also happens that maintenance and operations support will be more time consuming and difficult.

How to prevent the problem

One approach to prevention is to assess technology on a regular basis. In that way, you will at least know where you stand. Another approach is to give attention and priority to technology based issues. This can keep the heat and focus on fixing these problems as well as showing in graphic detail the problems and impacts that the current technology has.

How to address the problem

If you find that there are significant technology issues and problems, do not just deal with these one at a time. Instead, you should consider sitting back and defining what a more suitable technology architecture might be. Then you can build on this as a roadmap for the future.

Questions

1. Search the literature and Web to find examples in the following areas:

   - Identification of suitable technologies.
   - Evaluation and selection of new and emerging technologies.
   - Measurement of technologies.
   - Implementation of new technology.
   - Integration of new technology.
   - Phasing out of existing technology.

2. Search the Web and literature for guidelines in the above areas.

3. Research the Web on the issue: how to verify that lessons learned were used in later projects.
4. Research the Web on the issue: how to sell managers on the need to change technology.
5. Research the Web on the issue: how to ensure that technology acquired is used.

What to do next

1. If you have not done so already, develop a list of technology issues associated with the current architecture. These include the gaps, problems, and opportunities that exist. This is the first step toward improvements.
2. Again, consider the architecture from the standpoint of obsolescence. Define a new architecture that is desirable. Identify both the benefits and the problems addressed by the new architecture.
3. Review your vendor relations in terms of the support provided and the quality of the products and services. Consider implementing a regular measurement process of the technology performance.

Summary

Technical issues involve requirements, performance, support, vendor products, integration, and interfaces. Today, the situation is too complex and the business is too dependent on the technology to risk taking a reactive, *ad hoc* approach. You must be proactive not only in addressing problems, but also in defining the future direction.

24
Vendor and consultant issues

Introduction

Dependence on vendors, contractors, and consultants is not new in systems projects. It occurred when there was a limited number of programmers for a small number of mainframes in the 1960s. Also, many firms outsourced all of their computing to service bureaus. Times have changed, as have the nature and extent of the dependence.

- There is a greater reliance on vendor-supplied application software.
- The use of software tools has increased. These tools are supplied by different vendors but used by the same people.
- Specific systems activities have been outsourced, making the company more dependent because the outsourcer has much of the knowledge of the systems.

In fact, if you consider your own company, you would probably find that it is dependent on multiple vendors for key systems and business processes. With downsizing and limited resources, it is both infeasible and impractical to consider having all of these functions performed by internal support. The goal must be to better manage, coordinate, and direct external support. This will be the theme in the issues addressed in this chapter.

Issue: there is a lack of support from the vendor

Lack of support here means that the vendor is not providing sufficient resources to handle the work or that the resources provided cannot address the requirements. This can occur during normal or crisis times.

How this occurs

The vendor may take you as a customer for granted. The vendor may have supplied support in previous cases, but was not adequately compensated in the vendor's opinion. There may be no formal understanding related to support or how the support will be coordinated. It can also occur that the vendor's staff is stretched thin in that it does not include many senior technical people. The vendor may be concentrating its top people on getting new work and generating proposals. For technology you may be using a version of the product that is being phased out, limiting support.

Potential impact

Minor problems can fester for some time and lead to a major problem. This has happened with wide area networks, applications software, and operations support. Typically, many facets of the problems with the vendor surface as the situation deteriorates. The effects can spill over to other projects and other vendors. Relations with business units may suffer. People may question the vendor's product and even want to seek a substitute. If not resolved quickly, both you and the vendor may paint yourselves into opposing corners.

How to prevent the problem

It seems obvious that the problem might be prevented by defining support requirements and the rules for managing support in the contract. However, people come and go and the ones who may have established such rules on both sides may be gone—long gone. It is important to review and reinforce the rules and guidelines for support each time there is a change, as well as periodically. Important here is the escalation process for problems.

How to address the problem

If you detect a pronounced lack of support, sit down and determine when the problem worsened and how it worsened. Did your staff hold up its end in terms of providing information and so on? What events and factors led to the current situation? Go back to the vendor's management and work on the rules for support as well as the current incident. The steps in determining support requirements, providing a vendor with the necessary information, and getting support must be put into procedures. You will also want to institute a logging process for all incidents and problems, if you do not have one already.

Issue: the vendor attempts to take over the project

This phenomenon is most common in consulting and development projects wherein the vendor sees an opportunity to expand the business and relationship by filling any gaps in project management. This is not all bad, if managed properly, because you do want such vendors to jointly manage the project with you. Also, you may not have the people to address additional tasks that arise.

How this occurs

Frequently, the situation arises as additional, new tasks surface that require near-term attention. The vendor may volunteer to take on these tasks. If you do not resist, then a pattern may be established. From lessons learned, the most frequent cause of the problem is the lack of a defined role for the vendor and insufficient monitoring of the boundaries between the vendor and the internal staff.

Potential impact

In some cases, having the vendor take over some tasks can result in excellent work. You are in essence contracting out the additional work as well as some of the control of the project. A basic question is, "Who is liable if something goes wrong?" This question must be answered early before problems surface.

A more difficult situation occurs when the vendor takes over the project and guides the selection of technology and consultants. This is why it is difficult for hardware technology vendors to be project managers. The impact of an expanded role for the consultant can demoralize the internal staff. They may even begin to wonder who they are working for.

How to prevent the problem

Clear definitions of roles of the vendors as well as the process for handling new work are required at the start of the project. Who is in charge must be spelled out. In addition, procedures for handling new situations must be established before the vendor assumes responsibility. These procedures must be reinforced by the internal project manager.

How to address the problem

The internal staff and project manager are the first to detect any effort at a takeover. Try to handle this at the project leader level. Look for the cause in terms of a gap in management. Then you can escalate it upward in the organization. However, if not addressed, upper management should become involved.

Issue: the vendor delivers something different from what was promised

This is the case with an application development effort. It can also happen with systems or utility software where features delivered fail to match promises.

How this occurs

This issue can have several sources. The vendor staff doing the programming are removed from the people who are gathering requirements and specifications. Miscommunications results—you lose. Technical specifications can be misinterpreted. In addition, there can be several alternative means of implementing the same feature— some of which you don't like. What was promised? This may not be clear. Requirements may have changed, but the contract was not updated.

Potential impact

It is easy to say that you can reject the software or product and send it back. That may delay the project. If what you do receive is workable, you will be tempted to use it if the vendor promises fixes. That may entail developing workarounds (software or procedures that gets around the missing feature). You may be waiting a long time for fixes. In one case, a development editor and debugger lacked features related to testing. Another software tool had to be purchased to cover the testing—raising project cost and lengthening the learning curve. More effort is required to convert work between tools.

How to prevent the problem

For development projects try to get through the vendor salespeople and analysts to the programmers. Write as detailed specifications as you can. Carry out frequent work reviews. Implement a strenuous testing program. Insist on early delivery of design products for evaluation. Conduct the evaluations as soon as you receive them. This shows the vendor that you are involved.

How to address the problem

This will depend on the nature of the project. In general, you are faced with the following questions:

- Should you accept the product and attempt to use it as is?
- What is the minimum that must be fixed or changed for acceptance?
- How do you work around the shortcomings in the interim?

Develop an approach jointly with the vendor for dealing with deliverables prior to problems.

Issue: the vendor provides the wrong staff

Whether it is operations, network support, development, or consulting, the vendor is providing people to your organization to perform work. Even if the people are qualified, there can be personality clashes and other problems. The staff provided may not get along with each other.

How this occurs

The situation may arise because the company did not implement a review process for the vendor staff. There was an assumption that the company was being provided with highly qualified people. Some consulting firms put in a mixture of senior and junior people. Then they may pull out the senior staff. You are left with the remains. Also, the contractors may not be internally monitored.

Potential impact

Productivity can suffer along with work quality. If the project leader is not on top of the situation, management can wake up too late and the schedule and budget suffer. Moreover, the credibility of the vendor is at stake. Costs escalate as well due to delays and potential additions to staff.

How to prevent the problem

Requirements and qualifications must be in place and reviewed. There must also be an escalation process for replacing vendor staff along with a regular review process with vendor management. Access to the most highly qualified people must be a condition. This is especially true with application software packages. Monitor who is working on the project.

How to address the problem

All work by the vendor staff must be halted by the project leader. The vendor provided the wrong people. The project leader draws up a list of the problems and concerns along with a list of possible solutions and meets with vendor management. Don't resort to the power of the purse—holding money back until you attempt to solve the problem at this level and even with upper management.

Issue: the vendor takes a different business direction, leaving you adrift

Vendors are independent companies who set their direction based on their goals and management, their perspective of the marketplace, and competition. There is nothing to prevent them from changing direction. They may, for example, stop supporting different hardware or software environments. They may stop providing interface support for specific networks.

How this occurs

Although the vendor can be blamed or singled out for criticism, it can also be the fault of your organization. If you fail to keep pace with technology, then you are using workable, but obsolete products. To you this is fine because it works. For vendors it is a nightmare because they cannot continue to support all interfaces.

Potential impact

One potential impact is that you have to switch vendors and products to continue operation and growth. A second impact is that you, like the vendor, must also change direction. In either case, there can be impacts across multiple projects. In one instance, a company was forced to quickly change network operating systems. This change was disruptive. Not only was development impacted, but electronic mail and network management software also had to change, requiring extensive training. It was a major upheaval lasting six months.

How to prevent the problem

Key to the situation is defining and implementing an architecture that employs mainstream technology. You are less likely to run into vendor problems. Maintain regular contact with vendors to sense their direction and learn about their new products.

How to address the problem

If you are caught napping, then you must move to quickly redefine your architecture and technology direction—with and without the vendor. Consider the alternative of continued use versus replacement.

Issue: the vendor's staff members are absent from the project too much

Absence can mean lack of physical presence. It can also mean that they are there, but are not working very hard.

How this occurs

Here are some possible causes:

- You have selected a "hot" software package that is in demand. The vendor staff are in demand and are spread too thin.
- The vendor staff are not being properly managed and so are not as productive as they can be.

- The work environment has such pressure that the vendor staff are burned out or are absent.
- There may be management conflicts or payment problems.

Potential impact

Lack of productivity is one impact. Perhaps, more serious is that issues that can be resolved remain festering because of the lack of attention by vendor staff. If you were highly dependent on the vendor staff, then your staff may not be able to fill the gaps.

How to prevent the problem

Lay out rules for when and where people work. If you are paying for end products and not time and materials, then insist on intermediate deliverables. If you are paying on a time and materials basis, then you must follow up with frequent reviews.

How to address the problem

The project leader is responsible for tracking vendor staff and their work. When a problem occurs, the project leader contacts the vendor manager and informs internal management. If the project is being managed jointly with the vendor, then both can track the people. The vendor should make up for the absence. Here the project leader again evaluates new people assigned to the project. By being the loudest complainer you are more likely to receive attention in the short run. In the long run you must establish the rules for vendor staff involvement.

Issue: the vendor's work is of poor quality

Quality problems can result in failure to function. It can also mean that there are many marginal problems. There is also the question of what constitutes acceptable quality, and if the vendor agrees about this.

How this occurs

"Quality" is a relative term that may mean different things to the vendor and customer. Quality standards may not have been spelled out and agreed to at the start. There may also be ambiguity as to what quality applies to.

For example, the vendor product may not adequately support a network interface. There may be problems with software interfaces. The actual software may have bugs or lack code to process-specific transactions. It may not be the conscious fault of the vendor. You may be the pioneer user of the particular combination of technology in the specific environment.

Potential impact

Quality issues may impact performance, cost, or functionality. The issue is the extent to which quality problems affect the business and project. It may mean that the software is unusable until the problem is repaired.

How to prevent the problem

Define what "quality" means for your setting. This may mean setting testing terms for throughput, response time, range of transactions, and error rates. These should be included in the contract. Implement testing and evaluation as soon as you receive the product.

How to address the problem

You must quickly determine the impact of a quality program. Without the vendor you must decide on potential courses of action. Then you can involve the vendors to see what steps they can take. Consider the most severe option of stopping part of the project until the problem is repaired.

Issue: the vendor's skills are insufficient, producing a gap

Skills are not restricted to training in a technology. Skills mean proficiency to cope with problems as well as employing lessons learned to use the technology effectively. Skills also mean that the vendor staff can function as a team.

How this occurs

The vendor delivers people to work on a project. You assume, based on vendor representations, that these people are qualified. Late, you find out that they are junior and lack sufficient experience. The vendor may have misunderstood the project requirements.

Potential impact

You relied on the vendor staff. They let you down. You typically find out about this at the worse time—when they cannot solve a problem. Relations with the vendor can deteriorate quickly. More problems emerge. Project progress is affected.

How to prevent the problem

Whomever the vendor provides must be tested in terms of experience as well as knowledge. The project leader designs some initial task that covers this testing in addition to having technical interviews conducted. Areas where the vendor staff lack expertise must be identified.

How to address the problem

When a problem or gap appears, contact the vendor manager to set the situation right. The vendor must not only address the immediate problem, but also come up with a longer-term staffing solution that can be monitored.

Issue: the vendor's staff members seem to remain on the project forever

Projects in systems and technology can drag out due to additional requirements or slippage. Work can come in peaks and troughs. The vendor staff remain through all of this. They may stay on during implementation after their work has been completed.

How this occurs

Why do vendors remain on the project? Because they are needed. Also, they can stay on because of the desire to continue the relationship with the customer. The project may have been poorly planned so that they have substantial downtime or lapses in activity. They may be retained because of their knowledge and as insurance against future problems.

Potential impact

Costs rise. Morale internally can sink. People begin to ask, "Why are they still here?" Confidence in the project leader can drop. Unnecessary tasks can be created.

How to prevent the problem

As the project leader, ask when people can leave the project. This includes both vendor staff and internal employees. Identify the final vendor milestone at the start of the project. Don't mention it too often after that, as it can sour the relationship. Keep the vendor focused on near-term tasks, but always remember the final milestone.

How to address the problem

If there is a gap without work or if vendor staff seem to be hanging on, then define final end products and apply the pressure. Begin to phase them out of the project meetings.

Issue: there is no committed schedule from the vendor

At the start of the project there may be contractual dates for the vendor. These are different from a schedule. The schedule must back up the contractual dates and provide more detail along with interim milestones.

How this occurs

Committed contractual dates may not be updated due to project changes—affecting their credibility of dates and schedule. The vendor may not have been asked to prepare a plan for work. Or if there was a plan, it was never updated. Also, the vendor plan may not have been combined or meshed with your plan.

Potential impact

Problems or disagreements are almost inevitable in larger projects. Vendor staff are focusing on near-term tasks. No one is watching the overall schedule. There is now substantial slippage.

How to prevent the problem

Create an overall schedule that includes the vendor work at a summary level. Next, have the vendor manager define detailed tasks to fit under these summary tasks. Review the task and their meanings with the vendor. The next step is to have the vendor assign resources, durations, and start and end dates. Review these. Each week have the vendor staff update their part of the schedule.

How to address the problem

Let's assume that the project has started without a vendor schedule. Don't wait for problems. Insist that they develop a plan to be included in your schedule. Make sure that this plan is updated on a regular basis.

Issue: there is substantial turnover of vendor staff assigned to the project

Like your organization the vendor can experience turnover of staff. Because the vendor may have no extra or spare resources, this can have a major impact.

How this occurs

A person who works for the vendor may desire more stability and steady work. They may not like the pressure or being moved between organizations. They may seek a position with higher pay from a user of the technology. They may be attracted by one of the vendor's competitors.

Potential impact

When a person leaves a project, you not only lose the set of hands, you also lose that person's mind, experience, knowledge, and expertise. This is a problem with internal staff. With vendor staff there may be warning. The people may just stop showing up or the pace of their work slackens. It has happened. You as the customer may be the last to know. You may be left with vague assurances that the problems will be handled.

How to prevent the problem

As project leader, track the mood and temperament of vendor staff. If you sense dissatisfaction, you have several options. You can consider hiring them yourself. However, you may be precluded from doing this by contract. You may want to talk to vendor management. However, this can make the situation worse. Perhaps, you may continue to track the problem and work with the person so as to transfer his or her knowledge to your staff.

How to address the problem

Assume that turnover will occur. When it happens unexpectedly, assess the damage internally. Carefully identify what you expect from the vendors. Then contact the vendor and follow up. Strive for as continuous coverage as possible.

Issue: there are delays in vendor responses to problems, affecting the project

There is a problem in the project with the vendor's product. It may require in-depth technical support or a fix. The project can be held up.

How this occurs

The vendor staff may be stretched thin. They may feel that your problem is unique and so they assign it a lower priority because it does not affect other customers. They may also lack the expertise to deal with it. The problem may involve products of other vendors. The vendor could have even contracted out that area of the technology. All of these can produce a non-response.

Potential impact

The project team is forced now to work only on tasks that are not impacted by the problem. These may not be the most important tasks. The schedule can slip like sand through your fingers.

How to prevent the problem

Design a problem-handling process at the start of the project with the vendor. Try to find out how the vendor's internal problem-resolution process works and what methods are used. The more you know, the easier it will be for you to navigate within the vendor's organization.

How to address the problem

When a problem occurs, get right on top of it. Don't let up for a minute. Otherwise, the vendor may think that you do not think that the problem is important. Establish an escalation process within your organization before a problem surfaces.

Issue: the vendor's staff members are locked into their own methods, which are incompatible with the project

This can occur with planning, reengineering, and other consulting types of work. You thought that you were hiring experience, expertise, and knowledge. To your chagrin you find that you are getting mainly a method and not the experienced staff.

How this occurs

Vendors often train their staff in their own methods. This has a number of advantages. First, they present a standard front to any problem. Second, the vendor staff appear more interchangeable. More importantly, they believe that the method provides a competitive edge. When you select them for the project, you may fail to understand how they are dependent on their method and how it fits into the project.

Potential impact

The result can be a lack of fit between the method of the vendor firm and the situation at the customer firm. This can yield continuous conflict. Either the project is restructured around the method, or the method is dropped or modified. The project team members from the customer firm must take time out from the project to learn the method and then educate others as well. The method and consultant may be dropped because the project received a false start.

How to prevent the problem

Spend time understanding the method. See how it meshes with your culture and environment. Work with the vendor on the project schedule to see what the impact is of learning the method on the schedule. The method as well as the vendor is evaluated during the proposal stage.

How to address the problem

The method turns out to be a problem. It seems that the vendor is force fitting the project situation into the method. The reverse is the right course. Your staff lacks both experience and confidence in the method. What should you do? Consider killing the use of the method before more damage is done.

Issue: the project is overdependent on the vendor

Dependence on the vendor can be for the vendor's products or knowledge and expertise. It is a necessity for software, hardware, and network components.

How this occurs

You become overdependent when you cannot make project decisions and must rely on the vendor for tactical and strategic direction. This can arise because the internal staff are not adequately trained in the technology. It can also happen because you outsourced the technical support.

Potential impact

You can lose control of the schedule and the project. Confusion can reign among your own staff while the vendor calls the shots.

How to prevent the problem

Define vendor dependencies as well as the vendor's role at the start of the project. Review these roles with your team. Make the role part of the agreement. Think about a backup approach. Solicit the team's support in monitoring the vendor's work.

How to address the problem

If a problem arises, you must meet with the vendor manager to review roles and responsibilities. You may want to define a plan for transitioning some duties from the vendor to internal staff. You may also wish to involve more than one vendor to obtain backup support.

Issue: vendors don't cooperate among themselves

How this occurs

More IT projects involve several vendors, consultants, or contractors. ERP, E-Business, and process improvement projects are examples. Each vendor typically looks out after their own interests. They may not have estimated or taken into account working with other vendors in the project. Thus, they may be reluctant to cooperate with each other.

Potential impact

The potential problems can slow the project down and create political problems within the team and with management and business units. In some severe cases, the projects have actually been cancelled.

How to prevent the problem

Define at the start before the vendors are brought on board the project what you expect in terms of them working together. But this is not enough. You also have to have them work on issues and common tasks together. Try to identify these issues and tasks early and then have the vendors work together. Monitor their work and how they get along. You are after instilling a successful pattern of working together.

How to address the problem

If the problem arises, you should identify specific issues and instances of problems and then work on these. Don't try to address the problem generally—it probably will not work because of the generality. By addressing and solving specific issues you can work on building up the cooperative behavior.

Issue: vendor subcontracts out the work and then disappears

How this occurs

This occurs when the main vendor lacks the expertise and/or staff and has to bring in a subcontractor. In such cases, the vendor manager may not set up how the subcontractor is to work with the client firm. Problems begin to mount, but because the vendor is not on the scene, the problems get worse.

Potential impact

The progress of work can slow down. Subcontractor staff may make promises and commitments that cannot be honored by the contractor. Misunderstandings with business unit managers and staff can arise. Sorting it out directly with the subcontractor will probably fail unless you get the vendor involved.

How to prevent the problem

Define at the start whether and how any subcontracting will be done. Then the method for managing and dealing with subcontractors will have to be addressed. After the subcontractors are lined up, identify potential problems in meetings with both the vendor and the subcontractors. Define how these problems will be addressed. Monitor the initial work of the subcontractors closely to head off problems.

How to address the problem

If the problem is detected, then you should immediately involve the main vendor and implement the issues management approach discussed here and in previous chapters.

Issue: vendor uses what they did on your project with their next client

How this occurs

This may occur in E-Business where the vendor takes the analysis results or code and uses it to gain an advantage over other firms in bidding for the next job. This next job could be a competitor. People have after all a natural tendency to employ their experience as they move on to more work.

Potential impact

If competitive information is involved, this is serious and may call for legal remedies. In less severe situations, you may find that the staff who worked with you are gone and that when you require additional assistance, you receive resources that lack the experience.

How to prevent the problem

To prevent the problem you should first assess the type of work that they are doing and what the risks are to your organization. If there is no potential problem, then you can move on. If there is a problem, you can beef up the contract. Another better step is to raise this as an issue with the manager of the vendor firm and determine how it will be detected, prevented, and addressed.

How to address the problem

Each situation for this issue is unique. While legal action may be needed, the major club that you have with the vendor is future work and references. You can employ these to get some control over the situation.

Issue: vendor turns over work products that are not usable

How this occurs

There may be junior staff assigned by the vendor. The vendor manager on your account may not be reviewing their work closely. He or she may be concentrating on marketing to other firms. It may be that their earlier work was not carefully reviewed. Maybe they thought that you really didn't care. Another situation is when the client firm has no one technically on the staff who can evaluate their work.

Potential impact

Unacceptable work can mean later rework. This affects both the schedule and budget. It also creates management problems between the vendor and the client firm.

How to prevent the problem

At the very start you should identify what constitutes acceptable work. You should also define an evaluation approach for assessing their work and review it with the vendor. Then when the initial work comes in, you should evaluate it in detail. Another tip is to employ a single consultant if you do not have the appropriate person on board.

How to address the problem

Raise the quality of work right away as an issue the first time you notice a problem. In addition, take steps to implement a review process.

Questions

1. Search the literature and Web to find examples in the following areas:
   - Vendor identification.
   - Vendor evaluation.
   - Vendor selection.
   - Contract negotiation.
   - Managing vendor work.
   - Issues, decision-making, and actions involving vendors.
   - Measuring vendor performance.
   - Evaluating vendor work.
   - Turnover of work and knowledge from vendors.

2. Search the Web and literature for guidelines in the above areas.
3. Research the Web on the issue: internal staff are jealous of the vendor staff.
4. Research the Web on the issue: the vendor goes over the head of the project leader to upper management.
5. Research the Web on the issue: the vendor continues to interpret project issues differently from the project leader.

What to do next

1. For each major vendor, develop a list of issues that you have addressed or that are pending with the vendor. Review your approach for issue resolution with each vendor. Look for any patterns that indicate where you can improve your approach to dealing with vendors.
2. Assume that critical vendor staff were to be reassigned or become unavailable. What would be your backup plan?

Summary

Outsourcing in IT can now constitute 25 percent to over 50 percent of the total systems budget. Once you outsource, you lose control while, perhaps, gaining skills, flexibility, and technical support. However, success requires not only careful planning at the start, but also constant monitoring and measurement.

25

Global, cultural, and political issues

Introduction

Global projects have become common in the past 20 years with the growth of multinational corporations. However, if you look back into history, you can find examples of global projects related to the growth and expansion of empires: Persian, Roman, Chinese, Mongol, and more recently British. Global projects have always presented a challenge. A good portion of that lies in cultural and political factors. Such factors are shared with that of local projects. Project management, if successful, results in the implementation of the results of the work. The key word here is Change. That is why change management is so closely linked to project management as well as to process improvement. The methodologies such as PRINCE2 recognize change and change management as part of their processes. If you successfully complete a project, that does not mean it was successful. To be successful, change must occur. While there are many issues related to global projects, culture, and politics, space allows us to limit these to some of the most common.

Issue: there are project teams in different countries and cultures

How this occurs

For many years and even to some extent today, global projects are often treated the same as local projects. One reason is that the management thinks that their hierarchical structure and discipline can handle any cultural issues. Unfortunately, this is not the case. At the core of the issue is the fact that the management and staff in a specific country face issues that are similar to, but not identical to, those faced in the headquarters country. Culture here includes factors such as:

- Attitudes toward work.
- Commitment to projects versus their other work.

- Existing standards and procedures within a country.
- Value structure.
- Ability and willingness to participate in work in a team.

In one project we worked on in Mauritius, many of the employees took Friday off to go to the beach and not to work. That left four days of real work. Now you could try to insist that employees work the full five days, but soon you would realize that this would be like "paddling a canoe upstream". So the approach was to focus on the four days of productive work. Fridays were centered on lessons learned, issues, and training.

Political issues are major problems and are not addressed by the methodologies discussed in previous chapters. Here are some examples of political issues:

- People often tend to resist change brought about by a project.
- If the project is successful, some managers may fight over taking credit for the project.
- Team members can fight over assignments and getting management visibility. They can also struggle for credit and recognition.

Potential impact

If these cultural and political factors are ignored, then the project will suffer. Through-out much of the project, management may gloss over these or interpret the issues as technical or business issues. This is reinforced in project management classes and seminars which gloss over or ignore the political and social implications of projects. As such, they may address symptoms, but the underlying problems keep recurring. Examples of this occurred when auto makers, retailers, and other firms expanded or introduced new products or expanded into new countries. Wal-Mart experienced this in their initial expansion into Latin America. The impact of not recognizing or solving the issues include the following: project failure, project delays, and project implemented but insufficient change to warrant the project cost.

How to prevent the problem

One step in prevention is to identify potential cultural and political issues at the very start of the project. This is useful since the work has not started and people tend to be more calm and detached. There is another benefit in that you can involve the relevant managers in each country and get them to start working together. Better to do this before the project starts than to run into problems after the start. From experience, we have first circulated a list of potential cultural and political issues and then had the managers comment, add, and respond to the list. This often led to establishing more formal communications procedures related to issues, status, review of work, and so on. It also increased awareness of political and cultural factors.

How to address the problem

Let's suppose that work on the project has begun. A new issue or issues surface. You could choose to deal with the specific issue(s). However, that is a local solution. It is better to treat these as symptoms of bigger problems. Taking this approach, you would review all current issues and identify new ones with an emphasis on cultural and political issues. Thus, you can get at the root causes of the issues that surfaced. If you identified potential issues at the start as mentioned in the previous section, then new issues are not likely to emerge. Rather, the so-called "new" issue will be a version or variant of one of the potential issues.

Issue: the business staff do not want the project

How this occurs

If management wants the project, then the employees in business units and departments should go along, right? They may say they support the project, but deep down, they perceive the project as a threat to the *status quo*. An international project can be accepted in some countries, be indifferently received in others, and rejected in still other countries. Most people are comfortable in the work they do and do not feel that they should change. They feel change will just mean more work and effort for the same pay. Some may feel that their informal power is threatened by the project. This is because projects result in change; change can alter the power structure in a business unit.

Potential impact

In many methodologies this is not addressed. It is assumed that if management wants the project, the business staff and employees will go along. If you ignore the issue and assume this is true, then you could get a rude awakening later when results of the project are rolled out to the business units. They will raise many questions and problems. Technical managers and staff who don't think politically may then want changes to the project work instead of identifying and resolving their questions. Yet, what may be needed is to deal with the resistance to change. There may not have to be any project changes at all. The situation can get worse. If the employees succeed in delaying the project through the above methods, they may continue to try to disrupt the project by raising more questions and issues. Their underlying goal may to have the project fail altogether. The project manager and team then can be caught in an endless cycle that ends when the project timeline runs out.

How to prevent the problem

You should assume at the start of the project that at least some of the employees will resist the change that the project brings. You should raise this as a possibility with management before work begins on the project. Raise it also with the team. When work starts, you should consider raising the potential issue with the business employees. To head it off, the benefits of the project have to be clearly explained to the employees in terms of the benefits to them rather than just to management. Examples are the elimination of routine work and being able to perform their work without supervisory assistance.

How to address the problem

Once the project is on and you note that there is resistance to the change and project, here are some steps you can take. Gather the team together and determine how widespread the problem is. Consider holding a meeting to go over how the new work will be performed after the project is completed and the changes are implemented. Get the business employees to focus on the future and not on current tasks. This will help take the pressure off the project tasks.

Another approach is to find some business employees who support the change and clearly understand how the future work will be done. Use these people as "reference sells" to the other employees.

Issue: senior business employees undermine the project

How this occurs

Let's suppose that you have been an employee in a business department for over 10 years. You have seen supervisors and managers come and go. More junior employees come to you for assistance and advice. Supervisors also seek out your advice and experience. You have informal power and you enjoy it. Now management and IT come along with a project that will change the work in your department. Your job will be affected. Your informal power will diminish. How do you feel? In such cases, it is not unusual to find the senior business people see little or no benefit to themselves from the project or from their participation in the project. Even if management supports the project, we have found that in over half of the projects we have managed or been involved in, this occurs. It is natural in that, just like the employees, they feel threatened.

Potential impact

Many projects are often dependent on the cooperation and information that the senior business employees possess. They need to incorporate their knowledge of business rules into a new business process and/or system. If they do not cooperate or only partially participate, then the project schedule and budget will be negatively impacted. Moreover, problems are likely to surface in the late stages of a project as more information on business rules and practices dribbles out.

It can get worse. The senior people can encourage resistance by junior employees by being negative on the project. They see no need for change—so why should not the junior people feel the same? The project is undermined.

How to prevent the problem

This is such a serious and often common problem that it should be addressed at the very start of the project. You should assume until shown otherwise that the senior people will attempt to undermine the project.

Experience has shown that "the best defense is a strong offense". Thus, you would want to take steps to get the senior business staff on the side of change resulting from the project. Most of the time the advice given to you is to pitch the benefits of the project in general. However, this can fail since the benefits cited are for management and are too general. What is key is to define how employees' jobs and roles will change. This is not only more understandable, but also can generate more enthusiasm since they can get a vision of their future. The second part of this is to get people to understand the problems in the current situation. This will help them to see why change is needed.

How to address the problem

In several projects we turned around, the problem surfaced because the senior people thought that their working lives after the project was completed would be worse. We employed the guidelines under the prevention heading above to turn the situation around. We also involved senior business employees in training and coaching of the junior staff.

Issue: there is political conflict between different business departments

How this occurs

In organizational design it is often useful to have departments that have different views and purposes which seem to conflict. This is part of the checks and balances in an organization. This is especially true in international organizations where there are often conflicts between headquarters and local business units and departments. Headquarters wants consistency in the implementation of projects along with some level of standardization. Local units want some autonomy in how projects are done and results are implemented locally. Both are right.

Potential impact

These conflicts appear in the appearance of issues. For example, tures are said to be unsuitable in country X. The immediate impact enlargement of active issues for the project. This then takes time away from overseeing the work by the project leader. Since political issues are often intractable, the amount of time consumed can be very substantial.

If the issues cannot get resolved, a project can die. The project implementation can also be dropped from certain countries. The benefits of the project are diminished.

How to prevent the problem

At the start of the project, you should define the roles of the various departments involved. For global projects you should identify the roles of headquarters as well as that of local, in-country managers.

Another step is, at the start of the project, to establish two groups or task forces. One deals with issues that surface. The second is to share lessons learned about the project during project work. This was done successfully in the rollout of DirecTV in Latin America. For the issues task force the first order of business is to simulate how some common issues will be resolved. This will clearly define the issue management process.

How to address the problem

The conflict between business units will appear through new issues. You should be ready and anticipate these. Remember from earlier in the book the last thing a project leader wants is a surprise. These tend to be unpleasant.

Instead of working on the new issue, research the issue to determine the underlying cause as well as to identify related issues. If you see that there is political basis to the issues, then you should consider identifying these as such to management. This can avoid issue avoidance and can help address multiple issues at the same time.

Issue: some people are adverse to taking chances

How this occurs

This can be a cultural factor. In some countries there is a very conservative streak in which citizens are told about all the risks if they take a chance on something new. Locally in a company many people are risk adverse since they have a comfort zone in the work they are doing right now.

Potential impact

You should assume that most are unwilling to take chances. This applies not only to business employees, but also to technical staff and team members. The latter is often very comfortable with the methods and tools that they employ. They have a lot of time and effort invested in these and do not want to change.

The impact of inertia or unwillingness to change often leads the leader and team to only consider standard solutions. For example, for many IT staff the solution to user problems often only lies in IT solutions. Projects often ignore simpler, more direct solutions. There is substantial wasted project effort in programming exceptions to work that could have been eliminated.

How to prevent the problem

In projects involving business departments have the team trained in the basic work of the department. Then hold meetings to uncover some of the problems faced by the business employees. Then have the attendees define small changes that can be made to ease the problems. These are called "Quick Hits" or "Quick Wins". This exercise shows both the business and technical staff that there are other approaches to problem solving beyond a systems solution. Another benefit is that the project team better understands the business.

How to address the problem

Unwillingness to change often will not show up in the early stages of the project. Many people do not take the project seriously then. It more frequently shows up later when project results and systems are shown to people. You should anticipate this. When it does surface go back to the problems in the current work and the impacts that will continue to occur if the project results are not implemented.

For the team members the problem surfaces in the resistance or half-hearted acceptance of new methods or tools. To address this use a similar approach as for the business employees. Show what happens if the new methods and tools are not used effectively rather than just the benefits of the new methods and tools.

Issue: the project team is spread over different time zones

How this occurs

Not much has to be said here. This is just a characteristic of global projects.

Potential impact

The impact most often falls on the project leader. We have seen the wear and tear on project leaders first hand many times. One project leader had project teams in Europe, Asia, and North America. The guy tried to be available at all times. His wife threatened to divorce him if the situation continued. This was despite email, instant messaging, and video conferencing.

How to prevent the problem

If you have a global project, then you should plan at the start on how you will communicate on the following while getting a decent night's sleep.

- Planning for work;
- The use of methods and tools;
- Status determination and reporting;
- Milestone reviews;
- Project change control;
- Resource and work management;
- Issues management.

For each of these, walk through a simulation with the managers in different countries so that there is a common understanding.

The next step is to plan how to deal with emergencies and exceptions. Here you can give some examples and discuss what could be done if these arose.

How to address the problem

The problem will surface when there starts to be off-hours contacts. It just starts with a few incidents. Then it expands to cover regular work since this is most comfortable to the managers and employees in the remote location. You need to keep the contacts in off-hours to real exceptional situations.

While you can use e-mail, video conferencing, and other means of communication, there is still nothing like face-to-face contact. If you notify the remote office that you will be showing up, they will be ready and you may just get a canned set of information. This happened with a female project leader in Singapore. We advised her to have unscheduled visits so that she could get the truth. She did this, was surprised at how bad the situation was, and took corrective action.

Issue: the same problems seem to keep recurring

How this occurs

When a problem surfaces, it is often dressed in either or both technical and business clothing. The tendency is then to treat the problem that way. Later, you find that the issue recurs and just keeps coming up, dressed differently. Underneath it is the same issue. This happens because many are taught to take the issue as is and not to probe further. This is especially true for political and cultural issues.

Potential impact

The impact on the project leader can be substantial. Time is consumed dealing with the symptom issues, rather than the root cause. More of the symptom issues appear, more time is consumed.

How to prevent the problem

The approach for prevention is to assume that each issue that surfaces is a symptom not the cause. For example, if your child says he or she does not want to go school because of a headache or upset stomach, probe deeper and see what is happening at school to give rise to the symptom. If you let the student stay home, he or she may try another excuse next time since that one worked before.

Beyond looking for the root issues, at the start of the project make a list of cultural and political issues. Then when a new issue appears, try to map to one of these issues. Then look at the other open issues and see if they are related to each other.

How to address the problem

The best advice here is to follow the steps in prevention.

Issue: there are language barriers in the project team

How this occurs

While English is the common language in many projects, this does not eliminate the problems resulting from language. Language and its use are affected by culture. This means that the same terms and phrases that are very common get interpreted differently in different countries and cultures.

Let's take an example. Suppose that you are a project leader in Europe and are managing an outsourced software development effort in Asia. You go to the Asian development team and hold meetings. You review the project requirements. They seem to understand because they nod their heads and keep saying "Yes." Several months later you return and conduct a review. They show you parts of the new system and it does not match the requirements. You state that there are requirement problems. They say "Yes, yes."

Potential impact

This problem or issue(s) frequently occurs in outsourcing arrangements—even within one country. You can see the impact of the issue from the example. In the example there will have to be substantial rework, extra work—impacting both the schedule and the budget.

How to prevent the problem

At the start of the work, raise the language issue and give examples such as the one in this section. Have a discussion on how to ensure that messages are conveyed accurately. Perform several simulations on status and issues to verify that there is a common understanding.

How to address the problem

When you are trying to work through an issue or status, get down to the actual work. At the detailed level, we have found that there are fewer language problems. Have them give examples to ensure that there is a common understanding.

Issue: the team members are torn between their in-country duties and the project

How this occurs

After you read this issue, you might think, "Look management at headquarters is paying for the project and they run the company. Therefore, they call the shots and set priorities." This sounds OK, but reality is often very different.

Team members in remote locations already have existing duties. The project work is in addition to their regular work. Often, their regular work is driven by events—event- or incident-driven. This takes time away from the project work. Moreover, it is urgent and has to be done NOW to keep the business running.

Potential impact

The most direct impact is that less time is available to the project than was planned. This can affect quality of work, the schedule, and the budget. There is also the ancillary impact of loss in morale as the project slips and nothing or little is getting done.

How to prevent the problem

Before the project starts and is just getting organized, raise the resource management issue. Raise the level of awareness to this issue. Point out that conflicts of interest are natural given limited remote resources and pressing needs. Develop a strategy for the following:

- How and what resources will be allocated to the project;
- How the time of the resources will be divided between non-project and project work;
- How emergencies will be handled;
- How resource changes and substitutions will be accomplished.

How to address the problem

If this issue becomes active, one tendency is to show up at the remote location and take control of the team. This is a bad idea for several reasons. First, there can be multiple locations. You cannot be everywhere at once. Second, you demean the local project leader when you take over. Third, you confuse the reporting relationships in the organization between headquarters and the remote site.

A better approach is to show up and go through resource allocation with the project leader and in-country management. Get to the project level overall and not to individual tasks and work. When you get commitments to the project, then you should explore what will happen if emergencies arise. This is key since it is possible, even likely, that the remote location management will revert to their old ways.

Questions

1. Search the literature and Web to find examples in the following areas:

    - Project identification across multiple countries.
    - Project definition and the project concept on an international scale.
    - Global team acquisition.
    - Communications across multiple countries.
    - Determining status of a global project.
    - Managing work on a global basis.
    - Dealing with issues for a global project.
    - Evaluating milestones for a global project.
    - Implementing project results on a global basis.
    - Gathering lessons learned for a global project.

2. Search the Web and literature for guidelines in the above areas.
3. Research the Web on the issue: organizations in different countries use different methods and tools.
4. Research the Web on the issue: there are steady and constant communications issues.
5. Research the Web on the issue: decisions are not implemented consistently in different countries.

What to do next

1. For a current or recently completed project, review the list of issues. Try to map these to the political and cultural issues. You will probably find that several issues that you thought were unrelated to each other were in fact just symptom issues of underlying cultural and political issues.
2. Start with the list of issues in this chapter and expand this to get a more comprehensive list of political and cultural issues. Then employ this as a checklist at the start of your next project.

3. For your current and future projects, try to include more change management concepts and methods to deal with resistance to change.

Summary

Political and cultural issues are often not treated in classes, seminars, or books. Yet, they often represent the root causes of many business and technical problems. We have a database of over 450 issues and those related to politics and culture constitute the largest group in the database.

26
Quality issues

Introduction

"Quality" in most books and articles, and for most people applies to the end products of the work in the project. However, quality has specific meanings for each project and within each project. Quality also applies to the project plan, the work, the end products, communications, and other aspects of the project. Here we discuss a number of issues based on the more general application of the term.

Quality problems in IT work are often difficult to detect. You would have to exhaustively test programs, develop test scripts, and so on. Often, this is not feasible. As was suggested in Chapter 13 on Project Quality, you can resort to indirect means to detect quality problems. For example, let's suppose that a system analyst has prepared requirements and you are reviewing them for accuracy and quality. Use the body language and tone of voice guidelines in Chapter 11 on Project Communications to provide clues as to which areas may potentially have problems.

In terms of prevention of quality issues, many times problems result from miscommunications and misunderstandings. For example, a business employee gives a requirement to the system analyst who in turn conveys it to the project leader. Then the designers and programmers are told. There can be many errors in the transfer of information. From experience, it is best to have the project team understand the business process through limited training. Another measure of prevention is to have reviews with users prior to development work.

Issue: it is difficult during planning to deal with project quality

How this occurs

During project planning, you define the major end products for the work. Often, people concentrate on the final end products of the project in terms of quality. Quality of the plan, the interim milestones, and the work too often is not given adequate attention. There is too much time pressure to get the plan completed and approved.

Potential impact

If quality of the work and major end products is not addressed, there will likely be problems later—not only at the end, but also during the project. Team members, vendors, management, business units, and the project leader may have different definitions of quality. This is particularly true with outsourced projects. The impacts can lead to major rework and extra effort that was not included in the plan. The project schedule slips; the budget grows. Morale sinks.

How to prevent the problem

A key to prevention is to pose the question, "What constitutes minimal acceptable levels of quality?" You first ask this of the final end products of the project. You do this from three perspectives: business units/customers, management, and IT. The business unit/customer view is based on the new business processes that change due to the project work. The management view is often in terms of process performance and costs. The IT view is based on maintenance and operations. You would then expand from the final end products to major milestones. Here there are often two perspectives: business unit/customer and IT.

How to address the problem

If quality problems occur at the end of the project, then you should concentrate on the minimal work required for the project changes to be implemented. Other fixes will have to be done in maintenance or, even, as a new project.

If quality problems occur during the project, then you have some time to determine what to do. You would concentrate on the minimal level of acceptable quality. In addition to rework and project changes, you want to implement a new emphasis on quality reviews for later work.

Issue: it is hard to determine the appropriate level of quality

How this occurs

As has been stated, "quality" is a general term, like risk. It depends on perspective and the position and role of the person. People often ignore this until some major milestone is reached. Unfortunately, it is often too late. This happened in a different context with a friend of ours who was having a custom house built for his family. We advised them to stay on top of the work every day. Instead, they took a vacation for a month. To their discomfort and pocket books, they later found many problems—the sources of which occurred during their vacation. The major problem was that the air conditioning and heating were not properly installed which required jack hammers of the foundation and major rework. This consumed two additional months during which time they could not live in their house. Not to mention lawsuits with the contractor and subcontractors.

Potential impact

In many IT projects quality is not covered in detail until it is too late. The results are the same as in the last issue—problems with the budget, schedule, and morale.

How to prevent the problem

At the start of the project identify the major end products and identify what constitutes the minimal level of acceptance. Since this is often too general, turn to a discussion of what is unacceptable quality from a business unit and process view. Then move into a discussion of IT work. Expand this then to include the work and methods and tools.

How to address the problem

After the project starts and you can see during meetings that quality is not discussed or there are different viewpoints, start holding meeting and one-on-one contacts to focus on quality. Ignoring this is at your and the project's peril.

Issue: there is a lack of tools to assess work quality

How this occurs

Good examples of this are at the earlier stages of the project and toward the end during testing, integration, and implementation. There are more tools that relate to the software, training materials, and end user documentation. Determining the quality of requirements is more difficult and to some more abstract. Thus, quality does not receive the additional attention that should be given to it.

Potential impact

If you have uneven quality, then you pay the price later. For example, let's suppose that the quality of requirements is poor. This can lead to misunderstanding during design, development, and implementation. It is a cascading effect.

How to prevent the problem

During planning at the start of work along with the planning that goes on during the project, have specific meetings devoted to quality. Identify areas where quality is difficult to assess. Rather than talk about the positive aspects of quality, discuss the negative side. Have people identify potential quality problems based on their previous experience. Use lessons learned to uncover what they did in the past. Also, get some idea of the impacts of the quality problems in past work. That should raise the fear factor so that the team will take quality seriously.

How to address the problem

The problem often surfaces when there is a milestone completed, but there is no clear idea of how to review quality. Examples are requirements, testing plans, and implementation plans. You could spend hours trying to brainstorm quality approaches. A bad idea—takes too long. Instead, focus on how things could go wrong later. Make a list of these. Then map backward into the content of the milestone.

Issue: there is no time to evaluate all end products

How this occurs

We have said many times that time is the worst enemy of projects, more than money. If management gives you more money, they usually want something in return, often faster results. The issue most frequently occurs in projects where there has been a lack of forward planning on issues. Then each milestone has to be examined as to whether there should be a quality review.

Potential impact

Assuming that the issue arises, it typically turns up repeatedly each time a milestone is completed. This can delay the project. Moreover, it diverts the project leader from doing other work.

How to prevent the problem

At the start of the project you should identify the potential issues with the work tasks and milestones. During the project the issues are updated along with their status. The presence of issues can help you to rate the milestones and work for quality reviews. This avoids the *ad hoc* approach of doing it for each milestone.

How to address the problem

If you find that you are asking yourself, "Should this be reviewed for quality?" or saying, "There is too much to review in terms of quality." then you know that you have a problem. You should take steps to identify all issues with not only the current work and milestones, but also the future ones as well. Follow the steps in prevention.

Issue: how do you assess quality for work in progress?

How this occurs

Team members accept their tasks. They report back on progress—often in terms of percentage complete. We have seen that this is a bad measurement. The problem often occurs with junior project leaders who may be intimidated by technical members of the team. They just accept what they are told and hope for the best. Related to this is the fact that it is more complex and difficult to measure work in progress as opposed to completed work.

Potential impact

If you have no method for reviewing the work being done, you are more subject to being surprised in a negative way later. Miscommunications, lack of skills, being over-committed, and other factors can lead to problems. The impact goes beyond rework, additional work, and so on. It also reduces or eliminates the trust and confidence that the project leader and other team members have for a specific person in the team.

How to prevent the problem

If you are doing a project where the team location allows for face-to-face meetings, then you should go to each team member individually and ask, "How is the work going?" Use the tips on tone of voice and body language to see if they are having problems. For example, if they look away or down and talk in a low voice, this may be a sign of problems. By going to their office or cubicle, you can see what they are working on by viewing their desk surface.

An additional step is to ask them what they have learned so far. Have they experienced any surprises? Is there any change in the issues?

Then you can consider asking questions about their time. Ask what else they are working on. Ask what is causing them to spend more time on certain things.

How to address the problem

If you get surprised by a team member after he or she said multiple times that everything was fine, don't lose trust in them. Use the techniques under prevention with them. Also, show up more frequently at their office. Have more meetings with them. This shows that you are serious about the work. Ask if they need help or advice. This attention change will send a clear message to the other team members that you are taking the work quality seriously.

Issue: work quality in the project is of mixed quality

How this occurs

People on a project team have different levels of skills, ambition, motivation, and energy. This translates into a variation in the quality of work. People working on a project part-time may have less desire and energy for the project than full-time team members. This is natural and to be expected. The problem occurs because the project leader does not take this into account before and during the project.

One of the authors had three sons. At almost no time were they treated equally. At any one time, one or two had more problems in school, play and social activities than the others. You find that you have to throw fairness and equal time to get problems addressed.

Potential impact

If the project leader treats all team members equally, then you might have project democracy, but you are also more likely to have project failure. By devoting time to project team members who have little issues and whose work is routine, you are taking time away from other members who have issues and problems. These do not get attention and the impacts and surprises grow.

How to prevent the problem

At the start of the project you identified issues in the work and milestones. When you created the plan, you had the team members create their detailed tasks under the project template or work breakdown structure. At this time you can have them identify potential issues based on their lack of knowledge or experience. In that way you can determine where quality problems are likely to surface.

How to address the problem

If you are experiencing quality problems, review the list of issues for the tasks and milestones. Review the work of each team member to uncover more problems related to their work, experience, and knowledge. This will help you focus your attention and time in the future.

Issue: given the schedule and budget, it is difficult to improve the quality

How this occurs

Management often imposes unrealistic or tight budgets and schedules. It is sometimes and even common for the project leader to give these more attention than quality. Later quality problems surface.

Potential impact

The impact is that with less attention to quality, more quality problems will appear and this will impact both the schedule and the budget. Remember too that once the project starts, the team gets a vision of the quality expected by management and project leader.

How to prevent the problem

Use quality along with issues as trade-offs with management on both the budget and schedule. Try to define what is a minimal level of acceptable quality. In manufacturing this is defect analysis and standards.

In addition, think of potential countermeasures to potential quality problems in the future. How do you determine where the problems might surface? Use the list of potential issues for the tasks and milestones as a guide.

How to address the problem

The answer here depends on where the problem occurs in the project life cycle. If the problem occurs at the start or toward the middle of the project, then you can employ the guidelines under prevention. If the problem occurs late in the project, then you have to center your attention on what the minimal amount of work is to fix the problems or the most important parts of the problem. Unfortunately, to meet the deadlines some parts of the system will have to be fixed after the project. This is common enough that many projects have lingering issues after they are completed since people focus on "What is the minimum amount of work needed to go live with the system?"

Issue: quality issues surface after the work is completed

How this occurs

This relates to the previous issue. Quality issues appear after a project is completed for a number of reasons. One is that the requirements were incomplete or misunderstood. Another reason that is fairly common is that after exposure to the new system, the business unit staff and management see the need for more change to improve quality. This can be viewed as new requirements and is often more frequent than problems with the system.

Potential impact

One response to quality issues is to blame the project leader and team for the projects. This is misguided and does no good. The project is over and the people have moved on to other work. However, if the blame game starts, other project leaders will be reluctant to jump in to fix the problems.

For the business unit the quality problems may be sufficiently severe as to impact their use of the system. Expected benefits may not fully materialize.

How to prevent the problem

At the start of the project and throughout the work, the project leader should point out that many projects have lingering issues after the project is completed. They can give examples of roads and other infrastructure work. Let's suppose that a city is going to repave a street. They block or restrict traffic to do the repaving. They often lead faint white lines to indicate lanes and crosswalks. Traffic resumes. They later do the painting on the street. In that way traffic is less disrupted. For projects you also want to point out that after the project is completed, the attitude of the business unit staff to their jobs and work will change. This will then likely lead to requests for more systems work.

How to address the problem

As the work is completed, make a list of outstanding issues. Identify those that have to be fixed for minimal quality. Don't stop there. Take the rest of the list to the business unit manager and the IT manager and indicate that they may want to plan on how to deal with these later.

Questions

1. Search the literature and Web to find examples in the following areas:

   - Identifying and determining quality for the project.
   - Defining what is minimally acceptable quality of work.
   - Measuring quality of work in process.
   - Measuring and evaluating quality of completed work.
   - Dealing with quality problems for work in process.
   - Dealing with quality problems with completed work.
   - Modifying the project plan to incorporate rework and extra work due to quality problems.

2. Search the Web and literature for guidelines in the above areas.
3. Research the Web on the issue: there are different opinions as to what constitutes acceptable quality of work.
4. Research the Web on the issue: people waste too much time in reviewing routine work and milestones.
5. Research the Web on the issue: how to communicate with management on quality issues.

What to do next

1. For a recently completed project, identify quality issues that became active during the project as well as at the end. Identify any surprises related to quality. This will help you give more emphasis to quality in project planning and execution.
2. Examine the methods and tools for determining and assessing work quality during all parts of a project. Use this to identify the gaps and weaknesses in quality measurement.
3. On your current projects, hold separate team meetings on quality. For an upcoming significant milestone, hold a meeting with the team to discuss how quality will be assessed.

Summary

Unfortunately, it is often the case that quality issues do not have the same priority as other issues. This is probably because they are not as time pressing. This is one of the reasons for unpleasant surprises later in the project or after project completion. Quality issues should be treated equally with other issues. You can never assume everyone has the same idea of what constitutes minimal acceptable quality.

Part six
What to do next

27

How to implement improved project management

Introduction

This chapter begins the mission and vision of you and your work in projects. We and others have found that this can be valuable over the long and intermediate term.

A number of ideas and suggestions have been provided in the different chapters. Rather than attempting to use and implement these in a piecemeal way, consider using a more systematic approach. This is the subject of this final chapter. There are three time frames to consider. The first consists of near term quick hits that can be employed with little effort and hassle. The second consists of intermediate steps that can be taken after the quick hits. These draw upon the quick hits. The third category consists of the longer-term changes that complete the modernization of your project management process. For each we discuss the benefits and give tips on getting it started.

Implementing change of any significant kind is challenging. This can be even more apparent in IT projects that are political. Thus, we have included points of potential resistance to change and how to address these.

A vision for you

Let's assume that you are involved in projects or are a project leader. Do you have a vision of where you want to go and what you want to be relative to projects? This is an important question, because if you don't answer it, you may just move from project to project and never really advance.

What is your vision vis–a–vis project management in the next 5 years? What do you see as your involvement in projects? Here are some examples.

- You see yourself becoming a project leader for larger and more complex projects.
- You see yourself moving out of project management and into IT management.
- You see yourself as becoming an expert in project management who turns failing projects around and who guides others in their project work.

We initially chose the third one and turned around a number of failing project efforts. This worked well for 5 years, but then we got tired of it. It can be depressing if all you get is failing projects and projects in trouble. Then we reset the vision to the second one. We moved into IT and business management. This lasted for 10 years. Then again, we got tired of it so we moved to the first one as the vision.

If you have a vision, then you have direction. This can help guide you in deciding what projects you want to pursue as well as help in your project work.

Remember you, yourself, are your most important project. Thus, we recommend that you treat more of your everyday life outside of work as projects. We don't mean that getting gasoline or grocery shopping are projects. However, taking classes or seminars are. Planning and taking trips are projects. Learning a new skill or language is a project. Examples of our projects have been travel, learning to dance tango, and learning a foreign language. By merging your work and personal life in terms of projects and project management, you enrich both areas. You gain more expertise, lessons learned, and knowledge. This will make you more valuable at work and more productive at home. Life will become more enjoyable since you will get more out of life.

A vision for your projects

Let's move from you to your projects. What is your vision for your projects? You want them to be successful. What does "success" mean? To many it means getting the work done on time and within budget. It should mean that you successfully address issues such as the ones in the previous part of the book.

But that is not enough. You should include as part of the vision successful change in the business and organization as a result of the project. This may seem inappropriate since you often don't have control over what happens after the project. But as we have seen, you can plan, arrange, and orchestrate the situation so that the change occurs. One step to do this is to include the change within the scope of the project.

The mission of your project work

Let's move to your projects. Your goal should be CUMULATIVE IMPROVEMENT. What does this mean?

- You will get better at recognizing issues and addressing them.
- You will become better at estimation and creating project plans.
- Your project success rate will increase.
- You will be in greater demand as a project leader and member.
- In your future project work there will be fewer surprises.
- There should be fewer new issues since you should see the same ones recur again and again.
- Your interpersonal skills will improve with team members, management, vendors, and business units.

How do you determine how you are doing? Use the measurement checklists and scorecards of Chapter 15 as a starting point.

Quick Win implementation steps

Here is a list of things you can do right away. Note that these apply for whatever project management methodology you are using.

- **Identify the projects and non-project work.**

  You need to identify all of the work that critical staff are doing in order to allocate their time between regular work and projects. Attention must be given to smaller projects as well. Start with the approved projects and then identify the work performed by each staff member. This will pave the way for general reporting on routine tasks that are not part of a project.

- **Define and use the standardized project binder.**

  The tabs and contents of the project binder were identified in the book. By standardizing on the binder you can retain project files for reuse and lessons learned. The project binder can either be in paper or electronic form.

- **Customize the project management software and adopt standard abbreviations.**

  Customization is necessary in order to be able to use the data in a database type form. Custom data elements for issues, lessons learned, and so on can then be employed to filter and analyze project data. Without customization there is a lack of standardization and an inability to do multiple project analysis using project management software.

- **Establish a resource pool.**

  A common resource pool is necessary for multiple project analysis just as the customization above is. The pool contains both general and specific resources. In IT projects these resources are people related. However, in other applications you can identify calendar resources that allow you to customize the schedule down to the level of a specific task.

- **Create templates.**

  Recall that the approach to creating templates is to extract high-level tasks and gain consensus on the template. Existing project plans can then be retrofitted into the templates. Templates support both lessons learned and multiple project analysis. Templates also generate collaborative effort and a common understanding of tasks.

- **Identify a checklist of issues.**

  Start with the checklist in the appendix. Then add your own issues by identifying those of the current projects. Use the issues checklist at the start of each project in the project concept. As you find additional issues, add them to the checklist. The checklist reinforces the analysis and emphasis on issues.

- **Modify the approach to project meetings.**

  Several guidelines for project meetings were given. Meetings should focus on either issues or lessons learned. Status should be gathered prior to the meeting and summarized at the start of the meeting. Only team members involved in issues and lessons learned need to attend the meetings. Meetings can be held at a frequency based on the state of the project so that if the project is in trouble, there are more frequent meetings to resolve issues. By adopting these and the other guidelines your meetings will be more productive and get better results.

- **Standardize the reporting on projects.**

A one-page project reporting summary was identified along with issues analysis and various tables related to issues, projects, and business processes. Follow up on these. By having standardized reporting, management can focus on content of the information rather than trying to understand different formats.

- **Adopt templates and outlines for documentation and presentations.**

Start with your own projects and develop outlines for all major project documents and presentations with the team. Presentations should include status, budget, project concept, project plan, and issues meetings. Review the previous presentations and documents to see how they fit with the outlines and templates.

- **Set up a model project on the network.**

Having a project to review and use as a guide is very useful. You should establish a project on the network. The information should include the issues, lessons learned, project plan, and key events in the project. Encourage people to visit the site and provide comments.

- **Gather initial lessons learned from one or two projects.**

Use the guidelines in the book as ideas for you to gather lessons learned. You will normally identify experience that you gained. Then you will extract the lessons learned. This will provide structure for gathering lessons learned on a routine basis. Also, you will gain experience in establishing the lessons learned database.

- **Develop a project concept from an existing project.**

Take a current project and identify the business purpose, technical purpose, scope (business and technical), issues, roles, and benefits. Then review this to see how the project has changed. Pay careful attention to the scope and how it changed over time during the project. This will prepare you to develop the project concept for future projects.

- **Evaluate your contacts with managers and use a forward planning approach.**

Many of us get caught up in the daily work of projects and normal work. We often do not take time to assess our communications with management. Each week you should review what management contacts you had. You should also plan for contacts in the next week. This will raise your level of awareness and attention for management contacts.

- **Implement the project scorecard.**

Of the various scorecards presented (project, process, vendor, and business unit), the easiest one to start with is the scorecard for your project. On a monthly basis evaluate your project. You can use a spreadsheet in which the rows are the criteria and the columns are the months. You can then assess how you are doing and become more aware of measurement. You can see the forest through the trees.

- **Create a list of bookmarks for Web sites for project management and lessons learned.**

  Begin with the Web sites that we have included. On a regular basis add to these bookmarks. Print out the content and distribute these to your team.

Intermediate term actions

Let's now move to what you can work on after doing the short-term actions. Here is another list.

- **Using the issues information, create the issues graphs and tables.**

  Having begun to collect issues from projects you can now construct the graphs and tables developed in the book. This is good material for presentation to management. It is also useful to the project team to see the characteristics and trends of issues. It also paves the way for issues analysis later across projects.

- **Implement the project concept.**

  Having created a project concept out of a current project you can now implement the project concept as a structured approach to review project ideas. Try this out on smaller projects such as network extensions and upgrades, and enhancement requests.

- **Create the lessons learned database and relate it to the tasks in the template.**

  Previously, you had gathered lessons learned and created a template. Now you can implement the lessons learned database and link these lessons learned to the template. Review the project regularly to see if you can identify more lessons learned.

- **Set up and conduct meetings on lessons learned.**

  You have already modified the approach on meetings and are addressing issues. It is time to raise the level of awareness of lessons learned. Have team members give the results of their experience in team meetings. This should improve morale and facilitate information sharing.

- **Implement a collaborative approach in which team members define and update their own tasks.**

  With the template in place and the changes in project meetings you are prepared to have team members define their own tasks. Begin with a paper-based approach. Then after everyone is comfortable with this you can move on to updating the tasks by individual team members. Following this you can implement online task definition and updating by team members.

- **Scan the literature and collect information on project successes and failures.**

  Use the Web to gather lessons learned. We put this as an intermediate task since you will have gained experience in collecting lessons learned. Use magazines such as Information Week, Ziff-Davis Publications, and others. Circulate articles to the team members. Encourage them to search for articles as well on the Web and in print media.

- **Employ the process scorecard.**

    Previously, you had implemented the project scorecard. You can now assess the underlying business processes that your projects are supporting. Do this with team members casually as it will be politically sensitive. This work helps the team focus on tangible benefits of systems and technology and become more aware and focused on the business process. Suggest to management that this be implemented for new projects.

- **Use the vendor scorecard.**

    Another project measurement is the vendor scorecard. Begin with an internal assessment of vendor performance. Share it with the team and then with the vendor. Use the scorecard for new projects.

- **Formalize the approach of bringing new team members onto the project and getting them out of the team.**

    Often new team members are brought onto the project team in a casual way. Implement the structured approach that we have identified. Have them discuss their lessons learned from past projects with the team and assign joint tasks for them with other team members. This will support collaboration.

- **Review the methods and tools used in projects to assess their effectiveness and determine where you have gaps.**

    Create a table of methods and tools. For each area identify the methods, tools, experts to call on, guidelines, and expectations. Also, identify relevant lessons learned. This will support standardization.

Long-term steps

Building on both the short- and intermediate-term actions, you can begin to take more major steps. Here are some:

- **Begin to address the gaps in methods and tools in projects.**

    Having identified the current methods and tools, you will uncover the gaps in these. Work with the team and others in IT to fill the holes. This will begin to fill in the holes and encourage people not to invent their own.

- **Review projects and non-project work and eliminate those that do not contribute to critical business processes.**

    Now that you have identified the work being performed, you can move to eliminate or reduce work that does not add to the performance of the group. This supports focusing on critical activities.

- **Develop process plans to determine the long-term future of processes and use these to identify candidates for new projects.**

    Recall that a process plan is an approach for understanding the future direction of a business process. By developing these process plans you can get the users centered on the longer-term requirements for their business and away from submitting marginal requests.

- **Establish master schedules on the network for all projects.**

  With the templates in place and people updating the schedules, you are in a position to do multiple project analysis and create master schedules. This is a major step toward affecting the strategic direction of IT.

- **Implement a weekly or other regular resource allocations.**

  With the templates and a collaborative approach, there is a sufficient basis for holding meetings to allocate critical staff resources to project and non-project work on a regular basis. This will not only provide more consistent direction to the staff, but will also yield performance improvements.

- **Begin to involve team members in issues resolution.**

  Issues resolution follows from the collaboration in building and updating the project plan. Team members are now sharing lessons learned. Therefore, it is appropriate to get them involved in analyzing issues.

- **Develop a semiannual or annual report on business processes.**

  Previously, you have implemented the process scorecard. Drawing upon this you can start to analyze business processes on a regular basis. This will help both management, the business units, and IT to determine the most beneficial new project opportunities.

- **Implement comparative business unit assessments.**

  This is the scorecard for business unit involvement in projects. Begin doing the assessment and sharing it among IT managers. Then raise the level of awareness among business units for new projects by using the scorecard assessment. This should improve the business unit participation in the projects.

- **Review the list of issues and see if they can be eliminated or handled through lessons learned.**

  Now that you have been gathering and assessing various issues and lessons learned, it is time to consider seeing if some recurring issues can be headed off or prevented using lessons learned.

- **Develop an overall assessment of project effectiveness.**

  Taking the various scorecards, issues analysis, and lessons learned, you can begin to assess how effective project management and project performance are.

Points of potential resistance and what to do

Listed below are some potential areas of resistance to change in general. While this may appear negative, it is not. By reading this material, you become more aware of what arguments you may face and how to address them when they arise.

- **We have no time to learn and employ new methods.**

  People on projects are very busy. Some may feel that they do not have time to consider new project management approaches. However, if they keep doing the same things, there will be no improvement. Point this out. Also, indicate that the methods do not really take more time. Instead, they provide structure for what they are already doing.

- **Our situation is unique.**

This argument is employed to resist a template and standardization. The approach in the book is standardization at the higher levels of project activities and flexibility in the detail. They can still be unique in the detail.

- **You cannot force the use of a method or tool.**

No one wants to force people to do things. It does not work. The methods here support people's self-interest. They provide a framework for managing projects and doing project work.

- **We have tried something similar before and it did not work.**

This may be true. However, you will note that the method is composed of themes that are self-sustaining and supporting. Once you start using the techniques, you will establish successful patterns of behavior.

- **There are not enough resources to implement the changes.**

The approach can be implemented in small steps without any major change or upheaval. No additional resources are required.

- **Implementing a collaborative approach results in too many interfaces.**

When you collaborate, you do interface with people. However, there are no more interfaces that you would face without these methods.

- **There is no benefit in the approach.**

The approach has been successful in firms in many different industries, countries, and cultural settings. Improved productivity, morale, and performance are the most tangible benefits.

- **The method is too complicated.**

The approach is common sense. There is no jargon. It is a step–by-step approach.

- **Change will slow me down.**

By implementing the approach in small bite-sized parts, you should not be slowed down. Over time as you gain experience, you will become more efficient and effective.

- **Reduced scope to make decisions**

When structure is provided, some people may feel that they have less room to make decisions. The approach provides a general framework to address issues.

- **The approach is not how we do things.**

In general, the method does not change how you do your work. It provides a framework to support you in doing your work better.

- **The method restricts creativity.**

Creativity lies in the detail not in general activities. Creativity and flexibility are both supported in the templates, issues, and lessons learned.

- **Change in project management is threatening.**

  Any change is threatening to some people. This is understandable. Here we mitigate this by a phased approach to implementing the approach.

- **What's in it for me?**

  This is a key question and deserves some discussion. The approach frees you up to do more creative work. With the lessons learned your work quality and skills should improve. It should take you less time to do more routine tasks. Knowing that the same issues have been recurring gives some a feeling of comfort that you are not alone.

Summary

While technology changes and new business initiatives emerge, many characteristics of IT projects remain the same. The goal is to gather and employ lessons learned to reduce the overhead and increase the effectiveness in future systems and technology projects. You have seen how different IT projects are from regular projects. You have also seen the following themes throughout the book.

- Collaborative effort in defining, doing, and reviewing work.
- Managing multiple projects and normal, non-project work.
- Addressing issues across projects.
- Using the templates, issues and lessons learned databases, and other techniques to reduce the workload and make you more effective and efficient.
- Lessons learned to improve future performance.
- Joint ownership of project work by business units, IT, and vendors.
- Tracking and measurement of work and issues analysis.

Appendix 1: Project management software

There are over 50 project management software systems available. These can be divided into two groups. One is a group in which the software is proprietary. The other is that of open source. Project management software can either be Web-based or not. The majority are proprietary and Web-based. Full-featured project management software should support the following capabilities:

- Collaboration;
- Issue tracking;
- Scheduling;
- Project portfolio management;
- Resource management;
- Document management.

By far the most popular is Microsoft Project which comes in two versions. Microsoft Project is for single computer users. Microsoft Office Project Server supports multiple users in an organization. Both are proprietary. The stand-alone version supports scheduling and resource management and is not Web-based. The server version is Web-based.

Other full-featured project management software includes the following:

- AtTask. Proprietary and Web-based.
- BrightWork. Proprietary and Web-based.
- Clarizen. Proprietary and Web-based.
- Endeavor Software Project Management. Open source and Web-based.
- Easy Projects.Net. Proprietary and Web-based.
- Genius Inside. Proprietary and Web-based.
- HP Project and Portfolio Software. Proprietary and Web-based.
- Journyx. Proprietary and Web-based.
- Merlin. Proprietary and Web-based.
- Onepoint Project. Proprietary and Web-based.
- Planisware 5. Proprietary and Web-based.
- Primavera Project Planner. Proprietary and Web-based.
- Principal Toolbox. Proprietary and Web-based.
- Project.net. Open source and Web-based.
- Project-Open. Open source and Web-based.
- Projektron BCS. Proprietary and Web-based.
- PSNext. Proprietary and Web-based.
- SAP RPM. Proprietary and Web-based.
- Severa. Proprietary and Web-based.
- Teamwork. Proprietary and Web-based.
- Tenrox. Proprietary and Web-based.
- Workengine. Proprietary and Web-based.
- WorkLenz. Not Web-based and proprietary.
- Workspace.com. Proprietary and Web-based.

Since these software packages are updated, you should check the Web sites for the specific software.

You can find useful reviews of project management software at the Web sites listed in that section. Cnet.com has useful reviews as does techrepublic.com. Another useful site for reviews of Web-based software is web-based-software.com as well as bright hub.com. Another source is isoftwarereviews.com.

Other signs of popularity of project management software are available certification, available training, and the number and range of books available for the particular software package. Choosing a package that has a limited audience can bring problems in terms of available training and support as well as questioning on the selection. As a project leader or manager with many other things to do, this can be very distracting.

Appendix 2: War strategies applied to project management

Introduction

Carrying out military campaigns are examples of projects. Thus, it is useful to consider the works of some of the most-noted military strategists and works from history. Here we consider eight of these. The sources for further reading are as follows:

- Machiavelli, Niccolo and D. Donno. *The Prince*. Bantam Classics, 1984.
- Sawyer, Ralph. *The Seven Military Classics of Ancient China*. Basic Books, 1993.
- Von Clausewitz, Carl. *On War* (Translated by J. Graham). Bn publishing, 2007.

T'ai Kung

T'ai Kung's book is the *Six Secret Teachings*. He gave political advice to two kings Wen and Wu of the Chou dynasty in the eleventh century BC—over 3000 years ago. These rulers used his work to defeat the Shang dynasty which had ruled for 600 years. He is the first famous general and beginner of strategic studies in China. His book was written to support revolutionary activity wherein limited resources were employed to overcome a vastly superior enemy.

Here are a few of the themes in the book that apply to project management.

- Profit to involve and benefit people. This supports collaboration in projects.
- Serve by personal example. This defines part of the role of the project leader.
- Set goals versus focusing on pleasure each day. Using this we would adapt more of our lives to project structure.
- Consume as little resources as possible. This shows a focus on resource management.
- Among the 7 Harms avoid any magical formula and strange techniques. This applies to methods and tools used in projects as well as employing common sense.
- Focus on evidence when interviewing. Evidence here in interviewing potential team members would center on issues and lessons learned.
- To protect secrecy send letters in three parts. This is a warning in projects to be careful what you communicate.
- In evaluating work focus on what and how people work, not just results. This really applies to projects and project management.

Ssu-Ma Fa The Ssu-Ma Fa is a relatively brief text dating from about 400 BC. The term Ssu-Ma Fa means "The Methods of the Minister of War". The work covers policies, control, planning, values, and strategy. Here are some of the relevant points.

- Importance of training. This applies not only to methods and tools, but also to lessons learned.
- Balance between execution and exhaustion. This would suggest not to have a project "death march" or to storm the work to meet a deadline.
- One achieves victory by being endangered. In projects team members should feel that they have something to lose with failure.
- In defeat do not punish. Avoid scapegoat in failed projects.
- Carry a minimum amount of tools. Methods and tools need to be selected carefully and judiciously.
- Do not reward great victories. Avoid over-rewarding for project success as it can raise expectations.

Sun-Tsu

The *Art of War* is one of most popular books on warfare and has been employed in other contexts such as business and finance. It was employed by Napoleon as well as the Germans during World War II. The book was written around the period of 600–500 BC. Sun-Tsu's focus was on careful planning before any military action or campaign. In the book he deals extensively with command and control—with emphasis on the leaders as well as soldiers. Some of the ideas in this book are as follows:

- If instructions are not clear, it is the fault of the leader. This applies to project leaders who need to validate that their messages get across. This can be through examples, feedback, and simulations.
- Avoid battle without planning. This supports the need for a clear project plan.
- Avoid long campaigns. One should avoid large projects, if possible.
- Minimize risk and exposure. This applies to focusing on issues management.
- A general should not be interfered with by the ruler. This speaks to the relationship between management and project leaders.
- Know when to fight and when not to. This applies to issues management in projects.
- Commanding many is like commanding a few. The same project methods can apply to projects of all sizes. Problems arise for small projects which lack project structure.
- In battle one engages with orthodox methods and one gains victory with the unorthodox. During a project the project leader must be adaptive to changes.

Wu-Tzu

Wu-Tzu (also called Wu Ch' i) was a legendary figure in China linked to Sun-Tsu. He was never defeated in battle. He is viewed by many as China's first great general. His work has been valued as one of the foundations of Chinese military thought. Three principles from the work are as follows:

- Stress on support and logistics. The comparison here is to give adequate attention to methods and tools.
- Impartial assessment of situations. This supports the stance in this book that the project leader should be positive and neutral.
- Align with common people. The project should align with the people who will use the results of the project.

Wei Liao-Tzu

This work was named after Liao Wei. He lived during the period of Warring States in China. His focus was on integrating both civil and military aspects to achieve victory. He lived in the latter part of the fourth century BC. He was apparently not a commander, but a strategist. Five relevant ideas are as follows:

- When defining goals, be all-encompassing. Projects should not only have defined business and technical goals, but also ones related to politics and social areas.
- Establish small squads of men. This supports the use of small teams.
- Create certainty and stability. This can be aided by lessons learned and issues management.
- Must prepare for change. Projects are all about change. That is why change management is closely tied to project management.
- Foster commitment. This speaks to team involvement.

Huang Shih-Kung

The book here is referred to as *Three Strategies*. It is thought to have been written around 0 BC. The work focuses mainly on administration and control. Three levels of strategy are presented—upper, middle, and lower. Here are four points in the book.

- Once a decision is made, act decisively. You should focus on the actions stemming from the decisions as well as the decisions themselves.
- Different people need different rewards. This applies to the project team members so it is important to understand what each team member hopes to get from the project at the start of the work.
- Cultivate and build the image of authority.
- Combine weakness, strength, softness, and hardness. This applies to the project leader.

Carl Von Clausewitz

Von Clausewitz lived in the late eighteenth and early nineteenth centuries. He was a Prussian soldier and military theorist. He served in the Napoleonic Wars and was captured by the French. He then returned to Prussia in 1808 and aided in the reform of the Prussian army. He later served in the Russian army in 1812–1813. Some of his key points that apply to project management are as follows:

- Commanders have to be ready for new developments on the battlefield. This is the "fog of war". This applies to project leaders who have to be prepared for the unexpected event or new issues.
- "War is not merely a political act, but also a political instrument." This applies to projects by including both social and political factors.
- Lessons learned are most firmly learned when its application turns a failure into a success.
- Avoid dogmatism. This applies to having flexibility in projects.
- War combines science and art. The same applies to projects.

Niccolo Machiavelli

Machiavelli lived in the late 1400s to middle 1500s. He was an Italian philosopher who is considered to be one of the founders of modern-day political science. His business duties centered mainly in Florence where he was a government official and organized the city's militia. His most popular work is *The Prince* in which he skillfully gives many historical examples to support his points.

Today, many firms employ outsourcing and consultants. He distrusted and mercenaries and held these views. It is useful to keep these things in mind when involved in outsourcing.

- A nation can defend itself with arms that are its own, auxiliaries, mercenaries, or a mixture of all three. Of these, one of the worst choices is mercenaries.
- Mercenaries are disunited and without discipline: bold among friends, yet cowardly among enemies
- Mercenaries are loyal to the wage and not the prince.
- This problem is even more stark when one contemplates the mercenary captain. If he is a capable man, he may aspire to princehood and take the prince's own nation by force. This could apply to using consultants as project leaders.
- Mercenaries were viewed as being socially corrosive. We have seen many cases when the morale of internal staff is reduced by both the actions and pay of consultants and contractors.
- Freelance service provision tended to generate an ethic of contractualism, in which rights and responsibilities are confined to clauses in written agreements at the expense of a sense of trust.

Some of his other points are as follows:

- A prince must constantly study the art of war. This applies to project leaders keeping current with trends in project management.
- A good prince must look ahead and recognize evils the minute they are born. This speaks to the early recognition of issues by the project leader.
- To be great, one must study the greats of the past, and in order to avoid pitfalls, one must examine the mistakes of failed predecessors. This supports the value of gathering lessons learned from past projects.

Bibliography

If you go to Amazon.com and search books for project management, you can find over 15,000 entries. Here are a very few of some of the more popular titles.

Brooks, Frederick. *The Mythical Man-Month*, 2nd Edition. Addison-Wesley, 1995.

Office of Government Commerce. *Directing Successful Projects with PRINCE2*. The stationery Office, 2009.

Goldratt, Eliyahu. *Critical Chain*. North River Press, 1997.

Kerzner, Harold. *Project Management: A Systems Approach to Planning, Scheduling, and Controlling*. John Wiley and Sons, 2009.

Lientz, Bennet and Lee Larssen. *Risk Management for IT Projects*. Elsevier, 2008.

Meredith, Jack and Samuel Mantel. *Project Management: A Managerial Approach*, 7th Edition. Wiley, 2008.

Project Management Institute. *A Guide to the Project Management Body of Knowledge (PMBOK Guide)*. Project Management Institute, 2008.

Schwalbe, Kathy. *Information Technology Project Management*, 6th Edition. Course Technology, 2009.

Wysocki, Robert. *Effective Project Management: Traditional, Agile, Extreme*, 5th Edition. Wiley, 2009.

Index